ACTIVISM IN THE NAME OF GOD

ACTIVISM IN THE NAME OF GOD

Religion and Black Feminist Public Intellectuals from the Nineteenth Century to the Present

Edited by Jami L. Carlacio

University Press of Mississippi / Jackson

Margaret Walker Alexander Series in African American Studies

The University Press of Mississippi is the scholarly publishing agency of the Mississippi Institutions of Higher Learning: Alcorn State University, Delta State University, Jackson State University, Mississippi State University, Mississippi University for Women, Mississippi Valley State University, University of Mississippi, and University of Southern Mississippi.

www.upress.state.ms.us

The University Press of Mississippi is a member of the Association of University Presses.

A longer version of chapter 2 was published in *Black and White Women's Travel Narratives* by Cheryl J. Fish, 24–64. Gainesville: University Press of Florida, 2004. This material is reprinted with permission of the University Press of Florida.

Copyright © 2023 by University Press of Mississippi
All rights reserved

First printing 2023
∞

Library of Congress Cataloging-in-Publication Data

Names: Carlacio, Jami L., 1964– editor.
Title: Activism in the name of God : religion and Black feminist public intellectuals from the nineteenth century to the present / edited by Jami L. Carlacio.
Other titles: Religion and Black feminist public intellectuals from the nineteenth century to the present | Margaret Walker Alexander series in African American studies.
Description: Jackson : University Press of Mississippi, [2023] | Series: Margaret Walker Alexander series in African American studies | Includes bibliographical references and index.
Identifiers: LCCN 2023012271 (print) | LCCN 2023012272 (ebook) | ISBN 9781496845672 (hardback) | ISBN 9781496845689 (trade paperback) | ISBN 9781496845696 (epub) | ISBN 9781496845702 (epub) | ISBN 9781496845719 (pdf) | ISBN 9781496845726 (pdf)
Subjects: LCSH: African American women—Intellectual life. | African American feminists—United States—Biography. | Womanist theology—United States. | Womanism—United States—Religious aspects. | Women and religion—United States. | Feminist theology—United States. | African American intellectuals. | African American women—Religious life.
Classification: LCC E185.96 .A23 2023 (print) | LCC E185.96 (ebook) | DDC 230.082—dc23/eng/20230405
LC record available at https://lccn.loc.gov/2023012271
LC ebook record available at https://lccn.loc.gov/2023012272

British Library Cataloging-in-Publication Data available

This book is dedicated to Black women,
whose inner strength, courage, and self-love
have been an inspiration to me.

CONTENTS

Acknowledgments ix

Introduction: Witnesses of the Spirit. 3
Jami L. Carlacio

Nineteenth Century

Chapter 1. More Than "Mere" Rhetoric: Jarena Lee's *Religious Experience* Read through a Womanist Lens 41
Neely McLaughlin

Chapter 2. Journeys and Warnings: Nancy Prince's Resistant Truth-Telling in New England, Russia, and Jamaica 60
Cheryl J. Fish

Chapter 3. "Fishers of Men": Understanding Frances Ellen Watkins Harper's Poetry as Vocational Autobiography. 93
Jennifer McFarlane-Harris

Twentieth Century

Chapter 4. Cultivating "Mass Intelligence": Nannie Helen Burroughs and the Quest for Racial Justice 119
Angela Hornsby-Gutting

Chapter 5. The Gospel According to Madame E. Azalia Smith Hackley 138
Lisa Pertillar Brevard

Chapter 6. Mothers and the God of the Oppressed: Carrie Williams Clifford and a Literary Theology of Black Freedom. 164
P. Jane Splawn

Chapter 7. Theressa Hoover: Black Feminist, Methodist, Southerner . . 181
Janet Allured

Chapter 8. The Life and Thought of Anna Arnold Hedgeman: A Pragmatic Christian Feminist 212
Hettie V. Williams

Chapter 9. "It Sings in Our Blood": Pauli Murray's Re-Mattering of the World 237
Darcy Metcalfe

Twenty-First Century

Chapter 10. Sandy Speaks: The Digital Resurrection of Sandra Bland's Religious History 267
Phillip Luke Sinitiere

Chapter 11. "Black Feminist Love Evangelist" and "Prayer Poet Priestess": Alexis Pauline Gumbs 286
Laura L. Sullivan

Chapter 12. "Love Wins" and Black Lives Matter: The Spiritual Underpinnings of Patrisse Cullors's Crusade for Justice 310
Jami L. Carlacio

About the Contributors. 337

Index. 341

ACKNOWLEDGMENTS

This project has finally come to fruition after several years, thanks in large part to the dedication of this book's contributors. Despite the twin collective traumas of a global pandemic and the persistent violence experienced by nonwhite and nonbinary persons—and the toll these took on our mental, spiritual, emotional, and physical well-being—they persevered. Always quick to respond to my emails and patient when the project hit a snag and slowed our progress, they demonstrated their commitment to this volume and the women celebrated therein. Without them, this book would not have been possible.

It goes without saying—but I'll say it anyway—that the book you're reading has been made possible through the collaborative efforts of the staff at the University Press of Mississippi. First, because she saw my vision and guided me deftly through the initial stages of preparing and editing the manuscript, I thank acquisitions editor Emily Bandy. Second, I appreciate the help of those who worked "behind the scenes," so to speak: Valerie Jones and Corley Longmire; Jennifer Mixon, Todd Lape, and Joey Brown; freelancer Lynn Whittaker, whose expert copyediting added polish; and the many others at the Press whom I've not named but have been instrumental in the book's completion and distribution.

I also owe a debt of gratitude to the two reviewers who offered excellent suggestions for improving the manuscript. Their insightful comments resulted in a stronger, historiographically centered book. Their professional generosity cannot be overstated.

I am grateful also for the moral support I received, especially from my friends and mentors Margaret Barrow, Trisha Brady, Alice Gillam (RIP), Christine Mottau, and Lori Ramos, who continually encouraged me to complete this book project because, in their words, it is "so timely" and "important." I thank all those others with whom I shared my vision because they, too, reminded me of the value of making visible the important work the women highlighted in these pages and in fact all Black women have accomplished to make the world a better place. Their self-love, their inherent dignity, and their insistence that all women belong in and make valuable intellectual contributions to the public sphere are unparalleled.

And I thank my son, Javier, who patiently waited for "me time" when I had to spend countless hours at the computer in order to meet deadlines. He thinks that what this book is about is "cool." So do I.

ACTIVISM IN THE NAME OF GOD

Introduction

WITNESSES OF THE SPIRIT

JAMI L. CARLACIO

> Once you know that your life is not about you, then you can also trust that your life is your message.
> —Richard Rohr[1]

> Nay, 'tis woman's strongest vindication for speaking that *the world needs to hear her voice.*
> —Anna Julia Cooper[2]

Since the nineteenth century, religious and spiritual Black feminist public intellectuals in the United States have called attention to and protested against the discrimination of African American women and men on the basis of their race, class, and gender, and particularly in the twentieth and twenty-first centuries, their sexual orientation.[3] Drawing on their spiritual inner resources, these Black women have attempted to dislodge the normative thinking that has occluded the presence of these injustices or at least has downplayed the depth of their gravity. Whether through organizing marches and protests; publishing pamphlets, articles, spiritual and secular autobiographies, books, poetry, stories, or digital content; preaching in- and outside of churches; or creating art in its various forms, their goal has been not just to challenge but to disrupt discriminatory practices in all areas of social, religious, and political life and galvanize the Black church, the government, and communities into action. The essays in this collection recognize and celebrate twelve such women whose lives have been forged by the hammer and anvil of experience; they have made an indelible mark not just in Black women's history but in American history writ large.

It is important to note that our use of "Black women" is not meant to suggest their homogeneity, as this would serve only to essentialize the extent and varieties of intersectional oppressions and elide differences in their lived experiences. As the twelve chapters in this book demonstrate, there are both similarities and differences among Black women, including the specifics of their age, level and type of education, and gender identity, as well as the economic, religious, political, and cultural contexts in which they thought, lived, and acted. In fact, this collection may heighten readers' awareness and appreciation of the complexity of Black women's experience, particularly as we trace the sociopolitical aims and concomitant intellectual production of twelve exemplars over the course of three centuries. To wit: in their discussion of the similarities and differences between the terms "womanism," "Black feminism," and "Africana womanism," Maria D. Davidson and Scott Davidson acknowledge that "these perspectives [womanism, Black feminism, and Africana womanism] have a point of interest in common—the experience of Black women—but a close examination reveals some key philosophical and political differences between them." They caution against "grouping all Black women writers or theorists together under any one of these headings." That said, these writers add that "Womanism, Black Feminism, and Africana Womanism [are] compatible and complementary discourses."[4] For the purposes of this collection, when the adjective "Black" is used, as opposed to the more specific "African American," the reference is to Black women in the US, unless otherwise specified.

As compatible discourses, Black feminism and Africana womanism function both as descriptors of Black women's standpoint and as ideological critique. Though some of the Black women studied in this volume would not necessarily characterize themselves as Black feminists in a confessional way, their intellectual output and their work in the public sphere distinctly demonstrate the Black feminist standpoint. This critical stance makes visible oppressions that capitalist systems of production and consumption perpetuate on people of color and other minoritized groups. As producers of knowledge, Black women promulgate the value of multiple narratives as well as expose and widen the cracks and fissures that exist in oppressive structures, thereby weakening their hold. Indeed, Black women's way of seeing and being in the world is exactly what gives them the impetus and the *authority* to advocate and demand justice for the oppressed. Their desire for dynamic and revolutionary change fueled their efforts to create the necessary rhetorical space to intervene in the master narrative that has justified the marginalization of Black and, in fact, all oppressed people, regardless of their social location.[5] Importantly, while the Black feminist standpoint illuminates intersectional oppressions, it also recognizes the multiplicity of positions that Black women and men occupy. In the context of a culture that has historically rendered them virtually powerless to express themselves and to live their lives as self-determined individuals, the twelve women highlighted in this collection either ignored or circumvented cultural proscriptions by implicitly or explicitly calling out racism and sexism and calling for justice.

It is their standpoint of nondominance that has allowed these women to critique that which they have known both intellectually and experientially. They could do what privileged white women who benefited from the system could never do because those within the system cannot possess a dual perspective any more than fish can see the water in which they swim. What is more, those who benefit from the system cannot eschew their privilege. To be sure, the perspective of members of dominant groups is limited by their privilege; at the same time, history has shown that cross-racial collaboration has occurred between members of historically dominant and oppressed groups since the eighteenth century when persons of African descent critiqued and struggled against racist violence. This cooperation continues to exist—to greater and lesser degrees—in the present.[6] At the same time, Black women have straddled, and still do, two disparate worlds: one saturated in white patriarchal heteronormativity and the other in exploitation and violence by virtue of their intersectional identities. And for the women in this collection, fueled by their religious and spiritual convictions—whether the reference is to the Judeo-Christian God or an African ancestor God—they find liberation and connection. As womanist theologian Kelly Brown Douglas explains, God offers Godself to Black people to unite in relationship, and their "yes signals black people's belief in the power of God to right what is wrong in the world. . . . [It is] a testimonial of the divine/human interaction between God and black people. As such, it is a witness to black reality and black hope."[7] If we expand the notion of "God" to include multiple understandings of the divine, we may see how both the Black feminist and the womanist standpoints illuminate Douglas's point.

Just as the Black feminist standpoint values ways of being, doing, and knowing in the world, so too does womanism. This identifier is derived from Alice Walker's description of a womanist in *"Everyday Use"*: "I am preoccupied with the spiritual survival, the survival *whole* of my people. . . . I am committed to exploring the oppressions, the insanities, the loyalties and the triumphs of Black women."[8] Clearly, the issue of survival is essential to understanding not just the theological underpinnings of womanism but more broadly Black lives. For womanists, survival is a first step toward their liberation. Equally important is that Black women are *subjects* with agency; they are not objects who are subject to the many indignities perpetuated on them historically from slavery to the present. Womanists share the ideals promulgated by Black feminists and celebrate their particular situated knowledge and experience. Out of this grew a new womanist theology of liberation, characterized as such by womanist ethicist Katie Geneva Cannon in the mid-1980s, who emphasized the role of *spirituality* in Black women's lives. Insofar as it is liberatory, womanist theology shares concerns with Black liberation theology, developed by James Cone as a response to the racism inherent in the prevailing heteronormative theology steeped in whiteness. Womanist theologians have rightly pointed out Black liberation theology's elision of the specific oppressions of women, some of which come from the Black church and its historically patriarchal structure.[9] Along these lines, womanist theology advances what the womanist ethicist Emilie Townes characterizes as "justice-based spirituality," calling attention not simply to the *in*justices experienced historically by Black women but, more positively, to the interrelationship of justice and God as expressed in the Christian tradition.[10] This point is particularly important because Christian womanists see Christ as a partner in their liberation.[11]

The womanist theological stance initially presupposed Black women's Christianity, yet later generations of African American feminist and womanist theologians expressed deep concern over its Christocentric and heteronormative orientations. For example, in 2006, womanist process theologian Monica Coleman challenged the term "womanist" and its inherent limitations as an implicit descriptor of all Black women's orientation toward the divine. In a roundtable discussion on her question "Must I Be Womanist?," the panelists—Coleman and her respondents Katie G. Cannon, Arisika Razak, Irene Monroe, Debra Mubashshir Majeed, Lee Miena Skye, Stephanie Y. Mitchem, and Traci C. West—plumb the complexity not just of the meaning of the labels "womanist," "womanism," and "Black feminist," but also of their historical, political, spiritual, and personal contexts.[12] What is more, the Black church, traditionally central to the lives of both Black women and men, has been de-centered since not all Black women are Christian; thus, womanism and womanist theology are rich descriptors of the various theological, spiritual, and political perspectives demonstrated by the women in this book and around the world. Cullors and Gumbs, for example, have embraced principles of the West African Yoruba religion for inspiration and succor, yet their orientation does not preclude them from the category "womanist."[13]

Though they express and their lives demonstrate womanist principles, none of the women studied here defines herself explicitly as a womanist. Townes herself asserts that "the term 'womanist' is confessional."[14] Womanist theology, however, has deep roots from the beginning of chattel slavery through Black women's racial uplift work as missionaries and club women in the early twentieth-century missionary work and in novels, stories, poems, and other intellectual production since the nineteenth century. As womanist theologian Cheryl Townsend Gilkes explains, "the term womanist names a critical perspective grounded in the African-American experience. 'Womanist' is a way of seeing that affirms the validity of the Black experience in spite of centuries of white supremacist negation."[15] As advocates of the oppressed and as promulgators of liberation and autonomy, they are, borrowing the words of Marilyn Richardson, "secular minist[ers] of political and religious witness."[16]

AIMS AND FOCUS

Our aims in this collection are several, each of which deserves some elaboration. First, we highlight the complex, multifaceted historical trajectory of Black women and their relationship to theology, politics, and the culture in which they lived and created intellectual work. While monographs, edited collections, and articles have appeared that plumb the treasures of African Americans in the US and throughout the African diaspora, only a few have centered women until relatively recently. These texts are discussed in a later section and mark a significant intervention in the received histories of Black religious activity, whether in politics or forms of cultural production including music, art, literature, tracts, and so on. The historian Judith Weisenfeld astutely points out that "add[ing] a few female figures alongside the men of the expected pantheon of major actors or to substitute a woman for a man to illustrate some aspect of the standard narrative is to miss the profound and significant [and unique] challenges" Black women faced, whether Jarena Lee in the nineteenth century or Patrisse Cullors in the twenty-first.[17] Along these lines, the chapters in this book implicitly resist the notion that all Black women's experience is the same or similar rather than historically, politically, and culturally contingent. In other words, we claim no "essential" notion of what it means to be Black, female, feminist, womanist, and intellectual. Yes, there are similarities among the women studied here, but it is their diverse ways of thinking (or theorizing) and acting (what is known as praxis) that help the reader to appreciate them as exemplars. Moreover, these chapters urge us to think about how, across the span of about two hundred years, Black women had to rely on their ingenuity in different ways based on proscriptions that would delimit what counted and counts as respectable behavior as well as overcome other obstacles to their goals. As their individual stories demonstrate, nothing came easily: they dealt with racism, sexism, classism, ignorance, and a host of other acts and attitudes that would otherwise dog their every step—but didn't succeed in stopping them.

Second, we want to intervene in the heretofore generally accepted assumption that public intellectuals are gendered male, emerge from a particular (privileged) social location, and produce a particular form of intellectual work. For many, the Italian Marxist Antonio Gramsci comes to mind when describing "intellectuals," whether traditional or organic.[18] The idea of the public intellectual has evolved since he theorized about the role of intellectuals in society, which was dependent on social class theory promulgated by Karl Marx and Friedrich Engels in the nineteenth century. Gramsci described two kinds of intellectuals—the traditional and the organic—based not on what they knew or how much intelligence they possessed but rather on their social location relative to others. The left-wing scholar and linguist Noam Chomsky took Gramsci's ideas a step further by identifying two types of organic intellectuals—hegemonic and counterhegemonic.[19] By the latter I am referring to the kind of intellectuals who may possess a measure of social and economic capital that positions them above lower- and working-class people but who are self-critical and committed to social change. That is, counterhegemonic organic intellectuals resist both ideological identification with capitalist, patriarchal, white supremacist ideology *and* align themselves with the classes most exploited by it, even if they themselves are not members of those classes. During the last decades of the twentieth century, the idea of the organic public intellectual began to expand as members of minoritized groups—women and people of color, mainly—were recognized for their contributions to the public's understanding of the political, social, and cultural issues of the day. At the same time, this expanded notion did not necessarily include the works produced by Black women from the nineteenth century and much of the twentieth.

In more recent history, intellectualism has been associated with the academy or think tanks; adding the descriptor "public" to it gave some purchase to the notion that so-called thought leaders could present complex ideas to the public. Sociologist Patricia Hill Collins discusses two strategies of intellectual activism. The first refers to the roles and responsibilities of elites—whether producing scholarship about Black women's intellectual work and activism or as Black feminist public intellectuals. Speaking for herself, she regards her role as an academic elite and public intellectual as political insofar as she "speak[s] the truth to power," meaning that she has used her academic training in precisely the opposite way that it was intended ("to serve the interests of the gatekeepers who granted [her] legitimacy").[20] Instead, she uses her academic writing "to develop alternative analyses of social injustices that scholarly audiences will find credible." More than this, her work "counts as truth about race and racism." The second form of intellectual activism "speak[s] the truth directly to the people," and those who do so "talk directly to the masses."[21] She is rightly concerned about the locus of public intellectualism; preaching to the choir simply isn't enough: "How different our ideas about families, schooling, immigration, and government would be if we presented them not simply at academic conferences but also at neighborhood public libraries, to groups of college students, at parent education classes—and even to our own families."[22] In fact, as the historian Keisha Blain explains, "Black public intellectuals were not all members of the Black intelligentsia." She continues, "Black working-class and impoverished women . . . were not only activists but also theorists and intellectuals."[23] The takeaway of Blain's and Collins's points is that what counts as public intellectualism includes both kitchen table and public sphere political activism drawn from both personal and professional experience. The chapters in this volume demonstrate this richness and diversity.

Relatedly, our third aim is to call attention to and honor the constellation of religious or spiritual Black women whose commitment to the social, political, and economic well-being of oppressed people in the United States shaped their work in the public sphere.[24] This collection offers readers exemplars—some well known and others less so—with whose minds and spirits we can engage, from whose ideas we can learn, and upon whose social justice work we can build. Catherine Squires's discussion of counterhegemonic action in the Black public sphere is instructive here. In her essay "Rethinking the Black Public Sphere," she examines three Black public spheres insofar as "they respond to dominant social pressures, legal restrictions, and other challenges from dominant publics and the state."[25] At any given moment, one or all of these spheres may operate simultaneously—the enclave consisting of marginalized Black people forced into restrictive, segregated spaces; the counterpublic sphere, whose members emerge from "hiding" to assert their (oppositional) politics in the broader public sphere in order to challenge its hegemony; and the satellite sphere, which privileges a separate space for activism and public participation. Significantly, the Black feminist and womanist activists featured in this book have created the necessary rhetorical space to assert themselves on the public stage as key actors and to occupy one or more of these spheres simultaneously. That is, as public intellectuals, they have demonstrated how different knowledges *lay claim to* the truth of experience. Their intellectual output, in whatever form, functions both as a necessary corrective to existing structures that have governed the lives of oppressed groups and as counterhegemonic discourses that disrupt dominant ways of knowing and being, thereby shifting critical emphases toward alternative standpoints.

To sum up, we aim to challenge traditional notions of *what* intellectual work is and *by whom* it is produced and then to validate the thought and action of Black women who produce it. This book joins the chorus of texts that have called attention to the exceptional Black women called to preach, testify, write, sing, create art, and march to the beat of their own words and ideas and to galvanize their readers, listeners, and fellow activists to seek both recognition of and justice for the oppressed. As the women highlighted in these chapters make clear, a commitment to change the world takes enormous courage and faith, in large part because speaking truth to power is never easy; disrupting power is even more difficult. But it is no match for their faith and intellect as well as the anger, passion, and love that drive them.

A TRADITION AND A NEW CANON

That there *is* a tradition of Black feminist public intellectuals was firmly established by scholars in the 1980s, and critical work on African American women's contributions in both the public and private spheres has gained significant traction and in fact is "a distinct and growing field of study."[26] Scholars in- and outside of the academy in many disciplines, including Africana Studies; English studies; feminist, gender, and sexuality studies; history; philosophy; religion; rhetoric; and sociology have been doing the important work of excavating the long-buried treasures of African American women's creative production in the form of essays, anthologies, monographs, conference presentations, and curricula. During the 1990s and into the first two decades of the twenty-first century, texts documenting the rhetorical and intellectual work of Black women began to proliferate, cementing in place a canon of critical analyses by African Americans, both women and men.[27] The earliest comprehensive treatment that demonstrates this is Beverly Guy-Sheftall's *Words of Fire: An Anthology of African-American Feminist Thought*, published in 1995.[28] More than five hundred pages in length, the book features original work produced by a wide range of Black feminists and proto-Black feminists from the nineteenth and twentieth centuries, beginning with the nineteenth-century abolitionist Maria Stewart and concluding with womanist novelist Alice Walker. Guy-Sheftall's work marks the first watershed in the recuperation of Black feminist intellectual history that includes a wide variety of genres—speeches, essays, fiction, nonfiction, poetry, journalism, and more—on subjects ranging from antislavery to sexual and gender politics to Black womanhood to the problematic of intersectional oppressions. It was the first to effectively canonize a rich and complex tradition heretofore unacknowledged. Previous to *Words of Fire*, other celebrations of Black feminists' intellectual creativity appeared as monographs, notably Paula Giddings's *When and Where I Enter* (1984) and Hazel Carby's *Reconstructing Womanhood* (1989), which center Black women's social activism and literary production, respectively. Both Giddings's and Carby's texts jump-started the conversation that took flight and shows no evidence of landing anytime soon.

Subsequent works centering Black women's intellectual production have traded breadth for depth, such as Kristin Waters and Carol B. Conaway's edited collection, published twelve years after Guy-Sheftall's, entitled *Black Women's Intellectual Traditions*. Unlike *Words of Fire*, Waters and Conaway's book features scholarly *interpretations* of the intellectual work of Maria Stewart, Harriet Jacobs, Frances Ellen Watkins Harper, Pauline Hopkins, Mary Ann Shadd Cary, Ida B. Wells, and Anna Julia Cooper. In fact, Waters and Conaway's volume situates the birth of religious Black feminist public intellectuals in the early decades of the nineteenth century, and specifically with that of Maria Stewart, whose work at the public podium and on the page demonstrated a distinctly sociopolitical activist ministry. The "interpretive works" in this collection, write the editors, "can expose systematic thought—trace the outlines, uncover the formal structures and themes, develop and build upon the original material until a body of work emerges that carries forces and power in contemporary argument."[29] Like *Words of Fire*, Waters and Conaway's volume demonstrates the eclecticism of Black women's feminist intellectual work, grounded as it is in experience coupled with ideological critique that challenges the practices of the dominant culture that have attempted to silence Black women's voices and elide their action in and impact on history.

Continuing this important work, Mia E. Bay, Farah J. Griffin, Martha S. Jones, and Barbara Dianne Savage published, in 2015, *Toward an Intellectual History of Black Women* with the aim of "recover[ing] the intellectual traditions of thinkers who were often organic intellectuals and whose lives and thoughts are only modestly documented."[30] Seeking explicitly to reveal the ways in which the physical and psychic oppressions imposed on African American women informed their intellectual productions, they look to exemplars in Africa and the African diasporas of the United States and the Caribbean to illustrate this. Bay and her coeditors claim in their introduction that "Black women thinkers remain largely neglected outside the field of literary criticism. Historical scholarship on Black women especially has yet to map the broad contours of their political and social thought in any detail, or to examine their distinctive intellectual tradition as often self-educated thinkers with a sustained history of wrestling with both sexism and racism."[31] This is true to the extent that existing monographs, anthologies, and collections have barely scratched the surface of the rich ore of Black feminists' intellectual and creative production; this is why the wave of scholarship on Black women continues to rise. There is more to be said; there is more to be learned; there is more to be celebrated.

One significant intervention that foregrounds Black women's intellectual output from the genesis of the Black women's club movement in the late nineteenth century through the Black power movement in the early 1970s is Brittney Cooper's *Beyond Respectability: The Intellectual Thought of Race Women*.[32] The author argues that the intellectual production of Black women went beyond the creation of associations, clubs, racial uplift organizations, and church societies. What warrants our attention, she explains, is their performativity in the public sphere, where "respectability" refers not just to propriety but to their dignity, intelligence, and action. Using Anna Julia Cooper as her theoretical model (in the same way that scholars use Karl Marx, Michel Foucault, or Jacques Derrida as theoretical lenses), Cooper delves into the embodied public intellectualism of Mary Church Terrell, Fannie Barrier Williams, Pauli Murray, and Toni Cade Bambara, demonstrating what true race leadership really is and why it matters.

Her project is to "construct both an *intellectual genealogy* of the ideas that race women produce about racial identity, gender, and leadership between the 1890s and the 1970s, and an *intellectual geography* that maps the deliberate ways that Black women chose to take up and transform intellectual and physical spaces in service of their racial uplift projects."[33] What is true of the women studied in Cooper's book, and those in the other books mentioned here, is that Black women intellectuals—author, activist, feminist, religious, church and club leader, and so on—have existed for centuries, but they were not necessarily visible in the racist, sexist, heteronormative social imaginary. By social imaginary, I am referring to the way people in a society or culture imagine themselves in relationship to others—their shared, implicit expectations of how things are or ought to be and what constitutes the "norm." The social imaginary is produced and reproduced in the stories we tell about ourselves; it determines who fits and does not fit within the parameters of agreed-upon acceptable social practices. The social imaginary, in short, legitimates or delegitimates persons based on what are often specious understandings or prejudices, which often go unquestioned. The Black women celebrated in this book, like many others who came before and after them, have interrupted these narratives and either rewritten them or devised their own. They have redefined respectability and intellectualism and have used their experience to reflect on the world, to take action based on that experience, and to transform it.

This is apparent in Hettie V. Williams's edited collection *Bury My Heart in a Free Land: Black Women Intellectuals in Modern American History*.[34] Along with twelve contributing scholars, Williams traces Black women's praxis—meaning their intellectual thought and action—as it is instantiated in the abolitionist, anti-lynching, and club women's movement; the New Negro era; the civil rights and Black Power eras; and the post-civil rights era into the second decade of the twenty-first century. *Bury My Heart in a Free Land* stands out in its attention to the complex activism of Black women both during and after the peak of the civil rights movement that centers not only on aspects of militant Black feminism but also on the power of self-definition. The latter is exemplified by bell hooks and Audre Lorde, testaments to the self-assurance and resiliency of the Black woman's spirit to resist, using the power of the word, racist and sexist notions of what it means to be Black, female, and lesbian. What is more, the collection is noteworthy in its attention to the late Nobel laureate Toni Morrison's work in the public sphere as well as to women in public service and specifically Admiral Michelle Howard, the first Black woman to become a four-star admiral in the US Navy.

In addition to these Black female-centered anthologies, other important collections exist that celebrate the intellectual interventions of Black people. For example, historian of Black theology Clarence Taylor's *Black Religious*

Intellectuals: The Fight for Equality from Jim Crow to the 21st Century highlights the contributions of religious Black male leaders who "are rarely studied for their intellectual contributions" and notes that "connecting religion to political struggle has remained an important element of analysis and the freedom struggle."[35] Among others, he examines the life and activism of A. Philip Randolph; Pentecostal preacher Bishop Smallwood Williams; the Reverends John Culmer, Theodore Gibson, and Al Sharpton; and "race warrior" Louis Farrakhan, who "used religion in some fashion when formulating ideas and ideology, interpreting political struggles, and constructing identities."[36] Taylor recognizes the chauvinism inherent in the attitudes of Black men and the Black church generally and concludes his book with a brief chapter outlining how Ella Baker and Pauli Murray addressed this problem directly, initiating a serious conversation and critique that continue to this day. At the same time, this gloss of Baker's and Murray's intellectual activism reflects the serious scholarly elision of religious Black women's sociopolitical critique in the midst (or in spite) of institutionalized patriarchy—hence the proliferation of studies that center Black women intellectuals since the publication of Taylor's book in 2002.

While Taylor's book centers the intellectual contributions of Black men, Keisha N. Blain, Christopher Cameron, and Ashley D. Farmer's *New Perspectives on the Black Intellectual Tradition* offers a broad, expansive treatment of both male and female public intellectuals whose activism traverses geopolitical boundaries, signaling an important contribution in Black diaspora studies.[37] The editors and contributors of the book analyze Black political thought along the planes of internationalism, religion and spirituality, racial politics, and radicalism. The collection "illuminates . . . the origins of and conduits for Black ideas, redefines the relationship between Black thought and social action, and challenges long-held assumptions about Black perspectives on religion, race, and radicalism."[38] Published under the auspices of the African American Intellectual History Society, which convened for the first time in 2014, the book features nineteenth- and twentieth-century males and females engaged in reform, revolt, and nationalism. What makes this collection unique is both its depth and its breadth of subject matter. In order to appreciate fully and take seriously Black intellectual production, one must understand the genesis of the *tradition* and the global connections among Africans and Africans in diaspora. Blain et al. rightly point out that Black intellectual history is not simply about the political, creative, and religious actions of Black intellectuals but about the deliberate thought that went into them: "They didn't simply act on a whim, but they carefully thought about their actions and they carefully devised strategies and tactics. They proposed solutions, they offered critiques, they challenged others—all the while resisting many of their contemporaries who dismissed their contributions on account of their education and social standing."[39] In other words, the intellectual thought and corresponding action resist racist and sexist sociopolitical and cultural notions of public intellectualism.

Though the anthologies published thus far have documented the variety of intellectual work that Black feminists have produced, they necessarily cover only part of this rich multicentury tradition. Because of this, the recuperative work of scholars will continue to expand. Moreover, as the current century progresses, scholars are turning their attention to leaders of international progressive social movements, to members of the US House of Representatives and Senate, to occupants in the White House, and to presidential candidates on major and minor party tickets.[40]

There is, understandably, much more work to do. The present volume responds to this call by highlighting Black women's creative and intellectual work as multiply informed by their political and social location, their dedication to social justice, *and* their religious or spiritual identity—a triple helix with identifiable separate strands that comprise a whole. This eclectic group of Black women, whose spiritual-political activism spans about two hundred years, is connected by the desire to strengthen the conditions that make possible the social good that affirms and embraces all people, grounded in ethics and love. It bears repeating here that Black women are a heterogeneous group: the possession of a certain quantity of melanin does not render them the same across various categories of identity or particular kinds of intellectual production. Quite the opposite. As this collection and the others discussed below demonstrate, Black women from the eighteenth-century enslaved poet Phillis Wheatley to the Duke University-educated Alexis Pauline Gumbs and activist-scholar-artist Patrisse Cullors differ markedly with regard to social location, cultural influences, class, and gender identity, to name but a few categories. They also differ in their response to and critique of oppression by virtue of the cultural and historical moment in which they lived or live.

That said, it may on first glance seem curious to connect Jarena Lee to Patrisse Cullors, for example, but as one reads each of the chapters in the book, it becomes quickly apparent that all of the women featured here are witnesses of the Spirit. Whether implicitly or explicitly, they addressed the complex intersection of oppressions that have confronted Black, Indigenous, and People of Color for centuries. As the Black feminist legal scholar Kimberlé Crenshaw explains, a "single-axis framework" of analysis that narrowly conceives of Black women's marginalization according to a single category without acknowledging the complex interplay of oppressions is problematic: "Any analysis that does not take intersectionality into account cannot sufficiently address the particular manner in which Black women are subordinated."[41] Using their rhetorical gifts to demand justice for the intersectionally oppressed, these Black women, whose beginnings range from servants of white families to highly educated ivory tower professors, must be taken seriously. One additional point deserves mention here.

Some might assume that the Black feminist public intellectual must or does speak *for* or represent the race, which essentializes and in fact collapses "Black" into one monolithic racial category as well as reductively presumes that the lived experience of all Black people is the same. To do so would presuppose a hierarchy of privilege or knowledge, or both, and is dangerous and unstable ground on which to stand. At the same time, it is instructive to consider the work of feminist philosopher Linda Martín Alcoff, who addressed this issue in her 1991 essay "The Problem of Speaking for Others." The question undergirding her thesis is whether someone more privileged can legitimately speak for others less privileged. Much of her argument relates to a more specious kind of ventriloquism, that of white feminists speaking "for" Black women (feminist or otherwise). Yet, we can take to heart the question of who has the authority to speak for whom, and in what circumstances. Without going too deeply into this question, which should be treated in depth in a separate publication, it is important to consider why this might apply to the Black feminist or womanist intellectuals in this book. To speak "for" others who share similar oppressions based on their class, race, and gender, for example, is to speak on behalf of Black women whose voices have gone unheard and unacknowledged and who still suffer the effects of living in a patriarchal, white supremacist society. As such, one might reasonably argue that it is their "duty" as public intellectuals to "take on" the establishment and call attention to the violence perpetrated on African Americans, regardless of their gender or social status. Thus, the Black feminist activists studied here and others like them could not reasonably *not* do this. Alcoff's rhetorical question is apt here: "If I don't speak for those less privileged than myself, am I abandoning my political responsibility to speak out against oppression?"[42] The answer must be "yes." Putting the question another way, is there a defensible reason for *not* speaking out or taking action? The answer must be "no."

This is no mean feat; in fact, the task that these Black cultural, political, and ideological critics have set themselves is herculean. Pushing back on centuries of institutionalized injustices requires more than outrage, indignation, and intellectual prowess. It requires a deeply ingrained sense of self-love, a passion for truth, and an insistence on being heard, whether in the public square, in the church, on the streets, or in the ivory tower. More than this, the work of the Black feminist or womanist public intellectual requires a commitment to the greater social good whose force reflects both Christian and non-Christian religious traditions that celebrate the wholeness of Black people.[43] In other words, these women's work may be what womanist systematic theologian Karen Baker-Fletcher envisions as "political act[s] of a spiritual nature."[44] Like so many of their race, they were and are guided by a Higher Authority—an instantiation of Love—that informs the activism and intellectual prowess of religious Black feminist intellectuals. It is their central motivation; it is what ignites their fire and their passion, their three-dimensional love: for themselves, the race, and the divine as it expresses itself in their lives. bell hooks rightly asserts that "we cannot effectively resist domination if our efforts to create meaningful, lasting personal and social change are not grounded in a love ethic."[45] In a similar vein, Nicole Jackson points out that "love [is] at the heart of activists' struggles for citizenship rights and justice."[46] Having been deprived of their civil rights, whether at the ballot box, as victims of the prison industrial complex, or in being treated as second-class citizens, African Americans have reached into their souls to find the spiritual fuel for their resistance and outright rebellion. And certainly, as hooks reminds us, "love does not bring an end to difficulties, [but] it gives [Black people] the strength to cope with difficulties in a constructive way."[47]

A CONTEXTUAL OUTLINE OF THE BOOK

Nineteenth Century

This volume is organized chronologically to highlight the historical, political, and religious trajectory of Black feminist and womanist public intellectual activism. The interpenetration of religiosity and church, social movements, and artistic production that shaped the warp and woof of the nineteenth century is complex, but an overview of the major movements may help readers appreciate the efforts, challenges, and successes of the three women in this section. The profundity of their work for racial justice and gender equality cannot be overstated. At the forefront of and undergirding their activism was their belief in God, in Christ as liberator, and in the Bible as a scriptural justification for their work. In fact, as Bettye Collier-Thomas puts it, "black women have woven their faith into their daily experiences," which was "centra[l] to the development of African American religion, politics, and public culture."[48] Whether it was the church, the abolitionist movement, or racial uplift and other non-church-based organizations, Black women were not just active participants in history; they shaped it and created the conditions for subsequent Black feminist and womanist activists to do the same.

Theirs was not an easy task. Black women's activism and leadership in the public sphere was met with no small amount of resistance and criticism. Not only did they have to endure the cultural and social proscriptions that came with being Black; they also had to navigate the complexities of gender- and class-appropriate behavior, most stringently in the nineteenth century but certainly throughout the twentieth and twenty-first as well. Notwithstanding the predominantly male-led institutions, which included the antislavery societies and churches, Black women were excluded from the socially constructed category of "pure" (white) womanhood. In an era when the Cult of Domesticity ruled supreme and elevated white women's status to the top of a pedestal based on the ideals of piety, purity, skillful domesticity, and a culturally proscribed level of submission to males, Black women did not even merit consideration. And yet, Black women such as Jarena Lee, Maria Stewart, and the numerous autobiographers, preachers, deacons, club women, missionaries, and writers demonstrated quite well these attributes or, better, appropriated these categories as rationales for their activism. Religiosity informed their work ethic and fueled their desire to serve others under the auspices of God's kingdom.[49] Sojourner Truth, for example, went so far as to take the stage, uninvited, at a woman's rights rally in Ohio to claim and value her Black womanhood while calling out the specious sexism and racism of the so-called supporters of women's rights.[50] This mantle was taken up even more explicitly toward the end of the century, as the outspoken Episcopalian educator, orator, activist, and public intellectual Anna Julia Cooper railed against the racism and sexism experienced by Black women across multiple institutions, including transportation, suffrage, education, and the church. In her 1892 collection of speeches and writings entitled *A Voice from the South*, Cooper adopted a Protestant womanist stance to level stringent critiques of white women's racism and Black (and white) men's sexism, as well as advocated for equal educational opportunities for African Americans.

Piety was at the forefront of both African Americans' and whites' consciousness thanks to two Protestant religious revivals that swept early American colonies and territories, the second of which occurred between 1790 and 1830. The Second Great Awakening, as historians refer to it, was especially instrumental in Black women's religiously oriented activism. For example, as the chapter on Jarena Lee demonstrates, Black women felt called to participate in the church as preachers and ordained ministers before it was institutionally sanctioned or condoned by male leadership. Though their efforts were met with resistance from Black male leadership, African American women such as Jarena Lee, Sojourner Truth, Virginia Broughton, Zilpha Elaw, and many others listened to God, not men. Lee, for example, petitioned African Methodist Episcopal (AME) bishop Richard Allen to preach the Gospel because she felt called by the Lord to do so. Initially turned down, he acquiesced nearly a decade later when he witnessed her preach.[51] Lee is simply one exemplar of many in the early development of women's involvement in the Black church. As both an institution and as a place of worship, the church was a locus for social justice, racial uplift, and missionary work, where Amanda Berry Smith and Nannie Helen Burroughs led efforts, for example, both domestically and abroad. As part of a larger movement founded by Wesleyan Methodists, this evangelically oriented social work provided Black women with the opportunity to spread the Good News and to improve the well-being of their African and African-descended siblings. In their racial uplift efforts, they necessarily developed leadership skills and organizational acumen, which Black women continue to exhibit in- and outside the church today. For example, women's activism within and on behalf of the church occurred in the form of women's divisions and conventions as auxiliary to mainline denominations including Baptist, Episcopal, Methodist, and Presbyterian churches. Despite the fact that women outnumbered men in Black, white, and biracial churches, men still held positions of authority. This did not deter Black women, however, who formed mutual aid and benevolent societies and developed other programs to support the Black communities where they lived.[52]

Religion also fueled Black women's agitation for temperance and women's suffrage and against slavery and lynching, a modern form of which exists to this day. As to slavery, though they did not form specifically Black divisions within or alongside the existing predominantly (or solely) white abolitionist societies such as the American Anti-Slavery Society (1833–70), a number of women participated in several ways. Maria Stewart and Sojourner Truth, for example, gave speeches and collaborated with white women and men to the extent that social proscription and trenchant sexism and racism allowed. In their spiritual autobiographies, both Stewart and Truth emphasized their leadership as women of faith, which fueled their abolitionist and nascent women's rights efforts. Sarah Parker Remond and Frances Ellen Watkins Harper, as well as Nancy Prince, the subject of chapter 2, wrote prolifically and dedicated themselves to racial uplift and social critique. And one cannot appreciate Black women's efforts in abolition without acknowledging the profound contributions of Harriet Tubman, a conductor on the Underground Railroad, who not only led nearly a hundred enslaved people to freedom but also worked tirelessly for women's suffrage, including working across color lines with Susan B. Anthony. Likewise, Black women joined white women in their efforts to curb excessive drinking and, later, suffrage through the Woman's Christian Temperance Union (WCTU). Though the WCTU was founded and run by white women, Black women joined the temperance cause on both moral and feminist grounds. Yet, their work was not easy. Despite their efforts, particularly with regard to suffrage, Black women were met with staunch implicit and explicit racism by the women alongside whom they worked. The National Woman Suffrage Association, for example, privileged white women's right to vote to the exclusion of their Black sisters, despite the latter's active participation in the cause. As Collier-Thomas points out, Black women "recognized that white America, including most white women, viewed them as black first and as women second."[53] Nevertheless, these women and their siblings in subsequent decades and centuries were role models inspiring future Black women to make history and attempt to dismantle the scaffolding that has upheld white political, social, and ideological hegemony.

White hegemony, while solid, underwent a severe test in the postbellum era of Reconstruction, which lasted barely a dozen years. After 1865, many of the more than four million enslaved people found themselves free but largely poor, unschooled, and disenfranchised. Struggling to find paid employment, Black men were often, if not always, underpaid. To be sure, some freed people did succeed, many by farming land and hiring themselves out as skilled labor. They were assisted in large part by the government, which established the Freedmen's Bureau in 1865 to address the financial, educational, and political needs of this population. Reconstruction also made possible more economic and educational opportunities for women, who went to work and even formed the first collective action.[54] That women could institute collective action implied that they enjoyed some measure of financial autonomy. Hence, Black women worked, owned businesses, managed bank accounts, continued to be activists in- and outside of church, and were intellectual producers.

Among the Freedmen's Bureau's most important contributions was the establishment of schools, which meant the rapid growth of literacy—heretofore out of reach for many. Educational institutions proliferated not just with the help of the short-lived Freedmen's Bureau but also through the efforts of both Black and white women and men who knew that literacy—both biblical and general—was paramount to establishing true freedom from slavery or servitude. In fact, literally thousands of schools were created. Formal instruction took place in barns, rooms, or built structures, and women were instrumental in both founding many of these schools and educating their students. Biblical literacy was particularly important; the epic rise of or increased participation in Black-led churches including the AME and AME Zion churches as well as the rise of Black Baptist churches (African Americans largely withdrew from the white [racist] Baptist churches) meant that literate preachers skilled in oratory and steeped in biblical knowledge were needed.[55] More than this, the rise in literacy and the proliferation of Black churches signified Black autonomy. Knowledge was power, and religion, as it had always been, was one of the key driving forces that undergirded women's activism and self-proclaimed God-given authority.

Along with the increase in Black women's and men's professional, educational, and religious leadership came other threats to white hegemony—of social and political control, that is—such as the electoral franchise. As African American men gained access to the ballot box with the passage of the Fifteenth Amendment in 1870, they availed themselves of political opportunities that granted them a say in the nation's legislative branch. More than 1,500 Black men held political office in the South before the failure of Reconstruction brought this to an end.[56] To regain total social, political, and economic control, White southerners fought back, with a vengeance. One of the most violent ways was through mob violence and in particular lynching, carried out by the Ku Klux Klan and other organized groups that took drastic measures to suppress African American men's right to vote and to extinguish all African Americans' basic civil and human rights. By the end of the century, more than three thousand Black men, women, and children were effectively executed for crimes, many of which were manufactured to appease a frightened southern white population who felt that *their* freedoms and their hegemony were threatened. Black women, such as the religious activist and journalist Ida B. Wells-Barnett, did not stand down. She led an anti-lynching crusade against white mob violence, which galvanized Blacks as well as whites sympathetic to the cause to fight against it. If lynching were not enough, however, the creation of "Black Codes" instituted directly after the war ended and the emergence of Jim Crow "laws" would serve to tamp down African Americans' efforts to establish autonomy or maintain some of the power gained in the decade after the war.[57]

This brief overview of the extent and power of African American women's religious activism in the nineteenth century necessarily amplifies the incredulity of it. In the face of such trenchant opposition to their moral leadership, outspokenness, and tireless sacrifice in the name of race, class, and gender justice, Black women did not just persevere—they succeeded. The three chapters in this section of the book demonstrate this. Jarena Lee, Nancy Prince, and Frances Ellen Watkins Harper, all of whom were born free in northern states—the first two in Massachusetts and the latter in Maryland—possessed an innate desire to uplift the race, preach the Gospel, and use their rhetorical gifts to galvanize their communities to resist the tyranny of racism. Lee, a mystic called to preach, had to overcome the patriarchal proscriptions of the Black church against women preaching and used her gifts not only to evangelize in communities in the North but also to join the abolitionist cause by working with the American Anti-Slavery Society. In her chapter on Lee, Neely McLaughlin focuses on Lee's spiritual autobiography as a significant contribution in Christian discourse that is also political, noting nuances that have not become evident in readings that see the narrative's Christian discourse as simply a rhetorical means to a political end.

Not unlike Lee, Nancy Prince used her writing—spiritual travel narratives specifically—to highlight political problems in Denmark, Russia, and the West Indies. Rhetorically speaking, Prince penned her narratives not so much to highlight her adventures but to call attention to the hypocrisy, corruption, and colonial violence perpetrated by the British in the West Indies. Cheryl J.

Fish focuses her chapter on Prince's "resistant truth telling" that draws on multiple traditions, including the missionary report, slave narrative, and spiritual conversion narrative. Moreover, Fish analyzes Prince's complex relationship to mobility and the body as she recasts domesticity through leadership roles and redirects the maternal. Her journeys to Russia and Jamaica exemplify this mobile subjectivity, through which she presents multiple narrative positions and interventions vis-à-vis each context in relation to power, authority, conflict, geopolitical position, and ethnic or racial identities. In a similar way, Frances Ellen Watkins Harper, the subject of the third chapter, worked for the abolitionist cause and dedicated her life to racial uplift, temperance, and women's rights through a variety of rhetorical means: poetry, fiction, essays, and speeches. Jennifer McFarlane-Harris centers her chapter on Harper's first-person autobiographical techniques to craft a practical theology meant to inspire her fellow African Americans to aspire to positions of leadership.

Twentieth Century

The violent turn of events during the post-Reconstruction era and the creation of the Jim Crow system—or institution—of social control did not deter Black women, who remained fueled by the desire to claim or retain a measure of independence. They continued in their racial uplift efforts in both secular and religious spaces, and joined—and often led—the struggle for desegregation and civil rights. As the legal scholar and carceral justice activist Michelle Alexander puts it, the African Americans' brief moment of "sun" postemancipation was replaced by "a system that put black people nearly back where they began, in a subordinate racial caste."[58] This caste system remains in place today, but this fact does not preclude Black women's religious and political efforts—and successes—to work within and around it.[59] They continued their work to uplift the race and improve conditions for African Americans not only through putatively secular institutions and organizations but also through their respective churches. They created clubs and organizations such as the National Association of Colored Women, whose motto was "lifting as we climb"; the Urban League; and the African American YWCA, which "emphasized nurturing young black women and improving the daily conditions and life opportunities of black women and men in New York."[60] In addition, the birth of the NAACP (National Association for the Advancement of Colored People) in 1909 in New York City included among its founding Black female members Mary Church Terrell, its first president, and Ida B. Wells-Barnett, whose antilynching campaign was one of the organization's first priorities. White people were also instrumental in the organization's founding, including Mary White Ovington, a white abolitionist, suffragist, settlement house founder, and friend of Du Bois, whom she recruited to the NAACP. This longest-running Black civil rights organization was founded in response to a race riot in Springfield, Illinois, in which two Black men accused (but not convicted) of crimes against white people were transferred to a jail in another city while a white mob burned forty African Americans' Springfield homes to the ground and murdered two Black men.

Black women's leadership in the early to mid-century years of the civil rights movement took many forms. Besides Wells-Barnett's anti-lynching campaign in the early years of the NAACP's founding, South Carolinian Septima Clark developed "citizenship schools" aimed at helping Black World War I veterans gain literacy skills. Her activism extended well beyond this to leading efforts to achieve wage equity for teachers, participating in the local YWCA's activist agenda, and most significantly leading the teaching and education division of the Southern Christian Leadership Conference (SCLC).[61] Other women were equally instrumental, including Fannie Lou Hamer, who led desegregation and voter access efforts in Mississippi as well as co-led the 1964 Mississippi Freedom Summer Campaign. One of her peers, Ella Baker, the director of branches in the NAACP in the 1940s, helped organize and found the first conference of the Student Nonviolent Coordinating Committee (SNCC). Its mission was to "affirm the philosophical or religious ideal of nonviolence as the foundation of our purpose, the pre-supposition of our faith, and the manner of our action." SNCC asserts that its philosophy is derived from "Judaic-Christian [*sic*] traditions [and] seek[s] a social order of justice permeated by love, . . . the force by which God binds man to himself and man to man."[62] Statements such as this reinforce and exemplify the importance of religion and faith as inextricably intertwined with activism. Many more Black women played key activist roles in the civil rights movement, including classical musician and vocalist Madame Azalia Smith Hackley, the subject of the fifth chapter; Anna Arnold Hedgeman, the subject of the eighth chapter; and Coretta Scott King and the actresses Ruby Dee and Josephine Baker, among others.

It is, in fact, hard to separate Black women's faith and their leadership activities from their activism both in- and outside of the church. As to the latter, notwithstanding their faithful commitment to their church, Black and white women alike were frustrated by the persistent sexism and racism they encountered. Thus, according to Collier-Thomas, women founded in 1941 an interdenominational and interracial organization, Church Women United (CWU), that existed *outside* religious institutions. "CWU represented an aggrandizement of Christian 'womanpower' that united and moved women beyond a mere focus on their denominational and organizational interests," she explains. "They began to tackle major social and political problems such as race and women's status in the church and society."[63] Significantly, notes Collier-Thomas, church women "recognized their power, and that it could only be exercised in an organization controlled solely by women."[64]

Black women contributed to the welfare of Black people not only through education and literacy, racial uplift, desegregation, and voter registration efforts but also through their labor union activism. For example, as the labor movement gained traction in the 1920s, the first federally recognized Black-led union, the Brotherhood of Sleeping Car Porters, led by A. Philip Randolph, organized Black Pullman porters, who worked for low wages and endured the familiar racial discrimination experienced by their African Americans forebears. Recognizing he needed the help of both men and women, Randolph recruited the wife of a Pullman porter, Rosina Corrothers. A Sunday school teacher, organist, and music teacher for the Liberty Baptist Church in Washington, DC, Corrothers became instrumental in growing and strengthening the union and creating the International Ladies' Auxiliary, which provided emotional and financial support to the union men. Other church women held leadership roles in the labor movement, including Nannie Helen Burroughs, who organized the National Association of Wage Earners, which agitated for better wages for women and functioned as an employment service and professional development resource.

Black women's activism continued into the years and decades of the full flowering of creative expression of the Harlem Renaissance, whose main hubs were in New York's Harlem, Chicago, and Kansas City. The mass exodus of African Americans from the Jim Crow South to what promised to be greater opportunities in the North for economic advancement and the chance to exercise their civil rights created the conditions for Black women and men to shine as artists, poets, musicians, and progressives. Church and faith were constants, undergirding women such as Georgia Johnson Douglas, who participated in the Pan-African movement and socially progressive Congregational Church meetings and published articles exposing lynching. Like Douglas, AME activist, noted lecturer, and eloquence teacher Hallie Quinn Brown lent her energy to several organizations: as seventh president of the National Association of Colored Women, promoter of the Colored Women's League, and activist in the temperance movement, among others.

As the Harlem Renaissance lost much of its fervor by the 1940s, Black women's participation in the civil rights movement seemed to gain even more force. From "Queen of the Gospel" Mahalia Jackson's inspirational music and as muse of Martin Luther King Jr. to National Council of Negro Women leaders Dorothy Height and Anna Arnold Hedgeman (see chapter 8), Black women refused to stand down in the struggle for rights. Perhaps the tipping point for Black women's activism in the second half of the century occurred around the time King was assassinated, in April 1968. The political foment and turbulence of this time equaled no other. The sexism that characterized the Black Power movement seemed to engender in Black women even more determination to achieve political, economic, and social parity as well as respect. Both in- and outside the church, they disrupted narratives that presumed Black power referred only to Black men and challenged household, church, work, and political hierarchies that attempted to subordinate them. One radical Black lesbian feminist group, the Combahee River Collective, crafted in 1977 a manifesto that voiced the concerns—frustrations, really—of Black women who sought their own freedom from intersectional oppressions and claimed that this freedom lay in identity politics.[65] Though not religious, their statement represented in some ways the anger many Black women felt because they had been struggling with the same issues for centuries. New voices emerged to take up the mantle of activism in the form of civil rights and criminal justice reform as well as sexism and racism in religious institutions. Included among them is Pauli Murray, the queer legal scholar whose work influenced that of Justices Thurgood Marshall and Ruth Bader Ginsburg and the first African American woman to be ordained in the Episcopal Church (see chapter 9). She and the myriad other Black womanists and womanist theologians foregrounded the survival of all Black people, the importance of a love ethic, and, for Christians, the rescue of Jesus Christ from values and images predicated on white supremacy. The Jesus known to African Americans is neither white nor blond-haired and blue-eyed. For some Black womanists and Black theologians, he is Black.

It is within this complex and complicated backdrop that the six chapters in this section are situated. They feature a diversity of activists, some of whom readers will be familiar with and some of whom they may not be. The task of the book is in fact to make visible the contributions of lesser-known Black feminist/womanists, including Madame Azalia Hackley, Carrie Williams Clifford, Theressa Hoover, and Anna Arnold Hedgeman, alongside the more well-known Nannie Helen Burroughs and Pauli Murray. The section begins with Angela Hornsby-Gutting's chapter on Nannie Helen Burroughs, whose public advocacy of economic and social justice fused practical education with woman-centered leadership; her work presaged the nonviolent, direct-action campaigns of the era and provided the Christian, moral armament for future generations of activist public intellectuals. Gospel ethics and music animated the work of Madame Azalia Hackley, whose uniquely situated activism demonstrates the richness of African American spiritual and intellectual work. Lisa Pertillar Brevard highlights Hackley's professed reliance upon biblical scripture and the teachings of Jesus as the engine propelling her tireless activities as a singer and social activist. A self-described "race musical missionary," Hackley's goal was to uplift fellow African Americans by creating massive, temporary community choirs to dignify and preserve spirituals—their history and peculiar folk inheritance—which had become largely ridiculed in American popular culture and were therefore at risk of being abandoned by its own people.

Around the time that Hackley was performing her gospel ethics, Carrie Ann Williams Clifford—a well-educated member of Washington's Black elite—committed her life to improving the educational, social, and economic condition of African Americans still facing the crisis of illiteracy sixty years after emancipation. P. Jane Splawn highlights Clifford's pedagogical activism aimed at ending racial injustice via education and strong Black community leadership. As a member of the Black community for whom she served as a teacher, Clifford was also part of a select vanguard of leaders within the African American community, engaging such issues in *The Crisis* as women's right to vote.

No less educated and determined, native Arkansan Theressa Hoover, a leading Black laywoman who challenged racial and gender barriers in both church and society, led the Woman's Division of the Methodist Church. Janet Allured traces the career of Hoover, who served for more than two decades as chief executive of the financially independent 1.2-million-member United Methodist Women. Allured argues rightly that Hoover deserves heretofore unacknowledged credit for her advocacy of women's full participation in church policy-making bodies; in her positions on the national boards of ecumenical organizations like Church Women United, the YWCA, the National Council of Negro Women, and the National and World Council of Churches; and, as an observer at the United Nations, her work to end racism and to promote feminism and LGBTQ+ rights. As much a theologian as many ordained preachers, Hoover analyzed how male-defined systems impacted Black women in particular and how white feminist theology, though illustrative, was incomplete.

The next chapter traces the achievements of religious feminist civil rights activist Anna Arnold Hedgeman. In her chapter on Hedgeman, Hettie V. Williams traces the civil rights activist's extensive contributions to the beginnings of the civil rights movement. She describes how Hedgeman's pragmatic feminist theology influenced her writings and activism and how she adopted an interracialist approach to human liberation that was juxtaposed with an intersectional approach to Black women's empowerment. As such, argues Williams, Hedgeman was arguably one of the more significant public intellectuals in the history of the Black freedom struggle.

The chapter that concludes this section seems startlingly different in its focus on race and materialism. In her chapter on Pauli Murray, Darcy Metcalfe analyzes the ways in which the legal scholar, civil rights activist, author, and Episcopal priest employed womanist and Black feminist methods for the purpose of reconfiguring history and the material world. Demonstrating how a singular person's commitment of will to the good of all people can reconfigure an entire nation's historical consciousness, Metcalfe contends, Murray used the concepts of countermemory/counternarrative in her poetry to "re-member" America's unique history of racism and sexism. Murray's formations of intersectionality emphasize its specific material elements, its countless variations in distinct locales, and the multiform ways that gender, race, and class are embodied in the becoming of the material world.

Twenty-First Century

The emphasis on materiality—and in particular the violence perpetrated on the Black body—continues in the book's third section. Carrying the torch of civil rights activism, criminal justice reform, and prison abolition, the religious and spiritual Black feminist activists on whom the three chapters center repeat the same refrain: justice for Black people in its myriad forms and an end to the intersectional oppression of Black women, who comprise the second poorest demographic of US society and who suffer the most from disparities in health care.[66] Their call for collective healing resonates loudly as two of the most pressing social problems of our time have reached epic proportions: the incarceration of people of color (mostly Black men) and the indiscriminate killing of Black women and men, whether by white supremacist vigilantes or at the hands of white law enforcement.

How does the church, or religion, fit into this racial justice framework? The meanings of both "church" and "religion" have always shifted to reflect the social, political, and economic vicissitudes of a given culture; neither the institution nor people's belief system is monolithic. At the same time, while neither carries the same weight or meaning for everyone, there are some common denominators. The beginnings of African American worship occurred in "hush harbors" where enslaved women and men met to practice a syncretized form of worship that combined the mainline religion of their enslavers with the customs and rituals of their motherland. These sites afforded some measure of independence from white dominance and created a space for foment.[67] They were also the seedbeds of activism that many African American-led churches from the nineteenth century to the present have carried or do carry out, to a greater or lesser extent. As the discussion thus far has shown, Black women's involvement in their churches or religiously affiliated institutions suggests that the moral imperatives of race and gender equality and justice under God inspired their activism. While it is true that Black politics may have its origins in some historically Black churches, it might be more accurate to gesture to the relationships between a Black theology of liberation, Black suffering, and Black resistance. And it is here that we find the locus of twenty-first-century Black feminist and womanist thought and action. In one way or another, the work centers Black lives because Black lives matter not only in the US but across the diaspora, across religions, across gender orientations and identities, across socioeconomic status, and across ability.

Whether spiritual or religious, twenty-first-century Black feminists, womanists, and womanist theologians have helped define the issues that demand serious attention. First, sexism in primarily Black male-dominated churches and racism within non-Black or predominantly white churches have continued to affect Black women's attitudes toward and participation in them. Womanist theologians have since the late 1980s pointed to the near elision of Black women's voices in the church despite their active work within and outside of this institution. They continue to voice concerns today, and joining them are members of the LGBTQ+ community who have experienced outright rejection in the very spaces in which they have sought solace and salvation. Womanist theologian Eboni Marshall Turman points out that, historically, "male power and sexism in the [Black] church have induced gendered violence against women, often with appeals to the name of God." She continues, citing a culture of misogyny and homophobia in the Black church, whose harms register on both emotional and physical levels. What is more, she writes, "the black church has tended to dismiss the significance of varieties of spiritual experience that exist outside of it. A decentering of the black church in womanist theology opens up space for asserting that not all black women are Christian."[68] Gumbs and Cullors (chapters 11 and 12) have found such a respite. (Sandra Bland, a member of the AME church in her native Chicago suburb of Lisle, Illinois, freely expressed her Christian beliefs in the videos she recorded.)

And so, the question of relevance arises. If Black lives matter, do all Black lives matter to the church? To God? In her book *Resurrection Hope: A Future Where Black Lives Matter*, Kelly Brown Douglas traces her journey of faith in a world where, despite a movement that began with a love letter to Black people and has grown to global proportions, one rightly questions whether "God is a white racist" and whether it is "possible to envision a society—and perhaps even a world—where Black lives can ever truly matter."[69] The answer is "yes," but the work will continue for as long as white supremacist culture dominates and corrupts what Douglas calls "the moral imaginary. . . . It is the reflexive moral response, that is, the nation's organic reaction to social issues and concerns . . . that palpable yet imperceptible force that defines the way in which a nation intuitively perceives and responds to matters of injustice as well as the way it envisions and enacts justice."[70] The animating forces galvanizing Black feminists and womanists are carceral justice, reparations, and the freedom to breathe, walk, run, drive, work, and sleep without one eye open. It is grounded in love and an ethic that centers salvation and life. That these dreams may become a reality are taken up in the book's final three chapters.

The first chapter in this section traces the events surrounding the contentious 2015 incarceration of Sandra Bland, whose subsequent death in a Texas jail cell sparked national outrage against state-sponsored violence. Phillip Luke Sinitiere explores the rich religious content of Bland's video blogs (vlogs) known as *Sandy Speaks* and presents Bland as a public religious intellectual who threaded religious conviction with social activism. Though the activist herself is dead, Sinitiere maintains, the concept of digital resurrection shows how Sandra Bland still leads the movement that bears her name.

Just as Bland's religious legacy and Black self-love live on in the hearts and minds of social justice advocates, Alexis Pauline Gumbs, the subject of the eleventh chapter, centers love and spirituality, which are inherent in Black women's intellectual production. Laura L. Sullivan brings much-needed scholarly attention to Gumbs, in particular her social justice activism embodied in her unique spiritual perspectives and practices. Gumbs is of the generation of younger Black women for whom scholarship, activism, and spirituality are inseparable and who are creating their own theories, pedagogies, rituals, and ways of organizing. Sullivan discusses Gumbs's Black Feminist Breathing Chorus, in which participants chant the words of Black women ancestors—for example, Harriet Tubman's "My people are free"—to connect with nonlinear time and thus reimagine liberatory possibilities.

Liberation from state-sanctioned violence in the form of this century's new civil rights movement is more than possibility. In the final chapter, I explore the relationship between Black feminist liberation theology and Cullors's spiritually grounded social protest activism in the context of criminal justice reform. #BlackLivesMatter was birthed in 2013 with a hashtag and a Facebook post in response to the acquittal of neighborhood watchman George Zimmerman, who shot an unarmed Black teenager named Trayvon Martin. Its cofounder Patrisse Cullors—now a household name and exemplar of community action and activism—describes the work of #BlackLivesMatter and criminal justice reform in general as "healing justice."[71] In addition to her leadership in the Black Lives Matter movement, Cullors has spent the bulk of her career on breaking down the prison industrial complex and working to reform a system that criminalizes mental illness. Together, the three chapters that conclude the book close a large and multifaceted circle of religious and spiritual Black change-makers and intellectuals whose work has shaped every institution in our society for nearly two hundred years.

RIPPLES IN THE POND

There is always more to be said and more to be done. Doubtless, scholars and other writer-researchers will discover more buried treasure and fill in more blanks on the pages of this nation's history. Let this book be one of many more to come. It is accurate to say that the remarkable women celebrated in this collection practiced "pebble ethics," a term coined by womanist theologian Katie G. Cannon. As Baker-Fletcher explains, "the premise of pebble ethics is that the small everyday acts that individuals and individual groups make in support of social justice spread out like ripples on a pond, having a profound effect on the larger society. Moreover, each small act for social justice adds up, with lasting, positive repercussions. More people than we can imagine benefit from one truthful act or word."[72] There is no denying that these womanist and Black feminist public intellectuals exemplify pebble ethics. Not only did (and do) they advocate for social justice by critiquing the structures of domination supported by a white supremacist patriarchal society, but they have embodied the spiritual ontologies that make them witnesses of the Spirit.

NOTES

1. Richard Rohr, OFM, "Initiation," Center for Action and Contemplation (May 25, 2016), blog.

2. Anna Julia Cooper, "Woman versus the Indian," in *The Voice of Anna Julia Cooper: Including* A Voice from the South *and Other Important Essays, Papers, and Letters*, ed. Charles Lemert and Esme Bahn (Lanham, MD: Rowman and Littlefield, 1998), 107. Italics in the original.

3. Arlette Frund also situates the gifted eighteenth-century poet Phillis Wheatley, whose verses and elegies attracted the attention and respect of elite public audiences from Colonial America to England and France, in the category of public intellectual, framing her work in the public sphere as defined by German philosopher and sociologist Jürgen Habermas. See "Phillis Wheatley, a Public Intellectual," in *Toward an Intellectual History of Black Women*, ed. Mia E. Bay, Farah J. Griffin, Martha S. Jones, and Barbara Dianne Savage (Chapel Hill: University of North Carolina Press, 2015), 50.

4. Maria D. Davidson and Scott Davidson, "Perspectives on Womanism, Black Feminism, and Africana Womanism," in *Introducing Ethnic Studies: African American Studies*, ed. Jeanette R. Davidson (Edinburgh, GBR: Edinburgh University Press, 2010), 255. The reader will also notice that the essays in this collection use the upper case "B" in reference to persons of African descent. See Patricia Hill Collins, *On Intellectual Activism* (Philadelphia: Temple University Press, 2013), xxiii–xxiv, for a brief discussion of capitalization of the word "Black." She admits that "there are still unresolved controversies surround[ing] the capitalization of the term 'Black'" and explains that she "uses [Blacks, African Americans, Black Americans, and U.S. Blacks] interchangeably when these terms are nouns referring to this specific historic and cultural group" (xxiii). The use of upper- or lowercase "B/b" is respected in direct quotations.

5. Though the chapters in this particular volume center on justice for African Americans, Black feminist activists are inclusive in their struggle; they demand justice for all members of nondominant groups.

6. It is also true that many members of dominant groups have used—and do use—their privilege for good, creating the conditions by which they can enter into solidarity with

members of oppressed groups. This is fraught with its own problems, of course, since privilege itself comes with blinders, and even the most well intentioned of us are liable to trip and fall (short). Therefore, it is imperative more than ever that whites and members of other privileged groups recognize and remain mindful of our social location and work actively to avoid harming members of nondominant groups. In addition, Black feminist and womanist intellectuals, such as those studied here, will continue to do as they have always done: call out instances of specious discourse and racial bias that elide the particularities of Black women's lives across social, economic, political, and gendered spaces as well as other markers of experience related to religion, ethnicity, ability, and so on. We do not live in a postracial society and the concept of color-blindness negates the possibility of acknowledging difference and being open to dialog and constructive criticism.

7. Kelly Brown Douglas, *Stand Your Ground: Black Bodies and the Justice of God* (Maryknoll, NY: Orbis, 2015), 139.

8. Alice Walker, *"Everyday Use,"* ed. Barbara Christian (New Brunswick, NJ: Rutgers University Press, 1984), 62.

9. See James Cone, *A Black Theology of Liberation* (Philadelphia: Lippincott, 1970; repr. Maryknoll, NY: Orbis, 2010); Jacquelyn Grant, "Black Theology and the Black Woman," in *Black Theology: A Documentary History*, ed. James H. Cone and Gayraud S. Wilmore, vol. 1, 1996–1979, 2nd ed. (Maryknoll, NY: Orbis, 2003); Delores Williams, "Womanist Theology: Black Women's Voices," in Cone and Wilmore, *Black Theology*, vol. 2, 1980–1992, rev. ed., 265–72; and Kelly Delaine Brown Douglas, "Womanist Theology: What Is Its Relationship to Black Theology?," in Cone and Wilmore, *Black Theology*, vol. 2, 290–99. To his credit, Cone acknowledged in the preface to the 1986 edition of *A Black Theology of Liberation* that he "fail[ed] to be receptive to the problem of sexism in the black community and society as a whole." He admonished Black theologians to "take seriously the need to incorporate into our theology a critique of our sexist practices in the black community" (xxiv).

10. Emilie Townes, "Womanist Theology," in *Encyclopedia of Women and Religion in North America*, ed. Rosemary Skinner Keller and Rosemary Radford Ruether (Bloomington: Indiana University Press, 2006), 1165.

11. Systematic theologian Jacquelyn Grant explores Black women's unique relationship with Jesus in *White Women's Christ, Black Women's Jesus: Feminist Christology and Womanist Response* (New York: Scholars Press, 1989). Her premise is that Jesus must be rescued from a sexist, elitist conception to one that values his servanthood. For Grant, Black women must foreground their relationship with God in the context of their own lives.

12. A thorough discussion of the Roundtable is too complex to reduce to an endnote, and readers are urged to read it in its entirety. See Monica Coleman et al., "Must I Be Womanist?," *Feminist Studies in Religion* 22, no. 1 (2006): 85–134.

13. Cullors was raised as a Jehovah's Witness but left the church due in large part to its exclusionary policies regarding gender identity. See Patrisse Khan-Cullors and asha bandele, *When They Call You a Terrorist* (New York: St. Martin's Press, 2017), 71.

14. Townes, "Womanist Theology," 1168.

15. Cheryl Townsend Gilkes, "Womanist Ways of Seeing," in Cone and Wilmore, *Black Theology*, vol. 2, 322.

16. Marilyn Richardson, qtd. in Kristin Waters and Carol B. Conaway, *Black Women's Intellectual Traditions* (Burlington: University of Vermont Press, 2007), 17.

17. Judith Weisenfeld, "Invisible Women: On Women and Gender in the Study of African American Religious History," *Journal of Africana Religions* 1, no. 1 (2013): 137.

18. See Antonio Gramsci, *Prison Notebooks*, ed. and trans. Joseph A. Buttigieg (New York: Columbia University Press, 1992).

19. See Dierdre O'Neill and Mike Wayne, "On Intellectuals," *Historical Materialism*, (blog), October 8, 2017, https://www.historicalmaterialism.org/blog/intellectuals. The blog is an excerpt from *Considering Class, Theory, Culture, and the Media in the 21st Century*, ed. Dierdre O'Neill and Mike Wayne (Boston: Brill, 2018).

20. Patricia Hill Collins and Gloria González-López, "Truth-Telling and Intellectual Activism," *Contexts* 12, no. 1 (Winter 2013): 37.

21. Collins and González-López, "Truth-Telling," 38.

22. Collins and González-López, "Truth-Telling," 41.

23. Keisha Blain, "Writing Black Women's Intellectual History," blog post, November 21, 2016, *Black Perspectives*, https://www.aaihs.org/writing-Black-womens-intellectual-history/.

24. One exception to this is Cheryl Fish's chapter on Nancy Prince, whose activism extends beyond the United States to Jamaica and Russia.

25. Catherine Squires, "Rethinking the Black Public Sphere: An Alternative Vocabulary for Multiple Public Spheres," *Communication Theory* 12, no. 4 (2004): 457.

26. Mia Bay, Farah J. Griffin, Martha S. Jones, and Barbara Dianne Savage, eds., *Toward an Intellectual History of Black Women* (Chapel Hill: University of North Carolina Press, 2015), 2.

27. One of the earliest scholarly contributions to Black women's intellectual thinking and activism appeared in a comprehensive anthology of rhetorical history in 1990, updated in 2001. See Patricia Bizzell and Bruce Herzberg's *The Rhetorical Tradition: Readings from Classical Times to the Present*, 2nd ed. (New York: Macmillan, 2001). Both the first and second editions include the rhetorical contributions of women and men of many races, ethnicities, nationalities, religions, and so on, dating back to Ancient Greece and covering several continents. The anthology's second edition is mentioned here because of its deliberate expansion of the number of women of African descent. Though not billed as "intellectual work" per se, the descriptor "rhetorical" signifies that their work is intellectual and comes in many forms, including (spiritual) autobiography, poetry, prose, and speeches. For a thorough list of monographs and anthologies of Black women's intellectual production, see Bay et al., *Toward an Intellectual History of Black Women*, note 7, p. 11.

28. Beverly Guy-Sheftall, ed., *Words of Fire: An Anthology of African-American Feminist Thought* (New York: New Press, 1995).

29. Waters and Conaway, *Black Women's Intellectual Traditions*, 2.

30. Bay et al., *Toward an Intellectual History of Black Women*, 3.

31. Bay et al., *Toward an Intellectual History of Black Women*, 1.

32. Brittney Cooper, *Beyond Respectability: The Intellectual Thought of Race Women* (Urbana: University of Illinois Press, 2017).

33. Cooper, *Beyond Respectability*, 9.

34. Hettie V. Williams, ed., *Bury My Heart in a Free Land: Black Women Intellectuals in Modern American History* (Santa Barbara, CA: Praeger, 2018).

35. Clarence Taylor, *Black Religious Intellectuals: The Fight for Equality from Jim Crow to the 21st Century* (New York: Routledge, 2002), 1, 6.

36. Taylor, *Black Religious Intellectuals*, 181.

37. Keisha Blain, Christopher Cameron, and Ashley D. Farmer, eds., *New Perspectives on the Black Intellectual Tradition* (Evansville, IL: Northwestern University Press, 2018).

38. Keisha Blain, "New Perspectives on the Black Intellectual Tradition," blog post, November 21, 2018, http://keishablain.com/archives/2637.

39. Blain, Cameron, and Farmer, *New Perspectives on the Black Intellectual Tradition*, 4–5.

40. Women who have sought the presidential nomination on major party tickets include Hillary Rodham Clinton (Democrat, 2008, 2012, 2016); Shirley Chisholm (Democrat, 1972); and Carol Moseley Braun (Democrat, 2004). Clinton was the Democratic candidate for president in 2016. California Senator Kamala Harris was a contender for the Democratic nomination in 2020. She dropped out of the race in December 2019 but was selected to be Joseph Biden's running mate on the Democratic ticket in 2020 and was sworn in as vice president of the United States on January 20, 2021. Other lesser-known African American women have run for president on minor tickets: Charlene Mitchell on the Communist Party ticket in 1968; Lenora Branch Fulani on the Alliance Party ticket in 1988; and Cynthia McKinney on the Green Party ticket in 2008. See Nadra Kareem Nittle, "Black Women Who Have Run for President of the United States," in *ThoughtCo.*, updated May 25, 2019, https://www.thoughtco.com/Black-women-who-have-run-for-president-4068508.

41. Kimberlé Crenshaw, "Demarginalizing the Intersection of Race and Sex: A Black Feminist Critique of Antidiscrimination Doctrine, Feminist Theory, and Antiracist Politics," *University of Chicago Legal Forum*, no. 1 (1989): Article 8, 140. In *Black Feminist Thought: Knowledge, Consciousness, and the Politics of Empowerment* (New York: Routledge, 2000), sociologist Patricia Hill Collins addresses this problematic in a nuanced way, naming it a "matrix of domination." Referencing Crenshaw, she "use[s] and distinguish[es] between both terms in examining how oppression affects Black women. Intersectionality refers to particular forms of intersecting oppressions, for example, intersections of race and gender, or of sexuality and nation. [These] paradigms remind us that oppression cannot be reduced to one fundamental type, and that oppressions work together in producing injustice. In contrast, the matrix of domination refers to how these intersecting oppressions are actually organized. Regardless of the particular intersections involved, structural, disciplinary, hegemonic, and interpersonal domains of power reappear across quite different forms of oppression" (21).

42. Linda Martín Alcoff, "The Problem of Speaking for Others," *Cultural Critique*, Winter 1991–92, 8.

43. For Alexis Pauline Gumbs and Patrisse Cullors, the spiritual underpinnings of their political and artistic intellectual production are informed in part by the West African Yoruba tradition, which is discussed in the chapters dedicated to their work. Gumbs also considers "Black feminism [to be her] primary spiritual practice, and it is informed by many other spiritual traditions." See Lisa Factora-Borchers et al., "Undivided State: A Conversation on Feminism and Spirituality," *Bitch Media*, December 12, 2017, https://www.bitchmedia.org/article/undivided-state/conversation-feminism-and-spirituality.

Notably, many more voices can be added to the chorus. For example, Black feminist Muslim women represent a large contingent of contemporary public intellectuals. One such exemplar is Su'ad Abdul Khabeer, who explicates the particular oppressions that confront Black Muslim women: "Intellectual racism and spiritual patriarchy intersect in deeply perverse ways and on a deeply personal level. Yet the 'personal is political,' and thus the experience of the Black Muslim woman intellectual reflects realities of even broader concern" (289–90). These broader concerns are those I have expressed earlier in the introduction: the interlocking oppressions of racism, classism, and sexism, as well as discourses of white normativity, all of which attempt—and sometimes succeed—in delegitimizing the work of the Black feminist public intellectual. See "To Be a (Young) Black Muslim Woman Intellectual," in *With Stones in Our Hands: Writings on Muslims, Racism, and Empire*, ed. Sohail Daulatzai and Junaid Rana (St. Paul: University of Minnesota Press, 2018), 289–90.

44. Karen Baker-Fletcher, *A Singing Something: Womanist Reflections on Anna Julia Cooper* (New York: Crossroad, 1994), 28.

45. bell hooks, *Salvation: Black People and Love* (New York: William Morrow, 2001), xxiv.

46. Nicole Jackson, "Black Love as Activism." *Black Perspectives*, February 28, 2018, African American Intellectual History Society, https://www.aaihs.org/Black-love-as-activism/.

47. hooks, *Salvation*, xvii.

48. Bettye Collier-Thomas, *Jesus, Jobs, and Justice: African American Women and Religion* (Philadelphia: Temple University Press, 2010), xiv. See also Judith Weisenfeld and Richard Newman, eds., *This Far by Faith: Readings in African-American Women's Religious Biography* (New York: Routledge, 1996).

49. See, for example, Judith Weisenfeld, *African American Women and Christian Activism: New York's Black YWCA, 1905–1945* (Cambridge, MA: Harvard University Press, 1997). The author examines forty years of Protestant Black women's commitment to serve women and men in New York, both to highlight the intricate connection between religion and activism and to show how Black women leaders operated outside the Black church.

50. For a specific treatment of Truth and her womanist ethic, see Jami L. Carlacio, '"Aren't I a Woman(ist)?': The Spiritual Epistemology of Sojourner Truth," *Journal of Communication and Religion* 39, no. 1 (Spring 2016): 5–25. For a thorough treatment of Truth and her life, see Nell Irvin Painter, *Sojourner Truth: A Life, a Symbol* (New York: W. W. Norton, 1996).

51. Jarena Lee, *Religious Experience and Journal of Mrs. Jarena Lee, Giving an Account of Her Call to Preach the Gospel*, rev. and corrected ed. (Philadelphia: Printed and Published for the Author, 1849), Google Books, https://books.googleusercontent.com/books/.

52. Collier-Thomas, *Jesus, Jobs, and Justice*, 27. The chapter entitled "Soul Hunger" (pp. 3–53) offers an extended discussion of this issue.

53. Collier-Thomas, *Jesus, Jobs, and Justice*, xvii–xviii.

54. "June 18, 1866. First Collective Action of Black Women Workers," in *The Black Worker: A Documentary History from Colonial Times to the Present*, vol. 1, *The Black Worker to 1869*, ed. Philip S. Foner and Ronald L. Lewis (Philadelphia: Temple University Press, 2019), https://tupress.temple.edu/open-access/labor-studies/28. To be sure, free Black women worked to support their families as early as the eighteenth century; they organized collectives officially in the postbellum years.

55. See Daniel W. Stowell, *Rebuilding Zion: The Religious Reconstruction of the South, 1863–1877* (New York: Oxford University Press, 1998), especially 73–79. For a thorough treatment of Black women's involvement in the Black Baptist church, see Evelyn Brooks Higginbotham, *Righteous Discontent: The Women's Movement in the Black Baptist Church, 1880–1920* (Cambridge, MA: Harvard University Press, 1994).

56. See Eric Foner, *Freedom's Lawmakers: A Directory of Black Officeholders during Reconstruction* (Baton Rouge: Louisiana State University Press, 1996).

57. See Jacqueline Jones Royster, ed., *Southern Horrors and Other Writings: The Anti-Lynching Campaign of Ida B. Wells, 1892–1900*, 2nd ed. (Boston: Bedford/St. Martin's, 2016).

58. Michelle Alexander, *The New Jim Crow: Mass Incarceration in the Age of Colorblindness*, rev. ed. (New York: New Press, 2012), 25–26. The "sun" Alexander is referring to comes from W. E. B. Du Bois's *Black Reconstruction in America: An Essay Toward the History of the Part Which Black Folk Played in the Attempt to Reconstruct Democracy in America, 1860–1880* (New York: Harcourt, Brace and Company, 1935; New Brunswick, NJ: Transaction Publishers, 2012), 26. He wrote, "The slave went free; stood a brief moment in the sun; then moved back again toward slavery. The whole weight of America was thrown to color caste. The colored world went down before England, France, Germany, Russia, Italy and America. A new slavery arose. The upward moving of white labor was betrayed into wars for profit based on color caste. Democracy died save in the hearts of black folk."

59. Du Bois (*Black Reconstruction in America*) couched African Americans' location in terms of a caste system; the subject of caste was later taken up by Michelle Alexander (*New Jim Crow*) and has been thoroughly researched and explored in Isabel Wilkerson, *Caste: The Origins of Our Discontents* (New York: Random House, 2020).

60. Weisenfeld, *African American Women*, 3. Weisenfeld studies specifically the New York City branch, but its aims mirror that of the organization in general. See Collier-Thomas, *Jesus, Jobs, and Justice*, 373–82, for a specific, historical treatment of the YWCA, including interracial cooperation and racism, Black church women's experiences, and the vicissitudes of the association's activist and uplift goals.

61. Grace Jordan McFadden, "Septima P. Clark and the Struggle for Human Rights," in Weisenfeld and Newman, *This Far by Faith*, 300–312.

62. Student Nonviolent Coordinating Committee, *The Voice* 1, no. 1 (June 1960).

63. Collier-Thomas, *Jesus, Jobs, and Justice*, 367.

64. Collier-Thomas, *Jesus, Jobs, and Justice*, 368.

65. Combahee River Collective, "The Combahee River Collective Statement," Library of Congress Web Archive, https://www.loc.gov/item/lcwaN0028151/.

66. See "Status of Women in the States," *Institute of Women's Policy Research*, updated 2022, https://statusofwomendata.org/women-of-color/#spotlightpowoc. Just over 28 percent of Native American women live in poverty, while 25.7 percent of African American women do. For information on health disparities, see Juanita Chinn, Iman K. Martin, and Nicole Redmond, "Health Equity among Black Women in the United States," *Journal of Women's Health* 30, no. 2 (February 2021): 212–19.

67. Laurie Maffly-Kipp, "An Introduction to the Church in the Southern Black Community," May 2001, *Documenting the American South*, https://docsouth.unc.edu/church/intro.html. Maffly-Kipp suggests as an exemplar the "self-styled preacher" Nat Turner, who led a slave rebellion in Virginia in 1831.

68. Eboni Marshall Turman, "Black Women's Faith, Black Women's Flourishing," *The Christian Century*, February 28, 2019, https://www.christiancentury.org/article/critical-essay/black-women-s-faith-black-women-s-flourishing.

69. Douglas, *Resurrection Hope: A Future Where Black Lives Matter* (Maryknoll, NY: Orbis Books, 2021), 180, xiii. Douglas is quoting the philosophical theologian William R. Jones, who posed the question "Is God a white racist?" Douglas's book asks this question implicitly.

70. Douglas, *Resurrection Hope*, 6.

71. Patrisse Cullors, "The Spiritual Work of Black Lives Matter," Interview by Krista Tippett, *OnBeing*, NPR, May 25, 2017.

72. Baker-Fletcher, *Singing Something*, 176. Baker-Fletcher is referring to Cannon's October 4, 1998, Zerby lecture delivered at Bates College entitled "Like Ripples on a Pond: Womanist Modes of Pebble Ethics."

SELECTED BIBLIOGRAPHY

Alcoff, Linda Martín. "The Problem of Speaking for Others." *Cultural Critique* no. 20 (1991): 5–32. https://doi.org/10.2307/1354221.

Baker-Fletcher, Karen. *A Singing Something: Womanist Reflections on Anna Julia Cooper.* New York: Crossroad, 1994.

Bay, Mia E., Farah J. Griffin, Martha S. Jones, and Barbara Dianne Savage, eds. *Toward an Intellectual History of Black Women.* Chapel Hill: University of North Carolina Press, 2015.

Beal, Frances M. "Double Jeopardy: To Be Black and Female." *Meridians* 8, no. 2 (2008): 166–76. http://www.jstor.org/stable/40338758.

Blain, Keisha N. "Writing Black Women's Intellectual History." Paper presented at the Association for the Study of African American Life and History, Richmond, VA, October 5–9, 2016. https://asalh100.org/annual-meeting/.

Blain, Keisha N., Christopher Cameron, and Ashley D. Farmer. *New Perspectives on the Black Intellectual Tradition.* Evansville, IL: Northwestern University Press, 2018.

Carby, Hazel. *Reconstructing Womanhood: The Emergence of the Afro-American Woman Novelist.* New York: Oxford University Press, 1987.

Carlacio, Jami L. '"Aren't I a Woman(ist)?': The Spiritual Epistemology of Sojourner Truth." *Journal of Communication and Religion* 39, no. 1 (Spring 2016): 5–25.

Chinn, Juanita, Iman K. Martin, and Nicole Redmond. "Health Equity among Black Women in the United States." *Journal of Women's Health* 30, no. 2 (February 2021): 212–19.

Collier-Thomas, Bettye. *Jesus, Jobs, and Justice: African American Women and Religion.* Philadelphia: Temple University Press, 2010.

Collins, Patricia Hill. *Black Feminist Thought: Knowledge, Consciousness, and the Politics of Empowerment*, 2nd ed. New York: Routledge, 2000.

Collins, Patricia Hill. *On Intellectual Activism.* Philadelphia: Temple University Press, 2013.

Collins, Patricia Hill, and Gloria González-López. "Truth-Telling and Intellectual Activism." *Contexts* 12, no. 1 (Winter 2013): 36–41. https://www.jstor.org/stable/41960420.

Combahee River Collective. "The Combahee River Collective Statement." Library of Congress Web Archive. https://www.loc.gov/item/lcwaN0028151/.

Cone, James. *A Black Theology of Liberation.* Philadelphia: Lippincott, 1970. Reprint, Maryknoll, NY: Orbis, 2010.

Cone, James. *A Black Theology of Liberation.* 50th anniversary ed. Maryknoll, NY: Orbis, 2020.

Cooper, Anna Julia. "Woman versus the Indian." In *The Voice of Anna Julia Cooper: Including* A Voice from the South *and Other Important Essays, Papers, and Letters*, edited by Charles Lemert and Esme Bahn, 88–108. Lanham, MD: Rowman and Littlefield, 1998.

Crenshaw, Kimberlé. "Demarginalizing the Intersection of Race and Sex: A Black Feminist Critique of Antidiscrimination Doctrine, Feminist Theory and Antiracist Politics." *University of Chicago Legal Forum* no. 1 (1989): article 8. http://chicagounbound.uchicago.edu/uclf/vol1989/iss1/8.

Cullors, Patrisse, and Robert Ross. "The Spiritual Work of Black Lives Matter." Interview by Krista Tippett. *OnBeing*, NPR, May 25, 2017.

Davidson, Maria D., and Scott Davidson. "Perspectives on Womanism, Black Feminism, and Africana Womanism." In *Introducing Ethnic Studies: African American Studies*, edited by Jeanette R. Davidson, 239–59. Edinburgh, GBR: Edinburgh University Press, 2010.

Douglas, Kelly Brown. *Resurrection Hope: A Future Where Black Lives Matter*. Maryknoll, NY: Orbis Books, 2021.

Douglas, Kelly Brown. *Stand Your Ground: Black Bodies and the Justice of God*. Maryknoll, NY: Orbis, 2015.

Douglas, Kelly Delaine Brown. "Womanist Theology: What Is Its Relationship to Black Theology?" In *Black Theology: A Documentary History*, Vol. 2, edited by James Cone and Gayraud S. Wilmore, 290–99. Maryknoll, NY: Orbis, 2003.

Factora-Borchers, zaynab shahar, Nyasha Junior, Alexis Pauline Gumbs, Danya Ruttenberg, and Krista Riley. "Undivided State: A Conversation on Feminism and Spirituality." *Bitch Media*, December 12, 2017. https://web.archive.org/web/20190810203530/https://www.bitchmedia.org/article/undivided-state/conversation-feminism-and-spirituality.

Foner, Eric. *Freedom's Lawmakers: A Directory of Black Officeholders During Reconstruction*. Baton Rouge: Louisiana State University Press, 1996.

Giddings, Paula. *When and Where I Enter: The Impact of Black Women on Race and Sex in America*. New York: Morrow, 1984.

Gilkes, Cheryl Townsend. "Womanist Ways of Seeing." In *Black Theology: A Documentary History*, Vol. 2, edited by James Cone and Gayraud S. Wilmore, 321–24. Maryknoll, NY: Orbis, 1993.

Gramsci, Antonio. *Prison Notebooks*. Edited and translated by Joseph A. Buttigieg. New York: Columbia University Press, 1992.

Grant, Jacquelyn. "Black Theology and the Black Woman." In *Black Theology: A Documentary History*, Vol. 1, 1996–1979, edited by James H. Cone and Gayraud S. Wilmore, 323–38. Maryknoll, NY: Orbis, 1993.

Grant, Jacquelyn. *White Women's Christ and Black Women's Jesus: Feminist Christology and Womanist Response*. New York: Scholars Press, 1989.

Guy-Sheftall, Beverly. *Words of Fire: An Anthology of African-American Feminist Thought*. New York: New Press, 1995.

Harris, Melanie. "Ecowomanism: Black Women, Religion, and the Environment." *The Black Scholar* 46, no. 3 (2016): 27–39.

Higginbotham, Evelyn Brooks. *Righteous Discontent: The Women's Movement in the Black Baptist Church, 1880–1920*. Cambridge, MA: Harvard University Press, 1994.

hooks, bell. "Black Women Intellectuals." In *Breaking Bread: Insurgent Black Intellectual Life*, edited by bell hooks and Cornell West, 147–64. Boston: South End Press, 1991.

hooks, bell. *Salvation: Black People and Love*. New York: William Morrow, 2001.

"June 18, 1866. First Collective Action of Black Women Workers." In *The Black Worker: A Documentary History from Colonial Times to the Present*, Vol. 1, *The Black Worker to 1869*, edited by Philip S. Foner and Ronald L. Lewis. Philadelphia: Temple University Press, 2019. https://tupress.temple.edu/open-access/labor-studies/28.

Khan-Cullors, Patrisse, and asha bandele. *When They Call You a Terrorist*. New York: St. Martin's Press, 2017.

Lee, Jarena. *Religious Experience and Journal of Mrs. Jarena Lee, Giving an Account of her Call to Preach the Gospel*. Rev. and corrected ed. Philadelphia: Printed and Published for the Author, 1849; Creative Media Group, 2021.

Maffly-Kipp, Laurie. "An Introduction to the Church in the Southern Black Community." *Documenting the American South*. https://docsouth.unc.edu/church/intro.html.

McFadden, Grace Jordan. "Septima P. Clark and the Struggle for Human Rights." In *This Far by Faith*, edited by Judith Weisenfeld and Richard Newman, 300–312. New York: Routledge, 1996.

Nittle, Nadra Kareem. "Black Women Who Have Run for President of the United States." *ThoughtCo*. Updated December 10, 2020. https://www.thoughtco.com/Black-women-who-have-run-for-president-4068508.

O'Neill, Dierdre, and Mike Wayne. "On Intellectuals." *Historical Materialism* (blog), October 8, 2017. https://www.historicalmaterialism.org/blog/intellectuals.

O'Neill, Dierdre, and Mike Wayne, eds. *Considering Class, Theory, Culture, and the Media in the 21st Century*. Boston: Brill, 2018.

Painter, Nell Irvin. *Sojourner Truth: A Life, a Symbol*. New York: W. W. Norton, 1999.

Richardson, Marilyn. *Maria W. Stewart, America's First Black Woman Political Writer: Essays and Speeches*. Bloomington: Indiana University Press, 1997.

Rohr, Richard, OFM. "Initiation." Center for Action and Contemplation, May 15, 2016. Blog. https://cac.org/your-life-is-not-about-you-2016-05-25/.

Royster, Jacqueline Jones, ed. *Southern Horrors and Other Writings: The Anti-Lynching Campaign of Ida B. Wells, 1892–1900*. 2nd ed. Boston: Bedford/St. Martin's, 2016.

Squires, Catherine. "Rethinking the Black Public Sphere: An Alternative Vocabulary for Multiple Public Spheres." *Communication Theory* 12, no. 4 (2004): 446–68.

"Status of Women in the States." Institute of Women's Policy Research. Updated 2022. https://statusofwomendata.org/women-of-color/#spotlightpowoc.

Taylor, Clarence. *Black Religious Intellectuals: The Fight for Equality from Jim Crow to the 21st Century*. New York: Routledge, 2002.

Townes, Emilie. "Womanist Theology." In *Encyclopedia of Women and Religion in North America*, edited by Rosemary Skinner Keller and Rosemary Radford Ruether, 1165–73. Bloomington: Indiana University Press, 2006.

Turman, Eboni Marshall. "Black Women's Faith, Black Women's Flourishing." *The Christian Century*, February 28, 2019. https://www.christiancentury.org/article/critical-essay/black-women-s-faith-black-women-s-flourishing.

Wallace, Michelle. "Anger in Isolation: A Black Feminist's Search for Sisterhood." In *Words of Fire: An Anthology of African-American Feminist Thought*, edited by Beverly Guy-Sheftall, 220–27. New York: New Press, 1995.

Waters, Kristin, and Carol B. Conaway. *Black Women's Intellectual Traditions*. Burlington: University of Vermont Press, 2007.

Weisenfeld, Judith. "Invisible Women: On Women and Gender in the Study of African American Religious History." *Journal of Africana Religions* 1, no. 1 (2013): 133–49.

Weisenfeld, Judith, and Richard Newman, eds. *This Far by Faith: Readings in African-American Women's Religious Biography*. New York: Routledge, 1996.

Wilkerson, Isabel. *Caste: The Origins of Our Discontents*. New York: Random House, 2020.

Williams, Delores. "Womanist Theology: Black Women's Voices." In *Black Theology: A Documentary History*, Vol. 2, 1980–1992, edited by James H. Cone and Gayraud S. Wilmore, 265–72. Maryknoll, NY: Orbis, 1993.

NINETEENTH CENTURY

Chapter 1

MORE THAN "MERE" RHETORIC

Jarena Lee's *Religious Experience* Read through a Womanist Lens

NEELY McLAUGHLIN

Jarena Lee, the first authorized woman preacher in the African Methodist Episcopal (AME) Church, was born free in New Jersey. Her critique of patriarchal views and racism in the context of nineteenth-century Christianity constitutes a broadly significant indictment of white supremacist power structures. Although she was a public political figure in her role as mystic traveling preacher, called and inspired by God, most of what is known of Lee comes from her autobiographical narrative *Religious Experience and Journal of Mrs. Jarena Lee, Giving an Account of Her Call to Preach the Gospel*, published in 1849.[1] Employing the genre of the nineteenth-century spiritual narrative, Lee focuses on spiritual matters such as her conversion, her call to preach, and her sermons, but she offers only tantalizingly rare personal information. She commences her narrative by recounting her obliviousness to her sinful state and continues on to describe her eventual awareness of sin and subsequent conversion, a trajectory that consists of five phases common in nineteenth-century evangelical texts, as Virginia Brereton describes:

> (1) life before the conversion process began, when narrators more or less ignored the question of salvation; (2) a period when narrators became acutely aware of their sinfulness and the possibility they would be damned forever; (3) the surrender to God's will in the conversion proper, during which converts felt the oppressive sense of sinfulness lifted and gained confidence or at least hope that they were saved; (4) a description of the narrator's changed behavior and attitudes, resulting from conversion; and (5) an account of periods of discouragement and low spiritual energy followed by renewals of dedication.[2]

Lee relates intense periods of spiritual discouragement tied to her search for a church and eventually finds her home in the AME Church under the leadership of Richard Allen. Although she felt that she was a part of this community, she wrote that, initially, Allen rejected her call to preach because she was a woman.[3] Eight years later, when he became bishop, he granted her permission to lead prayer meetings and to exhort (15). It is only after she delivered an impromptu sermon "aided from above" that Allen accepted her call to preach, after which she became a traveling preacher for the AME Church (17). As William Andrews notes, eventually Lee "seems to have found accommodation with the all-male A.M.E. hierarchy, not as a licensed preacher, but rather as an official traveling exhorter."[4]

A SPIRITUAL INTERVENTION

In her narrative, Lee characterizes herself as a preacher, called by God though consistently questioned by those who did not accept the legitimacy of women preachers. The majority of the narrative is a record of her work as a traveling preacher and includes notes on miles travelled and sermons preached. For example, in the busy year of 1835, she writes, "I travelled 721 miles, and preached 692 sermons" (77). She travelled in Pennsylvania, through parts of New England, into the "slave country" of Maryland, and as far west as Ohio (5). Lee's experiences and opinions as she sets them forth, and the very existence of the published narrative, are widely recognized as historically significant. As the first African American woman to publish a spiritual autobiography, Lee drew early attention to the controversy of licensing women preachers and ordaining women. She is recognized by historians as a key figure in discussion about the westward expansion of her denomination, given her extensive travels as a preacher speaking to "promiscuous audiences" of men and women, white and Black.

It is not surprising, given her historical significance, that scholars have paid significant attention to Lee's narrative and her achievements. For example, in "A Womanist Response to the Afrocentric Idea: Jarena Lee, Womanist Preacher," Lorine L. Cummings presents Lee as a womanist and Afrocentrist "role model," identifying her as a significant illustration of the "'in-spite-of' faith" of womanists and noting her refusal to accept gendered limitations regarding her role in the Black church.[5] This work establishes Lee as an important historical figure in the Black church. Lee's spiritual narrative is also regularly included among other African American women's spiritual narratives of the period, including those of Zilpha Elaw, Sojourner Truth, and Julia Foote, the studies of which emphasize their historical and political significance. Bettye Collier-Thomas contextualizes Lee among other early northern Black women preachers as crucial in the establishment and development of the Black church despite limits on women's leadership opportunities.[6] Of Lee, among others, she writes, "Antebellum women preachers were social activists arguing for the liberation of their people. . . . [They] protested against slavery and attested to the equality of women."[7] Because of the political and rhetorical power of Christianity in the nineteenth century, Lee's engagement in Christian discourse is interpreted as the rhetorical deployment of spirituality for political ends and is therefore a rich site for continued scholarly inquiry. As Joy Bostic argues, "I am familiar with the critique that certain black women such as Lee and [Sojourner] Truth are overly referred to in scholarly discourses. Given their importance within American religious culture, however, I contend there remains too little scholarship on these women, particularly as compared to the extensive scholarship currently available on male religious icons both black and white."[8] In a similar vein, Joycelyn Moody calls for "appreciation of . . . holy women's narratives" that foregrounds their religious work, and she suggests the importance of reading Lee's spiritual autobiography with an explicit focus on its significance within Christian discourse and an early instantiation of Black proto-womanist public intellectualism.[9]

To fully appreciate Lee's significance as such, her narrative must be interpreted as a spiritual intervention in patriarchal Christian discourse, inextricable from her public role. However, due to its significance in nineteenth-century American public life, Christian rhetoric has both liberatory and oppressive potential that gives rise to a tendency among some scholars to read Lee's participation in Christian discourse as "mere" rhetoric. Some of the scholarly conversation about Lee ignores the theological nature and import of the narrative; some even consider it problematic. For instance, Andrews couches Christian rhetoric within a political framework, one in which writers like Lee engage in "misreading" the Bible for the purpose of revisionary "self-creation."[10] Underlying Andrews's argument is the notion that the sacred text of Christianity is rightly read as oppressive, in which Black narrators gain credibility through their rhetorical critique of Christian texts.

Other scholars writing on Lee go further, arguing explicitly or implying that conflict exists between being Black and being Christian. Renee K. Harrison, for example, sees Christian conversion as a manifestation of dominant white Christian cultural oppression and problematizes Lee's conversion as one of the "prime examples" that undermine the convert's identity.[11] Similarly, Richard J. Douglass-Chin views Christianity as one of the "trappings of whiteness."[12] Quoting Andrews, Douglass-Chin argues that Lee's narrative "demonstrate[s] . . . a universalizing and depoliticizing trend common in black spiritual life-writing of the nineteenth century, in which 'the conventional image of the pilgrim for

Christ usurps the persona of righteously indignant African.'"[13] While acknowledging her religious power, Douglas-Chin's approach ignores Lee's contribution to the religious discourse in which she participates and thus diminishes the historical and rhetorical importance of her life and work.[14] This perspective does emphasize the political significance of Christian rhetoric, but Lee's theological interventions are obscured, dismissed, and characterized as inherently problematic.

Taking Lee's narrative seriously means recognizing her contributions to Christian discourse, which cannot occur when the fact that she is Black implies that Christianity is inherently a political capitulation rather than a spiritual commitment. Scholars' emphasis on political language can also obscure Lee's significance in less dramatic ways. In the introduction to her book *Nineteenth-Century Black Women's Literary Emergence: Evolutionary Spirituality, Sexuality, and Identity*, SallyAnn H. Ferguson explains that "Jarena Lee [and other writers] . . . instinctively fortified their black female identities by successfully negotiating Christianity's ethical morass in antebellum America."[15] While Ferguson's characterization of Christianity at the time as an "ethical morass" is apt, understanding Lee's participation in Christian discourse as a negotiation that is instinctive rather than as a deliberate contribution elides the significance of the underlying yet powerful political overtones of Lee's work.

LEE AS PROTO-WOMANIST

Certainly, Lee "fortified" her position through Christian rhetoric, but at least as significant are the ways and extent to which she both critiques and contributes to Christian discourse and, in so doing, participates meaningfully in the religious public sphere. The assumptions that underlie these readings of Lee reveal some combination of understanding Christianity as overtly politically oppressive and normalizing an apolitical Christianity that is itself politically oppressive. The language of power is so readily meaningful as a way of approaching Lee's *Narrative* that such language obscures the integration of her resistance and theology, even in the context of important attempts to foreground her religious work. When Lee's religious discourse is read as a relic of a religious time and place, the power of the narrative to contribute meaningfully to an ongoing theological conversation goes unseen, but historical awareness of political realities ought not frame Christian discourse as an artifact. In Lee's case, prioritizing political concerns tends at the very least to mask the significance of her participation in Christian discourse, which thereby minimizes her significance as a public intellectual.

A useful and particularly apt reading of Lee employs the lens of womanist theology, which foregrounds religious concerns and thereby enables us to appreciate the force of Lee's Christian rhetoric as spiritually significant—the autobiography of a Black Methodist woman preacher and writer who engaged in the public discourse of the time through her preaching and narrative. As she predates womanist theology, framing Lee's work in this context is complex, as womanist ethicist Emilie M. Townes cautions: "It is inaccurate to describe Black women from the nineteenth century as womanists," though they might have "employed an interstructured social analysis in their activism" that aligns them theoretically with womanism.[16] Nevertheless, Townes sees such figures as Lee as an integral part of the conversation, noting that "at best, these women embody a nascent womanism that provides a rich framework for womanists of this era to flesh out in their theologies."[17] Although "at best" might suggest that women like Lee are not truly womanists, it is helpful to view Lee as a proto-womanist as a way to contextualize her narrative as a meaningful contribution to Christian discourse rather than to reduce her work to an exemplar of Christian rhetoric or as an indication of political capitulation. Townes addresses the relationship between religion and politics, explaining that "womanist theology is a form of reflection that places the religious and moral perspectives of Black women at the center of its method."[18] What might be seen as political problems from other critical perspectives are here framed in religious terms. She explains further that "issues of class, gender . . . and race are seen as *theological* problems." The lens of womanist theology is a framework that enables religion to function as the larger category in which political issues signify, which is of particular importance in regard to Lee as it aligns with her own presentation of the relationship between religion and politics. Conversely, as Townes writes elsewhere, "spirituality *is* a social witness."[19]

Lee's critiques of patriarchy and racism are fundamentally spiritual, and her contribution to Christian discourse highlights its liberatory potential. Thus, the womanist theological paradigm brings coherence to the relationships between life experience, spirituality, theology, and cultural critique in Lee's autobiography because, as womanist theologian Stephanie Y. Mitchem explains, "womanist theology is the systematic, faith-based exploration of the many facets of African American women's religiosity. Womanist theology is based on the complex realities of black women's lives."[20] Viewed from the standpoint of womanist theology, then, the struggles and joys of Lee's life are not divorced from her personal spiritual journey, and that personal journey constitutes her theology. In her reading of Lee in *Spiritual Interrogations: Culture, Gender, and Community in Early African American Women's Writing*, Katherine Clay Bassard aims to bring "cultural specificity" to readings of Lee, arguing that "the narrative line which enacts a search for religious community becomes the point of entry for the cultural as Lee encodes black oral forms of preaching and spirituals as structuring devices for her texts."[21] Bassard's framework establishes the spiritual world as significant because of its political implications through the primarily political concepts of "self-empowerment" and "communal political engagement."[22] Robert J. Patterson also analyzes Lee from a womanist perspective, arguing for "a more sustained dialogue between nineteenth-century African American women writers and womanist theology," which has beneficial potential "in both literary and womanist theological studies."[23] Patterson demonstrates that the lens of womanist theology is empowering, leading him to read Lee as fully political and fully religious, showing "how Lee grants epistemological privilege to black women's subjectivity," which in his view is designed "to foreground black women's ability to talk with, to, and for God in order to argue for black women's civil rights."[24] He focuses on Lee as presenting "resistance to patriarchal authority," noting challenges she faces and how she responds to them.[25] Patterson's work integrates religious and political language and concerns in approaching Lee's narrative, indicating the powerful potential of reading Lee through the lens of womanist theology.

I build on this work of bringing womanist theology to bear as an analytic lens through which to appreciate the value of Lee's writings. Here, I read Lee's religious and political concerns as equally significant and fully integrated, thereby explicitly rejecting the imposition of a hierarchical relationship between religious and political concerns in her narrative. Womanism itself brings a political focus to religion, as Stacey M. Floyd-Thomas and Laura Gillman suggest: the very use of such modifiers as "womanist" when applied to a theology text, they write, "accentuate[s] the ways in which our reflection on the sacred is informed primarily by our secular context (race, gender, and class), and by the way in which the sacred and secular have informed each other over history."[26] While it may foreground secular politics, a womanist lens also foregrounds integration of political engagement with spirituality and lived experience. Here, I resist privileging secular politics by focusing on this integration, and in so doing implicitly and at times explicitly reject a hierarchical relationship between political and religious discourses. A focus on integration illuminates the agency and brilliance of the pragmatic political rhetorical savvy of spiritual writers like Lee by allowing later critics to fully recognize their ownership of the genre of the spiritual narrative. I consider how Lee and her narrative embody womanist theology through a web of interrelated ideas and realities. Her identity as a preacher is spiritually significant; the writing and publication of her autobiography are public assertions of herself as a spiritual leader; her perspective and experience are important within public discourse; and her response to the racism and sexism in her culture, within the church and beyond it, functions as cultural critique. I conclude by considering the significance of reading Lee through a womanist lens in the larger context of the critical conversation about her.

Considered through the lens of womanist theology, the structure, content, and stated purpose of Lee's autobiography clarify the importance of understanding Lee as a religious figure whose contribution to Christian discourse is experiential. However, in keeping with the genre of *spiritual* autobiography, the narrative includes minimal biographical material that is unrelated to spiritual matters. As Frances Smith Foster writes, "details such as family history, physical descriptions, education, occupations, the names and circumstances of siblings, spouses, or children, and even the dates and places of crucial incidents in the narrator's life are minimized."[27] In the narrative as a whole, Lee describes how she sometimes suffered from protracted periods of illness, mentions thoughts of suicide, and references her family a few times, but other personal details are revealed only in passing. Even the brief section of *Religious Experience* headed "My Marriage," which follows Lee's conversion and Allen's initial rejection of her call to preach, simply mentions Lee's marriage to Mr. Joseph Lee, a pastor, in 1811. Further, the section describes Lee's illness, the death of five family members including her husband, and the fact that she has two young children (13–15). Even here, every circumstance is framed and interpreted in spiritual terms. Though Lee minimizes personal matters, her experience makes up the bulk of the narrative, which consists of an extensive account of her travels and preaching. Clearly based on her journal, this section includes notes on where Lee went, how she was received, and what she preached on. Her critiques of racism and sexism are incorporated into this experiential record, an approach that womanist theology frames as significant in its centering of Black women's experiential perspectives.

The interweaving of personal narrative and theology thus characterizes Lee's spiritual autobiography. It is in keeping with the generic requirement of the conversion narrative that Lee opens with intense awareness of sin when, at age seven while working as a servant, she lies about having completed a task: "At this awful point, in my early history, the Spirit of God moved in power through my conscience, and told me I was a wretched sinner. On this account so great was the impression, and so strong were the feelings of guilt, that I promised in my heart that I would not tell another lie" (3). As an instance of sin, this lie is far from an example of human depravity and ostensibly harms no one, though the story is presented with emotional intensity. Moody's words are helpful here: "The sentimental pedagogy used by the traditional spiritual autobiographer depicts her radical conversion from a sin-sick soul using a heart-wrenching representation of her transition from sin to sorrow to salvation."[28]

Lee's recounting of her sin signals her acceptance of the concept of original sin, a theological idea further explored when she attends a Presbyterian service, of which she writes: "These were the words, composing the first verse of the Psalms for the service: 'Lord, I am vile, conceived in sin, Born unholy and unclean. Sprung from man, whose guilty fall Corrupts the race, and taints us all.' This description of my condition struck me to the heart, and made me to feel in some measure, the weight of my sins, and sinful nature" (3–4). In an implicit critique of Presbyterianism, Lee subsequently considers suicide in her despair as the sermon has provided her with no hope of moving beyond her sin and guilt; but she is, as she sees it, prevented from such a step by God, though she does become ill due to spiritual labor and fear of judgment.[29] This is but one instance of the way in which the narrative frames and interprets Lee's life experiences in spiritual terms and, likewise, is an oblique way to promulgate her theology. Her conversion story further illustrates this dynamic in her exploration of different denominations, when she implicitly rejects Presbyterianism and Catholicism, finding her spiritual home in the AME Church. Here, in this Black Methodist community, Lee's conversion reaches a triumphant climax, which coincides with her call to preach. Reflecting the experiential emphasis of womanist theology, Lee's narrative presents personal experience as a basis for spiritual interpretation so as to educate readers and to participate in public discourse, including her support of Methodism and her critique of racism.

The connection between Lee's religious belief and her public voice in *Religious Experience* is manifested in her conversion and call to preach. Lee records her salvation as empowering: she gains her voice at the moment of her salvation, which occurs at the "instant" of her forgiveness of others, when she has a metaphorical experiential vision of God's glory. In being saved, Lee gains the power to speak publicly: "That moment, though hundreds were present, I did leap to my feet and declare that God, for Christ's sake, had pardoned the sins of my soul" (5). Here she gains the temporary "power to exhort sinners." Her conversion experience, although personal, is also publicly shared in the context of a church service. At this time, "the minister was silent," giving Lee the opportunity to speak to those present. This initial power to speak points toward Lee's call to preach.

Lee's engagement with expanding the role of women in the church is foregrounded throughout the narrative. Lee presents her call as a "surprise," and she responds with the concern that "no one will believe me" about having been called to preach (10). Lee's modesty is predictable, given that she is a Methodist, and is especially important rhetorically as she is a Black woman. As Chanta M. Haywood notes, "Women in the nineteenth century simply were not expected to enter religious culture as preachers. African American women certainly were not."[30] Though she gains a public voice as a preacher, she carefully presents herself not as seeking a platform but as responding to God. Scholarly discourse focused on the political utility of Lee's Christian rhetoric attends to the effectiveness of this strategy; the lens of womanist theology foregrounds the fact that, for Lee, preaching is both inherently spiritual and inherently political. Preaching may look like other forms of public speaking, but in a Christian context, it is a specific category of speech. In *Weary Throats and New Songs*, a historical analysis of early Black women preachers who pursued "the inner quest to answer the call of God" in spite of all manner of obstacles, homiletitian Teresa L. Fry Brown explains that "proclamation is sacred speech differentiated from public speaking."[31] To be a preacher is not to be just a public speaker, although as a preacher Lee speaks in public, and what matters is not just that preaching is about God for the people of God: the divine involvement of the Spirit in the call to preach and in preaching distinguishes preaching as sacred speech.

When Lee asserts herself as a preacher, she proclaims that she has been chosen by God as an intermediary. Taking seriously her call, she demonstrates that she is not simply using the power of Christian rhetoric to obtain a public platform, but instead makes the case through her experience that she, as a Black woman, should be recognized as a spiritual leader with a special role and direct connection to God. As such, as Brown notes, Lee feels inspired by and is a conduit for God.[32] Her personal sense of God becomes something more than personal when the Spirit inspires her to share it, and in her argument in favor of women preachers, she specifically discusses inspiration, which I address below. The fact that as a preacher she receives a public platform, one that she expands through the publication of her narrative, must not obscure the significance of her claim to be called by God to preach, a significance that the lens of womanist theology brings to the foreground.

Womanist theology critiques patriarchal dominance in religious contexts, foregrounding the necessity of attending to the experiences of Black women and their contributions to Christian discourse. Lee's critique of sexism within the church includes experiences, direct argument, interpretation of scripture, and even humor. When Allen first rejects her call, he does so because she is a woman (11). Lee records that at first she is relieved, yet she also notes that in being prevented from preaching, "that holy energy which burned within me, as a fire, began to be smothered." Lee laments that the patriarchal church structure not only causes personal spiritual harm but also harms Christianity in the public realm: "O how careful ought we to be, lest through our by-laws of church government and discipline, we bring into disrepute even the word of life." That the politics of sexism within the church could harm the public reputation of Christianity impels Lee to distinguish between church structures and true Christianity.

Patriarchal church policy harms the witness of the church and causes Lee's spiritual struggle, and at this point in the narrative, Lee presents a developed argument in favor of women preachers. She writes, "For as unseemly as it may appear now-a-days for a woman to preach, it should be remembered that nothing is impossible with God" (11). Lee's reminder of God's omnipotence is a clearly liberatory move and if accepted would end any argument about the unsuitability of women as preachers. Lee, however, does not wish to present women preachers as so strange that the idea would require an extraordinary intervention from God. She continues, "And why should it be thought impossible, heterodox, or improper for a woman to preach? seeing the Saviour died for the woman as well as for the man." Immediately preceding this argument in the narrative, of course, is a record that the patriarchal power of the church in fact had initially made it "impossible" for Lee to preach.

Having eventually achieved what might be "thought impossible," Lee highlights the existence of established doctrinal and social norms that undermine her authority as a woman preacher. She goes on to point out that Christ died for women, not just men, implying that women are both as worthy of and as in need of redemption as men, and emphasizes a direct relationship, unmediated by men, between Christ and women. Lee then turns to Mary as an example of a woman preacher: "Did not Mary *first* preach the risen Saviour, and is not the doctrine of the resurrection the very climax of Christianity—hangs not all our hope on this, as argued by St. Paul? Then did not Mary, a woman, preach the gospel?" (11; italics in the original). Part of her argument in support of her interpretation of Mary as a preacher relates to Paul's view, presented in 1 Corinthians 15, that the resurrection is the essential component of Christianity. The way that Lee defines preaching as sharing the news of the resurrection through reference to Paul may be particularly significant because Paul's famous passages about the role of women in the church are often decontextualized and invoked by those who are against women preaching. Lee also responds to the potential critique that "Mary did not expound the Scriptures, therefore, she did not preach" (12). She argues that preaching has been erroneously defined, over time, in such a way as to undermine the interpretation of Mary as a preacher that Lee herself presents: "To this I reply, it may be that the term *preach* in those primitive times, did not mean exactly what it is now *made* to mean" (italics in the original). In this passage, Lee challenges the conventional definition of preaching, implying that it is limited by its development in the context of systemic patriarchy. In so doing, she interprets the Bible, critiques the theology of others, and presents her own.

Lee circumvents the patriarchal power of the church by presenting her call to leadership as coming directly from God, and in the course of this argument in favor of women preachers, she develops this point by addressing education and inspiration. Using Biblical evidence and rhetorical questions, Lee argues that inspiration—not education—qualifies men to preach, concluding, "If then, to preach the gospel, by the gift of heaven, comes by inspiration solely, is God straitened: must he take the man exclusively? May he not, did he not, and can he not inspire a female to preach the simple story of the birth, life, death, and resurrection of our Lord, and accompany it too with power to the sinner's heart" (12).[33] Sharing the "simple story" requires no special education, and inspiration means that Lee can "accompany" that story "with power to the sinner's heart." The proof of a call is reaching sinners and connecting God to them, not education and institutional imprimatur. On this aspect of the nature of preaching, Brown writes that preaching is "communication of the inward manifestation of a command by the Holy Spirit to relate to others something about God's . . . purpose, and power in one's life and in the lives of all humanity."[34] From this perspective, Lee is responding to the Holy Spirit—what qualifies her to preach is being called and inspired, and her ability to be a communicative intermediary between God and humanity illustrates inspiration.

The preacher's life is part of who she is as an intermediary, and her communication is not abstracted from that reality. As Lee concludes her argument, it is fitting that the invocation of inspiration brings it full circle to the opening claim that God is powerful enough to call a woman to preach, leading to a personal reflection in which she declares the power of God in her life: "As for me, I am fully persuaded that the Lord called me to labor according to what I have received, in his vineyard. If he has not, how could he consistently bear testimony in favor of my poor labors, in awakening and converting sinners?" (12). In this discussion, Lee contributes her interpretation, explanation, argument, and experience to Christian discourse. Lee's argument in favor of women preachers reflects her belief that she is called to preach and that she has seen God's blessing on her work and demonstrates the centrality of personal experience claimed by womanist theologians. Further, this approach frames the part of her narrative that reads as an extensive record of her work as a traveling preacher as evidence of the legitimacy of her call. She does not simply reflect on her life's work but includes a vast body of evidence of her experience as called by God. Lee's existence as a successful preacher reveals that male control of the church's hierarchy is a spiritual error.

In recording her pursuit of her call and her work as a traveling preacher, Lee continues to critique the church's understanding of the appropriate role of women. The failure of a male preacher facilitates Allen's eventual acceptance of Lee's call to preach. The Rev. Richard William, as Lee puts it, "seemed to have lost the spirit" in the middle of a service. As for Lee, "in the same instant, I sprang, as by altogether supernatural impulse, to my feet, when I was aided from above to give an exhortation on the very text which my brother Williams [*sic*] had taken" (17). That scripture is Jonah 2:9 (KJV): "But I will sacrifice unto thee with the voice of thanksgiving; I will pay that that I have vowed. Salvation is of the Lord."[35] Lee references this verse, paralleling her own deferred call to preach and Jonah's delay: "I told them I was like Jonah, for it had been nearly eight years since the Lord had called me to preach his gospel" (17). While Lee does not at this point explain that she was prevented from fulfilling her call by a patriarchal church structure, she bypasses church hierarchy by appealing directly to God: "During the exhortation, God made manifest his power in a manner sufficient to show the world that I was called to labor according to my ability, and the grace given unto me, in the vineyard of the good husbandman." Lee interprets this as her call—authorized by God—to preach. And yet, though she is confident in God and her call, she expresses concern about the reception she will receive, and Allen's response surprises her: "I imagined . . . I should be expelled from the church. But instead of this, the Bishop rose up in the assembly, and related that I had called upon him eight years before, asking to be permitted to preach, and that he had put me off; but that he now as much believed that I was called to that work, as any of the preachers present."

Lee's recounting of Allen's support lends legitimacy to her own assessment of her call, but receiving Allen's support does not eliminate the opposition she faces as a woman preacher. For example, of one place where she preached, she writes, "On Thursday night, I filled an appointment. It was altogether a strange thing to hear a woman preach there, so it made quite an excitement, which made my labor very heavy, as the people were all eyes and prayed none" (87). Lee argues for the normalization of women preachers while neatly and humorously undermining a potential argument that women should not be preachers because they are distracting. In another instance, she incorporates a joke in her defense of her role and her opinion:

> I met with many troubles on my journey, especially from the elder, who like many others, was averse to a woman's preaching, And here let me tell that elder, if he has not gone to heaven . . . his objections to female preaching were met by the answer—"If an ass reproved Balaam, and a barn-door fowl reproved Peter, why should not a woman reprove sin?" I do not introduce this for its complimentary classification of a poor woman, who had once been a slave. To the first companion she said—"May be a speaking woman is like an ass—but I can tell you one thing, the ass seen the angel when Balaam didn't." (23)

Lee's decision to include this anecdote functions as a Biblical comeuppance that implicates her critics' obliviousness to spiritual reality, using humor as a mask for the seriousness of its problematic nature. Lee's experience as a traveling preacher brought her face-to-face with church patriarchy, which she speaks and acts against throughout the narrative, integrating her critique of sexism in the church, her experiences, her understanding of God's role in those experiences, and her understanding of Christianity and scripture.

ANTISLAVERY ACTIVISM

The subjects of racism and slavery are less prominent in the narrative than the critique of sexism, though they are clear. A member of the American Anti-Slavery Society, Lee asserts that slavery is wrong and explicitly condemns racism and slavery in a specifically spiritual way.[36] She criticizes the injustice of slavery by sharing a story of an enslaved person who helped her: "I had no help but an old man . . . he died in the year 1825, and has gone . . . to rest where the slave is freed from his master" (37). Lee's clear sympathy with the man and the reference to heaven as a place of freedom reflect an understanding of Christianity that moves toward justice, a point she makes in the course of recording her experience. Lee also incorporates into her narrative an analysis of slavery as a great evil for the country, writing, "the wickedness of the people certainly calls for the lowering Judgments of God to be let loose upon the Nation and Slavery, that wretched system that emanates from the bottomless pit, is one of the greatest curses to any Nation" (63). Lee labels slavery as unjust and evil, presenting a contemporary political reality in Christian terms, as a "curse" referencing the sinful state of the world, and as a "wicked" behavior that deserves God's punishment. In a context in which Christianity is often understood to condone slavery, Lee's presentation of slavery as unjust and sinful is theologically as well as politically significant. She offers a liberatory interpretation of Christianity that challenges an already contested Christian discourse.

This contribution is significant in the larger culture in which Christian rhetoric held considerable sway and develops the social witness of Christianity. In turn, Lee's political opposition to slavery is grounded in her Christianity. She engages with pro-slavery and abolitionist arguments by presenting her very existence as a Black woman preacher as an argument against a slave owner who believes that Black people do not have souls: "At the first meeting which I held at my uncle's house, there was, with others who had come from curiosity to hear the woman preacher, an old man, who was a Deist, and who said he did not believe the coloured people had any souls—he was sure they had none" (19). Lee believes that hearing her preaching changes his mind: "He now seemed to admit that coloured people had souls." In her analysis, changing this opinion leads to behavioral change: "This man was a great slave holder, and had been very cruel; thinking nothing of knocking down a slave with a fence stake, or whatever might come to hand. From this time it was said of him that he became greatly altered in his ways for the better."

Through sharing this experience and others, Lee explicitly responds to a pro-slavery argument, expressing her agreement with abolitionist views. For example, she writes of another encounter: "I also had the pleasure of meeting an anti-slavery society where I heard some very able discussions on the rights of the oppressed, and also clear demonstrations of the cruelty of the slaveholder, which was exposed with all its horror by a young man by the name of L——" (72). Just as she offers a clear condemnation of slavery, Lee also identifies racism in the church. In her search for a church, Lee encounters the white Methodist church, and though the phrasing is perhaps elliptical, it is clear that she rejects its racism: "It appeared that there was a wall between me and a communion with that people, which was higher than I could possibly see over, and seemed to make this impression upon my mind, *this is not the people for you*" (4; italics in the original). Lee then encounters Black Methodism, specifically the congregation of her eventual mentor Allen, and finds her church, "the people to whom my heart unites" (5). The context of this part of Lee's story highlights the critique, described by Foster, of the racism in the white Methodist church.[37] Foster points out that "the African Methodist Episcopal separation from the Methodist Episcopal church was not from matters of theological principle but because of the attitudes of intransigent white racists and the resulting determinations by black Christians to establish a congregation wherein they would be respected." Notwithstanding the racism and sexism in the church, Lee's religious leadership gives her opportunities to work against these social problems.

Lee's narrative validates the integration of her experience as a preacher in religious and political discourse. Thelma Townsend notes this integration, citing Lee's spirituality as central: "While Lee's autobiography is certainly a personal narrative . . . its essence is religious with an abundant retelling of the political culture of American society. She leaves a record of her transcendence of the socio-political forces of nineteenth century society which relegated her and other women to a subordinate and inferior place."[38] Here, Townsend interprets Lee's religious work as enabling her to transcend political obstacles. On one hand, Lee's personal life does not feature prominently, and in a rhetorical move of self-validation, she frames her story as a spiritual one, potentially minimizing her embodied self because being a Black woman was a liability for her as a public figure. On the other hand, Lee's perspective as a Black woman is central to her narrative. Personal stories and analyses are integrated throughout the published religious narrative and thereby brought into public discourse. As Foster writes, "narratives [such as Lee's] began with an apologia for publication which was at once a denial of egotism and an assertion of special authority," noting further that Lee "clearly believed that her life was exemplary, her words were valid, and her written testimony merited publication."[39] By integrating political and spiritual concerns, a womanist perspective undercuts any temptation to interpret Lee's participation in this necessary rhetorical move as a political maneuver at odds with its spiritual significance or as irrelevant to it. As such, it illuminates the power and brilliance of the pragmatic political rhetorical savvy of spiritual writers like Lee by allowing later critics to recognize the acumen of Black women spiritual writers like her.

This confidence is evident in the very fact that Lee published the narrative as well as in her reflection on its purpose. Bringing her narrative to a close, she writes, "I hope the contents of this work may be instrumental in leaving a lasting impression upon the minds of the impenitent; may it prove to be encouraging to the justified soul, and a comfort to the sanctified" (97–98). Her gesture toward the significance of her narrative upon the lives of her readers constitutes a claim that her life and experiences warrant public attention. Such confidence positions Lee as transcending political limitations through spiritual power: "There was an 'anyhow' in the gift of preaching. There was a dialectic balancing of the weary throat and the new song. Preaching, teaching, and writing God's word made the journey worth the struggle" (16).

Although she does not focus on her struggles in the extensive chronicles of her work as a traveling preacher, she often alludes to financial and health problems. Lee's life journey is full of trouble, but she remains dedicated to her call to preach, and it is as a preacher that she speaks, writes, works, and lives. To be a preacher is to be empowered by the spirit and is life-defining. The narrative immortalizes Lee by preserving and presenting her spiritual experience and the intervention of God in her life. Her own view of its potential significance for readers both establishes the public nature of Lee's life and story and reflects her conception of herself as a religious leader and part of a community.

CONCLUSION: THEOLOGY AS PUBLIC DISCOURSE

In occupying the overlap of political and religious discourse in nineteenth-century America, Lee's narrative of her Christian journey richly foregrounds her spiritual work while maintaining the significance of political realities and her views on them. Achieving this balance can prove challenging. As Peter Kerry Powers notes, "Relationships between ethnicity, religion, and cultural studies in America [are] . . . often uneasy." In Powers's analysis, "ethnicity embodies those human things [such as theology] . . . that the West no longer sees in itself," while at the same time, "if religion does make its presence felt, . . . attention is given to the apparently more 'universal' and disembodied concerns of religion and theology."[40] The point here is that religion can or even must be "justified" by "ethnicity," but when religion is attended to, what Powers characterizes as "ethnic particularity" is lost in a focus on theoretically universal abstraction. Womanism—Black women's experiential theology—speaks precisely to this problem and constitutes an antidote to it. Applying the lens of womanist theology to Lee's narrative brings her personal narrative into focus as both theology and public discourse and enhances her significance as a public figure.

NOTES

1. This narrative updates her 1836 publication. In his 2017 analysis of archival evidence "The Many Names of Jarena Lee," Frederick Knight notes that such evidence regarding Lee's life is limited and complicated by the range of spellings of her name, such as "Gerenia" and "Geranna." I follow the dates he ascribes to the publication of Lee's autobiography as well as the dates of her birth and death. Knight concludes that Lee died in 1864 based on census and other records, explaining, "Though the discrepancies in age and birthplace between Jarena Lee's autobiography and this census record raise some questions, it is likely that the 'Geranna Lee' of the 1850 census is Jarena Lee" (67). He concludes: "While gaps in our knowledge about her remain, it is clear that Jarena Lee died in poverty in Philadelphia in early 1864" (68). Frederick Knight, "The Many Names of Jarena Lee," *Pennsylvania Magazine of History and Biography* 141, no. 1 (January 2017): 59–68.

2. Virginia Brereton, *From Sin to Salvation: Stories of Women's Conversions, 1800 to the Present* (Bloomington: Indiana University Press, 1991), 6.

3. Jarena Lee, *Religious Experience and Journal of Mrs. Jarena Lee, Giving an Account of Her Call to Preach the Gospel*, rev. and corrected ed. (Philadelphia: Printed and Published for the Author, 1849), 11. Subsequent citations to this book are to this edition and will be provided parenthetically in the text.

4. William Andrews, introduction to *Sisters of the Spirit: Three Black Women's Autobiographies of the Nineteenth Century* (Bloomington: Indiana University Press, 1986), 6.

5. Lorine L. Cummings, "A Womanist Response to the Afrocentric Idea: Jarena Lee, Womanist Preacher," in *Living the Intersection: Womanism and Afrocentrism in Theology*, ed. Cheryl J. Sanders (Minneapolis: Fortress Press, 1995), 64, 63.

6. Bettye Collier-Thomas, *Jesus, Jobs, and Justice: African American Women and Religion* (New York: Alfred A. Knopf, 2010), 26–27.

7. Collier-Thomas, *Jesus, Jobs, and Justice*, 29.

8. Joy R. Bostic, *African American Female Mysticism: Nineteenth-Century Religious Activism* (New York: Palgrave Macmillan US, 2013), 145.

9. Joycelyn Moody, *Sentimental Confessions: Spiritual Narratives of Nineteenth-Century African American Women* (Athens: University of Georgia Press, 2001), xi.

10. William Andrews, *To Tell a Free Story: The First Century of Afro-American Autobiographies of the Nineteenth Century* (Urbana: University of Illinois Press, 1986), 14.

11. Renee K. Harrison, *Enslaved Women and the Art of Resistance in Antebellum America* (New York: Palgrave Macmillan, 2009), 138. In Harrison's analysis of Lee, "the fullness of her personhood was suppressed [by the 'conditions' of her conversion] and further suppressed by black male clergy and the Bible" (141).

12. Richard J. Douglass-Chin, *Preacher Woman Sings the Blues: The Autobiographies of Nineteenth-Century African American Evangelists* (Columbia: University of Missouri Press, 2001), 24–25.

13. Douglass-Chin, *Preacher Woman*, 36.

14. Timothy Powell's review of *Preacher Woman Sings the Blues* reflects this concern: "To equate Christianity with 'the trappings of whiteness,' . . . fails to do justice to the integrity of the black church or to this fundamentally important form of early African American writing." Powell, Review of *Preacher Woman Sings the Blues* by Richard J. Douglass-Chin, *American Literature* 74, no. 3 (2002): 646.

15. SallyAnn H. Ferguson, introduction to *Nineteenth-Century Black Women's Literary Emergence: Evolutionary Spirituality, Sexuality, and Identity*, ed. SallyAnn H. Ferguson (New York: Peter Lang, 2008), xxviii.

16. Emilie M. Townes, "Womanist Theology," in *Encyclopedia of Women and Religion in North America*, ed. Rosemary Skinner Keller and Rosemary Radford Ruether (Bloomington: University of Indiana Press, 1986), 1168.

17. Townes, "Womanist Theology." Townes explores this legacy in "Finding the Legacy: Nineteenth-Century African American Women's Spirituality and Social Reform," in her *In a Blaze of Glory: Womanist Spirituality as Social Witness* (Nashville: Abingdon Press, 1995), 30–46.

18. Townes, "Womanist Theology," 1168.

19. Townes, introduction, *In a Blaze of Glory*, 10.

20. Stephanie Y. Mitchem, *Introducing Womanist Theology* (Maryknoll, NY: Orbis Books, 2002), ix.

21. Katherine Clay Bassard, *Spiritual Interrogations: Culture, Gender, and Community in Early African American Women's Writing* (Princeton, NJ: Princeton University Press, 1999), 8.

22. Bassard, *Spiritual Interrogations*, 4. Referring specifically to the relationship between religious conversation and political engagement in Maria Stewart's work, Bassard explains: "The sense of a dialogue between metadiscursive realms—between different 'worlds,' we might say—for the purpose of both self-empowerment and communal political engagement informs this book" (4). Bassard's conception of spiritual and political "realms" reflects an interest in both, though the "spiritual" in Bassard's title is clearly political in her framework.

23. Robert J. Patterson, "A Triple-Twined Re-Appropriation: Womanist Theology and Gendered-Racial Protest in the Writings of Jarena Lee, Frances E. W. Harper, and Harriet Jacobs," *Religion and Literature* 45, no. 2 (2013): 76.

24. Patterson, "Triple-Twined Re-Appropriation," 61.

25. Patterson, "Triple-Twined Re-Appropriation," 62.

26. Stacey M. Floyd-Thomas and Laura Gillman, "'The Whole Story Is What I'm After': Womanist Revolutions and Liberation Feminist Revelations through Biomythography and Emancipatory Historiography," *Black Theology: An International Journal* 3, no. 2 (2005): 176.

27. Frances Smith Foster, *Written by Herself: Literary Production by African American Women, 1746–1892* (Bloomington: Indiana University Press, 1993), 60.

28. Moody, *Sentimental Confessions*, 52.

29. Interestingly, the association of Calvinist doctrine and suicide has precedent. In 1842, the moderate Calvinist Episcopalian Reuel Keith died by suicide, resulting in some speculation that his Calvinism was responsible. According to E. Brooks Holifield, "When [Keith] fell into a depression in 1840 and took his own life, the rumor circulated that his doctrine was to blame." Holifield, *Theology in America: Christian Thought from the Age of the Puritans to the Civil War* (New Haven, CT: Yale University Press, 2003), 241.

30. Chanta M. Haywood, *Prophesying Daughters: Black Women Preachers and the Word, 1823–1913* (Columbia: University of Missouri Press, 2003), 38.

31. Teresa L. Fry Brown, *Weary Throats and New Songs: Black Women Proclaiming God's Word* (Nashville: Abingdon Press, 2003), 25, 17.

32. Brown, *Weary Throats*, 17.

33. Though the phrasing implies a question, the quoted material ends with a period, which suggests that it was meant less as a question than a statement.

34. Brown, *Weary Throats*, 17.

35. Jonah 2:9, Holy Bible, King James Version.

36. In her narrative, Lee mentions the society in passing: "My mind was somewhat divided about going to N. York as I wanted to see the convention of the American Anti-Slavery Society" (89). The fact that she focuses more on arguments and objections to women being preachers than she does on arguments against slavery warrants further analysis, for at least three reasons. First, it may suggest that she sees racism as more obviously wrong, thus requiring less support; second, she expects more opposition from her primary intended audience to the first point than to the second, perhaps related to her critique of sexism in the Black church; or third, she does not wish to emphasize her argument against racism because she believes that doing so could weaken her credibility, presumably among white audiences. Regardless, the significance of her identity as a Black woman more than informs her theology: her identity is integral to her theology.

37. Foster, *Written by Herself*, 68.

38. Thelma Townsend, "Jarena Lee, Forerunner," *NAAAS Conference Proceedings* (Scarborough, ME: National Association of African American Studies, 2010), 1431.

39. Foster, *Written by Herself*, 60, 69.

40. Peter Kerry Powers, *Recalling Religions: Resistance, Memory, and Cultural Revision in Ethnic Women's Literature* (Knoxville: University of Tennessee Press, 2001), 2–3.

SELECTED BIBLIOGRAPHY

Andrews, William. *Sisters of the Spirit: Three Black Women's Autobiographies of the Nineteenth Century*. Bloomington: Indiana University Press, 1986.

Andrews, William. *To Tell a Free Story: The First Century of Afro-American Autobiographies of the Nineteenth Century*. Urbana: University of Illinois Press, 1986.

Bassard, Katherine Clay. *Spiritual Interrogations: Culture, Gender, and Community in Early African American Women's Writing*. Princeton, NJ: Princeton University Press, 1999.

Bostic, Joy R. *African American Female Mysticism: Nineteenth-Century Religious Activism*. New York: Palgrave Macmillan US, 2013.

Brereton, Virginia. *From Sin to Salvation: Stories of Women's Conversions, 1800 to the Present*. Bloomington: Indiana University Press, 1991.

Brown, Teresa L. Fry. *Weary Throats and New Songs: Black Women Proclaiming God's Word*. Nashville: Abingdon Press, 2003.

Collier-Thomas, Bettye. *Jesus, Jobs, and Justice: African American Women and Religion*. New York: Alfred A. Knopf, 2010.

Cummings, Lorine L. "A Womanist Response to the Afrocentric Idea: Jarena Lee, Womanist Preacher." In *Living the Intersection: Womanism and Afrocentrism in Theology*, edited by Cheryl J. Sanders. Minneapolis: Fortress Press, 1995.

Douglass-Chin, Richard J. *Preacher Woman Sings the Blues: The Autobiographies of Nineteenth-Century African American Evangelists.* Columbia: University of Missouri Press, 2001.

Ferguson, SallyAnn H. Introduction. *Nineteenth-Century Black Women's Literary Emergence: Evolutionary Spirituality, Sexuality, and Identity*, edited by SallyAnn H. Ferguson, xiiv–xliv. New York: Peter Lang, 2008.

Floyd-Thomas, Stacey M., and Laura Gillman. "'The Whole Story Is What I'm After': Womanist Revolutions and Liberation Feminist Revelations through Biomythography and Emancipatory Historiography." *Black Theology: An International Journal* 3, no. 2 (July 2005): 176–99.

Foster, Frances Smith. *Written by Herself: Literary Production by African American Women, 1746–1892.* Bloomington: Indiana University Press, 1993.

Harrison, Renee K. *Enslaved Women and the Art of Resistance in Antebellum America.* New York: Palgrave Macmillan, 2009.

Haywood, Chanta M. *Prophesying Daughters: Black Women Preachers and the Word, 1823–1913.* Columbia: University of Missouri Press, 2003.

Holifield, E. Brooks. *Theology in America: Christian Thought from the Age of the Puritans to the Civil War.* New Haven, CT: Yale University Press, 2003.

Knight, Frederick. "The Many Names of Jarena Lee." *Pennsylvania Magazine of History and Biography* 141, no. 1 (January 2017): 59–68.

Lee, Jarena. *Religious Experience and Journal of Mrs. Jarena Lee, Giving an Account of Her Call to Preach the Gospel.* Rev. and corrected ed. Philadelphia: Printed and Published for the Author, 1849.

Mitchem, Stephanie Y. *Introducing Womanist Theology.* Maryknoll, NY: Orbis Books, 2002.

Moody, Joycelyn. Preface. *Sentimental Confessions: Spiritual Narratives of Nineteenth-Century African American Women.* Athens: University of Georgia Press, 2001.

Patterson, Robert J. "A Triple-Twined Re-Appropriation: Womanist Theology and Gendered-Racial Protest in the Writings of Jarena Lee, Frances E. W. Harper, and Harriet Jacobs." *Religion and Literature* 45, no. 2 (2013): 55–82.

Powell, Timothy. Review of *Preacher Woman Sings the Blues*, by Richard J. Douglass-Chin. *American Literature* 74, no. 3 (2002): 645–47.

Powers, Peter Kerr. *Recalling Religions: Resistance, Memory, and Cultural Revision in Ethnic Women's Literature.* Knoxville: University of Tennessee Press, 2001.

Townes, Emilie M. *In a Blaze of Glory: Womanist Spirituality as Social Witness.* Nashville: Abingdon Press, 1995.

Townes, Emilie M. "Womanist Theology." In *Encyclopedia of Women and Religion in North America*, edited by Rosemary Skinner Keller and Rosemary Radford Ruether, 1165–73. Bloomington: University of Indiana Press, 1986.

Townsend, Thelma. "Jarena Lee, Forerunner." In *NAAAS Conference Proceedings*, 1428–36. Scarborough, ME: National Association of African American Studies, 2010.

Chapter 2

JOURNEYS AND WARNINGS

Nancy Prince's Resistant Truth-Telling in New England, Russia, and Jamaica

CHERYL J. FISH

When Nancy Gardner Prince stood on the deck of the *Romulus*, leaving Boston for Russia in 1824, she must have felt the presence of a divine power that she trusted, as well as anticipation and fear. A freeborn African American woman from Massachusetts who had worked as a domestic and been part of Boston's tight-knit Black community, Prince was about to leave the United States for the first time. Her departure was a springboard for many important developments in her life and, in a larger context, serves as an example of how mobility for African Americans leads to the deployment of a critical voice within the global public sphere. Prince's travels and subsequent accounts of them in hybrid travelogues add a significant, gendered dimension to early Black Atlantic tradition to include women in a genre that had focused on men and point to a complex narrative strategy through which we can study the history of transnational agency for Black women.

Prince goes beyond prescribed notions, should we have them, of Black women's lives and work in the antebellum period. Her resistance to categorization—she was a traveler, worker, public speaker, writer, and philanthropist whose texts are not slave narratives or recently recovered fiction—may account for the silence surrounding the significance of her interventions into institutional and colonial practices. Why, we might ask, was she marginalized by her peers and, until the late 1990s, by scholars of literature, women's studies, African American studies, and cultural studies?[1] For Prince was free to travel away from her home, but she justified this move within a context of duty and then benevolent labor, a variation of what Michele Mitchell calls "the Black aspiring class."[2] First, she traveled as a wife accompanying her husband to Russia, where he was to be a guard for the tsar and where she would run her own garment-making business. Then she traveled as a widow to Jamaica to do missionary work, helping to educate and uplift emancipated Afro-Jamaicans and raise funds for a manual labor school for orphans she planned to establish in Kingston. Of her desire to leave New England in 1840 she wrote: "My mind, after the emancipation in the West Indies, was bent upon going to Jamaica. A field of usefulness seemed spread out before me. . . . I hoped that I might aid, in some small degree, to raise up and encourage the emancipated inhabitants, and teach the young children to read and work, to fear God, and put their trust in the Saviour."[3]

Although humble about her own contributions, Prince was virtually ignored in public conversations by her contemporaries and then again in research on early African American women's writing beginning in the mid-1990s. I am claiming, however, that Prince's writing is a significant contribution to social critique by Black women using the hybrid genres available to her. As traveler, ethnographer, and evangelist, Prince could foresee possible alliances emerging out of the work of "usefulness" or uplift, alliances that might disrupt certain discourses of racial stereotyping, colonial power, and the mechanisms of slavery. Thus, she works at what Mitchell calls the intersection of the "sociopolitical body."[4] If we gender Paul Gilroy's *The Black Atlantic* to include women as cultural agents, Prince's significant border and water crossings between the Americas, Europe, and Russia are an attempt to disrupt ethnic particularisms from a number of provisional home spaces.[5] Her evangelical New England voice registers outrage from the scenes of empire and emancipation in Russia and then Jamaica, taking to task those who fail to live up to her sense of Christian ethics or the ideals of the American Declaration of Independence.

HYBRID DISCOURSES

Prince's travelogues include an 1841 pamphlet, *The West Indies: Being a Description of the Islands, Progress of Christianity, Education, and Liberty among the Colored Population Generally*, and three editions (1850, 1853, and 1856) of *A Narrative of the Life and Travels of Mrs. Nancy Prince*. In addition, she wrote several letters to the abolitionist press that discussed the discrimination and ill treatment that took place during her travels, as in her 1841 letter to William Lloyd Garrison.[6] These works present us with complex, cross-cultural discourse on mobility, emigration, and the work of uplift in varying colonial contexts. An important factor to consider when assessing Prince's work is how she discursively negotiates with a particular readership cutting across race and gender, a literate public of Black New Englanders, and committed white abolitionists.[7] Her sensibility regarding gender roles and her attention to women's plight and mental health challenges might be said to form the basis of early Black feminist positionality and the gendering of women's racial and cultural agency. Unlike most other writers of travelogues in the antebellum period, she anticipates and expresses the anxieties that signify the complex realities of her Black readers' lives as free subjects who have great advantages over their enslaved counterparts, yet who as Americans experience racism, discrimination, mob violence, and under certain conditions the possibility of being enslaved. Like Harriet Wilson's heavily autobiographical 1859 novel, *Our Nig*, Prince addresses the hypocrisy of northern whites in their treatment of Blacks, but she does so less overtly by using cautionary tales and biblical allegory.

Prince's travel writing becomes more significant when we consider that the African American slave narrative, often written under the direction of white sponsors to move white northern readers to action, has been the dominant genre of antebellum African American writing studied and canonized since the late twentieth century and has come to be nearly synonymous with the African American's journey.

With that in mind, Prince's pamphlet, narrative, and letters to the abolitionist press based on her travels as a free northern subject are important vehicles that convey other African American experiences and compel us to recognize that other stories, in dialogue with the reality of slavery, were being produced and read. We might say that Prince's accounts are cautionary allegories for Blacks and examples of misuse of power that their white allies in the struggle needed to note. Prince puts Black readers on alert, pointing to mistakes, exaggerated promises, and faulty historiography promulgated by missionaries and colonial administrators in their dealings with freed Afro-Jamaicans as well as emigrants and, in doing so, engages in the discourse about emigration, one of the border crossings that mark the Black Atlantic. Prince encouraged Black readers to stay in the United States, even though she found travel a liberating, albeit dangerous, experience that enabled her to perform active philanthropy between stints as a needlewoman.[8]

My reading of Prince begins with a brief biographical sketch, meant to be partial and subjective. Then I shall discuss how Prince fashioned a form of "resistant truth telling" that draws on multiple traditions, including the missionary report, slave narrative, and spiritual conversion narrative. Finally, I read her journeys to Russia and Jamaica as examples of mobile subjectivity through which she presents multiple narrative positions and interventions vis-à-vis each context in relation to power, authority, conflict, geopolitical position, and ethnic or racial identities. (In between these two trips, she lived in Boston and was involved in the abolitionist movement there, but she commits only one paragraph in her narrative to those activities. I also analyze the implications of this significant omission.)

Through closely reading these shifting locations and Prince's relationships to various forms of imperial and colonial rule, we can understand the complex relationships between gender, the body, and cross-cultural examples of compliance and resistance. In challenging racism and other forms of corrupt or unethical behavior, Prince might be grouped with Black women Lauren Berlant calls "diva citizens," such as Harriet Jacobs, Frances E. W. Harper, and Anita Hill. The diva citizen "renarrates the dominant history as one that the abjected people have once lived sotto voce, but no more; and she challenges her audience to identify with the enormity of the suffering she has narrated and the courage she has to produce, calling on people to change the social and institutional practices of citizenship to which they currently consent."[9]

What is striking about Prince is the outspoken defiance and unshaken faith she displays in the face of all kinds of danger; she was a survivor who took public action to try to create more just communities at home and abroad, applying what William Andrews calls the "moral absolutism" of the antislavery movement to that cause and others as she saw fit.[10] Prince's body, as a Black woman's body engaged in work, mobility, and struggle, is both a presence and an absence in her text. Her writing voice often seems disembodied but empowered by a spiritual and moral force that enables her to resist oppression and "talk back," not unlike the way contemporary Black women—including but not limited to feminists and public intellectuals—assert their dignity, their personhood, and their inherent value in the face of a white supremacist culture that would have them believe otherwise.

THE EMERGENCE OF A WRITING VOICE

Prince was the daughter of first-generation Massachusetts-born African Americans. Her father died when she was but three months old, and her mother remarried twice and bore many children, so at the age of eight Prince was forced to leave home and find work to support herself. Throughout her youth she worked as a servant for some of the most prominent New England families.[11] She wrote in her *Narrative* that her kin "were scattered all about" (9), but she kept track of their whereabouts, finding suitable homes and domestic positions for her siblings. Out of necessity, she became a maternal figure as a young girl, forgoing the comforts she longed for. She and her older sister Silvia had been abused by their stepfather. Prince looked older than her years and learned to be practical and self-sufficient. Accustomed to hard physical work and aware of the value of her labor, at the age of fourteen she traveled by herself from Gloucester to Salem to find a higher-paying domestic situation—but the family she ended up with worked her so hard that "in three months, my health and strength were gone" (11). We know that Prince was physically strong and had a will to match. She could use her body as an active barrier, physically separating other bodies from wrongdoing and harm. At seventeen, she traveled from Salem to remove her sister Silvia from a Boston brothel; when she was forty-eight years of age, she apprehended a slavecatcher who attempted to kidnap a formerly enslaved man for return to the South. Thomas Hilton, an observer, described how Prince, "with the assistance of the Black women who accompanied her [from the Smith Court houses in Beacon Hill], dragged [the slavecatcher] to the door and thrust him out of the house," telling the women and children who had gathered at the scene to "pelt him with stones and any thing you can get a hold of."[12] This incident, however, was not included in her *Life and Travels*; such active resistance to the Fugitive Slave Law of 1850 could have resulted in danger for herself and her friends and would have created a self-portrait of a physical and mental resistance that contradicted the image of a physically frail but spiritually empowered Prince with whom the reader is left at her narrative's end. An image of suffering is one with which readers were familiar; it was expected in the Black narrative industry.[13] Furthermore, Prince was asking for her reader's patronage as a form of financial support.[14]

At age twenty, she had become an evangelical Baptist, converted by Thomas Paul, the founder of the first independent African American church in the North and an important leader and missionary who had traveled to Haiti in 1823.[15] Her happy memories included religious instruction and guidance from her maternal grandfather, and in fact it was her faith in God that drove her, brought her comfort, and authorized her defiant voice. She concludes the second and third editions of her narrative with a poem, "The Hiding Place," in which the material world and all her journeys lead to a heavenly hiding place. The tropes of presence and absence, of revealing and hiding, are consistent strategies in her texts. She began her career as a public figure by speaking about her nine-year residence in Russia. Likewise, in her letters to the abolitionist press after returning from Jamaica, she is clearly moved to publicly express her indignation and desire for justice for African Americans and Afro-Jamaicans—revealing a different agenda and experience from the ones in Russia.

In representing her travels, Prince mixes elements of the itinerant preacher and colonial missionary—both of whom emphasize enlightened self-improvement and civilizing through Christianity—with the discourse of the adventurer/explorer. She includes accounts of dangerous journeys, incidents of deceit, and remarkable escape and survival. Surprising events are put in a religious framework that invests them with meaning, placing Prince's writing in what Paul Hunter calls the "providence tradition": according to him, providence literature reflects the pattern of Christian experience central to the Puritan myth and organizes experience into a teleological narrative based on a historical cycle.[16] Puritans believed that history revealed God's providence by rewarding the chosen and punishing those who were evil.[17] These varying strands are juxtaposed in Prince's writing, as she weaves stories of personal stability and instability, sin and virtue, chaos and order, in text that harkens back to the Bible and, at times, reads like a Black woman's version of John Bunyan's *The Pilgrim's Progress* or a narrative of Thomas Cole's famous series of paintings *The Voyage of Life*, a fixture in many homes in the increasingly religious milieu of the Jacksonian era.[18] Her writing voice emerges out of familiarity with oral discourses including preaching, political oratory, and itinerant Evangelicalism; the interplay of the sacred and secular, as practiced by Black preachers and members of the community, was also a tradition in many African cultures and no doubt was an important syncretic influence on African Americans.[19] Intellectually, although Prince's formal education was limited, she moved in abolitionist and reformist circles with Blacks and whites, and she was a member of the First African Baptist Church, a center for education, benevolence, and political activism in Boston's Black community.

TRAVEL AND "RESISTANT TRUTH TELLING"

Prince's travel texts are significant additions to the African American intellectual literary tradition. They are unique and yet familiar, containing generic elements from slave and spiritual narratives. They also draw on the popular travelogue, creating a hybrid form that uses mobility and outrage to chart a course for alternative social visions. In addition, Prince's works include themes that David S. Reynolds calls "popular subversive fiction," featuring deceitful authority figures and oppressed characters.[20] As other scholars of hybrid texts by African Americans have noted, drawing on the work of Victor Turner, in liminality, betwixt and between normative positions or categories, the marginalized person can imagine and is often forced to articulate alternative realities. Travel, with its disorienting liberation, is a free passage into the liminal state, allowing one to escape the everyday self and be transformed into an(other). Through her use of displacement, rupture, and textual gaps, Prince creates a liminal text that can induce a state of transition for her reader as well.[21] Prince shapes the flexible genre of travelogue to create a model of social criticism that I call resistant truth telling—a form of agency that derives its power from correcting abuses and misuses of power with a sensibility grounded in righteousness and self-marginalization. The higher, God-ordained power grants her authority to revise hypocrisy, but she does not consciously acknowledge her own complicity with some aspects of imperialism and assumed Western and Christian superiority.

Prince's travelogues diverge from those written by white men and a few white women who traveled to similar locations in the late eighteenth through mid-nineteenth centuries. Gender, race, class, and identity as a freeborn African American Christian from New England are the lenses through which Prince constructs her narratives. The 1841 pamphlet and *Life and Travels* affirm her place in the lineage of African American and Afro-Caribbean women who were educators, abolitionists, and outspoken social critics.[22] Even as Prince writes as a free African American, she continually emphasizes the contingent nature of that freedom. She or any free Black person in antebellum America could be enslaved, depending upon his or her geographic location, perceived threat to the dominant order, and visibility. For example, in returning from the West Indies, Prince's ship was unexpectedly detained both in Key West and near New Orleans; from the ship's deck she describes in her *Narrative* how she watched "the awful sight, which was the vessel of slaves laying [*sic*] at the side of our ship! the deck was full of young men, girls, and children, bound to Texas for sale!" (80). She had to stay on board to avoid her own possible beating and/or enslavement but was constantly taunted and threatened by whites from the shore.

A Narrative of the Life and Travels of Mrs. Nancy Prince opens with scenes of Prince's youth in a familial context, creating a dialogue with the experience of slavery and its narrative tradition. Attention to forced as well as chosen relocations connects her personally to the commercial deportation of slaves, signifying involuntary transport of human beings.[23] Family members and friends of Prince's youth appear and disappear as shadowy presences. However, family identity is mediated in this case through separation, and Prince's power comes through the management of bodies engaged in productive work. In the opening five pages, Prince uses the words "stolen," "captive," "escape," "voyage," "missing," "drowned," and "scattered" to convey the history of African Americans who are being uprooted against their will, as well as to give the particular circumstances of her family (5–9). For example, her maternal grandfather, Tobias Wornton, "or Backus, so called," was both an enslaved man and a soldier in the Revolutionary Army and served in the Battle of Bunker Hill (5). An unnamed maternal grandmother described as "an Indian of this country . . . became a captive to the English, or their descendants."[24] Mobility here incorporates forced relocations and body snatchings, conveyed in stories her grandfather told her about "how he was stolen from his native land." Her origins are both native and foreign, and contain the American paradox of captivity and escape, slavery and freedom, interracial mixing, and a genealogy from which to base her claim to American citizenship.[25] Prince's articulated identity as an Enlightenment subject, a granddaughter of the American Revolution, is connected to the men in her family who heroically fight and survive. Her mother's third husband, nicknamed Money Vose, "succeeded in making his escape from his captors, by swimming ashore" (6), after being stolen from Africa while the boat was at anchor in what turned out to be a free state. He eventually became a sailor; "his name may be found on the Custom House books in Gloucester" (7). Vose is seen as a heroic figure and the only one of her mother's husbands who provides a home for his wife and small children; however, he was also abusive.

An important contrast to make between Prince and the most canonical writers of American slave narratives Frederick Douglass and Harriet Jacobs is that Prince had more leverage than the enslaved, who needed to emphasize moral character, intelligence, and honesty to a white northern readership. Throughout her work, Prince alludes to the hypocrisy of northerners, despite their being her readers. Literacy is key to the enslaved person's perception and knowledge of the possibility of freedom; it enables Douglass to read about abolitionist support in the North. Learning to read and write was a decisive political act mentioned in the slave narrative; writing was a principal sign of reason, and in order to signify as full members of Western humanity, African Americans had to prove it through their writings. Nevertheless, narratives by Douglass and Jacobs featured authenticating prefaces by white abolitionists to testify on behalf of the formerly enslaved and introduce them to their readers.

Prince seeks the patronage of friends in the preface to the second and third editions of *Life and Travels* as well as acknowledging their part in revising her narrative. Though she mentions no specific names, we know from a petition she signed along with other members of the Boston Female Anti-Slavery Society and a record of money she donated to an antislavery fair that her circle included Black and white abolitionists such as the Garrisons, Maria W. Chapman, Lydia Maria Child, and Susan Paul.[26] Prince does not appeal directly for the abolition of slavery in the same way the slave narrative directly states that goal, usually by inciting readers to take action. That is not to say that her narrative does not offer a scathing critique of slavery and its many paradoxes and repercussions. These generic conventions point to the way travelogues and spiritual narratives provide other outlets for the critique of slavery, from those whose freedom and mobility have permitted them to see and compare international contexts.

To validate her desire to travel, Prince acts as a free agent who passes on literacy and religious instruction to other Blacks. This freedom, literacy, and citizenship qualify her to judge the character of Afro-Jamaicans and the economic conditions in Jamaica since emancipation. But most important, Prince claims authority from God, the basis for the spiritual autobiographer to write as witness. In addition, she believes she is writing not only with gratitude to "my Heavenly Father" but as a "duty to myself" (1850, 5), consistent with the individualistic Western autobiographical tradition. Her stance testifies to the amount of confidence she had developed as a traveler who survived adversity and the commanding impression she made on figures such as the tsar and empress of Russia, English and American missionaries, and a variety of Afro-Jamaicans. These affirmations and her grounding in a utilitarian, benevolent African American tradition contributed to her ability to talk back and point out deceit wherever encountered. In addition, as one who risked death and survived as she traveled, she would have a right and duty to act in public life. Moreover, her travels point to the need for building community, an "over ground" railroad of support, in transnational and US locations, cutting across race, class, political affiliations, and gender. In her narrative, she mentions meeting with and asking for help or receiving support from Lucretia Mott, Theodore Wells, Nathaniel Southard, and Lewis Tappan, among others. These friends help the traveler survive and provide material aid to counter the deception, cruelty, and racism she faces. Most likely *A Narrative of the Life and Travels of Mrs. Nancy Prince* was classified by readers as autobiographical and therefore perceived as insignificant as a political tract that engaged with current debates. In addition, Prince did not appear to try to promote herself, nor did she associate regularly with white women activists as did Sojourner Truth, although Prince did speak briefly at the 1854 National Women's Rights Convention in Philadelphia. The very use of classification and the politics of genre and placement could explain why, to this day, Prince's narratives are excluded from some anthologies of African American and American literature.

Prince's writing is related as well to the conversion narrative. For freeborn African American women in the 1830s and 1840s, public social criticism was expressed in the form of speeches, most likely to "promiscuous" or mixed audiences of both men and women, or in writing the autobiographical subgenre of the religious conversion narrative. Women such as Maria W. Stewart and Jarena Lee, writes Sue Houchins, "seized authority to depict their religious conversions and manumission from the bondage of sin, entering into both a spiritual and political discourse, using a discursive form suited to extend their vocation to teach, pray publicly and testify."[27] Prince's pamphlet and narrative would build on this model; however, her faith becomes the means, not the end, to justify her authority as a resistant truth teller. Typically, in spiritual autobiographies, the narrators indicate that, before conversion, they had been inclined to indulge in socializing or "the ways of the flesh."[28] Prince's paradigm is different: she always portrays herself as serious and hardworking, while her mother and sister represent bodily indulgence and succumb to sexual temptation only to be rescued by her. Speaking of Black women's emigrationist writing to Africa, Mitchell claims that "the concept of racial destiny stressed collectivity, yet it enabled African-American women and men to judge—often harshly—what they perceived as weaknesses, failing and pathologies on the part of other Black people."[29] Thus, Prince focuses on the moral rehabilitation of others, including family members.

Decorporealizing her own body makes sense as a strategy for negotiating her public exposure as a writer, and it allows her to shift the focus to her mission of racial uplift, away from the stereotyped sexualization of the Black female body, one of the products of slavery, and in her own case from the memories of a stepfather's blows.[30] Prince's attempt to decorporealize and transcend the body in order to emphasize her spirituality is only partially successful. References to the body emerge, suggesting its materiality and fallibility, creating a dialectic between empowered corporeality and the infirm body. These falls exemplify what Frances Bartkowski calls the "underside" of the traveler's sublime—"that moment when the headiness of motion turns into fear, disavowal and into the abyss in the ground."[31] There are several literal falls into pits, or into holes in the ground, which may be read as a revision of forms of "backsliding" or signs of Satan that we see in spiritual narratives like Jarena Lee's.[32] Prince's tropes of falling into pits are vehicles that materialize Christian repentance and deliverance, as if the corporeality of the body suddenly tempted or thrust into an "underworld" signifies a return of repressed fears and temptations. Her ability to survive these falls and accidents becomes proof of God's greater design. In spiritual narratives, there are many metaphorical and literal references to mobility, particularly walking, that lead up to the conversion and through the decision to preach Christian gospel. Jarena Lee writes of a dream of walking on the summit of a beautiful hill, when a man of "grave and dignified countenance" approaches her, convincing her to have her husband "take care of these sheep, or the wolf will come and devour them."[33] Similarly, Zilpha Elaw has a vision in which God says to her: "This is the way; walk ye in it."[34] Once she is a preacher, Lee tells us how many miles she walked to prove her dedication to the cause—often she walks more than twelve miles to conduct a service. Likewise, Prince emphasizes the number of miles she has to walk in the cold to rescue her sister from prostitution. For Prince and the spiritual narrators, walking is the most accessible and self-generated form of movement; walking as pilgrims walk leads to greater good. It is physically demanding proof, a test of one's commitment to God and to fighting corruption.

RUSSIA: NEGOTIATED POSITIONALITY

More than in any other section of her *Narrative*, in representing Russia, Prince turns to the Western tradition of observing and documenting difference by noting the exotic customs of foreign cultures. She manages to maintain an awkward kind of distance, struggling, it seems, to refrain from making generalizations in favor of simply highlighting the exotic for her readers, such as elaborate holiday celebrations, burial practices, and feasts. But because she lives and works for an extended period in St. Petersburg, the ethnographic term "participant-observer" is appropriate for her stance. Laboring and dwelling in a home place separates Prince from most of the male narrators of the era's travelogues to Russia; the men position themselves as flâneurs, observing as they roam the countryside, dine out, and encounter others.

Prince's affiliation with the court positions her to assume a life that appears middle class, a striking change from her domestic situations in Boston before and after her travels abroad. In Boston, Prince's work as a seamstress would have been construed as an acceptable and even "genteel" profession, though work would have been sporadic and the remuneration "trifling," notwithstanding ill effects on the health of the needlewomen.[35] It was, as Virginia Penny asserts, "a bitter reflection on those who employ them."[36] In contrast, in St. Petersburg, Prince writes in her *Narrative* that she took in children as boarders and employed a servant; her sewing business was so successful, in fact, that she employed a journeywoman and apprentices (26, 39).[37] The empress purchased from Prince "garments for herself and children, handsomely wrought in French and English styles, and many of the nobility also followed her example" (39). Early on, Prince makes the claim that "there was no prejudice against color" (23). Black people, according to Albert Parry, were viewed by Russians as "rare and exotic, yet useful and ornamental."[38] However, Prince reports no such overt attitudes and gives little information on her husband's service in the tsar's guard, except to say they go to court in the morning and "take their station in the halls, for the purpose of opening the doors . . . when the Emperor and Empress pass" (23–24). In the sanctity of her lofty role within an aristocratic hierarchy, the empress seems to present Prince and her readers with a comforting and seductive model, in contrast to the corrupt colonial administrators and forms of religious teaching that Prince will rail against in Jamaica. Despite the racial difference, Prince appears more sure of her own position in Russia than in Jamaica.

The compelling cause of the Russian peasantry did not stir in Prince the same passion as did American slavery. While alluding to comparisons between the two and noting the plight of the serfs, she never develops a thorough analysis or makes connections between the different parts of her narrative as the questions of slavery and emancipation arise in each location. Nor does she compare slavery in the West Indies with the type of bondage she witnessed in Russia. She does, however, make a statement that gets at the heart of the tragedy of slavery in America, and it is connected to her own concern over forced relocations, divided and broken families, and the trading of human beings as commodities. In Russia, she writes, the peasants "till the land, most of them are slaves and are very degraded. The rich own the poor, but they are not suffered to separate families or sell them off the soil. All are subject to the

Emperor, and no nobleman can leave without his permission" (38). Thus, she does identify as a major difference between Russian peasants and American slaves the fact that the Russian peasants stay together in one place. Although mobility in each class, even the aristocracy, is regulated by the tsar, the serfs can at least develop a community identity and solidarity with others of their class.[39] And families can remain together—unlike in America, where the separation of families, especially the parting of mothers and children, is one of the most tragic aspects of slavery.

Before and during the time Prince published her narrative, it was not unusual to see comparisons of American slavery with slavery in Russia published in both the popular and the abolitionist press. In one account, the fact that Russian slaves were white, not Black, qualified that form of slavery as "the very worst kind" that prevails in the "largest empire in Europe. These forty-two million white people are in a state of the most abject slavery. They are taught in the schools to the slaves—their catechism teaches them to worship the emperor as their first duty, and the entire nation bows under his despotic power."[40] In a piece in *The Liberator* of May 3, 1839, the popular travel writer John Lloyd Stephens also foregrounds the race question in his comparison of slavery in the two countries, using the example of the degradation of Russian serfs to refute any assertions of intrinsic white superiority: "I was forcibly struck with a parallel between the white serfs of the north of Europe and African bondmen at home. The serfs in Russia differ from slaves with us in the important particular that they belong to the soil, and cannot be sold except with the estate; they may change masters, but cannot be torn from their connexions or their birth-place."[41]

Unlike the other writers, perhaps Prince wanted to avoid questions of which kind of slavery was the "worst" because she was committed to the emancipation of African American slaves and was struggling against assumed white supremacy. She felt passionate about proving that the freed slaves of Jamaica were intelligent, industrious, and God-fearing people, and may have felt it was not within her power or interest to take up the cause of the Russian peasantry. Perhaps she felt it would have diluted her later arguments and the cause of abolition to which her readers were most committed. Or, because of her position at the court of the emperor, she may have hesitated to go too deeply into a historical analysis of the exploitation of the Russian serfs. In Russia, where her color marks her as exotic, she writes approvingly not only of what she sees as racial tolerance but of religious toleration and of the opportunity for children of all classes to be educated.

Her experience as a Black woman living in the orbit of Eastern Europe gives her another kind of protection: a secular, transnational identity that transcends racial categories, with immunity from white-supremacist American law. At one point during her nightmare voyage home from Jamaica, near the book's conclusion, the ship unexpectedly docks in New Orleans, and she faces the possibility of being imprisoned as a Black woman in a slave state. But she possesses a document of "protection" from the Russian government that seems to make an impact on the authorities. However, Prince feels an even greater protection from God, saying: "the Lord will take care of me" (78).

RUSSIA, BOSTON, JAMAICA

One of the most frustrating aspects of analyzing Prince's texts is weighing the importance of information that has been left out. In Russia, she was concerned with proving that she remained busy at all times; in her *Narrative*, details of her body engaged in work, prayer, and philanthropy are juxtaposed with descriptions of holidays, the marketplace, and awareness that "licentiousness" was common (40). In contrast, her resistant truth-telling is most overt when she represents her travels to Jamaica, which form the longest part of her narrative, incorporating the 1841 pamphlet and adding a lot more. Rhetorically, she moves from emphasizing her own industriousness in Russia to proving that the formerly enslaved Jamaicans are decent and hardworking, community-minded and intelligent. Race and racialized identities become key in the Jamaica section, whereas in Russia racial difference was minimized. Moreover, the Jamaica section contains overt warnings to African American readers and challenges the validity of emigration schemes offered by colonial administrators and plantation proprietors. In the Black Atlantic, Prince's journeys between the United States and the Caribbean point out possible alliances and interventions, but also illustrate hypocrisy and deceit and, finally, thwarted attempts to organize across national boundaries.

Here I want to mention that the textual bridge between the Russia and Jamaica sections is brief—only a few paragraphs—but it is nonetheless an intriguing description of her time in Boston after her return on October 23, 1833. Prince did not depart for Jamaica until seven years had passed; what she only hints at is her involvement in the abolition movement and in the bitter divides that were taking place. Since the narrative emphasizes travel, she does not dwell on her life at home. Her comments about contention within the movement in the light of some information that she left out suggest her ambivalence toward the women's movement as it relates to questions of race and gender as well as her apparent discomfort with polemical factions or organizations. It is telling that when she left for Jamaica, proclaiming "a field of usefulness seemed spread out before me" (43), the debate over women's participation in the abolition movement was heating up, and questions were being raised about the need to go abroad when there was much one could do locally for the free Black community. The words "usefulness . . . spread out" are appropriate because Prince did cover a lot of territory in Jamaica, moving from location to location and engaging in philanthropic ventures, educational enterprises, and religious proselytizing.

Prince never mentions that she was a member of the biracial Boston Female Anti-Slavery Society during the 1830s. Of her life when she returned from Russia, she writes only this:

> There had been an Anti-Slavery Society established by W. L. Garrison, Knapp, and other philanthropists. These meetings I attended with much pleasure, until a contention broke out among themselves; there has been a great change in some things, but much remains to be done; possibly I may not see so clearly as some, for the weight of prejudice has again oppressed me, and were it not for the promises of God, one's heart would fail, for He made man in his own image, in the image of God, created he him, male and female, that they should have dominion over the fish of the sea. This power did God give man, that thus far should he go and no farther; but man has disobeyed and become vain in his imagination, and their foolish hearts are darkened. The sins of my beloved country are not hid from his notice. (42–43)

This passage is compressed and enigmatic. Hazel Carby points out that there is irony in Prince's remark about not seeing so clearly as others because of being oppressed by prejudice, since Prince's experience with racism had sensitized her to its manifestations.[42] The biblical quotations signify Prince's displeasure with the internal contention regarding gender and the way it possibly interrupted the important antislavery work that remained to be done. What she leaves out is that by the fall of 1839, the Boston Female Anti-Slavery Society (BFASS) had divided into two factions over the "woman question." One sided with Garrison and his followers in the Massachusetts Anti-Slavery Society and the other sided with the more conservative clerics, led by Amos Phelps, Lewis Tappan, and others. The clerical faction used the argument that sexual integration and the full participation of women as speakers would distract abolitionists from their original goal.[43]

Part of the competition between the two sides was to secure the support of African American members, although they were generally not in leadership roles within the BFASS. According to Debra Hansen, the African American members were more interested in developing programs that directly assisted the Black community than in debating policy issues that consumed the white women.[44] This would account for Prince's anger at the disruptiveness of the split. African Americans who sided with the clerical group were called "coloured peelers"; several women whose husbands were Black ministers aligned with the proclerical forces.[45] Another reason some African Americans broke with Garrison was his adherence to a policy of nonresistance, which emphasized using only nonviolent means to overthrow slavery; some Black abolitionists felt that violence might be necessary to end slavery. Although Prince was in the same circle as these "peelers" and their husbands—for instance, she gave a talk on her Russian travels at Reverend Beman's church—her actions and external documents provide support for her alignment with the Garrisons, Lydia M. Child, and Maria Weston Chapman, advocating women's public participation in antislavery work. In fact, Prince was one of the seventy-eight members of the BFASS, and one of at least seven Black women, who signed a letter printed in *The Liberator* of November 15, 1839, declaring the election of pro-cleric Mary Parker as president of the BFASS invalid because of a miscounted vote.[46] After this dispute, Parker's faction formed the Massachusetts Female Emancipation Society, and Chapman's faction regrouped to reconstitute the BFASS. By all accounts, the organization never regained its prominence after the split. One of the first results of the split was the organization of two separate antislavery fairs for the year 1839. These fairs, the major fundraising events for antislavery and benevolent causes, had begun in 1834 and, according to Lee Chambers-Schiller, "crystallized as a desideratum of Boston's social season and a lucrative moneymaker that raised up to five thousand dollars a year for the abolitionist cause."[47] In October 1839, Chapman and the Garrisonian faction organized a fair that preempted the usual Christmas one. Prince is listed in the acknowledgments in *The Liberator* on November 22, 1839, as an individual donor to that fair, contributing seven dollars.[48]

To analyze Prince's support of women's public participation and the way she alludes to a patronizing form of racism within the movement, I return to her excerpted quote about the antislavery society. There Prince uses a passage from Genesis that forms the basis of one of Sarah Grimké's arguments in her *Letters on the Equality of the Sexes*. Grimké's argument is that "in all this sublime description of the creation of man (which is a generic term including man and woman), there is not one particle of difference intimated as existing between them. They were both made in the image of God; dominion was given to both over every other creature, but not over each other."[49] Prince herself implies that by enslaving humans, people have wickedly overstepped a God-given dominion over animals. She particularly singles out the "sins of my beloved country" (43). which are noticed by God, who will repay the hypocritical American sinners on the Day of Judgment. While supporting the right of women to speak and stand as men's equals in the abolition movement, she expresses her dissatisfaction with the split, noting the "contention" and that "much remains to be done" (42) for the antislavery cause. This shows a concern that the gender question could preempt, or divert attention from, antislavery work. Since her next passage introduces her determination to go to Jamaica to be useful, I read the biblical quotation and her subsequent remarks about vanity as working on a second level, as a denigration of the Boston abolitionists and their bitter divides—and part of a justification for going abroad to work for the cause of racial uplift there. The combination of domestic quarreling and lack of opportunity at home feeds Prince's restlessness. She feels she can be of greater good elsewhere, in the Caribbean where slavery has recently been abolished.

Tension among the Boston women also centered on the question of where one could do the most significant reform work, locally or abroad. In the 1840 Seventh Annual Report of the reconstituted BFASS, Maria Chapman tried to give the impression of a healthy organization: "Meanwhile, to the repentant and the undeceived, the old platform stands where it did. We sympathize with the self-denying labors of a Wilson or an Ingraham. But we need not go to Canada or Jamaica for a field of benevolent effort among the free colored people. They are among ourselves—a suffering remnant, in the grasp of a despotic people, whose hearts are hardened towards them."[50] There is no way of knowing for certain if Chapman was referring to Prince's plans to go to Jamaica, but Prince may be one of those whom Chapman had in mind, as she was recruited by David Ingraham. Chapman sets up an interesting paradox, yet her calling free Blacks "a suffering remnant" does not reflect the vitality and activism of Boston's free Black community. This patronizing tone may have contributed to Prince's distaste for the changes she had seen. At any rate, by traveling away from Boston and displacing her dispute with American women, Prince signals her difference from their approach and develops a larger, transnational position that includes negotiating among a variety of ideologies and value systems. She may also have consciously or subconsciously left Boston for Jamaica precisely because she could feel a sense of importance that was denied by rigid hierarchies at home; while free Blacks in America were second-class citizens, in Jamaica they could be valued for their experience and accomplishments. In Jamaica, Prince's independent thinking and her refusal to be absolutely aligned with one particular faction would serve her as an observer and fuel her anger at the oppression and deceit among the missionaries.

It is telling that one of the first incidents that Prince narrates of her travels to Jamaica involves a dispute with a female class leader in Reverend Abbott's missionary station in St. Ann's Harbor. The dispute is over the method of religious teaching, and Prince refuses to "yield obedience" to this female class leader:

> As I lodged in the house of one of the class-leaders I attended her class a few times, and when I learned the method, I stopped. She then

> commenced her authority and gave me to understand if I did not comply I should not have pay from that society. I spoke to her of the necessity of being born of the spirit of God before we become members of the church of Christ, and told her I was sorry to see the people blinded. She was very angry with me and soon accomplished her end by complaining of me to the minister; and I soon found I was to be dismissed, unless I would yield obedience. I told the minister that I did not come there to be guided by a poor foolish woman. (46)

In this instance, her anger is directly expressed at a "poor foolish" Black woman rather than at the white English clergyman himself. When Prince tells Abbott about her dispute, he says she should not express herself except to him, which is a form of silencing her that she does not directly acknowledge. Then Abbott comments: "I do not approve of women's societies; they destroy the world's convention; the American women have too many of them" (47).[51] Part of the tension comes from the difference between American abolitionists of the Garrisonian variety and the more traditional English abolitionist-missionaries. As a widowed African American traveling alone, Prince was atypical; she was neither a missionary's nor a magistrate's wife or daughter, and yet she had the audacity to question the authority and morality of the English Baptist system. She gave away Bibles, "not knowing that I was hurting the minister's sale" (47). On one level, Prince seems to threaten Abbott and stands for the disruptive American woman; on another, she is so marginal as to be easily dismissed, and she gives up teaching there and moves on to another part of the island.

In challenging the class leader's moral conduct, Prince displays her own ambivalence about women's leadership in a religious tradition outside her own New England Calvinist brand of Christianity—the tradition of Afro-Jamaican myalism, a Creole synthesis of evangelical Christianity and African religious experience that evolved over time to combat the effects of obeah, which could be seen as a form of resistance and Black identity in a so-called free society.[52] The class leaders, Abigail Bakan writes, were "spiritual guides similar to those in myal groups. Individual rebels could be expelled . . . who did not fully accept the leader's authority."[53] Prince may have found the method too full of superstitions, as the idea of spirit was elevated above written gospel, which was dear to Prince. In her *Narrative*, she does not mention the race of the class leader, but almost certainly she was Black: Abbott's congregation was composed almost exclusively of Black workers, and Prince was a lodger in the class leader's home (46). At another point, she goes into more detail about the Baptist class leader and ticket system, suggesting a lack of piety and a commodification: "They have men and women deacons and deaconesses in these churches; . . . some of these can read, and some cannot. Such are the persons who . . . urge the people to come to the class, and after they come in twice or three times, they are considered candidates for baptism. Some pay fifty cents, and some more, for being baptized; they receive a ticket as a passport into the church" (73).

In these descriptions, Prince's anger at the class leader and her refusal to "yield obedience" is narrated as a moment of defiance against a system she finds coercive. It is also a way to validate her own moral superiority in almost physical terms, the will and body in conjoined agency, refusing to submit.[54] At the time Prince traveled to Jamaica, Christian and myal elements were being blurred: according to Philip Curtin, "the elements of Christianity became stronger in myal practice-preaching, Christian hymns, Christian phraseology, 'prophesying' in the name of the Christian God—but the basic African elements were also retained."[55] In part, Prince's anger at the class leader is a displaced critique of the white English missionaries and the colonial practices of using Blacks to raise money and gain power. She may have felt this was not entirely unlike practices employed by white women in Boston, although the parameters were different. As she describes charitable giving in Kingston, where she went next, "The colored people give more readily, and are less suspicious of imposition, if one from themselves recommends the measure; this the missionaries understand very well, and know how to take advantage of it" (49).

Elsewhere in the *Narrative*, she contrasts the Maroons' position of a rightful claim to the island with the view of an innkeeper she meets outside Kingston, "an Englishman, with a large family of mulatto children," who expresses anger and fear that the "negroes will have the island in spite of the d- [devil]" (54). She mourns the racialized tragedy of the mulatto children of white fathers, who "were allowed great power over their slave mothers and her slave children; my heart was often grieved to see their conduct to their poor old grand parents" (58). These passages and the relationship of Blacks in Jamaica to colonial authorities raise the question of who has the right to citizenship and rule. The contestation of national identity and its relation to race connects to her Black readers' anxieties about their status as American citizens. Other travelers to the West Indies in the postemancipation period reported that the newly freed people were industrious and the whole country was better off since emancipation, but they did not address or anticipate the wide array of concerns Black readers might have had about their own status.

At the time Prince first published her pamphlet about Jamaica, advertisements and letters appeared in the abolitionist press by Blacks and whites noting both advantages and disadvantages to be derived from emigrating to the West Indies. Questions were being raised even before the Fugitive Slave Law of 1850 about free Blacks and what would happen should slavery end. Was it most prudent to leave New England or to stay put? Where was the greater economic and educational opportunity? Would there be more respect for Blacks in a country with a Black majority, such as Jamaica? Colonization schemes, limited employment opportunities, and the possibility of mob violence and kidnapping were realities in the lives of free Blacks. During the 1850s, when Prince published her three editions of *Life and Travels*, the nationalist-emigration debates were heating up. When the Fugitive Slave Law was passed in 1850, Martin R. Delany advocated emigration to places like Central and South America as part of a Black nationalist movement removed from US slavery and the perpetual threat of recapture and re-enslavement.[56]

Prince seems particularly sensitive to the exaggerated promises and empty rhetoric that would lure Blacks to Jamaica. She offers a striking contrast with her description of the realities in Jamaica for immigrants who

> on arriving here, strangers poor and unacclimated, find the debt for passage money hard and unexpected. It is remarkable that whether fresh from Africa, or from other islands, from the South or from New England, they all feel deceived on this point. I called on many Americans and found them poor and discontented,—rueing the day they left their country, where, notwithstanding many obstacles, their parents lived and died,—a country they helped to conquer with their toil and blood; now shall their children stray abroad and starve in foreign lands. (51)

This passage suggests a practical and more deeply rooted rationale for staying home. For African American families who sacrificed their lives in slavery, hoping it would be better for their children in the country where they had been enslaved, there would be a particular irony in leaving that country only to starve abroad. Prince suggests that the sacrifices made with African blood and toil helped contribute to the prosperity of America and give African Americans a right to call that country their home; as an abolitionist, she would also want free Blacks to stay home to support the cause of their fellow African Americans still in bondage.

Prince cautioned Black readers against emigration schemes in her narratives, whereas William Lloyd Garrison and his supporters used the pages of the abolitionist press to do so, embedding warnings in obituaries; both must thus be credited with obstructing Barclay's efforts to attract free Blacks to Jamaica and with keeping African American labor at home. For instance, when James G. Barbadoes, one of the leading Black abolitionists in the Boston community, died, a notice in the *Pennsylvania Freeman*, reprinted in *The Liberator* on August 20, 1841, stated that "contrary to the advice of his friends, he emigrated with his wife and family to Jamaica. They soon sickened with the fever of the country, and two of his children died. And now the last intelligence from there informs us of his own decease by the same malady." Prince's tone is one of surprise. She calls the emigration policy a "mistake," then notes with irony the reality facing those who have relocated. Prince focuses on the economic difficulties of the emigrants, while commenting elsewhere that her "injured brethren in Jamaica" show self-sufficiency and industriousness: "They have bought land and built houses. They raise all kinds of vegetables. They have no need to let themselves on plantations. They are extremely kind to each other, and have shown an excellent capacity to take care of themselves."[57] This is a message to Black readers and to whites in power: it is prudent to work the land in your own nation, as self-reliance and national identity come through hard work and the claim to land. Kindness and mutual, communal support are also essential.

In keeping with her theme of Black workers engaged in productive labor, Prince notes in her *Narrative* how Black women work in the market, tending the vegetable and poultry stalls; she counts the number of stalls, exceeding two hundred, to convey the scope and to emphasize the organizational and managerial skills of the Afro-Jamaicans, specifically women. She italicizes the words "surely we see industry" to emphasize that "it may be hoped they are not the stupid set of beings they have been called" (50). The equivalent work for African Americans of northern cities was in small businesses and trades, supporting each other, even though economic survival in a climate of intense racism would have been difficult. After writing that the emancipated Afro-Jamaicans "are enterprising and quick in their perceptions, determined to possess themselves, and to possess property besides," she includes a dialogue that, in effect, demonstrates how she revises the ethnographic gaze in relation to the Afro-Jamaicans when examining and questioning them (44). This inversion is an example of what I call resistant truth-telling. She advocates their interests in the United States and corrects false representations. In addition, she creates transatlantic links between the formerly enslaved Afro-Jamaicans and readers at home, dispelling stereotypes of laziness and the foreign other, noting in her book on the West Indies: "They wished to know why I was so inquisitive about them. I told them we have heard in America that you are lazy, and that emancipation has been no benefit to you; I wish to inform myself of the truth respecting you and give a true representation of you on my return."[58]

Besides connecting the freed Afro-Jamaicans to classic republican ideology on possessing the self and the desire to work the land—and arguing, by implication, that the same would be true of enslaved Americans—Prince's pamphlet and narrative validate the point of view of an elderly freedwoman, another kind of maternal voice filled with faith based in experience. In contrast to the Russia and Boston sections of her *Narrative*, Prince here makes sure to quote Black women who are not in positions superior to hers. The words of the woman, who has just survived a violent storm in which houses have been destroyed and families separated, are an example of righteousness that must be heard loudly and clearly by white New Englanders: "Not so bad now as in the time of slavery, then God spoke very loud to Bucker [*sic*] [white people] to let us go. Thank God, ever since that, they give us up, we go pray and we have it not so bad as before."[59] Prince follows with a sassy antislavery comment in the midst of her conventional travelogue descriptions of Jamaican landscape:

> I would recommend this poor woman's remark to the fair sons and daughters of America, the land of the pilgrims. "Then God spoke very loud." May these words be engraved on the post of every door; in this land of New England God speaks very loud, and while his judgments are in the earth, may the inhabitants learn righteousness! The mountains that intersect this island seem composed of rocks thrown up by frequent earthquakes or volcanoes.[60]

She authorizes the Black woman's words about buckra as the ones that should be engraved on every door. She is simultaneously making a narrative space for a transgressive ex-slave voice as she coopts this voice from an ethnographic perspective. That God speaks loudly in New England is a comment on racism and hypocrisy in the North. Letting this woman speak also shows readers that these newly freed individuals are pious, decent people who seek a chance; freedom to them is sweet. The comment also emphasizes the twisted logic of proslavery forces in the United States, who often claim those enslaved were better taken care of in bondage than as free women and men.

In the final third of her *Narrative*, the danger and bodily harm that threaten or are inflicted upon Prince become more central, as does psychic pain, for the journey home includes unexpectedly witnessing the transport of a group of enslaved persons. The dreadful homecoming leads to her conclusion that "fearful indeed is this world's pilgrimage" without refuge in God, her most comforting "hiding place" (87, 89). As she journeys from Jamaica back to the United States, Prince exhibits her most powerful resistant truth-telling and confrontations with those who enforce white supremacy and brutality, but back in Boston she has "been broken up in business, embarrassed and obliged to move, when not able to wait on myself" (85).

Chaos and disorder in Jamaica force Prince to abandon her philanthropic project. She returns to Kingston in May 1842 to find

> everything different from what it was when I left; the people were in a state of agitation, several were hanged, and the insurrection was so great that it was found necessary to increase the army to quell it. On this

> occasion there was an outrage committed by those who were in power. What little the poor colored people had gathered during their four years of freedom was destroyed by violence; it seemed useless to attempt to establish a Manual Labor School, as the government was so unsettled that I could not be protected.[61] (57–60)

As her narrative comes to a close and moves toward home, Prince's discussion of treachery en route from Jamaica to New York stresses racial difference and the tenuous relationship between slavery and the unofficial "criminal status" of free Blackness.[62] Alone among the passengers on board, Prince guesses the captain's deceitful plans to detain them in Key West: "The whites went on shore and made themselves comfortable, while we poor Blacks were obliged to remain on that broken, wet vessel" (76) because of laws requiring free Blacks to be put in custody. Her suspicions reinforce a pattern we have seen: Prince as a shrewd detector of avarice and deceit, who heroically stands as God's agent. This oppression is based on race rather than on gender and conveys a model of heroism in the face of adversity; it is a model emphasized in slave narratives and includes isolated heroism, stark courage, and keenly edged rationality. Prince resists oppression by speaking and acting even as her mobility is restricted. Her empowered voice intervenes from the troubled ship and sounds again in her narratives.

A severe storm forced the waterlogged ship to stop on the Mississippi near New Orleans. Prince observes Black men from ships being dragged to prison; Captain Tyler forces her to see the "awful sight" of a vessel full of "young men, girls, and children bound to Texas for sale!" (80). Prince is warned not to say anything to the Blacks she sees on land, and once again in Key West she is told by the captain that, had she gone ashore, "they intended to beat you" (81). She responds to threats of violence, interrogation, and surveillance by calling out and asking if her taunters believe in God and by reproaching them for their violent actions and the suffering they have caused: "There is a God, and a just one, that will bring you all to account" (79). Her body's mobility halted, and with the threat of violence and re-enslavement, voice becomes the unbound lash of verbal retribution and emancipation. Prince "kills" her taunters with rhetoric: drawing on a form of signifying in the African American tradition, in her *Narrative* she repeats and reverses their claim to believe in God: "I asked them if they believed there was a God. 'Of course we do,' they replied. 'Then why not obey him?' 'We do.' 'You do not'" (79).[63]

In 1843, after returning to New York and then Boston, Prince is left "poor in health, and poor in purse, having sacrificed both, hoping to benefit my fellow creatures" (82–83). She returns to the theme in the preface to the second edition (1853), where she reminded readers that she refused the support of the benevolent societies for widows, but solicited "the patronage of my friends and the public, in the sale of this work . . . as health and strength are gone."[64] In the preface to the 1856 edition, she wrote that she had lost "the power of my arms."[65] The mention of a disability and loss of physical power draws attention to the sacrifices Prince has made in her journeys. In her benevolent work, she has essentially given up a limb. The synecdoche of arms recalls Prince's heroic rescue of her sister, her leading the rock-throwing rebellion against the slavecatcher, and her experience of grasping a horse's leg to save her life. Powerful arms recall her strenuous work as a domestic servant, and later as a dressmaker, transforming "woman's sphere" into the masculinized Black womanhood symbolized by Sojourner Truth's bared, muscular arm as she demanded of her audience: "And ar'n't I a woman? Look at me! Look at my arm!"[66] The loss of Prince's arms and strength marks the aging body's boundaries and its immobility after a life of hard physical labor. In losing physical power, she must become more dependent on the kindness of friends and strangers, linking her material well-being with the purchasing of her book, which might be said to stand in as a phantom limb.[67]

The cathexis of arms and hands used to write the narrative emphasizes and denotes the limits of Prince's utilitarian body. The mobile African American woman's body, even when one is "free," cannot sustain its vigor under such substandard conditions. We can also surmise from Prince's accounts that her poor health and perhaps the loss of the power of her arms were long-term effects of several injuries described in the narrative and in at least one account of mistreatment aboard a boat detailed in a letter to *The Liberator* in 1841 in which a fall resulted in a dislocated left shoulder (56). Her injury was compounded by the exposure she endured while on deck all night, because Captain Comstock, on her passage from New York to Providence, refused to let her have a cabin ticket or her money back, and, as she says in her letter, two Black chambermaids refused to find a bed for her "and behaved with great rudeness and violence. In consequence of this exposure, I took cold, and have ever since been much worse."[68]

In the face of this infirmity of body and dearth of material welfare, as she describes it in her *Narrative*, the outraged daughter becomes childlike, bowed in silent humility and prayer, "willing to be purified though fire, and accept it meekly" (88). By transcending the physical realm of body and of material travel, this child can become a seraph, one of the highest orders of angels, which recalls saintly little Eva from Harriet Beecher Stowe's *Uncle Tom's Cabin*. In allegorized Christian myth, the stage of life denoted by childhood refers to a time of innocence, and therefore suggests a regressive, nostalgic conclusion. The achievement of salvation and knowledge of God's saving grace was a convention from spiritual autobiography that bestowed a fundamentally positive identity on its subject, such as access to love and forgiveness.[69] Prince seems to perceive life and death as on a continuum, which is part of the African and African American religious traditions.[70] In the allegorical poem "The Hiding Place," on the final page of the second and third editions of the narrative, the narrator forgoes the world's "tumultuous noise" and "wealth and honors I disdain"; "For peace my soul to Jesus flies; I want no other hiding place" (89).

The trope of hiding place is very similar to itinerant preacher Jarena Lee's "secret place" or "closet" that provides an alternative to the secular, capitalist world.[71] Later in the poem, Prince refers to her journey through the wilderness, returning to an Old Testament image used by both Puritans and enslaved persons and a theme that dominates Christian guidebooks:

> I'm in a wilderness below
> Lord, guide me all my journey through,
> Plainly let me thy footsteps trace,
> Which lead to heaven, my hiding place. (89)

Her hiding place in heaven turns out to be a "triumph in redeeming love. Thus the metaphor of a hiding place is ultimately a heavenly one, suggesting an eternal home in submission and death that promises peace no material existence can provide. The domestic homecoming in New England is minimized and elided as she time-travels to imagine the final rest. However, in "hiding/place" we are reminded of Prince's success in remaining hidden in her narrative and in history even as she reveals her special places to us. For Prince, as for the enslaved Harriet Jacobs, hiding is a site of doubleness, of presence and absence, a useful strategy to ensure that by choosing where and when to hide, she will eventually arrive at her desired destination.

CONCLUSION: MOBILE SUBJECTIVITY LEADS TO COMMUNAL ACTION

We are left with the complexities of the meaning of mobility, work, and subjectivity for Prince, who has told her readers much, but leaves us yearning for more details and answers. By embracing and yet exceeding categories, representations, and genres, Prince can be located but never pinned down without contextualizing her in a number of traditions and histories. And yet her bold unapologetic voice intervenes into established political and social practices, illustrating how the domestic and the foreign can be intertwined and how mobile subjectivity enables shifts in allegiance and agency to produce communal action, even if certain intentions are thwarted. As I have argued, there are numerous compelling reasons to claim Prince as a significant figure in African American and American literary, cultural, and intellectual history; she should not be left adrift at sea.

NOTES

1. Moira Ferguson was the first to devote extensive scholarly attention to Prince. See Moira Ferguson, *Nine Black Women: An Anthology of Nineteenth-Century Writers from the United States, Canada, Bermuda, and the Caribbean* (New York: Routledge, 1998); and *The History of Mary Prince, a West Indian Slave*, ed. with an introduction by Moira Ferguson (Ann Arbor: University of Michigan Press, 1997). Interdisciplinary scholarship on Prince has increased substantially since 1997.

2. Michele Mitchell, *Righteous Propagation: African Americans and the Politics of Racial Destiny after Reconstruction* (Chapel Hill: University of North Carolina Press, 2004), 9.

3. Nancy Prince, *A Narrative of the Life and Travels of Mrs. Nancy Prince* (Boston: Published by the Author, 1850), 43, 45. Unless otherwise indicated, all subsequent references to the *Narrative* are from the 1853 edition and are cited parenthetically in the text.

4. Mitchell, *Righteous Propagation*, 9.

5. Paul Gilroy, *The Black Atlantic: Modernity and Double Consciousness* (Cambridge, MA: Harvard University Press, 1993).

6. Nancy Prince, Letter to Mr. Garrison, *The Liberator* 1, no. 38 (September 17, 1841): 151.

7. The Black population of Boston in 1850 totaled approximately two thousand. The 1850 census reported that only 14 percent of the city's Black adults were unable to read and write; that number dropped to 8 percent by 1860. Massachusetts-born Blacks had a high rate of literacy because of strong public education in the state, but literacy in some cases referred to a rudimentary knowledge of reading and writing. See James Oliver Horton and Lois E. Horton, *Black Bostonians: Family Life and Community Struggle in the Antebellum North* (New York: Holmes and Meier, 1979), 2, 12–13.

8. Elsewhere, I have written about Prince's strategies to address the needs of African American readers. See Cheryl J. Fish, "Journeys and Warnings: Nancy Prince's Travel as Cautionary Tales for African American Readers," in *Women at Sea: Travel and the Margins of Caribbean Discourse*, ed. Lizabeth Paravisini-Gebert and Ivette Romero-Cesareo (New York: Palgrave, 2001), 225–43.

9. Lauren Berlant, *The Queen of America Goes to Washington: Essays on Sex and Citizenship* (Durham, NC: Duke University Press, 1997), 223.

10. William Andrews, "The Changing Moral Discourse of the Nineteenth-Century African American Women's Autobiography: Harriet Jacobs and Elizabeth Keckley," in *De/Colonizing the Subject: The Politics of Gender in Women's Autobiography*, ed. Sidonie Smith and Julia Watson (Minneapolis: University of Minnesota Press, 1992), 225–41. That includes the house of Captain FitzWilliam Sargent of Gloucester, in whose employ her stepfather Money Vose had also worked for twelve years as a sailor (Prince, *Narrative*, 7). FitzWilliam was the younger brother of Winthrop Sargent, who was the first territorial governor of Mississippi. Prince also "lived in the Rev. Dr. Bolle's family" in Salem (Prince, *Narrative*, 19). Lucius Bolles was minister of the First Baptist Church of Salem and secretary of

the Foreign Missionary Board from 1826 to 1844. He also actively raised funds for a benevolent society in Salem for female orphans. See the pamphlet *A Discourse, Delivered Before the Members of the Salem Female Charitable Society: Being Their Tenth Anniversary* (Salem, MA: Thomas C. Cushing, 1810). Prince was later engaged in similar benevolent causes.

11. See Anthony G. Barthelemy, Introduction, in *Collected Black Women's Narratives*, ed. Henry Louis Gates Jr. (New York: Oxford University Press, 1988). He writes, "Prince doubtless had to weigh the effect of the story of Smith Court on the marketplace for a Black woman to beat a white man and incite other Blacks to riot was too much even for the outspoken abolitionists" (xxxviii).

12. Thos. B. Hilton, "Reminiscences," *Woman's Era* 1, no. 5 (August 1894): 4.

13. Rosalyn Terborg-Penn, "Free Women Entrepreneurs from the 1820s to the 1850s: Nancy Prince and Mary Seacole," in *Crossing Boundaries: Comparative History of Black People in Diaspora*, ed. Darlene Clark Hine and Jacqueline McLeod (Bloomington: Indiana University Press, 1999), 165.

14. Barthelemy, Introduction, xxxviii.

15. As a leader of the African Baptist Church on Belknap Street, Paul was heavily involved in activities that connected the Black community, and no doubt he had an influence on Prince. Paul was a chaplain of the Masonic African Grand Lodge No. 459, of which Prince's husband, Nero Prince, was also a member and commander. See Larry G. Murphy, J. Gordon Melton, and Gary L. Ward, eds., *Encyclopedia of African American Religion* (New York: Garland, 1993); William G. McLoughlin, *New England Dissent, 1660–1883, Vol. II: The Baptists and the Separation of Church and State*, 766, n. 48; and J. Marcus Mitchell, "The Paul Family," *Old Time New England* 63, no. 3 (Winter 1973): 73–77.

16. Paul Hunter, *The Reluctant Pilgrim: Defoe's Emblematic Method and Quest for Form in* Robinson Crusoe (Baltimore: Johns Hopkins University Press, 1966), 73.

17. Kenneth B. Murdock, *Literature and Theology in Colonial New England* (1949; rpt., Westport, CT: Greenwood Press, 1970), 74.

18. See William H. Truettner and Alan Wallach, eds., *Thomas Cole: Landscape into History* (Washington, DC: Smithsonian Institution; New Haven, CT: Yale University Press, 1994).

19. Bonnie J. Barthold, *Black Time: Fiction of Africa, the Caribbean, and the United States* (New Haven, CT: Yale University Press, 1981), 27.

20. David S. Reynolds, *Beneath the American Renaissance: The Subversive Imagination in the Age of Emerson and Melville* (New York: Alfred A. Knopf, 1988), 361.

21. See Susan M. Marren, "Between Slavery and Freedom: The Transgressive Self in Olaudah Equiano's Autobiography," *PMLA* 108, no. 1 (1993): 94–105; she explores the liminal as space to create a "transgressive self" for Olaudah Equiano. See Carla Peterson, *"Doers of the Word": African American Women Speakers and Writers in the North (1830–1880)* (New York: Oxford University Press, 1995). Peterson suggests that Black women entered public civic debate by entering the state of liminality "consciously adopting a self-marginalization that became superimposed upon the already ascribed oppressions of race and gender and that paradoxically allowed empowerment" (17).

22. For theorizing on and laying out the development of this tradition, see, among others, Frances Smith Foster's *Written by Herself: Literary Production by African American Women, 1746–1892* (Bloomington: Indiana University Press, 1993); Peterson, *"Doers of the Word"*; and

Moira Ferguson, ed., *The Hart Sisters: Early African Caribbean Writers, Evangelicals, and Radicals* (Lincoln: University of Nebraska Press, 1993). Earlier groundwork was laid by Dorothy Sterling, ed., *We Are Your Sisters: Black Women in the Nineteenth* Century (New York: W. W. Norton, 1984).

23. Houston A. Baker Jr., *Blues, Ideology, and Afro-American Literature: A Vernacular Theory* (Chicago: University of Chicago Press, 1984), 24.

24. Although there is no Tobias Wornton listed among Black servicemen in the Revolutionary War records, there is a "Boston, Bachus" who served as a private in the Massachusetts Third Regiment. There are also listings for "Boston, Ceasar" and "Boston, Negro," suggesting that because many Black soldiers were enslaved, they were not listed by their full Christian names. See Debra L. Newman, comp., *List of Black Servicemen Compiled from the War Department Collection of the Revolutionary War Records* (Washington, DC: National Archives and Records Service, General Services Administration, 1974).

25. According to records from the Gloucester Archives, Prince's maternal grandfather "Bacchus," servant of Winthrop Sargent, married Dinah, servant of Samuel Sayward, on November 13, 1776. She mentions that Backus was stolen from Africa when a lad, and that her Native American grandmother served as a domestic in the Parsons family.

26. "Anti-Slavery Fair," *The Liberator* 9, no. 46 (November 15, 1839): 183.

27. Sue Houchins, Introduction, in *Spiritual Narratives*, ed. Henry Louis Gates Jr. (New York: Oxford University Press, 1988), xxix–xxx.

28. Foster, *Written by Herself*, 61–62.

29. Mitchell, *Righteous Propagation*, 15.

30. Peterson, *"Doers of the Word,"* 192.

31. Frances Bartkowski, *Travelers, Immigrants, Inmates: Essays in Estrangement* (Minneapolis: University of Minnesota Press, 1995), xx.

32. Jarena Lee, *Religious Experience and Journal of Mrs. Jarena Lee, Giving an Account of Her Call to Preach the Gospel*, rev. and corrected ed. (Philadelphia: Printed and Published for the Author, 1849).

33. Lee, *Religious Experience*, 13.

34. Zilpha Elaw, *Memoirs of the Life, Religious Experience, Ministerial Travels and Labours of Mrs. Zilpha Elaw, an American Female of Colour; Together with Some Account of the Great Religious Revivals in America [Written by Herself]*, in *Sisters of the Spirit: Three Black Women's Autobiographies of the Nineteenth Century*, ed. William L. Andrews (Bloomington: Indiana University Press, 1986), 88. Elaw was quoting Isaiah 30:21 (KJV).

35. Jacqueline Jones, *Labor of Love, Labor of Sorrow: Black Women, Work, and the Family from Slavery to the Present* (New York: Basic Books, 1985), 143.

36. Virginia Penny, *Five Hundred Employments Added to Women with Average Rate of Pay in Each* (Philadelphia: John E. Potter, 1868), 308.

37. Here my reading differs slightly from Carla Peterson's in *"Doers of the Word."* She claims Prince "openly acknowledges herself to be a commoner who observes and comments upon the customs of the Russian elite, in particular the imperial court" (95–96). While Prince is a "commoner" in relation to the status and power of the imperial court and in distancing herself from their customs, her affiliation with the court through her husband, and having her own employees, puts her in a relatively privileged position.

38. Albert Parry, Introduction, in Allison Blakely, *Russia and the Negro: Blacks in Russian History and Thought* (Washington, DC: Howard University Press, 1986), xii.

39. See Peter Kolchin, *Unfree Labor: American Slavery and Russian Serfdom* (Cambridge, MA: Harvard University Press, 1986). As Kolchin explains, the significant difference between American slavery and Russian serfdom was that American slaves were considered "aliens," taken from their homes in Africa against their will, and were of a different nationality, race, and cultural background from their masters. Russian serfs were generally of the same nationality as their masters, although in some regions there might be religious or ethnic differences. But Russian peasants were the lowest level of society, rather than outsiders, and while they did not own any property, most received from their owners allotments of land that they used to support themselves (43–45). Kolchin concludes that American slaves generally had a higher standard of living than their Russian or Latin American counterparts, but they also "suffered from much greater day-to-day interference than the serfs were usually subject to less regulation and were therefore freer to lead their lives as they wished" (156).

40. *Eliza Cook's Journal*, reprinted in *Ladies Repository* 14 (September 1854): 403.

41. John Lloyd Stephens, "Slavery in Russia," *The Liberator* 9, no. 18 (May 3, 1839): 69.

42. Hazel Carby, *Reconstructing Womanhood: The Emergence of the Afro-American Woman Novelist* (New York: Oxford University Press, 1987), 42.

43. Debra Gold Hansen, "The Boston Female Anti-Slavery Society and the Limits of Gender Politics," in *The Abolitionist Sisterhood: Women's Political Culture in Antebellum America*, ed. Jean Fagin Yellin and John C. Van Horne (Ithaca, NY: Cornell University Press, 1994), 54.

44. Hansen, "Boston Female Anti-Slavery Society," 46.

45. Hansen, "Boston Female Anti-Slavery Society," 56.

46. Shirley J. Yee, *Black Women Abolitionists: A Study in Activism, 1828–1860* (Knoxville: University of Tennessee Press, 1992), 102.

47. Lee Chambers-Schiller, '"A Good Work among the People': The Political Culture of the Antislavery Fair," in Yellin and Van Horne, *Abolitionist Sisterhood*, 250.

48. See Keith E. Melder, *The Beginnings of Sisterhood: The American Woman Rights Movement, 1800–1850* (New York: Schocken Books, 1977), 104.

49. Sarah Moore Grimké, *Letters on the Equality of the Sexes and the Condition of Woman, Addressed to Mary S. Parker* (Boston: Isaac Knapp, 1838; New York: B. Franklin, 1970), 4.

50. Boston Female Anti-Slavery Society, *Right and Wrong in Boston*, Annual Reports (Boston: Isaac Knapp, 1840), 30–31.

51. By "destroy the world's convention," Abbott most likely means the World Anti-Slavery Convention, often simply referred to as the World's Convention, held in London in June 1840, just months before Prince departed for Jamaica. At this convention, seven women representing Massachusetts and Pennsylvania as delegates were refused seats because the participation of women went against the traditions of the British antislavery movement. See Kathryn Kish Sklar, '"Women Who Speak for an Entire Nation': American and British Women at the World Anti-Slavery Convention, London, 1840," in Yellin and Van Horne, *Abolitionist Sisterhood*, 306.

52. Robert J. Stewart, *Religion and Society in Post-Emancipation Jamaica* (Knoxville: University of Tennessee Press, 1992), 144.

53. Abigail B. Bakan, *Ideology and Class Conflict in Jamaica: The Politics of Rebellion* (Montreal: McGill-Queen's University Press, 1990), 53.

54. Elsewhere in the *Narrative*, Prince characterizes any deluded or impertinent behavior on the part of former slaves as "the fruits of slavery, [which] makes master and slaves knaves" (62). I read Prince's gaze in relation to the Afro-Jamaicans as judgmental and corrective like a church elder's.

55. Philip D. Curtin, *Two Jamaicas: The Role of Ideas in a Tropical Colony, 1830–1865* (Cambridge, MA: Harvard University Press, 1955), 170.

56. See C. Peter Ripley, *Witness for Freedom: African American Voices on Race, Slavery, and Emancipation* (Chapel Hill: University of North Carolina Press, 1993), 20.

57. Prince, "To the Public," *Anti-Slavery Standard* (New York), May 25, 1843.

58. Prince, *The West Indies: Being a Description of the Islands, Progress of Christianity, Education, and Liberty among the Colored Population Generally* (Boston: Dow and Jackson, 1841), 11.

59. Prince, *West Indies*, 4.

60. Prince, *West Indies*, 4–5.

61. See Mervyn C. Alleyne, *Roots of Jamaican Culture* (London: Pluto Press, 1998), 88–89; Martha Warren Beckwith, *Black Roadways: A Study of Jamaican Life* (1929; New York: Negro Universities Press, 1969); and Monica Schuler, *"Alas, Alas Kongo": A Social History of Indentured African Immigration into Jamaica, 1841–1865* (Baltimore: Johns Hopkins University Press, 1980). The agitation that Prince describes is probably the aftermath of several "outbreaks" in 1842, when the natives openly practiced myalism (Alleyne, *Roots*), gathering together to "pull obeahs and catch the shadows from cotton trees" (Beckwith, *Black Roadways*, 158). During 1841 and 1842, revivals in that practice took place in twenty-two plantation villages, partly because of economic hardship, the result of a wage decrease and competition from the influx of African immigrants recruited by Alexander Barclay (Schuler, *"Alas, Alas Kongo,"* 40).

62. I am indebted to UC Berkeley professor Jenny Franchot (1953–1998) for this terminology.

63. On signifying, see Henry Louis Gates Jr., *Figures in Black: Words, Signs, and the "Racial" Self* (New York: Oxford University Press, 1987), 240–41.

64. Prince, Preface, *Narrative* (1853), 3.

65. Her work as a dressmaker and a tailor would have strained her physically where she was already vulnerable, given that her head would be bent forward and her arms bent at the elbow for long periods of time.

66. Sojourner Truth, quoted in Nell Irvin Painter, "Difference, Slavery, and Memory: Sojourner Truth in Feminist Abolitionism," in Yellin and Van Horne, *Abolitionist Sisterhood*, 141.

67. After the amputation of a functional extremity, the phantom limb is a sensation experienced in close to 100 percent of cases. Here I am using the term to suggest Prince's desire for her body's wholeness and restored power, and the use of the physical book as a "memorial" or replacement. See Elizabeth Grosz, *Volatile Bodies: Toward a Corporeal Feminism* (Bloomington: Indiana University Press, 1994), 70, 73.

68. Prince, Letter to Mr. Garrison, 151.

69. Nellie Y. McKay, "Nineteenth-Century Black Women's Spiritual Autobiographies: Religious Faith and Self-Empowerment," in *Interpreting Women's Lives: Feminist Theory and*

Personal Narratives, ed. The Personal Narratives Group (Bloomington: Indiana University Press, 1989), 140–41.

70. Peterson, *"Doers of the Word,"* 83.

71. Lee, quoted in Peterson, *"Doers of the Word,"* 83.

SELECTED BIBLIOGRAPHY

Andrews, William. "The Changing Moral Discourse of the Nineteenth-Century African American Women's Autobiography: Harriet Jacobs and Elizabeth Keckley." In *De/Colonizing the Subject: The Politics of Gender in Women's Autobiography*, edited by Sidonie Smith and Julia Watson, 225–41. Minneapolis: University of Minnesota Press, 1992.

"Anti-Slavery Fair." *The Liberator* 9, no. 46 (November 15, 1839): 183.

Bakan, Abigail B. *Ideology and Class Conflict in Jamaica: The Politics of Rebellion*. Montreal: McGill-Queen's University Press, 1990.

Baker, Houston A., Jr. *Blues, Ideology, and Afro-American Literature: A Vernacular Theory*. Chicago: University of Chicago Press, 1984.

Barthelemy, Anthony G. Introduction. In *Collected Black Women's Narratives*, edited by Henry Louis Gates Jr., xxix–xlviii. New York: Oxford University Press, 1988.

Barthold, Bonnie J. *Black Time: Fiction of Africa, the Caribbean, and the United States*. New Haven, CT: Yale University Press, 1981.

Bartkowski, Frances. *Travelers, Immigrants, Inmates: Essays in Estrangement*. Minneapolis: University of Minnesota Press, 1995.

Berlant, Lauren. *The Queen of America Goes to Washington: Essays on Sex and Citizenship*. Durham, NC: Duke University Press, 1997.

Bolles, Lucius. *A Discourse, Delivered Before the Members of the Salem Female Charitable Society: Being Their Tenth Anniversary*. Salem, MA: Thomas C. Cushing, 1810.

Boston Female Anti-Slavery Society. *Right and Wrong in Boston*. Annual Reports. Boston: Isaac Knapp, 1840.

Carby, Hazel. *Reconstructing Womanhood: The Emergence of the Afro-American Woman Novelist*. New York: Oxford University Press, 1987.

Chambers-Schiller, Lee. '"A Good Work among the People': The Political Culture of the Antislavery Fair." In *The Abolitionist Sisterhood: Women's Political Culture in Antebellum America*, edited by Jean Fagin Yellin and John C. Van Horne, 249–74. Ithaca, NY: Cornell University Press, 1994.

Curtin, Philip D. *Two Jamaicas: The Role of Ideas in a Tropical Colony, 1830–1865*. Cambridge, MA: Harvard University Press, 1955.

Elaw, Zilpha. *Memoirs of the Life, Religious Experience, Ministerial Travels and Labours of Mrs. Zilpha Elaw, an American Female of Colour; Together with Some Account of the Great Religious Revivals in America [Written by Herself]*. In *Sisters of the Spirit: Three Black Women's Autobiographies of the Nineteenth Century*, edited by William L. Andrews, 49–160. Bloomington: Indiana University Press, 1986.

"Eliza Cook's Journal." Rpt. in *Ladies Repository* 14 (September 1854): 403.

Ferguson, Moira, ed. *The Hart Sisters: Early African Caribbean Writers, Evangelicals, and Radicals*. Lincoln: University of Nebraska Press, 1993.

Ferguson, Moira. *Nine Black Women: An Anthology of Nineteenth-Century Writers from the United States, Canada, Bermuda, and the Caribbean*. New York: Routledge, 1998.

Fish, Cheryl J. "Journeys and Warnings: Nancy Prince's Travel as Cautionary Tales for African American Readers." In *Women at Sea: Travel and the Margins of Caribbean Discourse*, edited by Lizabeth Paravisini-Gebert and Ivette Romero-Cesareo, 225–43. New York: Palgrave, 2001.

Foster, Frances Smith. *Written by Herself: Literary Production by African American Women, 1746–1892*. Bloomington: Indiana University Press, 1993.

Gates, Henry Louis, Jr. *Figures in Black: Words, Signs, and the "Racial" Self*. New York: Oxford University Press, 1987.

Gilroy, Paul. *The Black Atlantic: Modernity and Double Consciousness*. Cambridge, MA: Harvard University Press, 1993.

Grimké, Sarah Moore. *Letters on the Equality of the Sexes and the Condition of Woman, Addressed to Mary S. Parker*. Boston: Isaac Knapp, 1838; New York: B. Franklin, 1970.

Grosz, Elizabeth. *Volatile Bodies: Toward a Corporeal Feminism*. Bloomington: Indiana University Press, 1994.

Hansen, Debra Gold. "The Boston Female Anti-Slavery Society and the Limits of Gender Politics." In *The Abolitionist Sisterhood: Women's Political Culture in Antebellum America*, edited by Jean Fagin Yellin and John C. Van Horne, 45–65. Ithaca, NY: Cornell University Press, 1994.

Hilton, Thos. B. "Reminiscences." *Woman's Era* 1, no. 5 (August 1894): 1–16.

Horton, James Oliver, and Lois E. Horton. *Black Bostonians: Family Life and Community Struggle in the Antebellum North*. New York: Holmes and Meier, 1979.

Houchins, Sue. Introduction. In *Spiritual Narratives*, edited by Henry Louis Gates Jr., xxix–xliv. New York: Oxford University Press, 1988.

Hunter, Paul. *The Reluctant Pilgrim: Defoe's Emblematic Method and Quest for Form in* Robinson Crusoe. Baltimore: Johns Hopkins University Press, 1966.

Jones, Jacqueline. *Labor of Love, Labor of Sorrow: Black Women, Work, and the Family from Slavery to the Present*. New York: Basic Books, 1985.

Kolchin, Peter. *Unfree Labor: American Slavery and Russian Serfdom*. Cambridge, MA: Harvard University Press, 1986.

Lee, Jarena. *Religious Experience and Journal of Mrs. Jarena Lee, Giving an Account of Her Call to Preach the Gospel*. Rev. and corrected ed. Philadelphia: Printed and Published for the Author, 1849.

Marren, Susan M. "Between Slavery and Freedom: The Transgressive Self in Olaudah Equiano's Autobiography." *PMLA* 108, no. 1 (1993): 94–105.

McKay, Nellie Y. "Nineteenth-Century Black Women's Spiritual Autobiographies: Religious Faith and Self-Empowerment." In *Interpreting Women's Lives: Feminist Theory and Personal Narratives*, edited by The Personal Narratives Group, 139–54. Bloomington: Indiana University Press, 1989.

McLoughlin, William G. *New England Dissent, 1660–1883, Vol II: The Baptists and the Separation of Church and State*. Cambridge, MA: Harvard University Press, 1971.

Melder, Keith E. *The Beginnings of Sisterhood: The American Woman Rights Movement, 1800–1850*. New York: Schocken Books, 1977.

Mitchell, J. Marcus. "The Paul Family." *Old Time New England* 63, no. 3 (Winter 1973): 73–77.

Mitchell, Michele. *Righteous Propagation: African Americans and the Politics of Racial Destiny after Reconstruction*. Chapel Hill: University of North Carolina Press, 2004.

Murdock, Kenneth B. *Literature and Theology in Colonial New England*. 1949. Reprint, Westport, CT: Greenwood Press, 1970.

Murphy, Larry G., J. Gordon Melton, and Gary L. Ward, eds. *Encyclopedia of African American Religion*. New York: Garland, 1993.

Newman, Debra L., comp. *List of Black Servicemen Compiled from the War Department Collection of the Revolutionary War Records*. Washington, DC: National Archives and Records Service, General Services Administration, 1974.

Painter, Nell Irvin. "Difference, Slavery, and Memory: Sojourner Truth in Feminist Abolitionism." In *The Abolitionist Sisterhood: Women's Political Culture in Antebellum America*, edited by Jean Fagin Yellin and John C. Van Horne, 139–58. Ithaca, NY: Cornell University Press, 1994.

Parry, Albert. Foreword to *Russia and the Negro: Blacks in Russian History and Thought* by Allison Blakely, xi–xii. Washington, DC: Howard University Press, 1986.

Penny, Virginia. *Five Hundred Employments Added to Women with Average Rate of Pay in Each*. Philadelphia: John E. Potter, 1868.

Peterson, Carla. *"Doers of the Word": African American Women Speakers and Writers in the North (1830–1880)*. New York: Oxford University Press, 1995.

Prince, Nancy. *The History of Mary Prince, a West Indian Slave*. Edited by Moira Ferguson. Ann Arbor: University of Michigan Press, 1997.

Prince, Nancy. Letter to Mr. Garrison. *The Liberator* 11, no. 38 (September 17, 1841): 151.

Prince, Nancy. *A Narrative of the Life and Travels of Mrs. Nancy Prince*. Boston: Published by the Author, 1850.

Prince, Nancy. *A Narrative of the Life and Travels of Mrs. Nancy Prince, Written by Herself*. 1853. In *Collected Black Women's Narratives*, edited by Henry Louis Gates Jr. New York: Oxford University Press, 1988.

Prince, Nancy. "To the Public." *Anti-Slavery Standard* (New York), May 25, 1843.

Prince, Nancy. *The West Indies: Being a Description of the Islands, Progress of Christianity, Education, and Liberty among the Colored Population Generally*. Boston: Dow and Jackson, 1841.

Reynolds, David S. *Beneath the American Renaissance: The Subversive Imagination in the Age of Emerson and Melville*. New York: Alfred A. Knopf, 1988.

Ripley, C. Peter. *Witness for Freedom: African American Voices on Race, Slavery, and Emancipation*. Chapel Hill: University of North Carolina Press, 1993.

Sklar, Kathryn Kish. "'Women Who Speak for an Entire Nation': American and British Women at the World Anti-Slavery Convention, London, 1840." In *The Abolitionist Sisterhood: Women's Political Culture in Antebellum America*, edited by Jean Fagin Yellin and John C. Van Horne, 301–33. Ithaca, NY: Cornell University Press, 1994.

Stephens, John Lloyd. "Slavery in Russia." *The Liberator* 9, no. 18 (May 3, 1839): 69.

Stewart, Robert J. *Religion and Society in Post-Emancipation Jamaica*. Knoxville: University of Tennessee Press, 1992.

Terborg-Penn, Rosalyn. "Free Women Entrepreneurs from the 1820s to the 1850s: Nancy Prince and Mary Seacole." In *Crossing Boundaries: Comparative History of Black People in Diaspora*, edited by Darlene Clark Hine and Jacqueline McLeod, 159–75. Bloomington: Indiana University Press, 1999.

Truettner, William H., and Alan Wallach, eds. *Thomas Cole: Landscape into History*. Washington, DC: Smithsonian Institution; New Haven, CT: Yale University Press, 1994.

Turner, Mary. "Chattel Slaves into Wages Slaves." In *Labour in the Caribbean, from Emancipation to Independence*, edited by Malcolm Cross and Gad Heuman, 14–31. London: Macmillan, 1988.

Yee, Shirley J. *Black Women Abolitionists: A Study in Activism, 1828–1860*. Knoxville: University of Tennessee Press, 1992.

Chapter 3

"FISHERS OF MEN"

Understanding Frances Ellen Watkins Harper's Poetry as Vocational Autobiography

JENNIFER McFARLANE-HARRIS

In the late 1860s, Frances Ellen Watkins Harper—a freeborn, middle-class, educated Black woman from the North who had already established her reputation as an outstanding lecturer on the antislavery circuit and published numerous poems, essays, and speeches—embarked on a southern lecture tour with the theme "Literacy, Land and Liberation."[1] Her letters from this period indicate that she traveled "almost constantly" across states such as South Carolina, Georgia, and Alabama, lecturing frequently to Black and white audiences of all ages and both sexes in many different venues, particularly Sunday schools and newly established schools for freepersons.[2] As historian Martha S. Jones describes, "After the Civil War, [Harper] became a conscience for the entire country, instructing her listeners . . . about what it meant to reconstruct the nation."[3] Harper saw firsthand the awful aftermath of that war, including widespread poverty for formerly enslaved people and poor whites alike, the continued violence of Rebel sympathizers and the burgeoning Ku Klux Klan, and even the "thickened graves" from what she called "that modern Golgotha," the stockade at Florence, South Carolina, where Union soldiers were imprisoned by the Confederates at the end of the war.[4]

Harper distilled her Reconstruction lecture tour experiences into poetic form in *Sketches of Southern Life*, first published in 1872. Although short, this book contains some of her most famous poems, a series featuring a first-person speaker named "Aunt Chloe." Significantly, these poems draw on the slave narrative tradition, depicting the horrors of slavery and the humanity of those enslaved; the characters speak in a kind of Black dialect, but without being reduced to stereotypes.[5] Although these poems are set during Reconstruction, Aunt Chloe's memories of the depravity of slavery, the trials of the Civil War, and the joys of emancipation are as fresh as ever. Claiming "Of course, I don't know very much / About these politics," Chloe is actually quite sharp on the topic of voting rights, and despite her age ("rising sixty"), she learns to read "The hymns and Testament."[6] By creating the Aunt Chloe character, Harper was able to draw on her encounters with formerly enslaved persons while voicing some of her own political and theological concerns.

In fact, Harper's *Sketches of Southern Life* is a melding of the personal and the political. As Valerie Palmer-Mehta argues in "'We Are All Bound Up Together': Frances Harper and Feminist Theory," Harper anticipates that famous call to arms of Second Wave feminism, "the personal is political," by using her own experiences of discrimination as examples in some of her most important speeches on women's rights, demonstrating to white women in the struggle that they must recognize the difference between their experiences of gender oppression and the multiple forms of prejudice Black women encounter at the intersection of race and gender.[7] Palmer-Mehta goes further, noting Harper's strategic deployment of the ordinary: "By using experience as evidence, [Harper] dips into the everydayness of people's ordinary lives to suggest how sexism and racism debilitated the quality of life for and endangered many of its citizens, clearly demonstrating how the personal is political."[8] In a similar way, through first-person poems in *Sketches of Southern Life*, Harper uses the "ordinary" to encourage the reader to recognize the nuances of oppression and concomitant activism that a Black woman like Aunt Chloe experiences. Indeed, *Sketches of Southern Life* may be construed as "an undeclared collective memoir, the composite testimony of freed African Americans Harper met in the course of her postbellum travels," according to Rebecka Rutledge Fisher.[9] Harper imagines a character in the person of Chloe who is paradoxically like herself, and yet not herself. Fisher continues, "Chloe's speech act is an essential overcoming of the negative. It negates silence on three discernible levels of consciousness: that of the author (Harper); that of the witness, narrator, and survivor of slavery (Chloe); and that of the collectivity of silenced slaves (the paradoxical human/non-human, those who speak but do not speak for themselves, those who survive in representation though they might have perished)."[10] Using Chloe as a mouthpiece allows Harper to ask difficult theological questions ("If God is good and just, / How it happened that the masters / Did grind us to the dust") and make credible claims about the consequences of slavery.[11] Harper's poetic technique is in the service of activism; the *first-person(al)* speaker is *political.*

METHOD AND MESSAGE OF HARPER'S POETRY

This chapter discusses Harper's poetic project as a moral, theological, and autobiographical one. In order to understand Harper's prowess as a public intellectual, we must interrogate the relationship between her method and message. Why was much of Harper's poetry so direct and plain-spoken, when her spiritual and political concerns were complex and demanding? The answer can be found in Harper's literary vocation. Like many other nineteenth-century authors, Harper composed highly accessible poems in ballad form with regular meter, perfect rhyme, and recurring tropes, the kind of poems that contemporary literary critics hesitate to scrutinize too intently lest they be found wanting in literary merit. Michael C. Cohen reminds us that nineteenth-century readers consumed, circulated, and valued poems differently than we do today, arguing that nineteenth-century poems must be subject to "historical readings" in social and political context(s) as they may not hold up to modern critical sensibilities: "I cannot reach these worlds of lived experience by reading poems in the way I normally would, using the protocols of close reading, since close reading emphasizes the careful analysis of formal, complex uses of language, while producing and valuing interpretation above all else. A large majority of nineteenth-century poems seem unable to hold up to the rigors of this kind of relation."[12] I argue, however, that the accessibility and predictability of Harper's verses in "'Fishers of Men'" and "Nothing and Something"—two of Harper's poems added to the 1886 edition of *Sketches of Southern Life*—are precisely the point. Harper understood sin as dangerous and predictable, and she crafted poems to help lead her readers away from sin and danger, toward the light. Through first-person speakers who encourage discipleship and social action—speaking positions that can be occupied simultaneously by the author and the reader—Harper relies upon her own well-honed spiritual vision to draw others closer to Christ. Her "I"-voiced speakers are both autobiographical and evangelical.

The memoir-adjacent Aunt Chloe sequence is just one example of Harper's continuing preoccupation with slavery after emancipation, part of her larger quest to inspire her readers toward political involvement and Christian excellence. Womanist theologian Cheryl Townsend Gilkes explains how Harper used religious language to communicate shared aims with other Black women: "Harper in particular asserted that in the process of adjusting to the social change associated with the new experience of freedom, African-American women drew upon their experiences in slavery as a source of militant solidarity evinced by African-American women of all backgrounds, and particularly privileged ones. Often that solidarity was expressed in the language of religious covenant and Christian mission."[13] One exemplar stands out. In "National Salvation," a January 31, 1867, lecture sponsored by the Social, Civil, and Statistical Association of the Colored People of Philadelphia, Harper delivered an amazing critique of Reconstruction, including this memorable sentence:

> Now slavery, as an institution, has been overthrown, but slavery, as an idea, still lives in the American Republic, and the problem and the duty of the present hour is this:—Whether there is strength enough, wisdom enough, and virtue enough in our American nation to lift it out of trouble; whether by its legislation and jurisprudence these distinctions between man and man, on account of his race, color, or descent, shall cease.[14]

The very "idea" of slavery continued to threaten the nation. And as Harper also suggested later that year in one of her letters (published on August 10, 1867, in the *National Anti-Slavery Standard*), the enslaved past was a "shadow" that might threaten the future: "The South is a sad place, it is so rife with mournful memories and sad revelations of the past. Here you listen to heart-saddening stories of grievous old wrongs, for the shadows of the past have not been fully lifted from the minds of the former victims of slavery."[15] Nevertheless, Harper was hopeful, "for the shadows bear the promise of a brighter coming day."[16] In order to get to that brighter day, however, there was much work to be done. For Harper, that meant everything from lecturing for free and "roughing it in the bush" to agitating for Black suffrage, women's rights, and temperance reform.[17] Operating through a Christian framework with Unitarian theology, Harper believed that Christian precepts could transform the sinful life of the individual and revolutionize corrupt social relationships.

Specifically, Harper was concerned about two types of sin that could jeopardize the individual and damage society: the "galling chain" of chattel slavery (and the ongoing legacy of this institution, as mentioned above), and the dangers of alcoholism, or "the bondage of the bowl."[18] In Harper's poetry, Christ has the power to rend these chains, and she encourages others to have their fetters broken by embracing Christian faith and modeling their lives on exemplary biblical figures such as the Syrophoenician woman, Ruth, Vashti, Moses, and Jesus himself. While she does not present intricate doctrinal systems like some of her near contemporaries, such as Julia Foote (sanctification/Methodism), Rebecca Cox Jackson (celibacy/Shakerism), or Zilpha Elaw (ecumenical holiness), Harper nevertheless impresses upon her readers the importance of holy living. Her first-person, "I"-voiced poetry allows for a kind of practical narrative theology, a clear-cut guide to salvation from what Harper called the "twin evils of slavery and intemperance."[19] Her poems were meant to inspire others, her fellow African Americans in particular, to act—that is, to take up positions of spiritual and political leadership.

Harper clearly believed in the intelligibility of the Bible, employing its stories and characters to lay the foundation for robust activism. Yet she also conceived of poetry as a crucial vehicle for theological and political thought, circulating ideas in the public square—in print, oratory, or both. As Meredith L. McGill demonstrates, Harper used savvy publication strategies in her antebellum work:

> Frances Ellen Watkins Harper's identity as a black woman poet was crucial to the role she played in the antislavery movement, but her poems' publication in cheap pamphlets, their frequent appearance in abolitionist newspapers, and the structure of the poems themselves all suggest that they were not intended to be read as lyrics, but rather as instruments of exhortation, nodes for the condensation and transfer of oral authority, and vehicles for collective assent.[20]

Here, McGill reads Harper's antislavery poems as largely against the interiority of the traditional lyric, arguing that poems like "The Slave Mother" are structured to "frequently abjure the lyric 'I' for a collective 'we'" in order to create "scenes of collective listening." I agree that Harper cleverly constructs such poems to include the reader-as-witness, but McGill's distinction between Harper's later work (postbellum) and earlier work (antebellum) is perhaps more important for her engagement with the lyric: "While in her later years, Harper worked to consolidate and preserve her literary legacy, the mid-nineteenth-century chapbook publication of her poems points at every turn *away* from the poet herself, *away* from a consistent poetic persona, and *away* from a stable poetic corpus toward frequently repeated oral performances and newspaper reports that helped strengthen opposition to slavery and knit together scattered communities of activists" (italics in the original). When examining "I"-voiced poems from "her later years" like those featured in *Sketches of Southern Life* (1886), I read Harper as using her own version of the lyric to carefully establish the importance of her literary vocation; poems like "'Fishers of Men'" turn *toward* "the poet herself" (to repurpose McGill's words), but in the service of an activist ethos that allows the reader to also become an "I" voice of her own, inward-looking (introspective Christian conviction) but outward-facing (future activism in the public sphere).

THE POETICAL *IS* POLITICAL—AND AUTOBIOGRAPHICAL

Harper continued using poetry as part of her personal political strategy after the Civil War. As Carla L. Peterson notes, "Watkins Harper occasionally and particularly in the postbellum period accompanied her lectures with recitations of her poetry, which she also collected in volumes for publication and sold at the close of her lectures."[21] According to Peterson, this method of distribution places Harper firmly in the African American autobiographical tradition:

"Just as other African-American writers sold their slave narratives or spiritual autobiographies after delivering antislavery speeches or sermons, so Watkins Harper sold her books of poems to the audiences that had come to hear her lecture. In this sense her poetry can be interpreted as autobiography, as an indirect account of individual life."[22] Following critics like Peterson, I read Harper's poems as crucial first-person accounts of her activist ethos. And as Frances Smith Foster explains in her groundbreaking anthology of Harper's work, *A Brighter Coming Day*, "from her earliest writings, Harper advocated a life in which the personal and the public were merged in an effort to realize the moral, social, and economic development of society. Her literature was an essential tool to that end, and it is her literature that must, finally, serve as her presentation of self."[23] Though Harper did not write an intentional autobiography and left behind no journals to tell the story of her life and work, we can glimpse her vocational process by turning to key poems. When read alongside her letters, essays, and prose fiction, we can piece together the elements that motivated her poetic sensibilities and pragmatic theological approach.

Considering Harper's poetry as autobiographical may seem unusual, even though much of her poetry contains an "I" speaker in a mode reminiscent of the self-referential but God-centered conversion narratives of conventional spiritual autobiographies in prose.[24] In fact, Harper's poetry conveys a process of continual revelation and increasing holiness in herself and others. Through this process (for Harper, a poetic process), a textual relationship between God, the believer/writer (through the speaker/supplicant wielded by that writer), and the reader/convert develops over time across multiple poems.[25] According to Foster, Harper seems to have taken more control over the publication and distribution of her work in the latter part of the nineteenth century; she regularly added new poems or essays to each collection when releasing new editions of her books, allowing her themes to reverberate across expanded texts.[26] Harper often included poems treating biblical themes, temperance, or her vocation in earlier volumes of her poetry that dealt heavily with the subject of slavery.[27] Given the content of these additional poems, I consider the poetic accretion across editions to be an autobiographical act (comparable to Walt Whitman's ongoing reworking of *Leaves of Grass* or Frederick Douglass's revision and expansion of his "life"—his *Narrative*—through three autobiographies).[28]

For example, consider "'Fishers of Men,'" one of the poems added to *Sketches of Southern Life* for the 1886 edition—fourteen years after the first edition was published. The poem begins with the speaker recalling a visionary state:

> I had a dream, a varied dream:
> Before my ravished sight

The city of my Lord arose,
With all its love and light.[29]

Using the word "ravished" in the sense of spiritual transport, Harper demonstrates that this speaker is seeing through a wondrous, God-given vision that allows her to go beyond the physical senses and tap into the spiritual world.[30] Like John, the speaker of the biblical book of Revelation who was transported through prophetic ecstasy and found himself before the heavenly city of the new Jerusalem, Harper's speaker finds herself before the "gates of light," ready to enter heaven.[31] Just as she is about to go through the gates, she hears an agonizing cry:

I turned, and saw behind me surge
A wild and stormy sea;
And drowning men were reaching out
Imploring hands to me.[32]

The anguished moans of these imperiled men seem to drown out the harps of the holy city. Turning to her angel guide, the speaker asks that she be allowed to return to earth and help "these wretched ones, / So wrecked and desolate."[33] Although the angel reminds her that going back will be difficult, the speaker is resolved. As she puts her back to heaven and faces the turbulent sea, her decision is rewarded:

I turned to go, but as I turned
The gloomy sea grew bright,
And from my heart there seemed to flow
Ten thousand cords of light.

And sin-wrecked men, with eager hands,
Did grasp each golden cord;
And with my heart I drew them on
To see my gracious Lord.

The streams of light pouring from the speaker's chest become lifelines for the drowning.[34] This imagery is striking, and Harper's speaker becomes a hero—with powers approaching those of a superhero—as her heartstrings pull others to safety. In the final stanza of this poem, the speaker again stands at heaven's gates, this time with a "rescued throng" beside her, all of whom will enter the holy city.[35]

"'Fishers of Men'" is an unusual piece for Harper. Although many of her poems include a first-person speaker depicting biblical stories or dramatic (and pathetic) scenes, they do not often include visions, dreamscapes, prophecies, and otherworldly impressions. A notable exception is the heretofore unknown poem "A Dream," which was published by a young Frances Ellen Watkins in her recently rediscovered first pamphlet *Forest Leaves*.[36] The first line of "A Dream" is precisely the same as that of "'Fishers of Men'": "I had a dream, a varied dream." However, "A Dream" presents a very different version of what happens on the cusp of the afterlife. Whereas "'Fishers of Men'" employs a first-person speaker who can actively choose to turn back from "the gates of light" to help those who might otherwise be lost in the "gloomy sea,"[37] the speaker of "A Dream" can only helplessly watch as a "judgement scene" rises before her eyes.[38] In the first half of this poem, those who are saved rejoice to be in Christ's presence, "Before his white and burning throne"; but in the second half of the poem, "glories" become "terrors" as the speaker repeats the phrase, "I had a dream, a varied dream," and then God's vengeance is on horrific display. The speaker describes the "terror, grief, and dread" as ineffable and unimaginable ("Tongue can't describe or pen portray"); she can only look on as earthly kingdoms are destroyed and sinners are doomed for all eternity:

> I heard the agonizing cry,
> Ye rocks and mountains on us fall,
> And hide us from the Judge's eye,
> But rocks and mounts fled from the call.
>
> I saw the guilty ruin'd host
> Standing before the burning throne,
> The ruin'd, lost forever lost,
> Whom God in wrath refus'd to own.[39]

The damned wish that the very mountains would crush and cover them from God's sight, but their cries go unheeded. And the speaker can do nothing to save the "guilty ruin'd host." The poem's end is quite sobering, as God's wrath has the final impact.

The trajectory of "'Fishers of Men'" is all the more remarkable when placed in contrast with that of "A Dream." The most provocative imagery in "A Dream" is uncanny: the dead rising up from the grave to be judged before the "burning throne."[40] But the captivating moments in "'Fishers of Men'" are those set in motion by the speaker as a heroic agent of the divine, pulling others to safety and light. The speaker of "A Dream" can only wish she had the aesthetic skill to fully describe the "joy and dread" of the judgment day ("Oh for an angel's hand to paint" the scene); the speaker of "'Fishers of Men'" truly becomes, in the words of Jesus calling his first disciples to leave their fishing nets and follow him instead, a "fisher of men," pulling drowning men from the sea.[41] With the "rescued throng / The Lord had given me" as proof of her evangelizing skill, the first-person speaker of "'Fishers of Men'" ends the poem with a "glad and free" heart.[42] Unlike the speaker of "A Dream," this speaker need not wish for the word-painting skills of an angel; instead, she negotiates with an angel, and saves a multitude.

"'Fishers of Men'" can be understood as an autobiographical exploration of Harper's discipleship, one of many examples from her poetry where the experiences, emotions, and beliefs of an "I"-voiced speaker seem to align with Harper's own knowledge and views. In this case, the "varied dream" related by the speaker of "'Fishers of Men'" can be read as an allegory about Harper's spiritual calling. A young Frances Ellen Watkins wrote "A Dream" as a poem with a first-person speaker who could not yet give shape to the "varied dream" or save the sinners therein; a more mature Harper took that same first line, and crafted an activist, evangelizing first-person speaker. Herself a "fisher of men," Harper cannot ignore the cries of those in distress, whether the "bitter shrieks" of an enslaved woman whose child has been sold away from her (e.g., her poem "The Slave Mother"), the whimpers of a young boy terrified of his drunken father (e.g., "Signing the Pledge"), or the sighs of a woman whose husband playfully mocks her desire for the vote ("John and Jacob—A Dialogue on Woman's Rights").[43] Her poems convey a kind of accessible, everyday theology in relation to important life events, both spiritual (the return of a prodigal son, signing a temperance pledge, the resurrection of Jesus, etc.) and social and political (the passage of the Fifteenth Amendment, the Emancipation Proclamation, commemorating the centennial of the African Methodist Episcopal Church, etc.).[44] For Harper, poetry is a tool of both self-expression and conversion, a way to rhetorically strengthen her relationship with the divine while pleading for the reader to take up her (and her Lord's) cause.

Moreover, Harper's poetic project seems to underscore the notion that personal salvation and social reform can—and should—go together.[45] The reader's potential to experience personal transformation (whether conversion to Christ or to a social cause) through reading a poem also involves the potential to become a social actor, a change agent in the material world. Harper continuously modeled the ways in which activism follows personal dedication to Christ in her literature and in her own life.[46] Before her marriage to Fenton Harper in 1860 at the age of thirty-five, Frances Watkins worked as a teacher in Ohio and Pennsylvania and toured across New England and parts of the Midwest as an antislavery lecturer. She apparently published her first pamphlet of poems in the late 1840s (*Forest Leaves*),[47] published more poetry in earnest in the 1850s (her popular and oft-reprinted *Poems on Miscellaneous Subjects* was first published in 1854), and then she began publishing fiction in 1859 with her short story "The Two Offers."[48] Though she cut back on her public activities somewhat during her four-year marriage, she resumed her lecturing career shortly after her husband's death, probably with their daughter Mary in tow.[49] In the 1870s, after her southern tour, Harper and her daughter settled in Philadelphia, and Harper joined the First Unitarian Church of Philadelphia.[50] Harper was instrumental in numerous activist organizations at the end of the century, becoming a leader in the Woman's Christian Temperance Union and the National Association of Colored Women (to name just two). She also continued to publish essays, poetry, and fiction. In addition to reprints of earlier poetry volumes like *Moses: A Story of the Nile* (1869) and *Sketches of Southern Life* (1872) and new poetry collections such as *Atlanta Offerings: Poems* (1895), she published three serialized novels in periodicals such as the *Christian Recorder* (the organ of the African Methodist Episcopal Church), as well as the novel *Iola Leroy; Or, Shadows Uplifted* (1892), before her death in 1911.[51]

UNITARIAN INFLUENCES AND MORAL GOOD

In light of her literary and activist objectives, Harper's apparent adoption of Unitarianism makes sense. In particular, one aspect of Unitarian theology involving the "Arminian concept of free will and free moral agency" seems to have informed Harper's vocation, bringing together her literature and social reform work: the idea, described by Nancy Hardesty, that "sin, disorder, and social evil would disappear if everyone would choose good, make unselfish choices, and convince everyone else to do likewise."[52] Harper saw her literary production as crucial to influencing others to make good choices that would better society, and she carried that desire into a Unitarian-like hermeneutic.

For an illuminating instance of her principles of biblical interpretation, take the sentiments espoused in Harper's mid-1850s essay "Christianity," where she notes that the Bible is "wonderful in its construction, admirable in its adaptation, it contains truths that a child may comprehend, and mysteries into which angels desire to look."[53] Katherine Clay Bassard uses this same passage as part of her argument that scholars sometimes overestimate the importance of Unitarian doctrine in Harper's poems.[54] However, even if we grant some tension between Harper's reliance on biblical stories as true and authoritative in her poetry and the ways in which nineteenth-century Unitarianism was turning away from biblical literalism (as Bassard notes), it is nevertheless important to examine how Unitarian concepts and theological elements may have resonated with Harper's poetic vocation in poems like "'Fishers of Men'"—a piece that becomes a creative *reimagining* of a Bible story rather than simply a rich *retelling*. In fact, I believe Harper would have found the following passage from the doctrinal guide *Unitarian Principles Confirmed by Trinitarian Testimonies* (1880) instructive:

> The Bible is not, throughout its various portions, a book only of dark and intricate passages leading to no certain conclusion. It abounds in narratives, whose beautiful simplicity and tender pathos are grateful to the ear of childhood; in pictures of divine heroism and disinterestedness which arrest the eye of youth; in songs of purity and piety which lift to higher realms the common mind of manhood; in words of comfort and consolation which impart heavenly strength and holy trust to the heart of feebleness and age.[55]

Harper's poetry also contains "beautiful simplicity and tender pathos" for her readers. She wanted to edify her readers by showing "pictures of divine heroism" from the Bible. But if her poem "'Fishers of Men'" is any indicator, Harper also fashioned herself into a hero in her own right, pulling her readers to safety by providing examples of human frailty and integrity, wickedness and righteousness, teaching her readers to choose the good and the light.

Most of Harper's poems are truth-conveying stories meant to convert her readers in some fashion. They often function like popular religious tracts and newspapers such as those published by the American Tract Society during the nineteenth century: "'simple, evangelical narratives, which unfold the plan of salvation to plain minds.'"[56] Alternatively, Harper's poems could serve a devotional purpose, much like nineteenth-century hymn collections—hymn texts without tunes—that could be used for private meditation.[57] Either way, in many of her poems, Harper's authorial/written "I" and the speaker's "I" entwine, and the reader's "I" is implicated through the act of "speaking" (that is, reading) this "I."

An illustration of how entwined "I" voices function in Harper's work to persuade the reader can be found in another poem that was added to *Sketches of Southern Life* for the 1886 edition: "Nothing and Something." One of the key activist causes of the late nineteenth century, temperance was one of the most important issues animating Harper's activism and literature, particularly during the period discussed in this chapter that coincided with Harper's membership in the Unitarian Church.[58] "Nothing and Something" is typical of Harper's temperance poetry in that it relies on the power of first-person narration to demonstrate the life-altering—and often life-threatening—consequences of liquor consumption, both for the (always male) alcohol abuser and for those around him (usually his wife and children). But the brilliance of this particular poem lies in the fact that five different "I" voices come together, each telling a story that seems interconnected with the others. These connections are made thematically across the narrative arc of the poem, as well as through regular meter and repetitive rhyme schemes.[59]

The poem consists of six stanzas of eight lines each (although the final stanza is divided into two parts). Except for the last one, each stanza begins with four lines in the voice of a first-person speaker, saying, "It is nothing to me," followed by a bold proclamation indicating that alcohol could never affect his/her life. The remaining four lines of the stanza are voiced by an omniscient third-person narrator telling of the hardship that later befell the first-person speaker of the previous lines, proving that the "nothing" of intemperance turned out to be "something" after all. To see the "dialogue" that takes place in each stanza, alternating between a first-person speaker and the third-person narrator, take the second stanza as an example:

> It is nothing to me, the mother said;
> I have no fear that my boy will tread
> In the downward path of sin and shame,
> And crush my heart and darken his name.
> It was something to her when that only son
> From the path of right was early won,
> And madly cast in the flowing bowl
> A ruined body and sin-wrecked soul.[60]

The effect of hearing multiple speakers, one after the other, whose stories end in disaster, is a powerful feeling of inevitable dread. All of the characters are caught up in the vicious circle of intemperance: the beautiful, grief-stricken young woman who fears the "staggering tread" of her alcoholic husband; the mother whose son becomes a drunkard (above); the young man whose drinking leads to imprisonment and separation from his family; the merchant unconcerned about selling liquor who later hears that his wife and child are dead because of the carelessness of a "drunken [train] conductor"; and finally, the man who "gave his vote for the liquor trade," completing the circle when his daughter marries an alcoholic (presumably she's the beauty from the first stanza). As already mentioned, the sense of inevitability is heightened by the regular meter (iambic tetrameter) and predictable rhymes that are paired every two lines and recur throughout the poem (for instance, "said," "head," "dread," and "tread" all appear more than once). Yet these seemingly simplistic devices are not because Harper lacked talent or did not want to experiment with verse forms.

In fact, this poem is a prime example of Harper's literary agenda. It can be seen as a devotional piece, a story full of pathos with lines that are easy to recall—something a reader could return to again and again. The force of this poem lies in repetition, and the inevitable rhymes are a device illustrating the trap of sin that it is easy to fall into. Only the last stanza (divided into two parts, a four-line question followed by a four-line answer) can break the cycle of grinding "a grist of sin" as the third-person narrator steps into the first-person speaker role, inviting readers into the story of the poem by using the word "us," asking, "Is it nothing for us to idly sleep / While the cohorts of death their vigils keep?" The speaker authoritatively answers her own question in the last four lines:

> It is something, yes, all, for us to stand
> Clasping by faith our Saviour's hand;
> To learn to labor, live and fight
> On the side of God and changeless light.[61]

The spondee in the middle of the first line of the final quatrain ("yes, all") adds an extra stress to the line, the only time in the entire poem where one line contains five strong stresses. This variation is significant; Harper is emphasizing just how important it is to join the temperance "fight." It is more than "something," the speaker suggests. It is everything. In the logic of the poem, choosing temperance means choosing the right side of the battle, the side of God and Jesus. The speaker seems to assume that her readers are already Christians ("Clasping by faith *our* Saviour's hand" [emphasis added]), but that they do not realize the extent of the damage that intemperance can wreak. Harper uses poems like "Nothing and Something" to convert her readers to the temperance cause.

CONCLUSION: POETRY AS VOCATION

Harper clearly used poetry as a medium for moral reform and social good. But as many of her writings attest, Harper also fashioned her poems into tools for racial uplift, encouraging her fellow African Americans to adopt virtuous behaviors in service of the reputation and betterment of the race.[62] Consider one of Harper's pieces of short fiction published in 1873 in the *Christian Recorder*, "Fancy Etchings," which contains a dialogue between a young woman, Jenny, and her aunt. Although Jenny is a fictional character, it is easy to imagine her words in the mouth of a youthful Harper, proclaiming her desire to be a poet.[63] For Jenny, poetry is a calling that will prove "'the best way to serve humanity'" while developing her own mental and spiritual faculties. When her aunt questions whether poetry will really have an impact on her fellow African Americans, considering that many of them are overburdened with work, having little time to devote to such "'songs,'" Jenny replies:

> It is just because our lives are apt to be so hard and dry, that I would scatter the flowers of poetry around our paths; and would if I could amid life's sad discords introduce the most entrancing strains of melody. I would teach men and women to love noble deeds by setting them to the music, of fitly spoken words. The first throb of interest that a person feels in the recital of a noble deed, a deed of high and holy worth, the first glow of admiration for suffering virtue, or thrill of joy in the triumph of goodness, forms a dividing line between the sensuous and material and the spiritual and progressive. I think poetry is one of the great agents of culture, civilization and refinement.[64]

This passage is one of the most straightforward presentations of Harper's understanding of her literary vocation, defined in both poetic and spiritual terms. In Jenny's words, we can see Harper's endeavor "'to teach others to strive to make the highest ideal, the most truly real of our lives,'" crafting enlightening words and characters in didactic fashion so her readers will choose to align their personal and religious goals with those of the race. Jenny's elucidation of the moral and social function of poetry in "Fancy Etchings" shows that the "I" of Harper's own experience can translate into the "I" of imagined life events for her characters (in this case, an important conversation between Jenny and her aunt), in turn allowing readers to inhabit and be inspired by the emotions of this complex "I" position. Harper entered public culture through her speaking circuits and activism, but also powerfully through the careful constructs of her first-person speakers—arguably the most moving enactment of her vocation.

These complex, inhabitable "I" voices in poetic form—these first-person experiences to *relate* and *relate to*, speakers to try on and dwell in, as Harper does herself—produce a lyric immediacy that not only captivated nineteenth-century readers but also intrigues academics today. Recent scholarship on Harper notes that her literary production and activist endeavors were, of course, "intersectional" before the term was coined, and part of a long tradition of Black protest for Black lives.[65] Martha S. Jones puts it simply and eloquently: during Reconstruction-era debates about whether Black men or white women should be the first to obtain voting rights, "Black women activists urged that their lives, which were lived at the nexus of sex and color, should define political culture. Frances Ellen Watkins Harper's vision . . . was that all the activists present were 'bound up together' submerged in a cauldron."[66] Harper shows that Black women's experiences of oppression are always already about race and gender intertwining in nuanced ways.[67] Thus, for Harper, liberation from oppression also requires a nuanced understanding of race, gender, class, and religion, deployed through multifaceted first-person subjectivity in her poems. Harper's readers can become activists-in-training who combine lived experience(s) of oppression, conviction of the rightness of their cause, belief in the power of God's word to change the world, and inspiration for the real work of organizing. Her combination of seeming aesthetic simplicity with deliberate accessibility creates an inclusive poetics that encourages her audience to *be active*, to, as she said in 1867, have "strength enough, wisdom enough, and virtue enough in our American nation to lift it out of trouble."[68]

NOTES

Sections of this chapter originally appeared in the author's dissertation. See Jennifer F. McFarlane-Harris, "Autobiographical Theologies: Subjectivity and Religious Language in Spiritual Narratives, Poetry, and Hymnody by African-American Women, 1830–1900" (PhD diss., University of Michigan, 2010). http://hdl.handle.net/2027.42/78821.

1. Melba Joyce Boyd, *Discarded Legacy: Politics and Poetics in the Life of Frances E. W. Harper, 1825–1911* (Detroit: Wayne State University Press, 1994), 120. My description of Harper's work during this period is based on her letters from 1867 to 1871 and the accounts of her southern lecture tours in Boyd, *Discarded Legacy*, 119–26, and in Frances Smith Foster, ed., *A Brighter Coming Day: A Frances Ellen Watkins Harper Reader* (New York: Feminist Press, 1990), 121–34.

2. Frances Ellen Watkins Harper, "'Almost Constantly Either Traveling or Speaking,'" [Columbiana, Georgia (?), February 20, 1870], in Foster, *Brighter Coming Day*, 126–27.

3. Martha S. Jones, *Vanguard: How Black Women Broke Barriers, Won the Vote, and Insisted on Equality for All* (New York: Basic Books, 2020), 113.

4. Harper, "Affairs in South Carolina," Wilmington [Delaware], July 26, 1867; "'Here Is Ignorance to Be Instructed,'" [Athens, Georgia, February 1, 1870]; and from the "Aunt Chloe" sequence, "The Deliverance"; in Foster, *Brighter Coming Day*, 124, 125, 202.

5. Following J. Saunders Redding, Frances Smith Foster explains that "Eschewing misspellings and linguistic signals that befuddle the reader and constrain the speaker within preconstructed dialectical boundaries of pathos and humor, Frances Harper avoided the problems that ensnared Paul Laurence Dunbar and worried James Weldon Johnson." See *Written by Herself: Literary Production by African American Women, 1746–1892* (Bloomington: Indiana University Press, 1993), 152. For more on Harper's "dialect" verse as her own version of Black speech, see Boyd, *Discarded Legacy*, 151. For a discussion of Harper's nonelite Black speakers as authoritative because they are not filtered through "Anglo-American standard speech," see Elizabeth A. Petrino, "'We Are Rising as a People': Frances Harper's Radical Views on Class and Racial Equality in *Sketches of Southern Life*," *ATQ: American Transcendental Quarterly* 19, no. 2 (2005): 144–45.

6. Harper, from the "Aunt Chloe" sequence: "Aunt Chloe's Politics" and "Learning to Read," in Foster, *Brighter Coming Day*, 204, 206.

7. Valerie Palmer-Mehta, "'We Are All Bound Up Together': Frances Harper and Feminist Theory," in *Black Women's Intellectual Traditions: Speaking Their Minds*, ed. Kristin Waters and Carol B. Conaway (Burlington: University of Vermont Press, 2007), 194–99.

8. Palmer-Mehta, "'We Are All Bound Up Together,'" 210.

9. Rebecka Rutledge Fisher, "Remnants of Memory: Testimony and Being in Frances E. W. Harper's *Sketches of Southern Life*," *ESQ: A Journal of the American Renaissance* 54 (2008): 57, http://doi.org/10.1353/esq.0.0014.

10. Fisher, "Remnants of Memory," 67.

11. Harper, "Deliverance," 200. For more on the "issue of *theodicy*, the justification of a loving and powerful God that allows evil and injustice to exist," see Juan M. Floyd-Thomas, *The Origins of Black Humanism in America: Reverend Ethelred Brown and the Unitarian Church* (New York: Palgrave Macmillan, 2008), 81. Also see Anthony Pinn, *Why, Lord: Suffering and Evil in Black Theology* (New York: Continuum, 1995). For an early reading of "Aunt Chloe's Politics" arguing that we may miss the importance of Harper's work if we fail to read her poetry through a historical framework, see Paul Lauter, "Is Frances Ellen Watkins Harper Good Enough to Teach?," *Legacy: A Journal of American Women Writers* 5, no. 1 (Spring 1988): 31–32, www.jstor.org/stable/25679013.

12. Michael C. Cohen, *The Social Lives of Poems in Nineteenth-Century America* (Philadelphia: University of Pennsylvania Press, 2015), 7.

13. Cheryl Townsend Gilkes, "The Politics of 'Silence': Dual-Sex Political Systems and Women's Traditions of Conflict in African-American Religion," in *African-American Christianity: Essays in History*, ed. Paul E. Johnson (Berkeley: University of California Press, 1994), 82.

14. Harper, "National Salvation," *Evening Telegraph* (Philadelphia), February 1, 1867, *Chronicling America: Historic American Newspapers*, Library of Congress, https://chroniclingamerica.loc.gov/lccn/sn83025925/1867-02-01/ed-1/seq-8/. For an analysis of this lecture (and the complete text of Harper's lecture itself), see Eric Gardner, "Frances Ellen Watkins Harper's 'National Salvation': A Rediscovered Lecture on Reconstruction," *Commonplace: The Journal of Early American Life* 17, no. 4 (Summer 2017), http://commonplace.online/article/vol-17-no-4-gardner/.

15. Harper, "Affairs in South Carolina," 124. For further reading that takes seriously Harper's personal, political, and professional "southernness," see Sherita L. Johnson, "'In the Sunny South': Reconstructing Frances Harper as Southern," in *Black Women in New South Literature and Culture* (New York: Routledge, 2009), 10–44.

16. Harper, "Affairs in South Carolina," 124.

17. Harper, "'A Room to Myself Is a Luxury,'" [Rural Alabama, 1871(?)], in Foster, *Brighter Coming Day*, 134. See also Boyd, *Discarded Legacy*, 202.

18. Harper, "The Dying Fugitive" and "The Ragged Stocking," in Foster, *Brighter Coming Day*, 176, 259.

19. Harper, "The Woman's Christian Temperance Union and the Colored Woman," in Foster, *Brighter Coming Day*, 281.

20. Meredith L. McGill, "Frances Ellen Watkins Harper and the Circuits of Abolitionist Poetry," in *Early African American Print Culture*, ed. Lara Langer Cohen and Jordan Alexander Stein (Philadelphia: University of Pennsylvania Press, 2012), 62.

21. Carla L. Peterson, *"Doers of the Word": African-American Women Speakers and Writers in the North (1830–1880)* (New York: Oxford University Press, 1995), 122.

22. Peterson, *"Doers of the Word,"* 128.

23. Foster, *Brighter Coming Day*, 23.

24. I have argued elsewhere that spiritual autobiography can be an expansive—often hybrid—genre, paradoxically redirecting focus away from the individual speaker and toward God, so that "the subject becomes a spiritual and textual agent by means of the divine." See McFarlane-Harris, "Autobiographical Theologies," 7.

25. F. Elizabeth Gray, *Christian and Lyric Tradition in Victorian Women's Poetry* (New York: Routledge, 2010), 138–39. Gray explains that this kind of "triangulated" textual relationship is crucial to the operation of devotional lyric poems: "The individual speaker's relationship with God, the primary focus, is triangulated by the speaker's relationship with his or her readers and co-believers—an unignorable secondary focus."

26. Foster, *Brighter Coming Day*, 235.

27. Consider, for instance, the poetic accretion from one edition to another in *Moses: A Story of the Nile*, which is extant in three editions: 1869, 1889, and 1893. The first extant copy of Moses (1869, actually marked "2nd ed.") included only one piece in addition to the epic poem about Moses: a short fable about a rose tree that feels so blessed to be a rose that she wishes all the other flowering plants would turn into roses too, not realizing that her "sister flowers" also have "their own missions." See Frances Ellen Watkins Harper, "The Mission of the Flowers," in Foster, *Brighter Coming Day*, 230–32. The 1889 volume of *Moses* then expanded the 1869 edition with the addition of two temperance poems, "The Ragged Stocking" and "The Fatal Pledge." Finally, in 1893, Harper added five more poems to *Moses*, all of which focused on biblical stories that reveal her Christology, fulfilling the promise of Moses (Old Testament) in the person of Christ (New Testament): "Christ's Entry into Jerusalem," "The Resurrection of Jesus," "Simon's Countrymen," "Deliverance," and "Simon's Feast."

28. For Whitman, see Jerome Loving, *Walt Whitman: The Song of Himself* (Berkeley: University of California Press, 2000). For Douglass, see William L. Andrews, *To Tell a Free Story: The First Century of Afro-American Autobiography, 1760–1865* (Urbana: University of Illinois Press, 1986).

29. Frances Ellen Watkins Harper, "'Fishers of Men,'" in Foster, *Brighter Coming Day*, 253.

30. Noah Webster's 1877 *An American Dictionary of the English Language* offers the following definition: "to bear away with joy or delight; to delight to ecstasy; to transport"; s.v. "ravish," def. 2.

31. Harper, "'Fishers of Men,'" 253. In the Book of Revelation 1:10, John says, "I was in the spirit on the Lord's day, and I heard behind me a loud voice like a trumpet" (New Revised Standard Version). For John's vision of the new Jerusalem, see Rev. 21:1–22:5. Note that just as Harper does in "'Fishers of Men,'" the John of Revelation has an angel guide.

32. Harper, "'Fishers of Men,'" 253–54.

33. Harper, "'Fishers of Men,'" 254.

34. For an interesting reading of key Harper poems featuring imagery of "light" as tied to activism and racial uplift, see Hannah Wakefield, "'Let the Light Enter!': Illuminating the Newspaper Poetry of Frances Ellen Watkins Harper," *Legacy: A Journal of American Women Writers* 36, no. 1 (2019), http://doi.org/10.5250/legacy.36.1.0018.

35. Harper, "'Fishers of Men,'" 254.

36. Frances Ellen Watkins [Harper], "A Dream," in *Forest Leaves* (Baltimore: James Young, 1849), 16–17. Images of the pamphlet's pages appear online in *Commonplace* courtesy of the Maryland Historical Society. See Johanna Ortner, "Lost No More: Recovering Frances Ellen Watkins Harper's *Forest Leaves*," *Commonplace: The Journal of Early American Life* 15, no. 4

(Summer 2015), http://commonplace.online/article/lost-no-more-recovering-frances-ellen-watkins-harpers-forest-leaves/.

37. Harper, "'Fishers of Men,'" 253, 254.

38. Watkins [Harper], "A Dream," 16.

39. Watkins [Harper], "A Dream," 16, 17.

40. Watkins [Harper], "A Dream," 16.

41. See Matthew 4:18–22, Mark 1:16–20, and Luke 5:1–11 (NRSV).

42. Harper, "'Fishers of Men,'" 254.

43. Harper, "The Slave Mother," "Signing the Pledge," and "John and Jacob—A Dialogue on Woman's Rights," in Foster, *Brighter Coming Day*, 59, 255–56, 240.

44. Harper, "The Prodigal's Return," "Signing the Pledge," "The Resurrection of Jesus," "Fifteenth Amendment," "President Lincoln's Proclamation of Freedom," and "In Commemoration of the Centennial of the A.M.E. Church," in Foster, *Brighter Coming Day*, 74–75, 254–56, 331–33, 189–90, 186–87, 243–44.

45. For more on the connection between personal conversion and social reform in writings by Harper's contemporaries, see Jennifer McFarlane-Harris and Emily Hamilton-Honey, *Nineteenth-Century American Women Writers and Theologies of the Afterlife: A Step Closer to Heaven* (New York: Routledge, 2021).

46. For a good overview of Harper's biography that draws on a number of sources, including the oft-referenced *Still's Underground Rail Road Records* (first published 1871), see Joan R. Sherman, "Frances Ellen Watkins Harper, 1824–1911," in *Invisible Poets: Afro-Americans of the Nineteenth Century*, 2nd ed. (Chicago: University of Illinois Press, 1989), 62–66. Also see Foster, Introduction, *Brighter Coming Day*, 3–40, and biographical details throughout Boyd's *Discarded Legacy*.

47. For more on the discovery of *Forest Leaves*, see Ortner, "Lost No More."

48. William Lloyd Garrison wrote a preface for Harper's *Poems on Miscellaneous Subjects*, which became "an immediate success, selling more than ten thousand copies and meriting reprinting in an enlarged version within three years. During Harper's lifetime the collection was reprinted at least twenty times." See Henry Louis Gates Jr. and Nellie Y. McKay, "Frances E. W. Harper," in *The Norton Anthology of African American Literature*, ed. Henry Louis Gates Jr. and Nellie Y. McKay (New York: W. W. Norton, 1997), 409. Harper's tale "The Two Offers" is often regarded as "the first short story published by an African-American." See Foster, *Brighter Coming Day*, 105.

49. For more on this four-year period as crucial to the development of Harper's political sensibilities and activism, see Eric Gardner, "Frances Ellen Watkins Harper's Civil War and Militant Intersectionality," *Mississippi Quarterly* 70, no. 4 (2017): 507, http://doi.org/10.1353/mss.2017.0025. Gardner delves into "the near-lynching of Frances Harper's sister-in-law and the chaos of [her husband] Fenton Harper's probate" following his untimely death.

50. Floyd-Thomas, *Origins of Black Humanism in America*, 69. As she grew older, Mary seems to have followed in her mother's footsteps, working alongside Harper as she lectured, taught, worked as an organizer, and promoted political causes. Mary passed away in 1909, two years before her mother's death.

51. For an overview of Harper's literary reputation and varying critical reception, including an explanation of the role of the Afro-Protestant press, see Foster, "Gender, Genre and Vulgar Secularism: The Case of Frances Ellen Watkins Harper and the AME Press," in

Recovered Writers/Recovered Texts: Race, Class, and Gender in Black Women's Literature, ed. Dolan Hubbard (Knoxville: University of Tennessee Press, 1997), 46–59.

52. Nancy A. Hardesty, *Women Called to Witness: Evangelical Feminism in the Nineteenth Century*, 2nd ed. (Knoxville: University of Tennessee Press, 1999), 34.

53. Harper, "Christianity," in Foster, *Brighter Coming Day*, 98.

54. Katherine Clay Bassard, "Private Interpretations: The Defense of Slavery, Nineteenth-Century Hermeneutics, and the Poetry of Frances E. W. Harper," in *There Before Us: Religion, Literature, and Culture from Emerson to Wendell Berry*, ed. Roger Lundin (Grand Rapids, MI: William B. Eerdmans Publishing, 2007), 133–36.

55. John Wilson, *Unitarian Principles Confirmed by Trinitarian Testimonies: Being Selections from the Works of Eminent Theologians Belonging to Orthodox Churches*, 10th ed. (Boston: American Unitarian Association, 1880), 228–29, Google Books.

56. Editors of the American Tract Society's *American Messenger*, quoted in David Paul Nord, *Faith in Reading: Religious Publishing and the Birth of Mass Media in America* (New York: Oxford University Press, 2004), 121. Tracts were one of many publication venues that temperance women utilized. Carol Mattingly notes that "In addition to writing for the WCTU's [Woman's Christian Temperance Union's] publication house, women published with the various tract societies, with Sunday school publication houses, and with the National Temperance Publication Association." See Mattingly, *Well-Tempered Women: Nineteenth-Century Temperance Rhetoric* (Carbondale: Southern Illinois University Press, 1998), 64.

57. June Hadden Hobbs, *"I Sing for I Cannot Be Silent": The Feminization of American Hymnody, 1870–1920* (Pittsburgh: University of Pittsburgh Press, 1997), 34. For more on the uses of hymns during the nineteenth century, see Hobbs, *"I Sing for I Cannot Be Silent,"* 34–69; Ann Douglas, *The Feminization of American Culture* (New York: Alfred A. Knopf, 1977), 217–20; and Gray, *Christian and Lyric Tradition*, 139–40, 172. Of course, hymns could also be a form of public worship. Peterson points out that "like other contemporary Unitarians and abolitionists such as Lowell, Longfellow, and Whittier, Watkins Harper wrote poems that are hymnal in nature and intent. As public poetry designed for oral performance and to move the entire congregation, the hymn is grounded in a literary philosophy of simplicity and clarity." Peterson, *"Doers of the Word,"* 129.

58. For more on Harper's temperance views and participation in the temperance movement, see her 1888 essay "The Woman's Christian Temperance Union and the Colored Woman," in Foster, *Brighter Coming Day*, 281–85. For more on Harper's role in the WCTU and racial tensions in that organization, see Mattingly, *Well-Tempered Women*, 85–95. For additional information on the participation of Black women in the temperance movement, see Ruth Bordin, *Women and Temperance: The Quest for Power and Liberty, 1873–1900* (Philadelphia: Temple University Press, 1981), 82–85, 159–60.

59. McGill makes a similar argument when discussing *Poems on Miscellaneous Subjects*: "[Harper's] poems depend heavily on stock figures . . . they strike generic postures and attitudes in predictable meter and simple rhymes (grave-slave, slave-save, strife-life, wrong-strong), and are jam-packed with rhetorical questions that seek to evoke a pragmatic, collective response from her readers." McGill, "Frances Ellen Watkins Harper," 63. I'm interested in the ways that Harper creates entwining first-person voices such that these "stock figures" become much more. As part of Harper's evangelizing impulse, they are recognizable characters, but not static.

60. Harper, "Nothing and Something," in Foster, *Brighter Coming Day*, 251.

61. Harper, "Nothing and Something," 252.

62. For an insightful history of racial uplift ideology, see Kevin K. Gaines, *Uplifting the Race: Black Leadership, Politics, and Culture in the Twentieth Century* (Chapel Hill: University of North Carolina Press, 1996).

63. Harper, "Fancy Etchings," in Foster, *Brighter Coming Day*, 224.

64. Harper, "Fancy Etchings," 225.

65. See Courtney L. Thompson, "'If There Is Common Rough Work to Be Done, Call on Me': Tracing the Legacy of Frances Ellen Watkins Harper in the Black Lives Matter Era," *Africology: The Journal of Pan African Studies* 12, no. 10 (March 2019): 93–109, https://www.jpanafrican.org/vol12no9.htm.

66. Martha S. Jones, *All Bound Up Together: The Woman Question in African American Public Culture, 1830–1900* (Chapel Hill: University of North Carolina Press, 2007), 141.

67. See Jen McDaneld, "Harper, Historiography, and the Race/Gender Opposition in Feminism," *Signs: Journal of Women in Culture and Society* 40, no. 2 (Winter 2015), 393–415, https://doi.org/10.1086/678147.

68. Harper, "National Salvation," February 1, 1867. Significantly, in the 1850s, Harper also published a poem entitled "Be Active," wherein she calls upon Christians (vocative: "Oh! be faithful!") to do the difficult and important work of activism, with God's help. See Harper, "Be Active," in Foster, *Brighter Coming Day*, 76–77.

SELECTED BIBLIOGRAPHY

Andrews, William L. *To Tell a Free Story: The First Century of Afro-American Autobiography, 1760–1865*. Urbana: University of Illinois Press, 1986.

Bassard, Katherine Clay. "Private Interpretations: The Defense of Slavery, Nineteenth-Century Hermeneutics, and the Poetry of Frances E. W. Harper." In *There Before Us: Religion, Literature, and Culture from Emerson to Wendell Berry*, edited by Roger Lundin, 110–40. Grand Rapids, MI: William B. Eerdmans Publishing, 2007.

Bordin, Ruth. *Women and Temperance: The Quest for Power and Liberty, 1873–1900*. Philadelphia: Temple University Press, 1981.

Boyd, Melba Joyce. *Discarded Legacy: Politics and Poetics in the Life of Frances E. W. Harper, 1825–1911*. Detroit: Wayne State University Press, 1994.

Cohen, Michael C. *The Social Lives of Poems in Nineteenth-Century America*. Philadelphia: University of Pennsylvania Press, 2015. Proquest Ebook Central.

Douglas, Ann. *The Feminization of American Culture*. New York: Alfred A. Knopf, 1977.

Fisher, Rebecka Rutledge. "Remnants of Memory: Testimony and Being in Frances E. W. Harper's *Sketches of Southern Life*." *ESQ: A Journal of the American Renaissance* 54 (2008): 55–74. http://doi.org/10.1353/esq.0.0014.

Floyd-Thomas, Juan M. *The Origins of Black Humanism in America: Reverend Ethelred Brown and the Unitarian Church*. New York: Palgrave Macmillan, 2008.

Foster, Frances Smith, ed. *A Brighter Coming Day: A Frances Ellen Watkins Harper Reader*. New York: Feminist Press, 1990.

Foster, Frances Smith. "Gender, Genre and Vulgar Secularism: The Case of Frances Ellen Watkins Harper and the AME Press." In *Recovered Writers/Recovered Texts: Race, Class, and Gender in Black Women's Literature*, edited by Dolan Hubbard, 46–59. Knoxville: University of Tennessee Press, 1997.

Foster, Frances Smith. *Written by Herself: Literary Production by African American Women, 1746–1892*. Bloomington: Indiana University Press, 1993.

Gaines, Kevin K. *Uplifting the Race: Black Leadership, Politics, and Culture in the Twentieth Century*. Chapel Hill: University of North Carolina Press, 1996.

Gardner, Eric. "Frances Ellen Watkins Harper's Civil War and Militant Intersectionality." *Mississippi Quarterly* 70, no. 4 (2017): 505–18. http://doi.org/10.1353/mss.2017.0025.

Gardner, Eric. "Frances Ellen Watkins Harper's 'National Salvation': A Rediscovered Lecture on Reconstruction." *Commonplace: The Journal of Early American Life* 17, no. 4 (Summer 2017). http://commonplace.online/article/vol-17-no-4-gardner/.

Gates, Henry Louis, Jr., and Nellie Y. McKay. "Frances E. W. Harper." In *The Norton Anthology of African American Literature*, edited by Henry Louis Gates Jr. and Nelly Y. McKay, 408–11. New York: W. W. Norton, 1997.

Gilkes, Cheryl Townsend. "The Politics of 'Silence': Dual-Sex Political Systems and Women's Traditions of Conflict in African-American Religion." In *African-American Christianity: Essays in History*, edited by Paul E. Johnson, 80–110. Berkeley: University of California Press, 1994.

Gray, F. Elizabeth. *Christian and Lyric Tradition in Victorian Women's Poetry*. New York: Routledge, 2010.

Hardesty, Nancy A. *Women Called to Witness: Evangelical Feminism in the Nineteenth Century*. 2nd ed. Knoxville: University of Tennessee Press, 1999.

Harper, F. E. W. "National Salvation." *Evening Telegraph* (Philadelphia), February 1, 1867. *Chronicling America: Historic American Newspapers*. Library of Congress. https://chronicلingamerica.loc.gov/lccn/sn83025925/1867-02-01/ed-1/seq-8/.

Harper, Frances Ellen Watkins. *A Brighter Coming Day: A Frances Ellen Watkins Harper Reader*, edited by Frances Smith Foster. New York: Feminist Press, 1990.

[Harper], Frances Ellen Watkins. *Forest Leaves*. Baltimore: James Young, 1849. Maryland Historical Society. In Johanna Ortner, "Lost No More: Recovering Frances Ellen Watkins Harper's *Forest Leaves*," *Commonplace: The Journal of Early American Life* 15, no. 4 (Summer 2015). http://commonplace.online/article/lost-no-more-recovering-frances-ellen-watkins-harpers-forest-leaves/.

Hobbs, June Hadden. *"I Sing for I Cannot Be Silent": The Feminization of American Hymnody, 1870–1920*. Pittsburgh: University of Pittsburgh Press, 1997.

Johnson, Sherita L. *Black Women in New South Literature and Culture*. New York: Routledge, 2009. ProQuest Ebook Central.

Jones, Martha S. *All Bound Up Together: The Woman Question in African American Public Culture, 1830–1900*. Chapel Hill: University of North Carolina Press, 2007.

Jones, Martha S. *Vanguard: How Black Women Broke Barriers, Won the Vote, and Insisted on Equality for All*. New York: Basic Books, 2020.

Lauter, Paul. "Is Frances Ellen Watkins Harper Good Enough to Teach?" *Legacy: A Journal of American Women Writers* 5, no. 1 (Spring 1988): 27–32. www.jstor.org/stable/25679013.

Loving, Jerome. *Walt Whitman: The Song of Himself.* Berkeley: University of California Press, 2000.

Mattingly, Carol. *Well-Tempered Women: Nineteenth-Century Temperance Rhetoric.* Carbondale: Southern Illinois University Press, 1998.

McDaneld, Jen. "Harper, Historiography, and the Race/Gender Opposition in Feminism." *Signs: Journal of Women in Culture and Society* 40, no. 2 (Winter 2015): 393–415. https://doi.org/10.1086/678147.

McFarlane-Harris, Jennifer F. "Autobiographical Theologies: Subjectivity and Religious Language in Spiritual Narratives, Poetry, and Hymnody by African-American Women, 1830–1900." PhD diss., University of Michigan, 2010. Deep Blue. http://hdl.handle.net/2027.42/78821.

McFarlane-Harris, Jennifer, and Emily Hamilton-Honey. *Nineteenth-Century American Women Writers and Theologies of the Afterlife: A Step Closer to Heaven.* New York: Routledge, 2021.

McGill, Meredith L. "Frances Ellen Watkins Harper and the Circuits of Abolitionist Poetry." In *Early African American Print Culture*, edited by Lara Langer Cohen and Jordan Alexander Stein, 53–74. Philadelphia: University of Pennsylvania Press, 2012. ProQuest Ebook Central.

Nord, David Paul. *Faith in Reading: Religious Publishing and the Birth of Mass Media in America.* New York: Oxford University Press, 2004.

Ortner, Johanna. "Lost No More: Recovering Frances Ellen Watkins Harper's *Forest Leaves.*" *Commonplace: The Journal of Early American Life* 15, no. 4 (Summer 2015). http://commonplace.online/article/lost-no-more-recovering-frances-ellen-watkins-harpers-forest-leaves/.

Palmer-Mehta, Valerie. "'We Are All Bound Up Together': Frances Harper and Feminist Theory." In *Black Women's Intellectual Traditions: Speaking Their Minds*, edited by Kristin Waters and Carol B. Conaway, 192–215. Burlington: University of Vermont Press, 2007.

Peterson, Carla L. *"Doers of the Word": African-American Women Speakers and Writers in the North (1830–1880).* New York: Oxford University Press, 1995.

Petrino, Elizabeth A. "'We Are Rising as a People': Frances Harper's Radical Views on Class and Racial Equality in *Sketches of Southern Life.*" *ATQ: American Transcendental Quarterly* 19, no. 2 (2005): 133–53. EBSCOhost.

Pinn, Anthony. *Why, Lord: Suffering and Evil in Black Theology.* New York: Continuum, 1995.

Redding, J. Saunders. *To Make a Poet Black.* Chapel Hill: University of North Carolina Press, 1939.

Sherman, Joan R. "Frances Ellen Watkins Harper, 1824–1911." In *Invisible Poets: Afro-Americans of the Nineteenth Century*, 62–74. 2nd ed. Chicago: University of Illinois Press, 1989.

Thompson, Courtney L. "'If There Is Common Rough Work to Be Done, Call on Me': Tracing the Legacy of Frances Ellen Watkins Harper in the Black Lives Matter Era." *Africology: The Journal of Pan African Studies* 12, no. 10 (March 2019): 93–109. https://www.jpanafrican.org/vol12no9.htm.

Wakefield, Hannah. "'Let the Light Enter!': Illuminating the Newspaper Poetry of Frances Ellen Watkins Harper." *Legacy: A Journal of American Women Writers* 36, no. 1 (2019): 18–42. doi:10.5250/legacy.36.1.0018.

Webster, Noah. *An American Dictionary of the English Language; Thoroughly Revised and Greatly Enlarged and Improved, by Chauncey A. Goodrich and Noah Porter*. Springfield, MA: G. & C. Merriam, 1877.

Wilson, John. *Unitarian Principles Confirmed by Trinitarian Testimonies: Being Selections from the Works of Eminent Theologians Belonging to Orthodox Churches*. 10th ed. Boston: American Unitarian Association, 1880. Google Books.

TWENTIETH CENTURY

Chapter 4

CULTIVATING "MASS INTELLIGENCE"

Nannie Helen Burroughs and the Quest for Racial Justice

ANGELA HORNSBY-GUTTING

In 1934, Mary Tilghman wrote the manager of the sewing unit at the Northeast Self-Help Cooperative, headquartered at Nannie Helen Burroughs's Christian-based National Training School for Women and Girls. In it, Tilghman expressed gratitude for the opportunity, through her labor, to "uplift this great work," while affirming the cooperative spirit of her fellow Black seamstresses. She further stated that "I am always glad when the days come for us to assemble together and work in harmony and I hope all the ladies feels [*sic*] the same way I do. For it is a great help."[1]

The Northeast Self-Help Cooperative, organized by Burroughs and Sadie Morse Bethel during the Great Depression, attracted four hundred members drawn largely from unemployed female laborers and homemakers with a yearly income between $500 and $1,000. Burroughs stated the cooperative's purpose was to provide "industrial education and the opportunity to work."[2] As such, it underscored Burroughs's lifelong investment in the intellectual, religious, and civic development of African Americans and working-class Black women.

Burroughs's oral and textual work supported and influenced the modern civil rights movement. Scholars have documented how, in her role as corresponding secretary and president of the Woman's Auxiliary of the National Baptist Convention (NBC), Burroughs used speeches, correspondence, the Black press, and religious publications to influence Black public sentiment on a variety of racial justice issues, from woman suffrage to race violence. Burroughs later used the training school's *The Worker* to update Black Baptists on the civil rights movement, including the burgeoning sit-in demonstrations, while educating subscribers about citizenship rights and responsibilities. She inspired some of the country's leading civil rights activists, including Congressman Adam Clayton Powell, Supreme Court Justice Thurgood Marshall, and civil rights activists Ella Baker and Martin Luther King Jr., the latter whom she addressed as "junior" in correspondence.[3]

Absent from such accounts, however, are analyses of how Burroughs, as a religious public intellectual, utilized the National Training School and other educational entities to inform her students and the Black masses about civil engagement, Christian moralism, economic justice, and nonviolent public protest, ideals that were emblematic of existing and future civil rights movement strategies and campaigns. The school's status as a meta-institution—it housed a printing plant, economic cooperative, community library, and laundry—stretched its pedagogy, as premised on a "discourse of resistance,"[4] beyond its physical borders. Her varied textual work, via educational missionary publications like the *Mission Herald* and writings produced at the school (including *The Worker*; *When Truth Gets a Hearing*, a student play; the *New Challenge*, an economic cooperative newspaper; and curriculum materials) imparted to an African American citizenry communal lessons in race ideology and strategy. Her writings also advocated for an elevated collectivist and feminist race consciousness. Her textual rhetoric as produced and performed at the school thus demonstrates the nexus, rather than divergence, of her religious activity, pedagogy, and communally centered political protests for racial justice.

A foremother of womanist theology, Burroughs's public sector work was likewise informed by biblical stories that empowered women and liberated them from restrictive roles in the church and society. While deploying familiar biblical references and imagery, such as the Hebrew exodus story to emphasize to modern African American audiences their relationship with God and the activism needed to realize the promised land, Burroughs also lent womanist theology to her rhetoric. Such theology held that religious men and women were equal in the eyes of God and thus should play active roles in foreign and domestic realms. Baptist women minimized traditional biblical narratives that cast women as subordinate to men, instead highlighting Old and New Testament female protagonists who held positions of power and displayed strength, military power, and prowess.[5] Mary V. Cook, recording secretary of the National Baptist Educational Committee and mentor to Burroughs, understood the Bible as an "iconoclastic weapon" wielded to rehabilitate women's public image.[6] Towards that end, Burroughs articulated in the public sphere a deep concern for Black working-class women who lacked economic and social advantages and promoted a philosophy of self-help among African Americans. In doing so, she joined her Christian values with a deep belief in the Black masses to produce an intellectual discourse typified by race cooperation, spirituality, self-determination, and Black male and female equality.

As a womanist Christian, Burroughs applied her educational philosophy to the male-centered discourse on race advancement by defying the conventional female constraints of her era. The National Training School taught students to probe and more deeply appreciate the significant actions of Biblical women such as Queen Esther, who saved the Jews of the Persian empire by urging them to rise up against their oppressors. At the same time, she recognized that Black female empowerment also necessitated "respectable" behavior by Black women due to their traditional exclusion from hegemonic gender norms. In this sense, Burroughs promoted traditional conceptions of "civilized" behavior for Black females while actively subverting white supremacist ideology and urging the eradication of Jim Crow laws.

Burroughs's public sector work is likewise informed by historians who have long illumined the dynamics of Black women's religious leadership. Scholars such as Evelyn Brooks Higginbotham, Bettye Collier-Thomas, Cheryl Townsend Gilkes, Rosalyn Terborg-Penn, Sylvia M. Jacobs, and Barbara Savage, among others, have disclosed the dual struggle for race and gender freedom among Black churchwomen of varied denominational affiliation. Stressing the import of Black churchwomen's organizational activity, which encompassed both domestic and foreign (missionary) concerns, these scholars demonstrated by what means and to what extent Black women could use evangelism to forward political and social reform at home and abroad. Such activism dovetailed with Black churchwomen's recurring challenge to overcome opposition and paternalism from Black and white male church leaders seeking to restrict their work.

A RELIGIOUS EDUCATION AND MOBILIZING "GOD'S ARMY"

Burroughs's pursuit of job opportunity, race equality, and self-determination for African Americans and Black women is a product of her relatives' individual striving and formal educational experience. She was born in May 1875 in Culpepper, Virginia, to John and Jennie Burroughs, an itinerant Baptist preacher and cook who were formerly enslaved. Burroughs's mother relocated Nannie at the age of five to the District of Columbia due to its better education system. Burroughs's maternal grandfather, Ligah, moved from being "the slave carpenter" to a land owner after Emancipation and enjoyed a comfortable living with his family as a skilled craftsman.[7] Burroughs selected the "scientific" track in high school, designed to "give a general education and prepare pupils for the Normal School and college."[8] Graduating with honors from the M Street High School, she founded the Harriet Beecher Stowe Literary Society to enhance her "literary and oratorical expression."[9] Moreover, at Nineteenth Street Baptist Church in DC, Burroughs's conversion to the Baptist faith at age fifteen introduced her to the linkage among religion, education, and public activism. The Reverend Walter Brooks, a formerly enslaved pastor, supported female education and established various study groups at the church; Burroughs learned the Bible through a "thoroughly graded" youth Bible study program. Known for its social activism, the church afforded Burroughs opportunities to develop skills as an educator and activist: she served as a librarian, Sunday School teacher, and secretary of the Young People's Society of Christian Endeavor. She "begged to get on programs and speak pieces."[10]

Based in part on her activist education at Nineteenth Street Baptist Church, Burroughs was determined to secure rights and liberties for all Americans. In *The Worker*, she framed this objective around four central democratic tenets: "freedom, an equal opportunity to education, an equal opportunity to employment, and an equal right to public accommodations."[11] She argued that of these four ideals, the last three "democratic rights" had been denied Blacks and required constitutional enforcement. Though human failings could be ascribed to the prevalence of race prejudice and discrimination in society, Burroughs believed that race equality and American democracy were inherently "Divine gifts" bequeathed by God and thus functioned as spiritual mandates. Denial of these rights, she continued, was therefore "the greatest insult to personal dignity." To protest systemic racism, or what Burroughs termed "a condition against which our very sense of decency revolts," she marshalled a variety of Black print media to spur Woman's Convention members, or "God's army," and other Black women to act on behalf of social justice.[12] *The Worker*, with some hundred thousand copies distributed quarterly, or four hundred thousand annually, was regarded as "the most widely read magazine by Negro women."[13] The *Mission Herald*, the official organ of the National Baptist Convention (NBC), was also read widely by millions of Black Baptists and became a repository for the assertion of democratic principles at home and abroad. It featured letters from NBC mission stations in Africa and the Caribbean and, as such, served as an educational forum wherein Blacks could discourse about colonial and postcolonial politics and their relation to Christian conversion activities. The *Herald* also functioned as a dialogical space where African Americans could enlarge their worldview, exchange ideas, and make critical connections between African and African American liberation ideology and strategy. In her position as bookkeeper for the NBC's Foreign Mission Board in Lexington, Kentucky, Burroughs routinely contributed commentary to the *Herald*'s "Woman's Page" (variably titled "Woman's Department") that focused on the plight of women and girls around the world. As importantly, Burroughs opined on domestic civil rights issues pertaining to race-based public accommodations such as railcars.

Aware of working-class Black women's frequent traversing of public space due to economic need, Burroughs editorialized about the inferior railroad car accommodations for Blacks that included a lack of step boxes for boarding the railcars and no separate toilet facilities for Black women. Like her peers in the Woman's Convention, Burroughs objected to legal segregation morally and philosophically. From a practical position, however, holding the country accountable for its existing laws was deemed an acceptable, if temporary, civil rights strategy. The Woman's Convention and other Black religious and secular groups such as the National Association for the Advancement of Colored People (NAACP) implemented such a strategy while the ongoing battle for full race equality persisted.[14] Burroughs thus initially endeavored to test the legitimacy of the "separate but equal" race doctrine by protesting its lack of enforcement on railroads. She opined in the *Mission Herald* that "There are some Negroes who are asking for improved conditions and will be satisfied with nothing less than first class accommodations for first class fare. We do not propose to give up, but shall unceasingly plead for fair treatment, and if the operating officials will not hear us, we will appeal to higher authority."[15] Her strategy of "gender deference," which argued for the equitable albeit separate treatment of Black women on public conveyances, ultimately evolved by 1918 to an unbridled call for the end of segregated rail travel. As she wrote in the same *Herald* article: "Nothing short of a repeal of the separate laws is going to bring permanent and satisfactory change in travel in those states where the law is in operation."

Besides critiquing railroad companies for their discriminatory behavior toward Black female passengers, Burroughs also informed *Herald* readers about environmental hazards within African American households and the resulting impact on childhood education. She sought the formation of a "Winter Time Fresh Air Association" to counter the poor ventilation of homes, churches, and public places, conditions that typically began at first frost and lingered through summer. She lamented that "poor little children who have got to go to school, and try to get something into their heads are stored away in a room at night, without a breath of air."[16] This left them in a "stupid and draggy" state. School lessons absorbed overnight had been "crowded out by impure air in which they have been compelled to fight for existence from twilight to dawn." Burroughs's statement is indicative of the belief that fresh air could promote race progress by allowing Black children's unfettered access to schooling. At the same time, as a member of the National Association of Colored Women, Burroughs would have been familiar with African American clubwomen's Fresh Air associations that provided rural retreats and farm visits for poor, urban Black children so that they could experience a wholesome, pure environment. Such activities also served to promote Black self-efficacy. Educator Booker T. Washington urged Black women to take outdoor jobs like raising chickens to, as Nancy Unger writes, develop "self-reliance, independence, and initiative."[17] Indeed, during the Great Depression, Burroughs relied on farm produce such as eggs and hogs purchased from her Aunt Rachel's Virginia farm to feed students, teachers, and staff.[18] Her aunt's farm work confirmed Burroughs's belief in the "Divine Plan" of labor where "The Negro will have to do exactly what Jesus told the man (John 5:8) to do—Carry his own load."[19] Thus, though not stated explicitly, the editorial by Burroughs suggested how the pursuit of fresh air was a source of Black agency, both intellectually and economically, including for working-class women who found themselves in industrial and other jobs where, according to Unger, the "planning and thinking is done for her" by supervisors.[20]

BIBLE, BATH, AND BROOM

The symbiotic relationship Burroughs drew in the *Mission Herald* between a physically stifling home environment and an impaired scholastic one reflected larger pedagogical aims centered on fashioning a more equitable and wholesome school experience for African and African American girls. Burroughs determined early that dignifying Black women and their labor was a Christian duty, a racial imperative, and a pedagogical necessity. In a 1902 lecture delivered at the Young People's Christian and Educational Congress, Burroughs juxtaposed Black working-class women with their idle counterparts. Unlike "parlor ornaments" or those who "flirt and loiter about the streets," she claimed that "self-supporting domestic servants" were "too honest, industrious and independent" to be "debased by idleness." They "have character enough for queens."[21] Her remarks demonstrated an opposition to narrow, middle-class constructions of femininity by placing domestic workers firmly in the center, rather than at the periphery, of Christian womanhood. Seeking to equip African and African American females for a proper life of public service at home and abroad, Burroughs opened the Christian-based National Training School (NTS) in the District of Columbia in 1909, concomitant with the founding of the NAACP.

Offering courses in the Old and New Testaments, Christian Education in the Local Church, Comparative Religions and Missions, theater, math, and history, the school also emphasized vocational training, including domestic service, given its low status in society and the stress placed on Black women as household servants. Touting domestic workers as formally trained was actually rhetoric intended to refute racist characterizations of Black women as incompetent, lazy, and immoral. The school, while providing a practical education to make Black women economically self-sufficient, also placed them beyond spiritual and moral reproach. Burroughs thus fashioned her Christian school on the three Bs—Bible, Bath, and Broom—which stressed her religious mooring and the import of embodying a clean life and industriousness to pupils.[22]

At the school, Burroughs both accommodated and contested dominant notions of female behavior. Like the Black female educator Charlotte Hawkins Brown, she followed secularist ideology that expected Black women to act and look feminine and be moral guardians of the home sphere.[23] At the same time, Burroughs inverted those same conventions when applied to the concept of Black women and work. In a catalog commemorating the forty-seventh anniversary of the NTS, she stated that the school aimed to "cultivate Christian graces" inclusive of the "fine art of Home-making," but not exclusive of training in business and other professional trades. The framing of all Black women's labor as respectable thus had the consequence of expanding Black women's economic opportunities in the public sphere while promulgating Christian-inspired social service activism. In the catalog she wrote, "the religion which stands the test consists in doing what Jesus said, rather than being content with what Jesus did."[24] Inverting middle-class, separate sphere formulations of female morality and respectability, Burroughs's corps of teachers also trained African and African American pupils as missionaries, social workers, shopkeepers, and insurance agents. This worldview was affirmed by Burroughs's religious instruction that encouraged students to view Biblical female characters in novel ways. For example, the final exam question "Who was responsible for the defeat of Ai?" had students reevaluate Rahab as a heroine who supplied a critical victory for the Hebrews rather than by her traditional depiction as a reviled prostitute or harlot.[25]

The broader education that Burroughs implemented suggested new routes to economic as well as personal autonomy for Black women outside those that traditionally had defined them. Departing from race leaders W. E. B. Du Bois and Booker T. Washington, who, respectively, endorsed a classical liberal arts and vocational education, Burroughs rejected strict adherence to either pedagogy. Addressing the Woman's Convention, Burroughs asserted that "an industrial and classical education can be simultaneously obtained, and it is our duty to get both."[26] Many students integrated both ideals as they opted for a diverse curriculum wherein they could craft an alternate female work identity. Acquiring skills in sewing, shoe repair, printing, and hairdressing might release them from a career in domestic service.[27] The flexible pedagogy that Burroughs endorsed shows how her intellectual ideas were produced in dialogue with her life experience and the race's social condition. Burroughs understood the tension inherent in maintaining a subjective and respectable Black female identity amid the reality of racially contested public spaces and ideology. As religious scholar Robert Orsi has observed, "The individual subjectivity is defined with reference to space, its qualities disclosed in the public theater of the neighborhood and pressed into the landscape." The work to give oneself "meaning," he writes, is at once an "inner process" as well as a "neighborhood contest."[28] Consistent with this spatial negotiation, Burroughs's writings were mindful of the lingering structural and ideological frameworks that collectively, and routinely, challenged Black women's claim to an autonomous civic and work identity.

AN ALTERNATIVE CURRICULUM

Burroughs's pedagogical contributions were both traditional and inventive, the latter reflective of a modern educational milieu that dismissed the idea of an indigenous Black culture. While Black scholars such as Du Bois believed in the cultural equality of all races, leading architects of curricula for social studies during the Progressive Era denied that African Americans had any cultural contributions to make to society. Though admitting to the "plasticity of racial types," academicians Thomas Jesse Jones (credited with coining the term "social studies"), John Dewey, and Arthur Dunn abetted those who held that, absent pedagogical intervention, African Americans constituted an inferior presence in society and were not yet prepared to assume the full responsibilities of citizenship. Their political limitations, Jones noted, was because African Americans, through no fault of their own, had "suddenly been transferred from an earlier form of society into a later one without the necessary time of preparation."[29] In other words, African American societies were culturally deficient because they represented a primitive form of living that had long been eclipsed by Western culture. Burroughs's contemporaries such as educators Mary Margaret Washington and Mary McLeod Bethune worked against such theories, in part, by founding the International Council of Women of the Darker Races. Members studied the conditions of women and children of color worldwide, from Nigeria to the Philippines, to foster heightened race consciousness and appreciation of different cultures.[30]

The adjudication of the historical identity, contributions, and treatment of African Americans in America also served as a corrective to a Progressive Era intercultural education movement that, while seeking to redress stereotypes of ethnic groups by highlighting each group's cultural contributions to America, tended to ignore nonwhite Americans and thus provided biased notions of their social behavior and norms based solely upon their place of origin.[31] Penned by Burroughs in 1916 and reprinted twenty-one times by 1972, *When Truth Gets a Hearing* was performed by the National Training School Pageant Players in school and church venues in and outside of the District of Columbia. Stressing race pride and Black female achievement, the play's text presented the "record of my race" to the court of public opinion.[32] In the play,

Burroughs used epideictic rhetoric, or demonstrative oratory, to debunk race-related essentialist arguments.

Reminiscent of the "character not color" argument famously promulgated by Martin Luther King Jr., *Truth* deems skin color a biologically indeterminate, mutable concept and thus not subject to reductionist, racist claims regarding Black servility. Rather, the play reasons that "color is incidental."[33] Burroughs, through *Truth*, provided anecdotal evidence suggesting that skin color was symptomatic of an array of environmental and cultural factors. Addressing the character "Error," the play claims that ancient Greeks and Romans used white slave labor, and as such, Africa was no more "a slave hunting ground than Europe of [*sic*] Asia." Further, the world's climatic zones dictated the varied pigmentation of the world's peoples: the "red Pygmies in the forest and yellow Bushmen on the cooler southern plateau. As far as race is concerned, but one race on this planet, the human race." Burroughs also addressed the impact of Christianity and race on Black America, invoking the character "Error" to tell the Biblical story of Black people's descent from the cursed Ham, which historically had been used by white supremacists to justify African American oppression.[34] In "12 Things White People Must Stop Doing to the Negro," Burroughs used the same Genesis account to argue against the so-called curse of Ham by God. "The Bible does not say that God cursed Ham," she wrote. "It says that 'Noah cursed his son, Ham.' God did not even appear on the scene while Noah was drunk."[35]

These lessons about race became part of the Negro History course that Burroughs's students had to pass before graduation. In this respect, Burroughs's play intervened in another critical pedagogical discourse. Anti-racist writings of the 1930s and 1940s tended to dismiss the legitimacy of Black history, reducing it to little more than political propaganda designed to ameliorate systemic racial enmities. For example, sociologist Gunnar Myrdal, who in *An American Dilemma* detailed the legal and extralegal discrimination directed against African Americans, panned Black history as an intellectual "waste land."[36] While lauding the research produced by Carter G. Woodson and other Black historians, Myrdal concluded that the facts generated from such scholarship had been distorted to the extent that "cultural achievements which are no better—and no worse—than any others are placed on a pinnacle; minor historical events are magnified into crises."[37]

In addition to explicating the ties between race identity, history, and religion, *When Truth Gets a Hearing* also emphasized the particular contributions of Black women throughout the world by invoking such regal figures as the several queens named Candace of the Meroe civilization in Kush, now northern Sudan. The Candace queens presided over a lucrative economy based on trade and ironworks.[38] By referencing magisterial Black women, Burroughs advanced the prospect of African American women eclipsing the narrow confines of domestic work as conscribed by a racially segregated society. At the same time, the play served to validate Black women's traditional labor roles as emblematic of a virtuous Black womanhood. In doing so, Burroughs problematized historical representations of Black women's public presence and the personal agency they exercised. The character "Negro Womanhood," for example, testified that "for 250 years I worked in the cornfields, kept the big house like a palace, nursed the children of my master and loved them with a love and tenderness such as the world has never seen and will never see again."[39] Within this context, Burroughs asserted the rightful historical recognition of Black women's labor, dating back to enslavement, as valued and respectable. Though risking the appropriation of such history to racist discourse that correlated menial Black female labor with white southern paternalism, *When Truth Gets a Hearing* depicts Black women as those who played significant communal and leadership roles domestically and abroad. The NTS's student body reflected the play's internationalist themes and expectations that pupils uplift their home communities. Jennie Somtunzi was among the first Africans to matriculate at the school, having enrolled in 1912. These students, along with Clara Walker and Victoria White from Liberia, returned to Africa as Christian missionaries.[40]

"GOOD RELIGION": THE COOPERATIVE ECONOMIC MOVEMENT

Shoring up the image of Black female laborers accompanied the weighty task of securing economic justice for Black women and African Americans generally during the Great Depression. Unemployment rates soared for southern rural and urban Blacks, the latter attaining jobless rates ranging 30 to 60 percent higher than that of whites.[41] In 1930, Burroughs editorialized that, though severe, the Depression paled when compared to the languid response of African American leaders to sufficiently address the crisis, which presented material and moral challenges. She noted, "they are so impotent in the present economic crisis" and groused that "the people are out of work; they are hungry; they are indulging in all kinds of vice; they are like sheep without a shepherd. Where are the leaders? What are they thinking and what are they doing?"[42]

Burroughs encouraged Black organizations to identify and deploy all available resources for the collective benefit of African Americans. One such strategy entailed erecting a factory and employing Black working-class women as seamstresses to produce apparel and uniforms for Black workers; this met the particular needs of domestic servants, who often wore uniforms they had to purchase from non-Black suppliers. Burroughs's vision of an all-Black factory led by Black working-class women presupposed their dominance and expertise in the domestic arena while also placing them in the nontraditional role of economic breadwinner. Black men, in turn, would be relegated to the "task of cleaning up the homes, yards and communities" to counter idleness.[43] The proposed gender inversion reveals Burroughs's feminist thinking when addressing the economic plight of poor Blacks and illumines the collectivist ethos informing such activism. She simultaneously paired traditional Victorian gender ideals with womanist theology to position nonelite Black women as integral to the race's economic salvation.

Not surprisingly, the financial collapse during the Depression ushered in the largest number of economic cooperatives for African Americans. African American educators and activists such as Du Bois, A. Philip Randolph, and Ella Jo Baker, who founded the Young Negroes' Co-operative League in the early 1930s, launched cooperative enterprises and/or gave sanction to cooperative economic practices and philosophy through the *Black World, Messenger, Crisis,* and other Black media. Du Bois noted that promulgating concepts of "intelligent cooperation" and "intelligent democratic control" on the part of economic leaders and institutions depended upon publicizing the movement and providing member education and training.[44] Such calls for instruction melded with Burroughs's beliefs, as she had long invested in achieving economic autonomy and, by extension, racial justice for African American women through a curriculum that regularly featured vocational courses in and outside of the domestic sciences and that stressed to her students the concept of purposeful, collective, and industrious Christian endeavor. Finally, African American cooperative activity and its associated values of race solidarity and sacrifice had traditionally been ascribed to Black churchwomen through womanist theology that stressed their supposedly heightened sense of morals and ethics compared to men. The Virgin Mary, for example, supplied moral guidance to Jesus throughout his life. Likewise, in a 1908 school fundraising memo outlining more diverse career paths for students, Burroughs wrote that "much stress will be placed upon the development of strong moral character, the Bible will be the standard classic, and no student will be permitted to take any training in any department who will not, in connection with such training, take the Christian Culture Course."[45] Depression-era cooperatives thus served to expand Black women's economic participation, increase their authority over familial resources, and reify their identity as spiritual beings.

The National Training School's structure allowed the creation and operation of the Northeast Self-Help Cooperative, later Cooperative Industries, Inc. Having begun the same year that the NTS reduced its operations due to the economic crisis, the cooperative remains distinctive among similar Black financial enterprises during the Depression years in that it was established by African American women and primarily served the needs of Black women and operated under the auspices of a private school for African and African American females. Like the school, the cooperative mirrored Burroughs's pedagogical principles of self-help, mutual aid, and skilled training for Black working-class women. While federal monies were still pending, the school granted the cooperative the use of its chapel, dining room, kitchen, club room and four classrooms. The cooperative's sewing unit occupied the four classrooms in Trade Hall three times a week.[46] While targeting jobless African Americans of both genders, the self-help group put more African American women to work than men through its efforts. The bylaws of the cooperative closely followed the Rochdale Principles introduced by a co-op in England. The organization allowed one vote per member, open membership and dividends in proportion to "the volume of purchases made during the period." Burroughs was elected president and Sadie Bethel served as secretary. Four out of the seven trustees listed as part of incorporation were women.[47]

Cooperative education classes, the *New Challenge*, and *The Worker* taught African Americans and Baptist women about the economic cooperative movement. The evening classes were conducted at the school for existing and potential members beginning in 1936. According to Burroughs, these sessions were designed to forward the "mass intelligence essential to mass cooperation" and to train individuals for leadership positions in the Cooperative movement. Of the fifty-four persons present at the January meeting, twenty-four enrolled in classes, the majority being women.[48] Having acknowledged by the mid-1930s that the federal government would provide limited financial assistance to impoverished Blacks, Burroughs purchased a federally subsidized farm in Maryland in 1936 with Federal Emergency Relief Administration money. The purchase allowed the hiring of poor and unemployed Blacks in the District of Columbia to labor on the farm and sell fresh produce to those in the city's neighborhoods. To solicit member-buyers, Burroughs, in explicit, candid, and persuasive prose, distilled the complexities of communal-based economics to out-of-work Black laborers. She wrote, "You might ask—what is the Cooperative Farm? It is simply an honest to goodness effort and determination on the part of some of us to help our own people out in their own present economic plight."[49]

Declaring that activism was the foundation for Black claims of American citizenship, Burroughs linked co-op membership to her religious faith and the larger goal of fully integrating African Americans into America's body politic. The co-op, Burroughs wrote, is a "democratic organization," one that found kinship with those who valued "justice and equity." As noted earlier, Burroughs understood conceptions of justice as imminently divine in origin and thus not subject to indiscriminate application by fallible human beings. As part of its bylaws, the co-op expressly forbade excluding potential members based on race, creed, or political identification. And like the National Training School, the cooperative required no affiliation with a religious denomination.[50] At the same time, as a devout and renowned Baptist leader, Burroughs did not sever her religious beliefs from the workings of the institution, relying on her extensive Baptist contacts to attract potential members. As part of rhetoric targeting the faithful Baptist women readers of *The Worker*, Burroughs consciously equated co-op values with Christian ones. In an editorial, she stated that "anything that will put hope, spirit and desire for better living in the masses is not only religion, but good religion."[51] Burroughs also invoked religious imagery to describe the cooperative enterprise. Though the "masses are slow to take the initiative for their own deliverance," Burroughs wrote that if equipped with the proper knowledge, they would "see the light." To that end, she endorsed the educational work of cooperative leader Toyohiko Kagawa of Japan, reporting that "American Christians sat at his feet to learn the 'brotherly' way in business."

Burroughs encouraged *Worker* subscribers to actively seek out more information about and discuss the cooperative movement by attending community meetings so as to "get the ABCs of it."[52] Those who ultimately joined the cooperative were prodded to participate fully and faithfully in its operations. In a poem titled "The Just Belong-ers," Burroughs playfully asked her audience, "Are you an active member, the kind that would be missed, Or are you just contented that your name is on the list?"[53] Speaking to members of a communal entity, Burroughs wanted her audience to reflect upon their personal motives for joining the co-op and concede that individualistic imperatives must give way to that which is "cooperative minded":

> So come to meetings often and help with hand and heart,
> Don't be just a member, but take an active part.
> Think this over, member, you know right from wrong,
> are you an active member, or do you just belong?

The *New Challenge* devoted its two known issues to educating readers on cooperative principles, explicating the nuts and bolts of the cooperative's various business operations and touting the larger aim of realizing economic freedom for African Americans. In an editorial titled "Negroes Can Save Themselves—If They Want To," Burroughs began by eschewing the idea that white America was to blame for African Americans' economic condition; rather, it "is due to what we are not doing for ourselves, in a united, intelligent, courageous way."[54] To acquire the "cooperative nature," Burroughs identified as a key component a communal-based education program premised on a philosophy in which African Americans assumed personal responsibility for the general welfare of the group. Other elements of a cooperative nature included not succumbing to infighting or petty jealousies, which functioned to compromise or rupture organizational unity. It also depended upon stimulating leadership among the masses rather than a few individual "Negro leaders for window dressing." These latter two co-op principles were particularly resonant for Burroughs, who, as leader of the Woman's Convention, constantly battled with the NBC's male hierarchy to retain the women's group's operational and financial independence. Such sentiment also reinforced the Biblical teachings of Ezekiel, who "came to his senses and saw the needs of his people."[55] Burroughs admonished the educated Black bourgeoisie to cease their indifferent, callous attitudes toward the plight of the masses; persisting in such behavior, she argued, ignored the race oppression that both groups shared, a fact that bound their fates together. Invoking the Bible, Burroughs asserted a democratic conception of race advancement, predicated upon individual responsibility and a group consciousness: "Don't wait for a deliverer. . . . We must arise and go over Jordan. We can take the promised land."[56] Her parting message in the *New Challenge* echoed that sentiment, noting that "as the masses are enlightened by the sacrifice of their enlightened leaders, the richness and fullness of the lives of the leaders depend absolutely on the development of the cooperative nature in the masses. Unless leaders and people rise tougher by working together, neither will get anywhere."[57]

CONCLUSION

In 1956, Burroughs demonstrated her abiding faith in the modern civil rights movement, proclaiming that Americans were "more Civil Rights minded today than they have ever been in the history of the nation."[58] Enforcement of civil rights legislation remained a "must," she continued, and no political party could ascend to power "unless it has in its platform a broad civil rights plank—not just a splinter." In her predictions that year, Burroughs nominated Martin Luther King Jr. as the most outstanding American and the Montgomery bus boycott as the most significant event. In a seven-point program for race progress in 1957, and indicative of her multipronged approach to race reform, which coalesced around personal and public matters, Burroughs encouraged the Black masses to seek out educational opportunities, shore up their domestic home life, combat injustice and race discrimination with "every practical, sensible, effective weapon at their command," and apply the religious teachings of Jesus to their daily lives.[59]

Burroughs's public advocacy of economic and social justice, as drawn from the currents of African American religious, Victorian, and feminist thought, and which fused a classical/industrial education with woman-centered leadership, both affirmed the nonviolent, direct-action campaigns of the era and supplied the Christian moralism reflected in America's core democratic principles. Upon her death in 1961, the educator Benjamin E. Mays praised Burroughs in a newspaper column for her lifelong civil rights advocacy. Mays noted how she had recently sought his assurance that "the sit-in demonstrations were not a fly by night thing" and urged "continuation of the sit-ins until every vestige of discrimination in eating establishments and lunch counters had been abolished."[60]

Motivated by the goal of fomenting "mass intelligence" among African Americans and produced under the auspices of the Christian-based National Training School, Burroughs's textual work presaged the direct-action, communally driven, moral suasion campaigns of the modern civil rights era. At the same time, her belief in racial justice, and Christian public service more broadly, was multifaceted—from conceptions of Black female education and the crafting of a noble and respectable Black womanhood to the pursuit of economic opportunity, equal public accommodations, and the eradication of domestic environmental hazards and the establishment of wintertime "fresh air" groups. Uniting all these endeavors was a belief that African Americans needed an intensive public education campaign to heighten their mental, moral, and spiritual capacities and help them acquire the fundamental principles of good citizenship. Burroughs's civic and religiously minded vocabulary secured the moral armament—her Christian character and dogged determination—for her students to emulate while inspiring future generations of race activists.

NOTES

1. "Tilghman to Sadie Mareze (Sewing Unit Manager)," 23 July 1935, Cooperative Industries Correspondence (1934–1936), Box 52, Nannie Helen Burroughs Papers, Manuscript Division, Library of Congress, Washington, DC. Hereafter cited as Nannie Helen Burroughs Papers, LOC.

2. Board of Directors, Cooperative Industries, n.d., Box 52, Nannie Helen Burroughs Papers, LOC. The roots of the cooperative movement among African Americans lay in the collective action that occurred in the wake of systematic race oppression and discrimination. Early African American economic cooperatives included mutual aid and benefit societies, mutual insurance associations, fraternal organizations and secret societies, buying clubs, and collective farming. For a comprehensive account of Black cooperative organizations, see Jessica Gordon Nembhard's *Collective Courage: A History of African American Cooperative Economic Thought and Practice* (University Park: University of Pennsylvania Press, 2014).

3. See Evelyn Brooks Higginbotham, *Righteous Discontent: The Women's Movement in the Black Baptist Church, 1880–1920* (Cambridge, MA: Harvard University Press, 1993); Bettye Collier-Thomas, *Jesus, Jobs, and Justice: African American Women and Religion* (New York: Alfred A. Knopf, 2010); Ann Michele Mason, "Nannie H. Burroughs's Rhetorical Leadership During the Inter-War Period" (PhD diss., University of Maryland, 2008); Karen A. Johnson, *Uplifting the Women and the Race: The Educational Philosophies and Social Activism of Anna Julia Cooper and Nannie Helen Burroughs* (New York: Routledge, 2000); Barbara Savage, *Your Spirits Walk Beside Us: The Politics of Black Religion* (Cambridge, MA: Belknap, 2008); and Rosetta E. Ross, *Witnessing and Testifying: Black Women, Religion, and Civil Rights* (Minneapolis: Augsburg Fortress, 2002).

4. For this concept and its application to Black Baptist women's early civil rights activity, see Higginbotham, *Righteous Discontent*, 222.

5. Patricia-Anne Johnson, "Womanist Theology as Counter-Narrative," in *Gender, Ethnicity, and Religion: Views from the Other Side*, ed. Rosemary Radford Ruether (Minneapolis: Augsburg Fortress, 2002), 197. The term "womanist" is credited to novelist Alice Walker. See Walker, *In Search of Our Mothers' Gardens: Womanist Prose* (New York: Harcourt Brace, 1983).

6. Mary V. Cook, "Woman's Work in the Denomination," in *Woman's Work: An Anthology of African American Women's Historical Writings from Antebellum America to the Harlem Renaissance*, ed. Laurie F. Maffly-Kipp and Kathryn Lofton (New York: Oxford University Press, 2010), 73; and Collier-Thomas, *Jesus, Jobs, and Justice*, 557.

7. Higginbotham, *Righteous Discontent*, 217–18; and Juanita Fletcher, "Nannie Helen Burroughs," in *Notable American Women: The Modern Period—A Biographical Dictionary*, ed. Barbara Sicherman and Carol Hurd Green (Cambridge, MA: Belknap, 1980), 125–27.

8. Letter from Nannie Burroughs to Booker T. Washington, 18 February 1896, Box 36, Booker T. Washington Papers, Manuscript Division, Library of Congress; and George F. T. Cook, *Report of the Board of Trustees of Public Schools of the District of Columbia to the Commissioners of the District of Columbia 1893–1894* (Washington, DC: Government Printing Office, 1895), 177.

9. Johnson, *Uplifting the Women and the Race*, 54.

10. "Walter Henderson Brooks," *Journal of Negro History* 30, no. 4 (October 1945): 460; and Mason, "Nannie H. Burroughs's Rhetorical Leadership," 45.

11. Editorial, *The Worker*, July-September 1954, 3, Box 334, Nannie Helen Burroughs Papers, LOC.

12. Collier-Thomas, *Jesus, Jobs, and Justice*, 423.

13. "President's Annual Message," *The Worker*, January-March 1961, Box 334, Nannie Helen Burroughs Papers, LOC.

14. "President's Annual Message," 433.

15. "Majors and Minors," *The Mission Herald*, June 1908.

16. "More Air on the Subject," *The Mission Herald*, June 1908, p. 5.

17. Nancy C. Unger, *Beyond Nature's Housekeepers: American Women in Environmental History* (Cambridge, UK: Oxford University Press, 2012), 93.

18. Burroughs to Rachel Winston, 1935, Box 1, Nannie Helen Burroughs Papers, LOC.

19. "12 Things the Negro Must Do for Himself," n.d., Box 46, Nannie Helen Burroughs Papers, LOC.

20. Unger, *Beyond Nature's Housekeepers*, 93.

21. Burroughs, "The Colored Woman and Her Relation to the Domestic Problem," in *The United Negro: His Problems and His Progress; Containing the Addresses and Proceedings of the Negro Young People's Christian and Educational Congress, Held August 6–11, 1902*, ed. I. Garland Penn and J. W. E. Bowen (Atlanta: D. E. Luther Publishing, 1902), 324–29.

22. See Higginbotham, *Righteous Discontent*, 187; and Opal Easter, *Nannie Helen Burroughs* (New York: Routledge, 1995), 100.

23. Audrey Thomas McCluskey, *A Forgotten Sisterhood: Pioneering Black Women Educators and Activists in the Jim Crow South* (Lanham, MD: Rowman & Littlefield, 2014), 105.

24. Souvenir Brochure, 1909–1956, 5, 11, Box 309, Nannie Helen Burroughs Papers, LOC.

25. Examination Questions, n.d., Box 311, Nannie Helen Burroughs Papers, LOC.

26. Report of Corresponding Secretary, Second Annual Woman's Convention, n.d., Box 331, Nannie Helen Burroughs Papers, LOC.

27. See McCluskey, *Forgotten Sisterhood*, 106; Traki L. Taylor, "'Womanhood Glorified': Nannie Helen Burroughs and the National Training School for Woman and Girls, Inc., 1909–1961," *Journal of African American History* 87 (Summer 2002): 395; and Victoria Wolcott, "'Bible, Bath and Broom': Nannie Helen Burroughs's Training School and African American Uplift," *Journal of Women's History* 9, no. 1 (Spring 1997): 88–110.

28. Robert A. Orsi, "The Religious Boundaries of an In-Between People: Street Feste and the Problem of the Dark-Skinned Other in Italian Harlem, 1920–1990," in *Gods of the City: Religion and the Urban American Landscape*, ed. Robert A. Orsi (Bloomington: Indiana University Press, 1999), 278.

29. Quoted in Thomas D. Fallace, "The Racial and Cultural Assumptions of the Early Social Studies Educators, 1901–1922," in *Histories of Social Studies and Race: 1865–2000*, ed. Christine Woyshner and Chara Bohan (New York: Palgrave, 2012), 37–40, 41, 51.

30. See Deborah Gray White, *Too Heavy a Load: Black Women in Defense of Themselves, 1894–1994* (New York: W. W. Norton, 1999), 135; and Michelle Rief, "Thinking Locally, Acting Globally: The International Agenda of African American Clubwomen, 1890–1940," *Journal of African-American History* 89 (Summer 2004): 215. See also Alana D. Murray, "Countering the Master Narrative in U.S. Social Studies: Nannie Helen Burroughs and New Narratives in History Education," in Woyshner and Bohan, *Histories of Social Studies and Race*, 99–114.

31. Fallace, "Racial and Cultural Assumptions," 49.

32. *When Truth Gets a Hearing*, n.d., 8, Box 47, Nannie Helen Burroughs Papers, LOC.

33. *When Truth Gets a Hearing*, 13.

34. *When Truth Gets a Hearing*, 10.

35. "12 Things White People Must Stop Doing to the Negro," n.d., Box 46, Nannie Helen Burroughs Papers, LOC.

36. Quoted in Jeffrey Aaron Snyder, *Making Black History: The Color Line, Culture, and Race in the Age of Jim Crow* (Athens: University of Georgia Press, 2018), 139.

37. Gunnar Myrdal, *An American Dilemma, Volume II: The Negro Problem and Modern Democracy* (New Brunswick, NJ: Transaction Publishers, 1996), 752.

38. *When Truth Gets a Hearing*, 9; and G. Mokhtar, *General History of Africa: Ancient Civilizations of Africa* (Berkley, CA: Unesco, 1990), 76.

39. *When Truth Gets a Hearing*, 28.

40. Enrollment records, n.d., Box 147, Nannie Helen Burroughs Papers, LOC.

41. Derrick Aldridge, *The Educational Thought of W. E. B. Du Bois: An Intellectual History* (New York: Teacher's College Press, 2008), 75.

42. Burroughs, "Leaders Mark Time with Many Idle, Says Nannie Burroughs," *Afro-American*, December 6, 1930.

43. Burroughs, "Leaders Mark Time."

44. Quoted in Nembhard, *Collective Courage*, 17, 97–98.

45. "Baptist Training School Needed," 3 May 1908, Box 315, Nannie Helen Burroughs Papers, LOC.

46. Letter to Citizens Associations, 24 April 1934, Cooperative Industries Correspondence (1934), Box 52, Nannie Helen Burroughs Papers, LOC.

47. Applications A-L, n.d., Box 53, Nannie Helen Burroughs Papers, LOC; Applications M-W, n.d., Box 54, Nannie Helen Burroughs Papers, LOC; Membership Lists, n.d., Box 54, Nannie Helen Burroughs Papers, LOC; and Constitution and By-laws, n.d., Box 52, Nannie Helen Burroughs Papers, LOC.

48. Meeting Minutes, 16 January 1936, Box 54, Nannie Helen Burroughs Papers, LOC.

49. Summary of the Non-Partisan Negro Conference, n.d., Box 47, Nannie Helen Burroughs Papers, LOC.

50. "Join the Cooperative," n.d., Box 54, Nannie Helen Burroughs Papers, LOC.

51. "What Do You Know about the Cooperative Movement?," *The Worker* 4, no. 14 (April–June 1937): 5, Box 333, Nannie Helen Burroughs Papers, LOC.

52. "Join the Cooperative," 6.

53. "The Just Belong-ers," n.d., Box 54, Nannie Helen Burroughs Papers, LOC.

54. "Negroes Can Save Themselves—If They Want To," *New Challenge* 9 (October 1937), Box 54, Nannie Helen Burroughs Papers, LOC.

55. The recurring battles between Burroughs and the NBC's male leadership for control of the Woman's Convention and National Training School are treated in depth in Collier-Thomas, *Jesus, Jobs, and Justice*, esp. 133–38.

56. Nannie Helen Burroughs, "Unload Your Uncle Toms," in *Black Women in White America: A Documentary History*, ed. Gerda Lerner (New York: Vintage, 1973), 551–53.

57. "Negroes Can Save Themselves."

58. "Here Are My Predictions for 1957," n.d., 1, Nannie Helen Burroughs Papers, LOC.

59. "Here Are My Predictions," 2–3.

60. Benjamin E. Mays, "My View," *Pittsburgh Courier*, June 10, 1961, Sec. 2, 9.

SELECTED BIBLIOGRAPHY

Aldridge, Derrick. *The Educational Thought of W. E. B. Du Bois: An Intellectual History*. New York: Teacher's College Press, 2008.

Brooks-Barnett, Evelyn. "Nannie Burroughs and the Education of Black Women." In *The Afro-American Woman: Struggles and Images*, edited by Sharon Harley and Rosalyn Terborg-Penn, 97–108. Port Washington, NY: Kennikat Press, 1978.

Burroughs, Nannie Helen. "Leaders Mark Time." *Afro-American*, December 6, 1930.

Burroughs, Nannie Helen. "Majors and Minors." *Mission Herald*, June 1908.

Burroughs, Nannie Helen. "More Air on the Subject." *Mission Herald*, June 1908, 8.

Burroughs, Nannie Helen. Papers. Manuscript Division, Library of Congress, Washington, DC.

Burroughs, Nannie Helen. "What Do You Know about the Cooperative Movement." *The Worker* 4, no. 14 (April–June 1937): 5.

Collier-Thomas, Bettye. *Jesus, Jobs, and Justice: African American Women and Religion.* New York: Alfred A. Knopf, 2010.

Daniel, Sadie Iola. *Women Builders.* Washington, DC: Associated Publishers, 1931.

Easter, Opal. *Nannie Helen Burroughs.* New York: Routledge, 1995.

Fallace, Thomas D. "The Racial and Cultural Assumptions of the Early Social Studies Educators, 1901–1922." In *Histories of Social Studies and Race: 1865–2000*, edited by Christine Woyshner and Chara Haeussler Bohan, 37–56. New York: Palgrave Macmillan, 2012.

Fletcher, Juanita. "Nannie Helen Burroughs." In *Notable American Women: The Modern Period—A Biographical Dictionary*, edited by Barbara Sicherman, Carol Hurd, Ilene Kantrov, and Harriette Walker, 125–27. Cambridge, MA: Belknap, 1980.

Higginbotham, Evelyn Brooks. *Righteous Discontent: The Women's Movement in the Black Baptist Church, 1880–1920.* Cambridge, MA: Harvard University Press, 1993.

Johnson, Karen A. *Uplifting the Women and the Race: The Educational Philosophies and Social Activism of Anna Julia Cooper and Nannie Helen Burroughs.* New York: Routledge, 2000.

Mason, Ann Michele. "Nannie H. Burroughs's Rhetorical Leadership During the Inter-War Period." PhD diss., University of Maryland, 2008.

Mays, Benjamin E. "My View." *Pittsburgh Courier*, June 10, 1961, Sec. 2, 9.

McCluskey, Audrey Thomas. *A Forgotten Sisterhood: Pioneering Black Women Educators and Activists in the Jim Crow South.* Lanham, MD: Rowman & Littlefield, 2014.

Murray, Alana D. "Countering the Master Narrative in U.S. Social Studies: Nannie Helen Burroughs and New Narratives in History Education." In *Histories of Social Studies and Race: 1865–2000*, edited by Christine Woyshner and Chara Haeussler Bohan, 99–114. New York: Palgrave, 2012.

Nembhard, Jessica Gordon. *Collective Courage: A History of African American Cooperative Economic Thought and Practice.* College Park: Pennsylvania State University Press, 2014.

Pickens, William. *Nannie Helen Burroughs and the School of the Three B's.* New York, 1921.

Savage, Barbara. *Your Spirits Walk Beside Us: The Politics of Black Religion.* Cambridge, MA: Belknap, 2008.

Taylor, Traki L. "'Womanhood Glorified': Nannie Helen Burroughs and the National Training School for Woman and Girls, Inc., 1909–1961." *Journal of African American History* 87 (Summer 2002): 390–402.

Wolcott, Victoria. "'Bible, Bath and Broom': Nannie Helen Burroughs's Training School and African American Uplift." *Journal of Women's History* 9, no. 1 (Spring 1997): 88–110.

Chapter 5

THE GOSPEL ACCORDING TO MADAME E. AZALIA SMITH HACKLEY

LISA PERTILLAR BREVARD

> It can not [*sic*] be denied that Divinity has specially endowed the Negro spiritually, but he does not consistently express it in all the forms that he might express it, especially in the great Race cause. He is full of heart, and will give his money, his food, his life, for God—but he does not yet realize that the same love for God that he puts into his gifts should be expressed and applied in his daily walks in life as Christ has expressly commanded.[1]
>
> —Madame Emma Azalia Smith Hackley

INTRODUCTION: HACKLEY'S DOCTRINE

Classically trained coloratura soprano, Episcopalian, and social activist Madame Emma Azalia Smith Hackley declared God's word sovereign, pairing it with the examples of Jesus Christ, the can-do-must-do spirit of the Industrial Age (1890–1915), and the urgent need for Black American socioeconomic uplift, during what historian Rayford Logan calls the nadir—the lowest point—of American race relations.[2] A Class of 1900 graduate of the University of Denver School of Music and well versed in the classics, French, piano, and emerging modes of mass communication—especially print media—Hackley was among the early Black American proponents of using the arts to combat racial prejudice. Her goal was to uplift fellow Black Americans by creating massive temporary community choirs to dignify and preserve spirituals—their history and peculiar folk inheritance—which had become largely ridiculed in American popular culture and were therefore at risk of being abandoned by their own people. A classically trained pianist and soprano and member of W. E. B. Du Bois's Talented Tenth, who believed that the most desperate classes of African Americans exhibited the most natural musical talents worthy of development, Madame Hackley nevertheless (to adapt a phrase from Booker T. Washington's "Atlanta Exposition Address of 1895") "cast her bucket" wherever her vast travels by train and steamship took her. Hackley's understanding and articulation of the big picture of faith, combined with applied, everyday strategies for success, enabled her to reach primarily Baptist African American communities, inspire her contemporaries, and pave the way for the next generation of African American classical musicians. Emphasizing self-examination, self-determination, self-expression, and community uplift, her doctrine inspired her audiences to integrate purposefully spirituality, or applied faith, into everyday life, with the dual aims of honoring God and fostering socioeconomic uplift.

Hackley's forays into both the arts arena and politics began at an early age and extended into married life and beyond. A native of Murfreesboro, Tennessee, Hackley (née Emma Azalia Smith) studied piano at home under the direction of her mother, Corilla Beard Smith, a school teacher and owner of a school for Black Americans, and performed concerts in the area. When racial tensions threatened her school, Corilla and her husband relocated the family to Denver, Colorado, where Azalia excelled and continued her studies in voice and piano. In Denver, Azalia, as she preferred to be called by her closest friends, met the man who would become her husband, Edwin Henry Hackley (1859–1940), at a concert featuring Sissieretta Jones, known as the Black Patti (after Adelina Patti, the Italian classical singer). Edwin was editor of the *Denver Statesman*, a Black newspaper known for its progressive stance on race advancement. Prior to eloping with Azalia in 1894, Edwin, who was also an attorney and the first Black American to be admitted to the Colorado Bar, had previously courted Ida B. Wells. Edwin's colleague was Ferdinand Barnett, who later became Wells's husband.[3] Assisting Edwin with the newspaper, Azalia contributed "The Exponent," a section that dealt with socioeconomic needs of Black American women navigating the modern age. Owing to the popularity of her articles, the newspaper eventually became known as the *Statesman-Exponent*.[4] Her work at the newspaper formed a basis of engagement from which she would turn, time and again, to foster her mission: write an article for the editor of a Black newspaper in exchange for free advertising to one of her upcoming concerts in a particular city or region. Such work also enabled Azalia to build a name for herself, thus reaching an increasingly widely dispersed group of the Black American elite. However, the Hackleys' outwardly progressive stance on racial uplift, which also included their organizing the Grand United Order of Libyans, an organization devoted to achieving justice for Black Americans, led to conflicts that forced the couple to relocate to Philadelphia.[5]

The Black American elite of that time constituted a minority within a minority, closely intertwined with each other and, as they well understood, with the fate of the Black masses. The history and culture of Philadelphia made it a suitable place for the newlyweds to explore intellectual, creative, and political pursuits. Edwin Hackley was also a poet and playwright, and in Colorado, he and Paul Laurence Dunbar, who was later renowned for his dialect poetry and lyric poems such as "Sympathy," both suffered and attempted to recover from tuberculosis by breathing the fresh mountain air.[6] Philadelphia was an important city for the Hackleys, serving as the location of The Peoples' Chorus, a massive temporary choir that Azalia organized and directed and which gave such classical greats-to-be as Marian Anderson and Roland Hayes their first audiences. Philadelphia was also the place where Edwin developed his skill as a playwright.[7] To foster her musical mission, Azalia plied her trade as a journalist and newspaper columnist to share her advice with Black audiences and to foster community organizing and concertizing in such additional hubs as Washington, DC, working with the nascent Washington Conservatory of Music; writing a popular series of articles, *Hints to Young Colored Artists* (1912–1914), for the *New York Age*; and eventually, relocating to Chicago, Illinois.[8] There she founded her own music settlement school, the Vocal Normal Institute (VNI), the first Black American music settlement school, established along the lines of Jane Addams's Hull House. The VNI was designed to serve as an acculturation center for Black musicians—especially Black women—desiring to move from plantation to city life and claim a place in classical music. Its central location in Chicago made it, Azalia, and her doctrine accessible by rail from all regions of the United States.

Nowhere is Azalia Hackley's doctrine more prominent and pointedly expressed than in her pioneering book, *The Colored Girl Beautiful* (1916), best known as the first etiquette book for Black American girls and women. Careful review of that book reveals that it also contains strategies for individual and cultural survival, which Hackley declares are ideally rooted in a spiritual sense that permeates all activities. Hackley says, "Each Negro must consider himself a spiritual missionary whose appearance, speech, actions, and surroundings will reflect the storehouse of the great Light within. . . . [Moreover], the religion that does not help toward the advancement of this persecuted race, and does not win the admiration and respect of other races, is not the religion of the colored girl beautiful, of today" (128). Written in spurts between her treks by train in Jim Crow cars (locomotive passenger cars specifically designated for Blacks, located near the coal-fed engine and therefore subject to the effluvia of coal dust) and manifesting her beliefs, training, philosophies, and experiences, the book, while nodding to the harshness of the past and acknowledging present inequities, purposely looks ever forward to the future, concretizing her work and status as a public intellectual.

AN INTELLECTUAL INFLUENCER

Hackley was a public intellectual because as an internationally recognized professional musician-performer, businesswoman, lecturer, newspaper columnist, author, and former public school teacher, she regularly and purposefully addressed the public at large—especially the Black American community—on moral and civic matters. Given her elevated social station, educational attainments, and business activities, her cohorts and audiences expected her to show leadership in that way. Careful analysis of her efforts shows that Hackley did not have the luxury of "just" singing or traveling; every aspect of her work as an artist necessarily entailed tangling with the politics and geographies of the times in which she lived, including the ever-present legacy and shadow of chattel slavery. Nor was she exempt from living the ideals that she preached in *The Colored Girl Beautiful*. Hackley wrote, edited, published, and distributed the book—at her own expense—despite a grueling travel schedule throughout the US that included raising massive, temporary choirs in Black communities to perform traditional Black American spirituals alongside selected folk songs from Western Europe. Her efforts fostered a repertoire later capitalized upon by world-renowned Black American music legends including Paul Robeson, Harry Belafonte, Kathleen Battle, Jessye Norman, and Sweet Honey in the Rock.

Along the way, Hackley had become widely known and sought after as a journalist and public speaker, adept at addressing a wide range of topics from comportment to professional courtesies to modern home economics to Black and women's empowerment, among many others. Such extensive experience cemented her status as a public intellectual. In fact, Hackley's book came about because Booker T. Washington, a widely recognized public speaker and founder and president of Tuskegee Institute, a Black institution of higher learning in Alabama, invited Hackley to the campus specifically to counsel and advise young Black women students about such matters as beauty, social etiquette, intellect, industry, education, religion, courting, wifehood, and motherhood. On the topic of beauty, she writes,

> Every colored girl would like to be beautiful. The so-called beauty is but skin deep. A burn, a scar, a disease, and beauty is fled, although contour and other evidences remain. We look at the photos of beautiful, smiling, round-faced children and then at the tired, many-lined unhappy faces

> into which they have changed. Women delight in showing us photos to prove how beautiful they were when they were sweet sixteen. As we look it is hard to believe. However, the camera, they say, always tells the truth, and we have later evidence before us. The inward tools, Thoughts, have carved the ugly pictures on faces. Ignorance is a terrible curse along all lines. Many have not learned the secret of preserving their bodies, along with other studies, yet the savage nations care for their bodies. (41–43)

The pages of *The Colored Girl Beautiful* share with African American girls and women that multifaceted, multilayered "secret."

According to Hackley, "A woman's mind should always be filled with a life plan, or else she is in danger. A busy woman is generally a safe woman. She must find her life work and keep busy. Even a hobby is better than nothing if time is on her hands. She should do something with all her might and not delay, for time is flying" (85). For Hackley, the aim of such a life plan is to "train herself to make a perfect social circle as far as she is able" (93). By word and by deed, Hackley taught that such a social circle should extend to include all aspects of the community, so that a woman not only fulfills her life's purpose, but does so in such a way as to recognize and address her implicit obligation to the home and the civic arena. Hackley's primary concern was Black American women working outside the home: this was the majority of Black American women, whom she believed had a special obligation to work diligently and efficiently, not only to earn money and practice the art of conservation to save in preparation for lean times, but to use their position in the larger working world to build crucial connections for additional paid work opportunities, as well make as other connections with people, to gain access to needed goods and services. She writes, "A bank account is always the most respected thing in the struggle of life," and "contact is often worth more than money" (133). According to Hackley's gospel, circumstances, however daunting, are no excuse for a woman failing to make this social circle.

Accordingly, Hackley's philosophies on industry, education, and religion are intertwined. She preached that for the colored girl beautiful, education and religion go hand in hand: "She will learn that the aim of education is the aim of religion: to lift one above the animal. She will endeavor to lift herself to the highest plane of true womanhood that she may pull others higher" (133). Moreover, she also asserts that such a woman should be prepared to take on leadership roles within the community:

> The colored girl beautiful will be taught her duty and relationship to the race, that she may be a living example of what right education and right training will do. She will study human needs and about the history and

> progress of her people that she may take her place in the affairs of her race if called upon, and then bequeath her knowledge and good qualities to succeeding generations. She will be taught lessons of self-control and modesty; to respect her womanhood and to conduct herself that she may command respect from all men and boys including those of her family.

Hackley's take on the importance of schooling meaningfully weds industry, piety, and creativity, laying the foundation for citizenship:

> The school that the colored girl beautiful should attend will have trees, grass, flowers, shrubs and a garden (even though a small one) that the girl may keep in close touch with the first teacher—Mother Nature. The care of the school campus as well as the windows, fences, and surroundings, will reflect the careful spirit of the school. The colored girl beautiful will select the school which fights flies, dirt, filth around back doors; the school which aims for sanitation before putting in electric lights; in fact, a school which has health and sanitation as its hobby. (134)

An intellectual influencer, she also delineates specific responsibilities of freedmen's schools: "Colored schools are supposed to correct the tendencies of children who have lived under careless, untidy conditions, to give them ideals of cleanliness and order" (136). By extension, as daughters and mothers in a historically matrilineal subset of American society, Hackley held Black women accountable for diligently ensuring that a holistic educational experience, encompassing harmonious and sanitary physical environs at home, school, and church, would serve as a foundation for what she called "right living" (155), which stimulates higher thought, thus fostering understanding of and adherence to spiritual, familial, and civic duties. Nor does she exempt girls and women who labor under especially heavy social, economic, or other constraints from attempting to manifest such a goal: "Be ready for the opportunity or crisis which is bound to come for the better. Stick to a position like a leech. Make it a bigger and better one than you found it and it will prepare you for greater openings. Someone is always watching good workers." She continues by explaining that Black women carry a special burden, in that the diction and comportment of Black women who work outside the home are the measure against which the entire Black race is judged (156).

In order to prepare Black women for carrying such burdens sufficiently, Hackley also preached on such topics as courting, wifehood, and motherhood, *in that ideal order*. She also makes particular effort to tell women who are living on their own that such a situation is no reason for them to discount or discredit themselves:

> In her relationship with men the colored working girl beautiful will put a higher appraisement on herself than may be necessary in the case of the more fate-favored girl who stays under her parents' roof. Because she works is no reason why she should be cheap, easily attained, or easily pleased, as far as men are concerned. She will demand much instead of little from men, that they will offer more for the pleasure of her society. Unless she is engaged she will be wise to permit no caresses and will try to conquer the tendency towards accepting "petting." She will bide her time for the recognition of her worth. (154–55)

To Hackley's way of thinking, such preparation forms the needed foundation for mutual respect in marriage, the foundation of a strong family and society.

Where the Black community is concerned, Hackley considers the role of the wife key to breaking the cycle of poverty, ignorance, and social neglect. Hackley's description of the ideal wife is one who serves as the household's chief health and sanitation officer; practices home economics, being thrifty and creative with home finances, food, and other resources; upholds her husband's name; and guides the husband and children in such a way that they respect her, themselves, and each other. According to Hackley's gospel, a Black wife is to do all of the aforementioned while maintaining her feminine charms:

> The protection of the name of any kind of a man, bad, no account, or cruel, is better than [being single]. The first duty of a wife is to keep healthy. Even if she is ailing, she must not complain . . . she must earnestly endeavor to discover the cause and . . . remove it. Many men are attracted by youth alone and after it has flown, they are not interested. A wife should study the fancies of her husband if she desires to hold him, and then begin work on herself, to hold her youthful looks. Many a woman has attracted her husband through singing, conversation, or other accomplishments and after marriage has permitted these to decline, and has not lived up to the ideal that she gave him before marriage. A wife should ask herself if she is living up to the ideal she suggested before she married, or if she is a disappointment, before she questions her husband's conduct. (172–76)

Hackley holds Black wives accountable for thorough self-assessment, instead of automatically blaming their husbands for dalliances outside the marriage. Describing divorce as a "terrible something" that erodes support, future opportunities, and confidence, she advises women to remain married for the sake of the children—at least, until the children reach the age of majority—and to bide her time serving the community or building a business of her own

(170). Admitting that these rules constitute a tall order, she exhorts: "There are four great laws given to a wife: Brace up! Brush up! Clean up! Look up!" (157). Careful readers wonder whether Hackley may well have been talking about herself.

Wifehood is the foundation of motherhood, which Hackley says is the most difficult and sacred of trusts, especially for Black women. On the matter of motherhood, Hackley argues, "To assume the position of colored motherhood is the greatest privilege and responsibility that can come to any woman in this age" (199). Nor does she exempt Black boys and men from doing their duty to assist in ensuring a harmonious home and hearth—*although she does hold Black women accountable for holding the boys and men accountable.* As is true of girls, she says,

> Boys, also, get their estimate of colored womanhood from their mothers. A whipping, striking, scolding, threatening "shut-up" mother presents him a wrong view-point of real motherhood. If it is expected that he should stand erect before any woman, he should before the women of his mother's race. Off will go his hat, if even asked a question. His voice, his eyes, his backbone, his heels, all reflect her training. In spite of protest he will never sit if a woman is standing, unless he is ill or a cripple.

Continuing this train of thought, Hackley acknowledges that Black boys and men are expected to defer to white women in public; correspondingly, she says, Black boys and men should also treat Black women with the same deference. Above all, she says that Black boys should be taught to respect themselves, body, mind, and spirit: "Early in the boy's life, the colored mother beautiful will teach him to keep in pure in thought and deed as girls are expected to be. He will be given a right idea of the sacred sex organs and will be taught their health—the value and price of their abuse. Self mastery [*sic*] will be the watchword in thought, even in sleep and recreation" (201–2). Hackley understood that, without strong families, there could be no strong communities and that Black freedom meant Black responsibility. Accordingly, she used public speaking to not only identify social inequalities, but to hold Black families and communities responsible for addressing, if not eradicating, them.

While perhaps considered harsh by today's standards, such advice was Hackley's antidote for a people barely a half-century removed from chattel slavery—a people defined by law as subhuman, slopped like hogs and made to breed for the slavery system. In effect, Hackley's work answered Sojourner Truth's pointed question, "Ain't I a woman?" with a declarative *Yes!* while also holding her sisters responsible for the health, well-being, education, and posterity of the Black race, both in their communities and as a whole.

When Hackley had visited the Tuskegee campus several times, she realized that the student body was consistently changing and that the knowledge needs of the women on campus far exceeded the number of times that she could visit. As a result, she took it upon herself to gather her ideas into a manuscript and publish it. The resulting book, *The Colored Girl Beautiful*, consists of eighteen concise chapters: "The Future"; "The Colored Child Beautiful"; "The Colored Girl Beautiful"; "Laws of Attraction—Vibrations"; "Love"; "Personal Appearance"; "Deep Breathing"; "Originality"; "Youth and Maturity"; "Self Control"; "Her Relationship with Men"; "The Religion of the Colored Girl Beautiful"; "The School of the Colored Girl Beautiful"; "The Home of the Colored Girl Beautiful"; "The Colored Working Girl Beautiful"; "The Colored Woman Beautiful"; "The Colored Wife Beautiful"; and "The Colored Mother Beautiful." When viewed holistically, each chapter builds upon the previous one, culminating in an exploration and exhortation of the role and status of the Black American mother. Viewed thematically, the order of chapters emphasizes four clusters of thought: beginnings and possibilities (first through third chapters); love and fidelity (fourth through eleventh chapters); faith and spirituality (twelfth through fourteenth chapters); and growth and posterity (remaining four chapters). The concepts in each cluster range from micro to macro and from abstract to concrete and coalesce into Hackley's gospel of Black motherhood, which appears in the book's final chapter, "The Colored Mother Beautiful." In that chapter, Hackley writes,

> To assume the position of colored motherhood is the greatest privilege and responsibility that can come to any woman in this age. The colored mother beautiful carries a heavy burden—the weight of future generations of a handicapped, persecuted people. She may bless or curse each succeeding generation; she may change race history; she may make a more beautiful race with the beauty that comes from beauty of character and right living. What a privilege to carve the destiny of a race! How glorious to look into the future and see lines of ancestry influenced and advanced by her thought and example, to see her stamp of personality upon a posterity which will point to her in pride and thankfulness! (181–82)

Adept at public speaking and swaying public opinion, Hackley acknowledges that many of her audience members were likely to become mothers (if they were not already) and that their academic work and social attainments at Tuskegee were just the beginning of Black elite societal expectations. Resonating like that of a church pastor addressing a congregation, Hackley's rhetoric is deliberately designed to pique the interest of and inspire her original audience:

women students at Tuskegee Institute, who undoubtedly continued to consider, discuss, and debate her preaching long after she had left the campus. Accordingly, the original 1916 version of the book differs considerably from digital online offerings in that each chapter of the printed version ends with a blank page—a thought page, of sorts, for the reader to pause, and take notes if desired, before moving on to the next chapter.

The fact that *The Colored Girl Beautiful* contains no pictures or photographs is also significant. At the time of the book's publication, Hackley's image had been widely circulated through decades of Black American newspapers and placards advertising concerts and other public programming activities in which she was featured. In fact, so well known was her image that a fictionalized version of Hackley appears as the "rich widow" in James Weldon Johnson's *The Autobiography of an Ex-Colored Man*:

> There was still another set of white patrons, composed of women; these were not occasional visitors, but five or six of them were regular habituées. When I first saw them, I was not sure that they were white. In the first place, among the many colored women who came to the "Club" there were several just as fair; and, secondly, I always saw these women in company with colored men. One of these in particular attracted my attention; she was an exceedingly beautiful woman of perhaps thirty-five; she had glistening copper-colored hair, very white skin, and eyes very much like Du Maurier's conception of Trilby's "twin gray stars." When I came to know her, I found that she was a woman of considerable culture; she had traveled in Europe, spoke French, and played the piano well. She was always dressed elegantly, but in absolute good taste.[9]

A very well-read and extensively travelled person who occupied the same elite social class as Johnson, Hackley was likely aware of this fictionalized depiction of herself. Not surprisingly, there is no record of her response to the portrayal, especially since it mentions her socializing with an unnamed man and not her well-known husband, Edwin. Azalia's lack of documented response to Johnson's book should come as no surprise, for, by the time it was published, she had undergone what was called a "polite divorce" from her husband. Legal divorce was not only messy and embarrassing, but it interrupted the flow of resources between exes; for this reason, the polite divorce, in which a couple agrees to socialize separately while still living under the same roof, was a popular solution. Such practice was in keeping with Hackley's statement in *Colored Girl Beautiful* that it was advantageous, in society as well as in business, for a woman to carry a husband's name (171). An established lady, Hackley would not dignify Johnson's depiction with a formal response. Deliberately choosing not to include an image of herself in her book, she encouraged each reader to see herself within its pages instead.

In the Foreword to *The Colored Girl Beautiful*, Hackley wrote, "The talks were very informal and personal and as the girls asked questions the thought came to me to jot down the points, that similar talks might be given to the girls in other schools. Then came the request, 'You come so seldom, can you print the talks?' Much of the talks could not be printed because many of the questions and answers were personal" (171). Reflecting her experiences as a traveling, working professional, and influenced by biblical precepts as well as concepts advanced by a range of public intellectuals predating the Common Era through to the early twentieth century, *The Colored Girl Beautiful* preaches the virtues of Black girls and women behaving in a Christ-like manner, while creating and taking responsibilities for self, community, and society as world citizens:

> It is not sufficient to say, "I am a Christian (I am spiritual—of the spirit)" unless one expresses this in countless ways each day. Not only in kind, helpful actions and gentle speech, but in the work-a-day life. . . . Race pride expresses the God in us. The Israelites were the chosen people because of blood ties. They were proud of their blood. Blood is thicker than water. The real Christian should be proud of his people. He should believe in them and uplift them as our Great Example did the lowly. (122)

Moreover, she says, "Once [you] convince the rankest Negro hater that the Negro undoubtedly has spirituality, which is surely advancing him and the race, and a certain respect will follow" (126). Hackley firmly believed that applied spirituality could turn the tide of race relations. The significance of her bold, declarative stance cannot be overstated, for during this period, *de facto* and often legal racial segregation and related socioeconomic exclusion were the norm for Black Americans. Ever aware of her influencer status, Hackley also realized that publishing such a book might extend her legacy. Indeed, while giving advice to her readers about the powers of thought and inscription, she says that "writing a thought intensifies its influence" (45). Writing *The Colored Girl Beautiful*, she may well have been talking about herself. Far more than an etiquette book, it was Hackley's attempt at courting posterity.

Despite her fame and influence, Hackley likely wondered about her legacy, and, while she embodied many of the ideals about which she publicly preached, she did not live up to all of them. An accident during her childhood had rendered her barren; and by the time of the book's publication in 1916, Hackley was divorced. Further, she had suffered a personal and public failure of her Vocal Normal Institute (VNI).

The failure of the VNI was not due to lack of interest from pupils. Rather, because Hackley believed that the least-prepared students had the most natural talent, were the most deserving, and made the best student musicians, she drew much of her student body from among the desperate class; thus, her pupils were too poor to pay for lessons. Moreover, having toured extensively throughout the United States as well as in Canada and Western Europe, she could no longer maintain the grueling schedule of arranging, publicizing, and presenting concerts as fundraisers for music scholarships and support for the VNI. Finally, by the time Hackley published her book in 1916, American popular music had changed; and, largely owing to the success of Scott Joplin, a Black American composer and pianist, ragtime had become the most popular American music form, eclipsing the former popularity of European classical music and American military music traditions and related cultural ideals upon which Hackley and her cohort had relied.[10]

Hence, during the ragtime era, Hackley redoubled her efforts to establish social etiquette as a cultural expectation for Black American families, with special emphasis on highlighting the roles of girls and women as moral and physical leaders of the race. In the preface to *The Colored Girl Beautiful*, she expresses her abiding allegiance to the spiritual and physical uplift of Black American girls and women: "If I had a daughter I would desire that she should know these things and more; that she might become a beacon light to her home and the race. As I have not been blessed with a daughter, I send these thoughts to the daughters of other colored women, hoping that among them there is some thought worthy of a racial 'Amen'" (ii). Such is all the more profound when we realize that Hackley easily could have passed for white but chose not to. Hackley's allegiance reflects her understanding of God and spirituality; scripture, tradition, and reason; and spirituality and agency.

GOD AND SPIRITUALITY

Hackley believed and taught that God is the Supreme Being, the ultimate embodiment of perfection and all that is good. An Episcopalian schooled in the catechism and observing the "via media," or middle way, between Protestant and Roman Catholic doctrines and practices, both Catholic and Reformed, she sought and taught balance among scripture, tradition, and reason. She also promoted the belief that Jesus Christ, as being at once fully human and fully God, is the "pattern of patterns" (130), whose unerring examples must be thoughtfully and purposefully followed.

Accordingly, her teachings especially emphasized the Great Commandment to love God and neighbor fully, as found in Matthew 22:36–40 (KJV):

35 Then one of them, which was a lawyer, asked him a question, tempting him, and saying,
36 Master, which is the great commandment in the law?
37 Jesus said unto him, Thou shalt love the Lord thy God with all thy heart, and with all thy soul, and with all thy mind.
38 This is the first and great commandment.
39 And the second is like unto it, Thou shalt love thy neighbor as thyself.
40 On these two commandments hang all the law and the prophets.

Hackley regarded adherence to this commandment an expression of faith or, as she taught it, *applied spirituality*—an awareness of which, she preached, should govern all activities, great and small, dignifying the mighty, and elevating the mundane.

Hackley declares, "The religion of the colored girl must be spiritual in every sense, that it may influence her every thought and act, and make her a true medium for race progress" (130). Combining the industry and piety of the Protestant work ethic with the teachings of the Gospel of Matthew, Hackley decidedly worked among, and sought to mold, model-minority Christian soldiers from among the raw "clay" of underdeveloped, underappreciated masses of Black Americans in the South. Like other Black American activists of her time, including Booker T. Washington, W. E. B. Du Bois, Ida B. Wells, and Mary Church Terrell, Hackley believed that the situation and disposition of the vast majority of Black Americans—many of whom were poor, illiterate, destitute, and transitioning from plantation to city life—determined the status and possibilities for Black Americans as a whole. Moreover, she believed that overcoming those limitations began in the home and that Black women, if properly trained in the ways of directed applied spirituality, could raise not only their standard of living and social status but those of their families and future generations.

Hackley was a living proponent of the biblical teaching that "Faith without works is dead" (James 2:25–18, KJV):

14 What doth it profit, my brethren, though a man say he hath faith, and have not works? Can faith save him?
15 If a brother or sister be naked, and destitute of daily food,
16 And one of you say unto them, Depart in peace, be ye warmed and filled; notwithstanding ye give them not those things which are needful to the body; what doth it profit?
17 Even so faith, if it hath not works, is dead, being alone.
18 For as the body without the spirit is dead, so faith without works is dead also.

Hackley activated her faith and practiced what she preached through many applications, one of which, in particular, continues to bear fruit. In 1913, she appointed Robert Nathaniel Dett, an Afro-Canadian composer, to the director of music position at Hampton Institute (now Hampton University), a Black institution in Hampton, Virginia. By so doing, she founded the Music Department there, which became and remains world-renowned for its studied and nuanced performance of the Black American spiritual. In the process, she established an American home base for Dett, who is best known for composing and arranging such original spirituals as "Listen to the Lambs," which Hackley had premiered during one of her grand folk music festivals. Of Hackley's influence and legacy, Dett wrote,

> There is probably no name in America which should be more honored for having stimulated respect for Negro music and musicians than that of Madame E. Azalia Hackley. . . . By going all through the country, especially the South, and personally organizing mammoth Negro choruses to sing spirituals in the largest available halls, before large audiences, [Hackley] not only dramatically focused attention on Negro native musical ability, but gave the Negroes themselves a thrill of pride in their own ability.[11]

Hackley's stalwart belief in the power of God and human ability to reason and grow gave hope to a downtrodden people struggling with the legacy of slavery.

SCRIPTURE, TRADITION, AND REASON

As Hackley taught, the Black American spiritual is a primary fount for Black history and culture. Since enslaved Black people were usually forbidden from studying the Bible themselves, whatever they learned about Christianity came mainly through the oral tradition and in such Black American folk songs as "Steal Away," "Wade in the Water," "Didn't My Lord Deliver Daniel?," and "Ezekiel Saw the Wheel," among many others. And, while some spirituals, like "Steal Away" and "Wade in the Water," functioned as coded language for the underground railroad—a loosely organized chain of hideaways for fugitives escaping slavery by making their way to freedom in Canada—others contained distilled interpretations of biblical tales, among them the story of God delivering Daniel from the lion's den. "Didn't My Lord Deliver Daniel?," with its counterpoint lyric "And why not ev'ry man?," expresses Black Americans' determination for equality under the law as under God. Black American spirituals thus constitute a common denominator cultural text, which, even when removed from its slavery origins, nevertheless retains its cultural significance.

Realizing their value, Hackley led and advocated performances of spirituals by temporary Black American choruses that performed such songs. She wanted Black Americans to know their worth as people and contributors to the US and world economies and cultures. Accordingly, she eschewed vulgarities and showiness and preached substance and economy. Nor were Hackley's influences and exhortations solely biblical in nature; careful examination of her book reveals that she also meaningfully incorporated select teachings and examples from a wide range of classical and contemporary public intellectuals, all of whom imbued their work with a sense of agency.

SPIRITUALITY AND AGENCY

Hackley's adaptation of the Anglican/Episcopalian "middle way" approach enabled her to meaningfully incorporate into her doctrine aspects of Aristotle's high-minded man; the Bible; John Ruskin's theories on work, ethics, and the arts; Ralph Waldo Emerson's musings on originality; and Frederick Douglass's views on God and justice, all the while straddling the Booker T. Washington–W. E. B. Du Bois dispute about the purpose of Black Americans' education. Aristotle's influence appears in her consistent appeal to higher-order thinking and living and to "vibrating" the good that it be returned. In *The Colored Girl Beautiful*, she writes:

> To be beautiful, one must fill her mind with beautiful thoughts.
>
> Race prejudice is the result of the vibrations of hate and anger sent out by strong minds. The world is what one makes it by the projection of one's thought. The magnetic, energetic, hearty person brings things about because he projects a stronger vibration of thought, will power and personality, whether in a hearty hand shake, sunny smile or display of interest.
>
> By helping others we help ourselves. We must learn to give, give, give, in order to receive.
>
> We must teach our minds to act upon the minds of others. We must learn the laws [of vibrations] and obey them, that we may send out strong thoughts of peace and love to counteract the overwhelming tide of thought against us. (56)

Hackley teaches her readers to be forthright, upstanding, and helpful, even in the midst of societal extremes, as well as to practice self-discipline: first, to control the self; and second, to practice high-mindedness in order to foster favorable social outcomes by gaining allies. In this, Hackley applied Aristotle's concept of high-mindedness: "The merits, then, of the high-minded man are extreme, but in his conduct he observes the proper mean. For he holds himself worthy of his exact deserts, while others either over-estimate, or else under-estimate their own merits."[12] In other words, an upstanding, thoughtful person knows what he or she deserves, knows the rules (of behavior), and behaves accordingly. An aspect of Aristotle's theory is reflected in this passage from Philippians 4:8 (KJV): "Finally, brethren, whatsoever things are true, whatsoever things are honest, whatsoever things are just, whatsoever things are pure, whatsoever things are lovely, whatsoever things are of good report; if there be any virtue, and if there be any praise, think on these things."

Hackley's emphasis on purity of thought, or high-mindedness, also extends to encompass that which Ruskin advocated. Ruskin's influence on Hackley's philosophies and on American thought in general bears consideration. A British public intellectual and the first Slade Professor of Fine Art at Oxford, Ruskin had lectured widely on subjects such as the meanings of humanity and work against the backdrop of the Industrial Revolution as well as on the forms and functions of art, broadly speaking, as evidence of what he called the "ethical state" of a country.[13] Quoting Ruskin, Hackley writes, "Ruskin's creed of work should be the universal creed. 'The man or woman who does work worth doing is the man or woman who lives and breathes his work; with whom it is ever present in his or her soul; whose ambition is to do it well and feel rewarded by the thought of having done it well. That man, that woman, puts the whole country under an obligation'" (87). Today's readers often attribute the phrase "The man or woman who does work worth doing" to President Theodore Roosevelt; actually, as Hackley indicates, Roosevelt was paraphrasing Ruskin.

Hackley's application of Ruskin appears in the following passage:

> Only a somebody "can" work well. We cannot get blood out of a turnip, and neither can a nobody "do" things. A slip-shod, half-hearted working woman is a curse to the race, because she gives it a bad reputation. She should put the "somebody" stamp on every portion of daily work and do the work as if she expected to get a diploma for it each night. She should not work mechanically or it will be drudgery. She should put pride and enthusiasm in her work, and let it reflect her inner self.
>
> A colored working girl is a racial trust. Her race burden is a heavy one. Her speech, actions and diligence constitute the measure by which the whole race is judged. (153)

Hackley's advice is reminiscent of that of Anna Julia Cooper, who proclaims, "Only the BLACK WOMAN can say 'when and where I enter, in the quiet, undisputed dignity of my womanhood, without violence and without suing or special patronage, then and there the whole *Negro race enters with me*'"[14] (italics in the original). Cooper also writes, "Let us insist then on special encouragement for the education of our women and special care in their training. Let our girls feel that we expect something more of them than that they merely look pretty and appear well in society. Teach them that there is a race with special needs which they and only they can help; that the world needs and is already asking for their trained, efficient forces. Finally, if there is an ambitious girl with pluck and brain to take the higher education, encourage her to make the most of it. Let there be the same."[15] Hackley's considerable and varied efforts echo Cooper's point of view. Understanding Aristotle, Ruskin, and Cooper as public intellectuals, Hackley, in presenting their ideas in popular forms ranging from public speeches and music performances to newspaper journalism and pamphlets, deliberately sought to place herself as a peer in their sphere.

In addition to adapting and expanding upon Ruskin's musings on work, Hackley appears to have adapted his views on the purpose and expression of human song. Ruskin declares that "with absolute precision, from highest to lowest, *the fineness of the possible art is an index of the moral purity and majesty of the emotion it expresses*. And that is so in all the arts; so that with mathematical precision, subject to no error or exception, the art of a nation, so far as it exists, is an exponent of its ethical state" (italics in the original).[16] As artist, activist, and public intellectual, Hackley takes Ruskin's concept of the "art of a nation" and pushes the boundaries to focus expressly on cultivation of the Black American spiritual—its content, history, and piety as the Black American voice to and for the world. Moreover, Hackley teaches that the colored girl beautiful "will learn that the aim of education is the aim of religion, that is, to lift one above the animal. She will endeavor to lift herself to the highest plane of true womanhood that she may pull others higher" (87). Such a plane included concentrated study and application of the spirituals, as Black American's unique evidence of human dignity and morality or high-mindedness.

For Hackley, originality is the highest expression of high-mindedness. Her emphasis on this also extends to her preaching on "Originality," which constitutes an entire chapter in *The Colored Girl Beautiful*. For Hackley, life purpose and originality were inextricably intertwined, so much so that one might even spend time "faking it," as it were, even if one has little or no chance of succeeding:

> No matter how poor a woman may be she may be original in her ideas. At first, of course, she must use the ideas of others, until she can show

> her cleverness through her adaptations, and employing her powers and gifts will add until larger powers and gifts result.
>
> She must try to get a new line of work for race advancement and dedicate herself to it. If she eliminates the Ego (Self) and will aim to work for the good of others, she will succeed.
>
> Each one should find a realm, something in which she shall be supreme, and be first. "It is better to be first in an Iberian village than second in Rome." The race needs daring original people, to think and speak.
>
> Emerson says, "Every man has a call to do something unique." (87)

Paraphrasing Emerson's "Self-Reliance," Hackley encourages readers to be authentic, not only for themselves, but also and especially for the larger community. She cautions against pursuing originality for its own sake, however:

> Originality does not include exclusiveness. Exclusiveness is deadly to originality. The exclusive woman is seldom of service to the race, and she is not always a congenial or an agreeable person. She may live so much to herself that she is uninteresting as well as selfish. She touches nothing vital excepting books and has nothing else to talk about. One should train herself to make a perfect social circle as far as she is able. The display of wealth is never original—only vulgar—and only an inborn vulgar woman would place her so-called friends at a disadvantage by entertaining them beyond their power of return.
>
> It is pathetic to watch the social efforts—"climbing"—of people with only money "sans" brains and originality. (93)

Hackley warns readers against becoming so focused on being authentic—developing individual talents and satisfying individual curiosities—that they ignore their responsibility to rejuvenate and advance not only themselves, but the larger community.

Emerson's "Self-Reliance" emphasizes a similar view of authenticity, minus Hackley's emphasis on community. In this essay, Emerson advises, "Insist on yourself; never imitate. Your own gift you can every moment with the cumulative force of a whole life's cultivation; but of the adopted talent of another, you have only an extemporaneous, half possession. Shakespeare will never be made by the study of Shakespeare. Do that which is assigned you, and you cannot hope too much or dare too much."[17] Developed against the backdrop of popular blackface minstrelsy and crude vaudevillian depictions of Black Americans, Hackley's philosophy necessarily included racial uplift because the lowest common denominator among Black people was often considered representative of the race. Taken in this light, then, Hackley's insistence upon Black authenticity is quite bold, indeed.

Hackley's views on authenticity echo what Søren Kierkegaard considered the authentic self: the expression of one's "ultimate commitment." According to Kierkegaard, "The self is defined by concrete expressions through which one manifests oneself in the world and thereby constitutes one's identity over time." In his view, "becoming what one is" and evading despair and hollowness are not matters of solitary introspection, but rather matters of passionate commitment to a relation to something outside oneself that bestows one's life with meaning. For Kierkegaard as a religious thinker, this ultimate commitment was his defining relation to God.[18]

Hackley's "ultimate commitment" was to educate Black American girls and women as representatives and leaders of what she calls in *The Colored Girl Beautiful* "a persecuted race" (130). In the book's concluding chapter, titled "The Colored Mother Beautiful," she says that, at the point of death,

> The peace and contentment that comes from having done her whole duty gives [the colored mother beautiful] a spiritual beauty of countenance that comes from the other world; the habit of right living through right thought, reflects in her face and gives her a physical beauty that comes in no other way.
>
> At the last, the Still Small Voice Whispers, "Well done, thou good and faithful servant of a persecuted race. You have done what you could. No one can do more. Receive your eternal reward," and the face is illumined with the beauty that shall endure forever. (206)

Hackley taught that real beauty results from a lifetime of right living: commitment to developing self and society to the best of one's abilities, with God and conscience on one's side.

On the matter of God and conscience, Hackley paraphrases Frederick Douglass when she writes, "With God, one is a majority" (87). Hackley must have read Douglass's 1852 speech given at the National Free Soil Convention in which he spoke about the Fugitive Slave Law:

> Could a law be made to pass away any of your individual rights? No. And so neither can a law be made to pass away the right of the Black man. This is more important than most of you seem to think. . . . It has been said that we ought to take the position to gain the greatest number of voters, but that is wrong.
>
> Numbers should not be looked to so much as right. The man who is right is a majority. He who has God and conscience on his side, has a

> majority against the universe. Though he does not represent the present state, he represents the future state. If he does not represent what we are, he represents what we ought to be.[19]

Here, Douglass invokes natural law, which states that a man, whatever his color, has the same natural rights as any other and that such law supersedes government law. By extension, he also says that a voting bloc, however fervent, cannot ensure that which is right; rather, he says, only that which is ethical and therefore, like natural law, also above governmental law, prevails. That Hackley paraphrases Douglass's statement "He who has God and conscience on his side, has a majority against the universe" should not surprise her readers; Hackley had been married to an attorney who likely had copies of these documents in his personal library to which she would have had access. In addition, such topics were certainly among those discussed among the Black American elite in salons like those in Europe during the Enlightenment. By quoting Douglass and representing what he calls the "future state," Hackley invokes his overall point: that Black Americans, regardless of the laws of the state or politics, have the same natural rights as any other human beings and thus the right to self-determination, as long as such self-determination is morally grounded. By the time *The Colored Girl Beautiful* was published, fifty years had passed since the abolition of slavery in the United States; moreover, Hackley, feeling her mortality and nearing her own year of jubilee, determined to ensure that the next generations of Black American girls and women would (pro)claim their rightful place in society.

MADAME E. AZALIA SMITH HACKLEY'S JUBILEE

In Black American culture, the year of Jubilee—the fiftieth year—is recognized as both a cultural and women's milestone. Leviticus 25:10 (KJV) says, "And you shall consecrate the fiftieth year, and proclaim liberty throughout the land to all its inhabitants. It shall be a jubilee for you, when each of you shall return to his property and each of you shall return to his clan." Fifty years after the abolition of slavery in the United States, Black Americans celebrated a tenuous freedom. Similarly, Black American women at or near the age of fifty celebrate their tenuous freedom—freedom from childbearing concerns, coupled with the fact that they are considered to have reached their highest mastery of skills and execution of their chosen vocation and/or avocation—a reward often claimed against the backdrop of considerable health and financial challenges. Driven by the concept of cultural jubilee and her own impending fiftieth birthday and frustrated by the lack of overall race progress, Hackley's *The Colored Girl*

Beautiful pushed for Black Americans, and Black American women in particular, not only to keep their eyes on the freedom prize but to (pro)claim it.

Advocating Black American personal and social responsibility, Hackley's book embodies the teachings of Titus 2:1–10 (KJV):

> [1] But speak thou the things which become sound doctrine:
> [2] That the aged men be sober, grave, temperate, sound in faith, in charity, in patience.
> [3] The aged women likewise, that they be in behaviour as becometh holiness, not false accusers, not given to much wine, teachers of good things;
> [4] That they may teach the young women to be sober, to love their husbands, to love their children,
> [5] To be discreet, chaste, keepers at home, good, obedient to their own husbands, that the word of God be not blasphemed.
> [6] Young men likewise exhort to be sober minded.
> [7] In all things shewing thyself a pattern of good works: in doctrine shewing uncorruptness, gravity, sincerity,
> [8] Sound speech, that cannot be condemned; that he that is of the contrary part may be ashamed, having no evil thing to say of you.
> [9] Exhort servants to be obedient unto their own masters, and to please them well in all things; not answering again;
> [10] Not purloining, but shewing all good fidelity; that they may adorn the doctrine of God our Saviour in all things.

According to Hackley, Black people rely too much on God and not enough on their own efforts, expressed this way in *The Colored Girl Beautiful*: "As a rule colored people expect entirely too much help from God. We must help ourselves more" (128). She reasons that God gave Black people common sense, innate physical and musical beauty, and originality—all worth cultivating not only to elevate self but especially to elevate the Black community. She explains, "Each Negro carries a three-fold burden; first, his own personal burden; second, the burden of his posterity; and third, the burden of the race. These follow each other and are dependent upon each other. God has given him physical strength, a strong backbone and strong shoulders to carry the heavy yoke of the three-fold burden, as well as a wealth of spirituality to cheer him and keep his heart light, along the way of life" (129). Accordingly, she commands, "The religion of the Negro should prompt less study of the desires of the personal Ego, and should teach other nations to respect his race, or, his religion is not spiritualizing as it could and should spiritualize."

Hackley's doctrine, which recognizes both God and the "Ego," an aspect of Freudian psychoanalysis, is not surprising. A lifelong learner and preacher-teacher, Hackley made it her business to acquaint herself with a wide variety of emerging trains of thought. In the years leading up to the publication of *The Colored Girl Beautiful* in 1916, American interest in Freudian psychology had sharply risen. In 1909, Freud visited the United States, and on the heels of his visit, related institutions and publications cascaded into existence: according to Ruth Hunsberger, "In 1910 the Psychopathological Association was organized in Washington, D.C., followed by the New York Psychoanalytic Society in 1911 and the American Psychoanalytic Association in Baltimore in 1914. In 1917, the Johns Hopkins Medical School offered regularly cataloged courses in psychoanalysis—the first medical school to do so."[20] In her ministry, Hackley briefly mentions Freud's concept of the Ego to show her engagement with contemporary thought, balance religious fervor, and simultaneously serve as evidence of her membership among the learned Black elite and status as an American.

Hackley's "gospel" also anticipates womanist theologies. Katie G. Cannon's "The Emergence of Black Feminist Consciousness" argues that Black feminist consciousness and related moral agency can be fully understood and appreciated only when taken in historical context.[21] Cannon states that the work of Black womanist theologians is to take up such challenges as "The Struggle for Human Dignity" and "The Struggle Against White Hypocrisy."[22] For historical context, she provides a womanist theological perspective on incongruities during the Jim Crow era: "Blacks were assigned a fixed place as an inferior species of humanity" and "Jim Crowism was contrary to nature and against the will of God"; yet "Was not the essence of the Gospel mandate a call to eradicate affliction, despair, and systems of injustice?"[23] Cannon shows how Black women, engaged in what contemporary scholars now recognize as womanist theology, championed the Gospel, simultaneously establishing themselves as uniquely positioned to fight against injustices while fighting for Black women's dignity and the health and strength of Black families and communities. By word and by deed, Hackley was such a woman.

Delores S. Williams's *Sisters in the Wilderness* offers another perspective: "Liberation is an ultimate, but in the meantime survival and prosperity must be the experience of our [Black] people. And God has had and continues to have a word to say about the survival and quality of life of descendants of female slaves."[24] Anticipating and embodying several aspects of Cannon's and Williams's philosophies, respectively, Hackley's "gospel" called for the eradication of Jim Crowism and related socioeconomic ills, largely through the focused, applied spirituality, industry, and agency of Black women.

Hackley's efforts also should be considered in relation to Black women's religious leadership traditions. TeResa Green reports, for example, that "No Black women prior to the late nineteenth and mid-twentieth centuries were ever formally endorsed or ordained as preachers and pastors by any denomination. Instead, they were obligated to take alternate paths to the ministry as exhorters, teachers, missionaries, evangelists, religious writers, and wives of clergymen."[25] Moreover, Green states that Black mothers, given their roles during the periods of slavery and Reconstruction, have an essential role to play in the spiritual and socioeconomic uplift of Black communities. A self-appointed lay preacher, Hackley took all these "alternate paths" to spread her understanding of the Gospel. While she did not give birth to children, she nevertheless became a surrogate mother to young Black women classical singers, as well as to the intended and extended readership of her book, *The Colored Girl Beautiful*. Moreover, her marriage to an attorney was socially akin to having married a clergyman.[26] Hackley openly acknowledged select theological, theoretical, musical, and spiritual predecessors, especially focusing on the roles of Black mothers as the backbone of Black families and communities. Her insistence on acknowledging such varied cultural inheritances deliberately countered prevailing prejudices against Black intellect and piety. Taken as a whole, Hackley's efforts contribute to our understanding of applied womanist theology and Black women's religious leadership.

CONCLUSION: "GREY MATTER" AND BLACK WOMEN'S UPLIFT

While marginalized due to race and gender, Madame Hackley nevertheless determined to place herself intellectually, if not socially, among the great thinkers, current issues, and arguments of the time. Her audience, comprised largely of formerly enslaved persons with little to no formal education, expected her to know and teach a great deal about the larger world and its workings, and she endeavored not to disappoint them nor allow herself to be intellectually pigeon-holed into talking solely about race or gender. Indeed, according to Hackley in *The Colored Girl Beautiful*, the "gray matter" in a Black woman's head is the same as that in any woman's head, and it can be cultivated to command itself to either uplift or drag down society, "according to the concentration of thought, and resulting habits" (20). Hackley, guided by the word of God and her own curiosity and talents, commanded her gray matter to uplift self and society, and she exhorted, inspired, and empowered her audiences to do the same. As she saw it, God allows people to know and grow their worth. Whether they (pro)claim and cultivate it is up to them. She expressly endeavored to give Black American girls and women the dignity, inspiration, roadmap, know-how, and agency to (pro)claim their rightful places as servants of God, citizens of the world, and shapers of destiny.

NOTES

1. Emma Azalia Smith Hackley, *The Colored Girl Beautiful* (Kansas City, MO: Burton Publishing Co., 1916), 124. Subsequent references to this book appear parenthetically in the text.

2. Rayford Logan, *The Negro in American Life and Thought: The Nadir, 1877–1901* (New York: Dial Press, 1954), 79.

3. Lisa Pertillar Brevard, *A Biography of Edwin Henry Hackley, 1859–1940, African American Attorney and Activist* (Lewiston, NY: Edwin Mellen Press, 2003), 31–32.

4. After Azalia's death in 1922, Edwin Hackley continued to write and publish, one of his most important books being *Hackley and Harrison's Guide*, a precursor of, and blueprint for, the Green Book, a travel manual designed specifically for Black people traveling by car, to inform them of places where they could stop for food, gasoline, and lodging during the era of Jim Crow and de facto racial segregation. See Brevard, *Biography of Edwin Henry Hackley*, 79–157.

5. Lisa Pertillar Brevard, *A Biography of E. Azalia Smith Hackley, 1867–1922, African American Singer and Social Activist* (Lewiston, NY: Edwin Mellen Press, 2001), 33.

6. Brevard, *Biography of Edwin Henry Hackley*.

7. In 1913, after a polite divorce from Azalia, he wrote and staged in 1913 in Philadelphia *The Ambassador: A Play in Three Acts*. See Brevard, *Biography of Edwin Henry Hackley*, 39–64.

8. Brevard, *Biography of E. Azalia Smith Hackley*, 157–215.

9. James Weldon Johnson, *The Autobiography of an Ex-Colored Man* (Boston: Sherman, French, 1912), 85.

10. Lisa Pertillar Brevard, *Madame E. Azalia Hackley's* The Colored Girl Beautiful *(1916)* (New Orleans: Monarch Baby Publishing, 2004), 57.

11. Quoted in Juanita Karpf, "For Their Musical Uplift: Emma Azalia Hackley and Voice Culture," *African-American Communities. International Journal of Community Music* 4, no. 5 (2011): 250.

12. Aristotle, *The Nicomachean Ethics of Aristotle*, Book IV, trans. and ed. Robert Williams (London: Longman's, Greene, 1876), 96.

13. John Ruskin, "The Relation of Art to Morals," *Wikisource*, accessed November 20, 2022, https://en.wikisource.org/wiki/The_Relation_of_Art_to_Morals.

14. Anna Julia Cooper, *A Voice from the South* (Xenia, OH: Aldine Printing House, 1892; Chapel Hill, NC: Documenting the American South, Academic Affairs Library, University of North Carolina at Chapel Hill, 2000), 31, https://docsouth.unc.edu/church/cooper/cooper.html.

15. Cooper, *Voice from the South*, 78.

16. Ruskin, "Relation of Art to Morals."

17. Ralph Waldo Emerson, "Self-Reliance," in *Self-Reliance and Other Essays*, ed. Stanley Appelbaum (New York: Dover, 1993), 35.

18. Søren Kierkegaard, qtd. in Somogy Varga and Charles Guignon, "Authenticity," in *The Stanford Encyclopedia of Philosophy*, ed. Edward N. Zalta, Spring 2020, https://plato.stanford.edu/archives/spr2020/entries/authenticity/.

19. Frederick Douglass, "The Fugitive Slave Law," Speech to the National Free Soil Convention at Pittsburgh, August 11, 1852, https://rbscp.lib.rochester.edu/4385.

20. Ruth Pedersen Hunsberger, "The American Reception of Sigmund Freud," 2005, http://www.hunsberger.org/freud-america.htm.

21. Katie G. Cannon, "The Emergence of Black Feminist Consciousness," in *Feminist Interpretation of the Bible*, ed. Lettie M. Russell (Louisville, KY: Westminster John Knox Press, 1985), 30.

22. Cannon, "Emergence," 31, 33.

23. Cannon, "Emergence," 30.

24. Delores S. Williams, *Sisters in the Wilderness: The Challenge of Womanist God-Talk* (Maryknoll, NY: Orbis Books, 1993), 245.

25. TeResa Green, "A Gendered Spirit: Race, Class, and Sex in the African American Church," *Race, Gender & Class* 10, no. 1 (2003): 122.

26. While a member of the clergy is obliged to preach and follow the laws of God, an attorney is obliged to observe and act in accordance with the law as the gospel of the land.

SELECTED BIBLIOGRAPHY

Aristotle. *The Nicomachean Ethics of Aristotle*, Book IV. Translated and edited by Robert Williams. London: Longman's, Greene, 1876.

Brevard, Lisa Pertillar. *A Biography of E. Azalia Smith Hackley, 1867–1922, African American Singer and Social Activist*. Lewiston, NY: Edwin Mellen Press, 2001.

Brevard, Lisa Pertillar. *A Biography of Edwin Henry Hackley, 1859–1940, African American Attorney and Activist*. Lewiston, NY: Edwin Mellen Press, 2003.

Brevard, Lisa Pertillar. *Madame E. Azalia Hackley's* The Colored Girl Beautiful *(1916)*. New Orleans: Monarch Baby Publishing, 2004.

Cannon, Katie G. "The Emergence of Black Feminist Consciousness." In *Feminist Interpretation of the Bible*," edited by Letty M. Russell, 30–40. Louisville, KY: Westminster John Knox Press, 1985.

Colored American Magazine 15, no. 3 (March 1909). https://nmaahc.si.edu/object/nmaahc_2014.63.64.5.

Cooper, Anna Julia. *A Voice from the South*. Xenia, OH: Aldine Printing House, 1892. Documenting the American South, Academic Affairs Library, University of North Carolina at Chapel Hill, 2000. https://docsouth.unc.edu/church/cooper/cooper.html.

Dett, Robert Nathaniel. *Listen to the Lambs*. 1914. https://imslp.org/wiki/Listen_to_the_Lambs_(Dett%2C_Robert_Nathaniel).

"Didn't My Lord Deliver Daniel?" Arr. Moses Hogan. Accessed January 12, 2019. https://www.musicnotes.com/sheetmusic/mtd.asp?ppn=MN0135169.

Douglass, Frederick. "The Fugitive Slave Law: Speech to the National Free Soil Convention at Pittsburgh, August 11, 1852." https://rbscp.lib.rochester.edu/4385.

Du Bois, W. E. B. *The Souls of Black Folk*. 1903. Project Gutenberg, January 29, 2008. Ebook #408. https://www.gutenberg.org/files/408/408-h/408-h.htm.

Emerson, Ralph Waldo. "Self-Reliance." In *Self-Reliance and Other Essays*, edited by Stanley Appelbaum. New York: Dover, 1993.

Finkelman, Paul, ed. *Encyclopedia of Black American History, 1619–1895: From the Colonial Period to the Age of Frederick Douglass*, Vol. 2. New York: Oxford University Press, 2006.

Fisk Jubilee Singers, performers. "Wade in the Water." *Wade in the Water, Vol. 1: Black American Spirituals—The Concert Tradition.* Washington, DC: Smithsonian Folkways Records CD, 1994, Track 7.

Florida A&M University Concert Choir, performers. "Ezekiel Saw the Wheel." *Wade in the Water, Vol. 1: Black American Spirituals—The Concert Tradition.* Washington, DC: Smithsonian Folkways Records CD, 1994, Track 17.

The Garretsonian 1, no. 1 (November 1908).

Green, TeResa. "A Gendered Spirit: Race, Class, and Sex in the African American Church." *Race, Gender & Class* 10, no. 1 (2003): 115–28.

Hackley, Emma Azalia Smith. *The Colored Girl Beautiful.* Kansas City, MO: Burton Publishing Company, 1916.

Howard University Chamber Choir, performers. "Wade in the Water." *Wade in the Water, Vol. 1: Black American Spirituals—The Concert Tradition.* Washington, DC: Smithsonian Folkways Records CD, 1994, Track 19.

Hunsberger, Ruth Pedersen. "The American Reception of Sigmund Freud." 2005. http://www.hunsberger.org/freud-america.htm.

Johnson, James Weldon. *The Autobiography of an Ex-Colored Man.* Boston: Sherman, French, 1912.

Karpf, Juanita. "For Their Musical Uplift: Emma Azalia Hackley and Voice Culture in African-American Communities." *International Journal of Community Music* 4, no. 5 (2011): 237–56.

Logan, Rayford. *The Negro in American Life and Thought: The Nadir, 1877–1901.* New York: Dial Press, 1954.

Ruskin, John. "The Relation of Art to Morals." *Wikisource.* 2008. https://en.wikisource.org/wiki/The_Relation_of_Art_to_Morals

Sneezby-Koch. "Azalia Smith Hackley—Musical Prodigy and Pioneering Journalist." *History Colorado,* March 27, 2017. https://www.historycolorado.org/

"Steal Away." Arr. Moses Hogan. Accessed November 20, 2022. https://www.musicnotes.com/sheetmusic/mtd.asp?ppn=MN0139363.

Truth, Sojourner. "Ain't I a Woman?" In *Sojourner Truth: Ain't I a Woman?* Washington, DC.

Varga, Somogy, and Charles Guignon. "Authenticity." In *The Stanford Encyclopedia of Philosophy,* edited by Edward N. Zalta. Spring 2020. https://plato.stanford.edu/archives/spr2020/entries/authenticity/.

Washington, Booker T. *Up from Slavery: An Autobiography.* Garden City, NY: Doubleday & Company, Inc., 1901; Documenting the American South, Academic Affairs Library, University of North Carolina at Chapel Hill, 1997. https://docsouth.unc.edu/fpn/washington/washing.html.

Williams, Delores S. *Sisters in the Wilderness: The Challenge of Womanist God-Talk.* Maryknoll, NY: Orbis Books, 1993.

Women's Rights National Historical Park, National Park Service. "Sojourner Truth: Ain't I a Woman?" Accessed November 20, 2022. https://www.nps.gov/articles/sojourner-truth.htm.

Chapter 6

MOTHERS AND THE GOD OF THE OPPRESSED

Carrie Williams Clifford and a Literary Theology of Black Freedom

P. JANE SPLAWN

INTRODUCTION: GOD IN HERSELF

Carrie Williams Clifford was an outspoken African American voice for racial and gender equality in the early decades of the twentieth century.[1] Moving within the influential Black social circles of Cleveland, Ohio, and Washington, DC, she was attuned to issues of concern to the African American community and boldly presented a vision of a strong Black womanhood for the new century. From articles such as "Votes for Children," in which she argued that, by empowering women with the right to vote, children would be the immediate beneficiaries, to her poetry collections *Race Rhymes* (1911) and *The Widening Light* (1922), she immersed herself in the pivotal concerns of the era: advancing the respectability of Black women alongside that of the race, promoting strong Black families, and providing a strong educational base for Black children. While she would not have claimed the term "womanist" for herself (conceptualized in the mid-1980s by womanist theologian Katie G. Cannon), her interests and concerns were consonant with that of other proto-womanist thinkers of the era. When we consider her body of work, it is clear that Clifford understood God to be closely aligned with what James Cone would later identify as the "God of the oppressed."[2] As some liberation theologians have argued, Christ, who was born in humble circumstances, shares a special affinity with the disenfranchised and the oppressed. For Clifford, God is not only a God of justice, but an advocate of equality. To follow God, then, is to stand up for racial and gender concerns. Clifford expresses her religious views by deploying themes of service and uplift in her writings, from which may be gleaned her literary theology of Black freedom.

The history of the United States, like that of other nations with diverse cultures, consists of an evolving mosaic in which new and heretofore unseen pieces are repeatedly added. Clifford's theology provides an important precursor to the liberatory theology prominent in the work of Black theologian James Cone in the 1970s. However, her work also provides a foundation for womanist theologians including Katie G. Cannon and Jacquelyn Grant in the 1980s and 1990s, revealing that, for Black women, liberation and theology have a long history and tradition of being intertwined. Clifford and other Black women activist theologians expand the texture and fabric of the American mosaic to reveal the hauntingly beautiful tapestry that constitutes this country. By doing so, they uncover strength where none had been imagined, a strong faith in the "God in [themselves]" and a belief in a world of unseen possibilities.

Clifford was born and raised in Chillicothe, Ohio. Though not much is known about her early life, historical evidence reveals that she was an honors student who, upon graduation, was prevented from teaching in the Ohio Public School System because of her race. For this reason, she became a teacher in Parkersburg, West Virginia, in 1883. She subsequently moved to Cleveland where she married William H. Clifford and became the editor of *Sowing for Others to Reap: A Collection of Papers of Vital Importance to the Race for the Ohio Federation of Colored Women's Clubs*.[3] Later, she moved with her husband and sons to Washington, DC. There, she set up her home as a "Sunday saloon" for various writers and intellectuals, with nearby Howard University providing access to many of the great thinkers of the period, including Mary Church Terrell, Alain Locke, Georgia Douglas Johnson, and W. E. B. Du Bois.[4] As Elizabeth McHenry has persuasively argued, these literary societies provided the foundations of literacy within the African American community in the nineteenth and early twentieth centuries, with figures like writer and literary salon host Georgia Douglas Johnson serving as a literary midwife for a number of aspiring writers in the first part of the twentieth century.[5] That Clifford was seen as an important voice is clear from her being selected as a contributor to a roundtable on women's suffrage titled "Votes for Children," which appeared in the 1915 edition of *The Crisis: A Record of the Darker Races*, the official publication of the NAACP.[6] The contributors to that column included a number of African American luminaries, including Alice Dunbar Nelson, Rev. Francis J. Grimke, Charles Chesnutt, James Weldon Johnson, William Stanley Braithwaite, Nannie Helen Burroughs, Josephine St. Pierre Ruffin, Blanche K. Bruce, and Mary Church Terrell. On key issues of women's suffrage, anti-lynching, and the racial stereotyping of Black people in popular, incendiary films like *The Birth of a Nation*, Clifford added her voice to the Black community's public outcry against injustice.

Indeed, by the early part of the twentieth century, Clifford had become what womanist theologian Cheryl Townsend Gilkes refers to as a "community mother," a role that Gilkes avers has not been fully addressed.[7] As she defines them, community mothers, according to West African tradition, were strong "mothers" who, alongside men, became the most powerful voices to speak out against inequality and injustice in society.[8] Given the numerous references to mothers in Clifford's poetry and essays, it is clear that she saw women as central to both the communal and spiritual needs of the Black community. Arguably for Clifford, to empower Black women is, by extension, to empower subsequent generations of African American women and men.

As noted, themes of service and uplift undergird much of Clifford's writing, frequently highlighting the key roles that Black women have played as community leaders, public intellectuals, and mothers. For Clifford, community mothers in particular were not only political leaders but also spiritual leaders in the Black community. In the poem "To Howard University," a sonnet intended to celebrate the intellectual and community achievements of the university, for example, God's love manifests itself via the very existence of the university, which Clifford presents as a loving mother that nurtures and sustains her students.[9] Additionally, she elevates the role of mothers in the poem "Little Mother," in which race and gender intersect as Clifford decries the savage lynching of an eight-months pregnant Mary Turner in Georgia in 1918.[10] The epigraph to the poem announces that "Little Mother" was written "upon the lynching of Mary Turner" and presents a "dark-faced mother" "trembl[ing]" in fear of the lives of her husband, her unborn child, and her own at the hands of "pale-faced demons." Here, Clifford's vision of strong Black womanhood encompasses her activism and service; as a Black woman, she must add her voice to this terrible crime against another Black woman and her family.

Clifford also speaks truth to power in her poetry and essays. For example, in the poem "Shrines," in which she distinguishes between false versus true shrines, she names her "shrine" as the "cross" on which John Brown's body was hanged. An icon of social justice within the Black community because of his armed stance against slavery resulting in his capture at Harpers Ferry and subsequent hanging, Brown was not only embraced by the African American community, but his "story" was enfolded into the African American oral tradition of the late nineteenth and early twentieth centuries. At the same time, Clifford is unafraid of calling out D. W. Griffiths and Thomas Dixon for producing hateful, inflammatory images of African Americans in their creative works like Griffiths's film *The Birth of a Nation* (1915) and Dixon's novel *The Clansman* (1905), upon which *The Birth of a Nation* was based. In her work as in her social life, she modeled middle-class African American core values of service and uplift. Even so, she was undaunted in speaking out against injustice during the era of Jim Crow in her two volumes of poetry. Hence, public outcries against injustice coupled with a strong sense of service formed the bases of Clifford's literary theology of Black freedom.

CRITIQUE OF RACIAL INEQUALITY

In recent decades, Clifford's poetry has been rediscovered owing largely to G. K. Hall's collection entitled *African-American Women Writers, 1910–1940* and to the re-issuing of *The Widening Light*.[11] However, for decades Clifford's voice has been overlooked as a public intellectual. There are some notable differences in the poetic style of *Race Rhymes*, her first volume, and *The Widening Light*, her second volume. In fact, at least one copy of *Race Rhymes* contains Clifford's own handwritten revisions to the text.[12] These revisions appear to reflect Clifford's continued efforts to hone her craft as a writer. Clifford published *Race Rhymes* in 1911 with R. L. Pendleton in Washington, DC.[13] She then published *The Widening Light* with Walter Reid Company in Boston in 1922.[14] In the preface to her first volume, Clifford makes the traditional apology for the "brochure" that she is "giving to the world, adding that she makes no claim to unusual poetic excellence or literary brilliance."[15] Referring to herself in the third person, Clifford states that "the author" of each of the poems in *Race Rhymes* "has been called forth by some significant event or condition in the history of the Negro in America." Echoing Chaucer's "go litel book," Clifford says that she "sends these lines forth," but that she does so "with the prayers that they may change some evil heart, right some wrong and raise some arm strong to deliver."[16] She names her mother as the source that undergirds her activism in the volume's "Dedication": "To My Mother . . . [whom] the gentle Saviour called . . . Home on high with saints to dwell."[17] Linking her mother's influence to her own desire for social change, Clifford invokes a Black ancestral mother throughout each of her two volumes of poetry. For Clifford and other Black women writers then as well as now, an ancestral Black mother is not only primal, but attends to her daughters in times of physical and spiritual need. Arguably, elevating the position of mothers with the Black community was not inconsistent with the Christian ideals of the Black community.

In her handwritten notes to the poem "America" in *Race Rhymes*, Clifford revises the line "America is not another name for opportunity / To all her sons!" to read "America! famed land of liberty, / Is not another name for opportunity / To all her sons!"[18] The speaker identifies her audience in the poem as "Christians," who for "too long your pretense have your acts belied."[19] Cautioning her white audience that Black people's "fate is irrevocably bound up with yours," the speaker reminds them that, in spite of "degrading slavery," Black people have been "humble, patient, loyal" to America, having fought in each of the nation's major wars. In the last two stanzas of the poem, Clifford raises rhetorical questions that are followed by a warning in the final stanza. She asks her Christian audience whether race is a sin or a crime sufficient to justify the "unjust laws" against African Americans and reminds them that, if this is so, then they are guilty of "despis[ing]" God's "handiwork"—a sin that they will repay "with generous measure overflowing." If retribution does not happen now, the speaker avers that it will certainly come in the hereafter, where

> For every act of cruelty you've done,
> For every groan you have from him [the African American] wrung,
> For every infamy by him endured,
> He [God] will you all repay, be thou assured!
> Not here alone ere time shall cease to be,
> But likewise There, through all eternity.[20]

A few decades later, Langston Hughes would express similar sentiments in his political poem "Let America Be America Again" by having his speaker attest, "America never was America to me."[21]

In "A Reply to Thos. Dixon," a poem addressed to the North Carolina novelist who used derogatory racial stereotypes to portray African Americans, Clifford's speaker says that Dixon spreads a "scandalous tale" about Black Americans because he dislikes the idea of Black progress. Even so, the speaker claims that Blacks will not lessen their struggle, but instead "will die for Justice, God and human right" by

> . . . confound[ing] theory with fact,
> *Prove* by thought, by word, by deed,
> The falseness of the vile attack.[22] (italics in the original)

Additionally, Dixon was not only a staunch advocate of "racial purity," but he portrayed African American men in his works as sexual predators who have an unbridled lust for white women. Clifford's torch against dehumanizing Black people in this and other poems would be taken up by future generations of African Americans.

"Atlanta's Shame," which succeeds "A Reply to Thos. Dixon" in *Race Rhymes*, can be read as a sustained critique of lynching, which occurs, the speaker argues, because of lies and unfair stereotypes. This poem was written after the Atlanta riot of September 22, 1906, in which more than twenty-five Black

Americans and two white Americans died. Clifford handwrites "(Written After the Riot)" below the title in one copy of her collection.[23] Casting the city of Atlanta as a haughty, disdainful woman, the speaker in the poem contrasts the "queenly" status of the city to the "bitter hate" that it exhibits toward its Black citizens. In spite of this, the speaker argues, Atlanta's Black citizens have fared well—perhaps referencing the success of higher education institutions like Spelman College, Morehouse College, Clark College, and Atlanta University as well as that of businesses along "Sweet Auburn Avenue," known for its prosperous Black-owned offices and establishments. The speaker claims that the city hates Black people because they "remind her of her shames" and because she resents their successes in spite of the racial injustice. Clifford concludes the poem by limning white Atlantans' three days of rioting against Black residents as "a carnival of crime."

"The Jim Crow Car" continues Clifford's lament against racial inequality in the United States. The speaker calls out the system of racially segregated seating on public transportation as "an institution infamous and more degrading far / Than aught I know of" in which "the good, the bad, the criminal are herded there together."[24] The speaker ends the third stanza of the poem by referring to this segregated car as "the 'Jim Crow' cage"—a jab at racialized institutions in which Black Americans are given the same accommodations as animals. Clifford's speaker cautions the wealthy and powerful even as she challenges those who are impoverished: the powerful are not justified because of their strength, and the disenfranchised must not "yield [their] God-given right to might."[25]

UPLIFT, CELEBRATION OF RACE, WOMEN

Clifford's activism in *Race Rhymes* continues in *The Widening Light* (1922), her second poetry collection, which she dedicates "To My Race." It includes such poems as "The Birth of a Nation," "Little Mother," and "Silent Protest Parade." The book's epigraph comes from *The Crisis*: "But above all comes the New Spirit," and the collection as a whole continues Clifford's outcry against injustice.[26] For instance, each of the poems in "Three Sonnets" is strategically crafted with the titles "Appeal," "Demand," and "Warning."[27] "Warning," the final sonnet in the sequence, forebodes the natural sequence of events should the speaker's "appeal" and "demand" not be met. Addressed to white America, "Appeal" makes the case of how Black people have given their lives as well as their brawn for the building of America:

> And tho' you scorned and spurned us, tried the more
> To love and serve you better than before.

Your children we have nursed, your evening meal
Set forth: your crops have reaped, your acres tilled,
Your burdens borne, your enemies have killed.[28]

"Demand" moves from the historical context in "Appeal" to make the case for Black equality, referencing the emergence of the Niagara Movement (1905–1908), a civil rights organization founded by W. E. B. Du Bois and Monroe Trotter that is regarded as the precursor to the NAACP:

Who with the volume of Niagara's roar
And strength with which her giant waters pour,
Demand, with vigor which shall not abate
All the prerogatives which are our due
Without regard to race or creed or hue.[29] (italics in the original)

The Niagara Movement got its name from Niagara Falls, Canada, the initial meeting place of the organization. At its first formal meeting in Harpers Ferry, Virginia, in 1906, a number of Black women were in attendance.[30] Finally, in "Warning," the last of the three sonnets, the speaker makes plain the small sore of perceived injustice that can fester into a gaping wound: "A tiny tendril creviced in the rock, / In time will burst apart a granite block."[31] As associates of Du Bois, the Cliffords understood the need for organized responses to racial injustice. That Carrie Clifford claimed her right not only to speak out but to feel outraged is evident in her two volumes of poetry, as these lines from "Warning" suggest.

Just as Clifford decries lynching and other terrorist acts against the African American community in her poetry, she also calls out gender inequality. For example, in "A Dream of Democracy," Clifford's speaker has an apocalyptic vision in which she sees injustice, cruelty, crime, and rape as the "debris" left behind over the course of human history.[32] This debris must, then, be named as such and discarded from the community, so that everyone can live in a safe and thriving environment. Indeed, speaking from the vantage point of the early decades of the twentieth century, Clifford signals "the problem of the color line" that her friend and contemporary Du Bois had identified earlier, in 1903.[33]

Other connections to Du Bois also appear in *The Widening Light*. For example, there are multiple references to "the veil" in such poems as "Soul-Growth," "Negro Players on Broadway," and "Within the Veil."[34] Here, Clifford construes the veil as unspoken codes within the Black community maintained for self-preservation. There is an aspect of mystery associated with the veil. In "Quest," for example, Clifford's speaker affirms,

My soul contains all thought, all mystery,
All wisdom of the Great Infinite Mind:
This to discover, I must voyage far,
At last to find it in my pulsing heart.[35]

This speaker is aware of and appreciates the mystery, but understands that only through deep inner reflection can she begin to penetrate "the Great Infinite Mind," whereas in Clifford's poem "Shrines," the speaker avers that her shrine is "the bitter cross where John Brown hung."[36] Clifford shows that she embraces those whites who have been willing to lay down their lives for the liberation of enslaved Americans. She likens her cross with Brown's in recognition that struggle is not easy, or to echo Frederick Douglass, it is necessary to bring about progress.[37] Yet the symbolism of the cross in the poem suggests that Clifford, like Brown, sees herself as sharing in Christ's struggle; however, that struggle for both Clifford and Brown was against what they saw as the evil of racial injustice and inequality. Similarly, in her poem "Like You," Clifford foreshadows 1970s and 1980s liberation theologians' views of the God of the oppressed in which parallels between the racially and economically oppressed are made to the life of Jesus. In "A Toast to Africa: Christmas 1920," for instance, she presents the view of Christ as being on the side of the oppressed.[38] Clifford writes:

I drink to my Race on this epochal morn,
Remembering the Christ-child who came lowly-born,—
Was despised, crucified and rejected of men,
But now to whom honor and glory—Amen!

In this poem, Clifford thus makes an argument similar to that of womanist systematic theologian Jacquelyn Grant in *White Women's Christ and Black Women's Jesus* and James Cone in *God of the Oppressed*.[39] Her vision is jubilatory in that the speaker seems to project, by extension, a higher position for African Americans in the future—if not in this world, then in the world to come.

To be sure, Clifford's vision of the future for African Americans situates Black women as the "cornerstones" of a stable and progressive African American community. Her view is in keeping with a long-standing tradition within that African American community in which there existed a Black communal desire for its "elder mothers" to provide wise counsel. Marita Bonner, African American writer and Clifford's contemporary, deploys an older Black woman, revealingly named "Cornerstone," in her 1928 play *The Purple Flower* to provide the voice of wisdom as well as stability to a Black community in crisis. Scholars have also noted this cultural trope within many African American communities. While discussing the roles of Black women in the church and community, Cheryl Townsend Gilkes argues that

> in both sacred and secular community settings, there are powerful and respected older women addressed by the title "Mother." In secular settings, such mothers are often the heads of Black women's organizations and hold positions of power and authority in more broadly based community and civil rights organizations. In sacred spaces, particularly the churches, they are occasionally pastors, sometimes evangelists, more often pastors' wives, but most often leaders of organized church women (missionaries, deaconesses, mothers' boards, etc.).[40]

While they may not have always taken center stage, Black women, nonetheless, provided the necessary undergirding and structural leadership needed in church and community organizations. As Gilkes puts it, "community mothers are the guardians of community political traditions. Their ability to function as power brokers stemmed from their leadership within historical Black women's movements and organizations."[41] Along these lines, the advent of such women's organizations as the National Association of Colored Women, founded in 1896 by Frances Ellen Watkins Harper, Mary Church Terrell (who became its first president), Harriet Tubman, and Ida B. Wells-Barnett, and the National Council of Negro Women, founded by Mary McLeod Bethune in 1935, helped facilitate networking and organizing among African American women. These churchwomen, writes Gilkes, used "secular organizations and agencies" to facilitate their outreach into the community.[42]

Service is integral to the Black clubwomen's conception of community, and Clifford's poem "All Hail! Ye Colored Graduates" (1911) provides a good example of this view. In this poem, the speaker plainly states that "*service*" must be the rule of Black high school and college graduates.[43] Clifford beckons women to join her in the call to service in "Duty's Call," yet in "Marching to Conquest" and "My Baby," she makes a traditional appeal to women as mothers.[44] In "We'll Die for Liberty," she makes plain that Black people are no longer seeking freedom from slavery, but are, rather, fighting for "'equal rights and equal justice, equal opportunity.'"[45] Hence, Clifford calls young Black graduates to "service" and to answer "duty's call." Additionally, as teachers, Black women have provided vital services to the larger Black community. Appropriating Richard Nice's term "educational capital," Hilton Kelly has discussed the value of education to African American teachers during the Jim Crow era and Black teachers' resourcefulness in their ability to "make a way out of no way," as the saying goes.[46] Noting that these teachers not only provided their students with "skills and knowledge," Kelly argues that they also "combined [their instruction] with good moral development, a positive racial identity, and a solid base education to enter a world of state-sponsored segregation, racial discrimination, and economic deprivation."[47] It is in this way that Jim Crow-era Black teachers advanced "educational capital," a form of capital that, according to Kelly, could not only uplift and serve the Black community, but also prepare students for possible access to mainstream white society.[48]

THE BLACK COLLEGE AS "MOTHER"

Returning to the poem "To Howard University," we see that Clifford presents Howard University as a Black mother with "full breasts" feeding Black men and women hungry for an education:

> Beloved Mother, you for whom we pray,
> Be fortified to meet our every need,
> At your full breasts the hungry children feed,
> Nor turn a single thirsting soul away![49]

In this section of the poem, the speaker addresses the university as though *she* is especially beloved by God for being a "Beloved Mother," able to sustain her supplicants. Gilkes has argued that nontraditional churches such as those within the Pentecostal and the Sanctified traditions, have roots that can be traced back to West African religions.[50] While her religious views were firmly rooted in traditional Christianity, Clifford nonetheless overtly pays homage to her African heritage in poems like "A Toast to Africa."

However, in poems like "To Howard University," more subtle precepts of West African religious traditions arguably can be gleaned. For instance, the poem's praise of the powerful role of women, especially in their role as mothers, suggests an indirect connection between Howard University and powerful African female deities like Osun and Yemoja who have the power (*ase*) to rescue their children in need of assistance. These Yoruba female deities are associated with childbirth, menstruation, and beauty. The speaker suggests that, as the unborn child receives nurture in its mother's womb, similarly students are nurtured and protected by Howard University.[51] The religious overtones in the poem are suggested by its syntactical rhythm that can be likened to that of the biblical psalms: "Be fortified to meet our every need"; "Nor turn a single thirsting soul away!" Here, Clifford underscores the connection between the power of God and the power of a good education in the concluding lines, in which she invites her readers to offer up "our thanks . . . to God and *You!* [Howard University]" (italics in the original).[52] As someone who moved within the prominent Black social circles of Washington, DC, Clifford was all too familiar with the social and educational enrichment that Howard University offered to students as well as the Black community. She draws parallels between Howard and African female deities whose "female power" has been associated with women in leadership roles. As Diedre Badejo writes in her discussion of a village's Queen Mother under the protection of the goddess Osun, "through the womb of a woman all humanity passes, so it is woman as mother who is responsible for knowing the character of men and, of course, other women."[53] Women's roles in childbearing and childrearing underscore their centrality to Yoruba society, and for this reason, according to Badejo, the Queen Mother plays a prime role in the selection of the future king.

As with the role of the Queen Mother in African communities, Clifford links her role as a teacher to her role as an activist in the African American community. Some of the poems in her two collections were written not only for a Black intellectual community but for Black church and community audiences. These poems, moreover, emphasize moral and ethical instruction to youth, decorum in society, and religious values. If, as has been noted, Clifford's God is clearly on the side of the oppressed, then humans are called to righteous living. She views God as a God of justice who calls humankind to stand up for equality and righteousness. Because women play vital roles in Clifford's vision of equal justice and mothers are granted a high status, she presents women as being more in tune with the operation of equality. For instance, the epigraph to "Mothers of America" in *The Widening Light* states that the poem is "A sonnet celebrating the heroism and valor of the women of America, Black and white, in the Great War for world democracy, 1917–1918."[54] White as well as Black women are referred to in the poem as "valiant" "Queens," who "bear the birth pangs of a world" and offer "succor." Here, Clifford's speaker seems to encourage coalition formation with white women who themselves were struggling against gender inequality in the early part of the twentieth century. Exceptions can be found in poems like "Silent Protest Parade" in which the speaker decries the active participation of white women, many who were themselves mothers, yet took part in the "hellish East Saint Louis 'show'" that condoned the "kill[ing of] / Poor Black workers, who'd fled in distress from the South" only "to find themselves murdered and mobbed in the North."[55]

Even so, Clifford infuses her poetry with a consciousness awakened by her vision of the God of the oppressed. For Clifford, that God is always near. She expresses her awareness of the Creator in the poem "God," in which the speaker feels God's presence in

> the low, sweet note
> In the thrush's throat—

The sun-beam's glory by a dew-drop caught!
He is the mighty tide
Gripping old ocean's side—
The mountain's thought![56]

Representing God as a "nurturer" and as a sustainer, Clifford invokes imagery of God's compassion and love. In her writings, God's agents on earth are frequently feminine. Alongside her appropriation of the God of the Oppressed is an ancestral Black womanspirit who guides Black women and anchors the Black community through the turbulent racial waters in the United States during the early decades of the twentieth century.

CONCLUSION: CLIFFORD AS A STRONG BLACK LEADER

Clifford's activism for women's rights extends back to the 1900s, never wavering from her vision of racial and gender equality, not least of which was suffrage. In fact, in "Votes for Children," published in *The Crisis* in 1915, Clifford is identified as the "Honorary President of the Federation of Colored Women's Clubs of Ohio." In this short essay, she employs syntactical repetition throughout, especially in the first paragraph.[57] Clifford uses affirmative rhetoric as well when she argues that "it is the ballot that opens the schoolhouse and closes the saloon," that "woman is the chosen channel through which the race is to be perpetuated," and that "the family is the miniature State, and here the influence of the mother is felt in teaching, directing and executing, to a degree far greater than that of the father." By repeating the phrase "It is the ballot" twice to make her point and later adding the preposition "by" in the third repetition of the phrase, her argument moves to an invitation to her readers to take action. Religious language of election is suggested as well in her allusions to women's role in the march for progress. For example, Clifford limns women as the "chosen channel through which the race is to be perpetuated" and whose "sacred and intimate communion with the unborn babe" sets the future child on the path to citizenry. Moreover, she argues that women seek the vote because of their need to care for their families. As she puts it, "more and more it is beginning to be understood that the mother's zeal for the ballot is prompted by her solicitude for her family-circle." She lists a number of civic concerns that mothers have fostered "*in spite of not having the ballot*" (italics in the original). Here, Clifford questions "why should [a woman] be forced to use indirect methods to accomplish a thing that could be done so much more quickly and satisfactorily by the direct method—by casting her own ballot?" She says that a mother's "dream" "is of a State where war shall cease, where peace and unity be established and where love shall reign." She concludes her argument by asserting that the family is "a miniature State" to emphasize that the role of the mother is primal, underscoring what she refers to as the "great mother-heart" that "demand[s] 'Votes for Women'. . . [because] fundamentally it is really a campaign for 'Votes for Children.'"

Scholars have noted that the presence of Black women in the early part of the twentieth century must be unearthed from oral and written historical accounts if we are to gain a better grasp of the profound contributions of African American women to social justice throughout American history. As Cheryl Wall argues on the reissuing of Zora Neale Hurston's texts in *Women of the Harlem Renaissance*,

> Hurston's recuperation intensifies the need to examine the lives and works of her female contemporaries: to identify common themes and metaphors in their writings, to determine who they were and where and how they lived, and to study the level of interaction among them. Hurston's achievement in *Their Eyes Were Watching God* and other books was the end result of a struggle enjoined by a generation of literary women to depict the lives of Black people generally and of Black women in particular, honestly and artfully.[58]

Thus, a re-examination of the writings of Black women from the years preceding the Harlem Renaissance like Clifford proves key if we are to provide a more complete vision of this era of American and African American imaginative writing. The positioning of writers like Clifford as "minor" within the African American literary canon should be interrogated, given the specific demands of their audiences and the historical contexts in which they wrote. Black women of the early twentieth century spoke to what they understood to be the pressing needs of the Black community—whether those needs were for reproduction rights or to raise an outcry against lynching.

Like many of her educated, elite Black women contemporaries, Clifford understood her duty of assisting with the uplift of the vast number of African Americans facing the crisis of illiteracy sixty years after emancipation. Alongside Black women teachers like Mary Burrill and Georgia Douglas Johnson in Washington, DC, Alice Dunbar Nelson in Delaware, and Carrie Law Morgan Figgs in Jacksonville, Florida, Clifford felt the urgency of ending racial injustice via education and strong leadership in the Black community. These women were also a part of the Black community, which they served not just as teachers in the classroom, but as role models and leaders. Clifford's activism as well as her desire to uplift and to serve her race were central to her literary theology of freedom, but ultimately, Clifford directs the question back to her reader: "What might God be asking of us all in an era filled with racial injustice?" To be sure, Clifford's literary theology of freedom for all Americans suffuses each of her major essays and volumes of poetry. As evidenced from her teaching in West Virginia to her strong stance against D. W. Griffiths's portrayal of Blacks in *The Birth of a Nation*, Clifford viewed her outspokenness as part of her charge to follow God. Long before Cone's *God of the Oppressed* and Grant's *White Women's Christ and Black Women's Jesus*, she envisioned a theology in which God was not simply a God for the affluent who enjoyed much of the world's prosperity, but a God that is equally a God of the downtrodden—a God that sees, sympathizes, and aligns God's Self with them in their suffering.

NOTES

1. I would like to thank my colleague Hilton Kelly for his helpful comments on this chapter. Clifford's corpus has been rediscovered recently owing largely to G. K. Hall's *African-American Women Writers, 1910–1940* series and to the reproduction and reissuing of *The Widening Light* in 2011.

2. James Cone, *God of the Oppressed* (Maryknoll, NY: Orbis, 1997).

3. Mary Murphy, "Biographical Sketch of Carrie Williams Clifford," accessed November 20, 2022, https://d3crmev29os45i.cloudfront.net/dorp/legacy/0/1c0a/a1cd/1007876620-I00001-size-original.jpg.

4. Elizabeth McHenry, *Forgotten Readers: Recovering the Lost History of African American Literary Societies* (Durham, NC: Duke University Press, 2002); and Lorraine Elena Roses and Ruth Elizabeth Randolph, eds., *Harlem Renaissance and Beyond: Literary Biographies of 100 Black Women Writers, 1900–1945* (Boston: G. K. Hall, 1990).

5. McHenry, *Forgotten Readers*.

6. Carrie Williams Clifford, "Votes for Children," *The Crisis: A Record of the Darker Races* 10, no. 4 (August 1915): 185.

7. Cheryl Townsend Gilkes, "The Roles of Church and Community Mothers: Ambivalent American Sexism or Fragmented African Familyhood?," in *African American Religion: Interpretative Essays in History and Culture*, ed. Timothy E. Fulop and Albert J. Raboteau (New York: Routledge, 1997), 373.

8. Gilkes, "Roles of Church and Community Mothers," 367.

9. Carrie Williams Clifford, *The Widening Light* (Boston: Walter Reid, 1922), 7. All page references are to this edition. Note that G. K. Hall's 1997 edition of *Writings of Carrie Williams Clifford and Carrie Law Morgan Figgs* incorporates the pagination from this edition alongside its own.

10. Clifford, *Widening Light*, 19.

11. P. Jane Splawn, ed., *Writings of Carrie Williams Clifford and Carrie Law Morgan Figgs* (New York: G. K. Hall, 1997). *The Widening Light* has also been reprinted by various presses from 2011 through 2018.

12. Boston University's library has a copy of Clifford's *Race Rhymes*, signed by Clifford to Braithwaite. Clifford's handwriting in her signature appears to be the same as that in the handwritten revisions to that copy.

13. "African American Book Publishers List," Stuart A. Rose Manuscript Archives and Rare Book Library, comp. by Randall K. Burkett, February 20, 2017; rev. August 25, 2017, http://rose.library.emory.edu/documents/African%20American%20Publishers.pdf. Burkett, who has researched Black publishing houses, has noted that Pendleton began the publishing house located on 609 F St., N.W., Washington, DC, in 1896.

14. Cary D. Wintz and Paul Finkelman, *Encyclopedia of the Harlem Renaissance* (New York: Routledge, 2004). Wintz and Finkelman describe the publisher as "a small vanity press based in Boston."

15. Clifford, *Race Rhymes* (Washington, DC: R. L. Pendleton, 1911), 7.

16. Clifford, *Race Rhymes*, 7. For Chaucer, see Geoffrey Chaucer, *Troilus and Criseyde: Book V*, accessed November 20, 2022, www.poetryfoundation.org/poems/43939/troilus-and-csiseyde-book-v.

17. Clifford, *Race Rhymes*, 5.

18. Clifford, *Race Rhymes*, 9. Handwritten notes in text.

19. Clifford, *Race Rhymes*.

20. Clifford, *Race Rhymes*, 9–10.

21. Langston Hughes, "Let America Be America Again," in *The Collected Poems of Langston Hughes*, ed. Arnold Rampersad (New York: Knopf, 1995), 189–91.

22. Clifford, *Race Rhymes*, 11.

23. Clifford, *Race Rhymes*, 12.

24. Clifford, *Race Rhymes*, 13.

25. Clifford, *Race Rhymes*, 14.

26. Clifford, *Widening Light*, ix.

27. Clifford, *Race Rhymes*, 32.

28. Clifford, *Race Rhymes*, 31.

29. Clifford, *Race Rhymes*, 32.

30. David Levering Lewis, *W. E. B. Du Bois: A Biography* (New York: Henry Holt, 2009).

31. Clifford, *Widening Light*, 32.

32. Clifford, *Widening Light*, 10

33. W. E. B. Du Bois, *The Souls of Black Folk* (New York: New American Library, 1982).

34. Clifford, *Widening Light*, 12, 13, 9.

35. Clifford, *Widening Light*, 49.

36. Clifford, *Widening Light*, 29.

37. Frederick Douglass, *Narrative of the Life of Frederick Douglass, An American Slave: Written by Himself* (New York: Dover, 2012).

38. Clifford, *Widening Light*, 1.

39. Jacquelyn Grant, *White Women's Christ and Black Women's Jesus: Feminist Christology and Womanist Response* (Atlanta: Scholars Press, 1989); and Cone, *God of the Oppressed*.

40. Gilkes, "Roles of Church and Community Mothers," 367–68.

41. Gilkes, "Roles of Church and Community Mothers," 373.

42. Gilkes, "Roles of Church and Community Mothers," 374

43. Clifford, *Race Rhymes*, 21.

44. Clifford, *Race Rhymes*, 22–24.

45. Clifford, *Race Rhymes*, 28.

46. Hilton Kelly, "What Jim Crow's Teachers Could Do: Educational Capital and Teachers' Work in Under-Resourced Schools," *Urban Review* 42 (2010): 329–50.

47. Kelly, "Jim Crow's Teachers," 343.

48. Kelly, "Jim Crow's Teachers," 347.

49. Clifford, *Widening Light*, 7.

50. Gilkes, "Roles of Church and Community Mothers," 370–72.

51. This is a common metaphor used for colleges and universities.

52. Clifford, *Widening Light*, 7.

53. Diedre Badejo, *Osun Seegesi: The Elegant Deity of Wealth, Power and Femininity* (Trenton, NJ: Africa World Press, 1996).

54. Clifford, *Widening Light*, 2.

55. Clifford, *Widening Light*, 16.

56. Clifford, *Widening Light*, 55.

57. Clifford, "Votes for Children," 185.

58. Cheryl Wall, *Women of the Harlem Renaissance* (Bloomington: Indiana University Press, 1995), 9.

SELECTED BIBLIOGRAPHY

"African American Book Publishers List." Stuart A. Rose Manuscript Archives and Rare Book Library. Compiled by Randall K. Burkett. February 20, 2017; rev. August 25, 2017. http://rose.library.emory.edu/documents/African%20American%20Publishers.pdf.

Carby, Hazel. '"On the Threshold of Woman's Era': Lynching, Empire, and Sexuality in Black Feminist Theory." *Critical Inquiry* 12, no. 1 (Autumn 1985): 262–77.

Clifford, Carrie W. "Cleveland and Its Colored People." *Colored American Magazine* 8–9 (1908): 365–80.

Clifford, Carrie W. "Love's Way: A Christmas Story." *Alexander's Magazine* 1, no. 9 (January 1906): 55–58.

Clifford, Carrie W. *Race Rhymes*. Washington, DC: Pendleton, 1911.

Clifford, Carrie W., ed. *Sowing for Others to Reap: A Collection of Papers of Vital Importance to the Race*. Ohio Federation of Colored Women's Clubs. Boston: Alexander, 1900.

Clifford, Carrie W. "Votes for Children." *Crisis* 10, no. 4 (August 1915): 185.

Clifford, Carrie W. *The Widening Light*. Boston: Walter Reid, 1922.

Cone, James. *God of the Oppressed*. Maryknoll, NY: Orbis, 1997.

Doyle, Laura. *Bordering on the Body: The Racial Matrix of Modern Fiction and Culture*. New York: Oxford University Press, 1994.

Gilkes, Cheryl Townsend. "The Role of Community Mothers: Ambivalent American Sexism or Fragmented African Familyhood?" In *Interpretative Essays in History and Culture*, edited by Timothy E. Fulop and Albert J. Raboteau, 366–76. New York: Routledge, 1997.

Grant, Jacquelyn. *White Women's Christ and Black Women's Jesus: Feminist Christology and Womanist Response*. Atlanta: Scholars Press, 1989.

Higginbotham, Evelyn. "African-American Women's History and the Metalanguage of Race." *Signs* 17, no. 2 (1992): 51–74.

Higginbotham, Evelyn. "The Black Church: A Gender Perspective." In *African-American Religion: Interpretive Essays in History and Culture*, edited by Timothy E. Fulop and Albert J. Raboteau, 201–25. New York: Routledge, 1997.

Honey, Maureen, ed. *Shadowed Dreams: Women's Poetry of the Harlem Renaissance*. New Brunswick, NJ: Rutgers University Press, 1989.

Hull, Gloria. *Color, Sex, and Poetry: Three Women Writers of the Harlem Renaissance*. Bloomington: Indiana University Press, 1987.

Kelly, Hilton. "What Jim Crow's Teachers Could Do: Educational Capital and Teachers' Work in Under-Resourced Schools." *Urban Review* 42 (2010): 329–50.

McDowell, Deborah E. *"The Changing Same": Black Women's Literature, Criticism, and Theory*. Bloomington: Indiana University Press, 1995.

McHenry, Elizabeth. *Forgotten Readers: Recovering the Lost History of African American Literary Societies*. Durham, NC: Duke University Press, 2002.

Peterson, Carla L. *"Doers of the Word": African American Women Speakers and Writers in the North (1830–1880)*. New York: Oxford University Press, 1995.

Philips, Layli, and Barbara McCaskill. "Who's Schooling Who? Black Women and the Bringing of the Everyday into Academe, or Why We Started *The Womanist*." *Signs* 20, no. 4 (1995): 1007–18.

Roses, Elaine, and Ruth Elizabeth Randolph. *Harlem Renaissance and Beyond: Literary Biographies of 100 Black Women Writers, 1900–1945*. Boston: G. K. Hall, 1990.

Smith, Jessie Carney. *Notable Black American Women*, Book I. Farmington Hills, MI: Gale, 1991.

Stetson, Erlene. *Black Sister: Poetry by Black American Women, 1746–1980*. Bloomington: Indiana University Press, 1981.

Terborg-Penn, Rosalyn. *African American Women in the Struggle for the Vote, 1850–1920*. Bloomington: Indiana University Press, 1998.

Wall, Cheryl. *Women of the Harlem Renaissance*. Bloomington: Indiana University Press, 1995.

Wintz, Cary D., and Paul Finkelman, eds. *Encyclopedia of the Harlem Renaissance*. New York: Routledge, 2004.

Chapter 7

THERESSA HOOVER

Black Feminist, Methodist, Southerner

JANET ALLURED

INTRODUCTION: A METHODIST LEADER

For Theressa Hoover, from Fayetteville, Arkansas, the Women's Division of the Board of Global Missions of The United Methodist Church and feminist theology were profoundly freeing. The Methodist Church's doctrines, creeds, practices, and policies provided opportunities for Hoover to become an African American feminist trailblazer, public intellectual, theologian, coalition-builder, and change-maker. By the time The Methodist Church merged with the Evangelical United Brethren to form The United Methodist Church in 1968, Hoover had been working for the Women's Division for twenty years.[1] When she agreed to accept the job of chief executive of the division upon that merger, she attained the distinction of holding the highest executive position ever held by a Black female in any mainline denomination in the country. From that position at the helm of the nearly two-million-member faith-based women's organization, she worked to overturn racial and gender discrimination in both church and society, justifying the need for equality with her own brand of Methodist-inflected theology.[2]

The Women's Division (WD), which governed the women's missionary associations in a federated structure of local and regional units, was generally more progressive than the rest of the church, and it influenced the General Conference (the church's official policy-making body that met every four years) to take more liberal positions on race and gender equality than it otherwise would have. The main reason for its extraordinary influence is that the WD retained sole control over its missionary organizations, and thus its independence from the male church hierarchy, longer than any other Protestant women's organization. Hoover proudly recalled the division's autonomy in her retrospective history: "Methodist women secured and controlled their own funds, generated programs, established separate mission institutions, and recruited and deployed their own commissioned workers. . . . Unified Methodist women also maintained their own educational programs with children and youth, and special relationships with college students." The WD flourished in this relationship, Hoover observed, growing in both membership and property, until 1964 when a General Board reorganization—against the wishes of the WD—folded the women's home and foreign missionary societies into the "male" ones operated by the general church. Before that hostile takeover, ostensibly done for efficiency of administration, the division was governed by its majority-female elected board. Even after the reorganization of 1964, the women raised their own funds—to the tune of millions of dollars per year—and decided how they would be disbursed. In this woman-led religious organization, Hoover found a base of power and a model for personal autonomy.[3]

Hoover steered The United Methodist Church toward ending white male privilege in houses of worship and in the hundreds of institutions it funded and administered, and she supported the goals of the larger women's liberation movement in her writings, speeches, and actions. Her influence was not confined to her own denomination either, for she used her seats on many national boards to push those organizations toward adopting feminist stances as well. Additionally, she and her staff, from their headquarters in New York City, encouraged Methodist women to create networks in their local communities in support of ratification of the Equal Rights Amendment (ERA) and other goals of second-wave feminism. In multiple ways, then, Hoover's influence stretched across regional, national, and even international boundaries.[4]

Hoover earned nothing but praise and abiding respect from those who worked with her. At her memorial service in 2014, Joyce Sohl, who succeeded Hoover as the head of the WD, nicely summarized Hoover's priorities: "[Theressa] worked diligently to enhance the role of women within the Church and to preserve and strengthen a highly visible organized body of women involved in the work of mission and justice to women and children."[5] Hoover was not afraid to speak truth to power, but she did so with "grace, compassion and respect," remarked Barbara Campbell, her second in command, almost reverentially, in an interview with me. Campbell added, "She didn't suffer fools gladly, but neither did she take herself too seriously." Despite her astonishingly successful and high-profile career, however, Hoover is little remembered today.[6]

This lack of attention is puzzling, given that her promotion to chief executive of a major Protestant women's organization garnered national attention. The January 1971 issue of *Ladies' Home Journal* recognized her as one of America's seventy-five most important women; the next year, two prestigious schools of theology—Perkins in Dallas and the Harvard Divinity School—invited her to give lectures; and she was interviewed on NBC's *Today* show several times within a few years of her appointment.[7] But the early seventies was the heyday of second-wave feminism. By the end of that decade, a resurgent conservative movement had emerged that thwarted further reform efforts, shushed the progressive movement, and buried the ERA. Hoover's feminism, no matter how faith-based, did not placate the ultra-conservative New Right, which may help account for the shade.

Perhaps scholars have neglected Hoover's pioneering work as a leading Black Christian feminist because she did not produce the kinds of academic writing or theory that scholars generally look for. Instead, she wrote short pieces in mass-produced magazines aimed at lay audiences. Yet these articles popularized for laypeople the theological zeitgeist among Black Christian women in a form of proto-womanism. A person who eschewed labels of any kind, Hoover never referred to her theology as womanist, but her writings indicate that she thought along those lines long before she ever heard the word. "Womanism," a term coined by writer Alice Walker, was a Black woman's philosophy grounded in her history, culture, and religious experience. A term picked up and used by many Black female intellectuals in the 1980s, "womanism" was a way of addressing interlocking oppressions that confronted Black women throughout their lives, a concept that prefigured the idea of "intersectionality," a legal expression created by attorney Kimberlé Crenshaw, civil rights advocate and scholar of critical race theory. *Christian* womanist thinkers like Hoover focused a critical eye on systems of oppression based not only on class, gender (including sex and sexuality), and race, but also on religion.[8]

Hoover was exceedingly bright and capable by all accounts, but for a Black girl growing up in the Jim Crow South, intelligence was not a ticket to success. Instead, it was her background and experiences and, ultimately, her denomination that explain her astounding achievements as an American Protestant leader and thinker. Her experiences in Fayetteville, a smallish Ozark mountain town with a tiny Black population; in a Black congregation (St. James Methodist Church); at Philander Smith College, a historically Black Methodist-affiliated school; with the racially diverse Little Rock Methodist Council, which first employed her to work with Methodist churches; and ultimately with the WD—all of these factors developed her critical thinking and leadership skills, and gave her the confidence and ultimately the platform to advance a far-reaching social justice agenda.

Hoover was a pivotal mid-century "bridge" figure in American religion in part because the church her family attended, St. James, was part of the Methodist Episcopal Church (MEC) in Arkansas, an overwhelmingly white denomination. Though the MEC is often casually referred to as the "northern" Methodist Church, there were quite a few MEC congregations and MEC-affiliated colleges in the South, nearly all founded for formerly enslaved persons by northern Methodist missionaries during Reconstruction. Hoover thus grew up in a denomination that was at least somewhat less racist than most religious groups in the South, an experience that led her to have hope that challenging racism in the United States was a worthwhile endeavor.

Hoover's Methodist belief system and connections to Methodist-affiliated institutions in her home state led to her remarkable success. Methodism, an offshoot of Anglicanism, began in England under the leadership of brothers John and Charles Wesley in the late eighteenth century. From the beginning, it appealed to women because, like Jesus, the Wesleys emphasized outreach to the poor and marginalized. Born during the Enlightenment, Methodism stressed education and rationality as paths to piety, and taught that education should be lifelong and available to everyone regardless of gender, race, or class. The purpose of gaining knowledge, furthermore, was to prepare for a life of service. This led Methodists to establish colleges, seminaries, and universities, many of them for educating newly freed African Americans. Hoover attended one of those colleges—Philander Smith, in Little Rock, Arkansas—founded and financed by the MEC.[9]

Born in Fayetteville in 1925, Hoover's experiences growing up in the Jim Crow South made her keenly aware of how patriarchal structures allowed white men to exploit ethnic minorities and the poor and allowed all men to subordinate and victimize women. But the Methodist Church, which had always been the most significant denomination in the South in terms of social justice activism, provided a vehicle for change. The WD, which governed the missionary associations in a federated structure of local and regional units, was generally more progressive than the rest of the church, and it influenced the General Conference to take more liberal positions on race and gender equality than it otherwise would have.

Hoover's family history also shaped her willingness to strive for something bigger than herself, to seek a more just world order: "I grew up in a home where I was taught that, even though I received formal education, I had a responsibility to the whole of society, to all those who may be marginalized because of circumstances rather than through their own fault."[10] Her father, James Hoover, a World War I veteran with a sixth-grade education, was a formative influence on her life. Hoover described her father as a strong, kind, gentle, and dignified man who always opened the door of his home to anyone in need. Though the family had no money, they did have middle-class values, including a strong appreciation for education. She later said, "It was just understood that we were going to go to high school and college." Fayetteville did not offer high school education for African Americans, so she and three of her siblings went to live with their aunt, a teacher in a small east Texas town, and attended the high school where she taught. Over the years, her aunt ended up hosting dozens of teenagers from Fayetteville—an example of "other-mothering," a form of mutual assistance that Black women provided for children in their communities. In 1942, when Hoover graduated at the top of her class, she packed her bags for Little Rock and Philander Smith College, a Black Methodist coed institution.[11]

The University of Arkansas did not admit African Americans then, but it is worth noting that Arkansas, despite the bad reputation it got as a result of the Little Rock integration crisis of 1957, was a fairly moderate state. The school board of Washington County, of which Fayetteville was the county seat, was the first in the nation to approve desegregation following the *Brown v. Board of Education* decision. Compared to other places in the former Confederacy, Fayetteville's race relations were relatively good, and desegregation outside of Little Rock proceeded calmly. "We didn't have a lot of the pressures you get in the Delta part of the state," Hoover said in an interview late in her life. "The strictures were not so obvious." In other words, she was not as limited as a Black sharecropper in the cotton belt would have been.[12]

Her birthplace in an area of the South that afforded greater opportunities to African Americans than did the Black Belt helps to account for Hoover's unusual career trajectory. She was fortunate, too, that her father insisted she go to Philander Smith. "He couldn't afford that," she recalled, "but he felt we could get a better break there" than at the one state-supported college for African Americans in Arkansas. Her father was right. Philander Smith was a far better school than the three other colleges open to Blacks in Arkansas. It boasted excellent professors and now has an impressive list of alumni that includes James Cone, the founder of Black liberation theology, and Joycelyn Elders, surgeon general of the United States under President Bill Clinton. Hoover attended a couple of decades before Philander Smith students lead the sit-ins in Little Rock, but she nonetheless racked up an impressive record of leadership achievement. She joined Delta Sigma Theta Sorority (a Black service-oriented sorority), served as office secretary at the Wesley Chapel, attended the National Methodist Student Conference at the University of Illinois, and was active in the Student Christian Association (the YMCA-YWCA on campus). Elected student body president her senior year, Hoover showed a talent for leadership that brought her to the attention of the Little Rock Methodist Council, an organization of nineteen Black and white Methodist churches and community representatives searching for ways to overcome the racial divide. The council hired her on a part-time basis to help Black churches improve their Christian education programs.[13]

The Methodist Church's connectional system made this possible. Unlike evangelical denominations such as the Baptists, where individual churches are relatively autonomous and are controlled largely by the local congregation,

Methodists are governed by a federated system reminiscent of the Anglican church (Episcopal in the United States) from which they emanated. In the Methodist Church, every congregation is part of a district; groups of districts are annual conferences; groups of conferences are grouped as jurisdictions. Annual conferences are composed of all ordained ministers and an equal number of lay representatives in each conference area. Delegates are elected from various units to represent them at the General Conference. This hierarchy meant that every member of the Methodist Church was structurally and doctrinally connected (through *The Book of Discipline*, the constitution of the church) to every other member. Thus, decisions made by the General Conference were of great importance to local congregations. It also meant that individual units had access to the enormous wealth and resources of the larger church body.[14]

For Hoover, Methodism's connectional system opened educational and career opportunities and provided a sense of community and belonging that might otherwise have been dedicated to place or to family. For example, the campus church sent her to a national student conference in Urbana, Illinois, which exposed her to a diversity of ethnicities and cultures and to possibilities beyond her little neck of the woods. One attendee at this conference told historian Sara Evans, "We were all persons of faith in search of common answers and a quality of liberated life that was faithful before God. We sought social justice, growth, and affirmation for all persons."[15] Students left this conference and started or participated in sit-ins in their own communities. They were literally "acting out their convictions," something John Wesley had always encouraged.

A few months before her graduation from Philander Smith in 1946, Hoover began working for the Little Rock Methodist Council.[16] The council, made up of representatives of all the Methodist churches in the area, including Christian Methodist Episcopal and Central Jurisdiction churches, had been organized a few years before to coordinate Christian social relations initiatives in Little Rock and to promote interracial understanding by providing opportunities for different racial groups to work together. Before she was turned loose in the field—travelling over a wide area helping Black churches with leadership training and program development—the council paid for her to train during the summer at Garrett Seminary in Illinois (home of feminist theologian Georgia Harness) in religious education. Impressed with her intelligence as well as her excellent interpersonal skills, the council hired her as associate director after her graduation from college. On the council board was Rev. James E. Major, president of Philander Smith. Together with Hoover, he persuaded the board to locate and develop a rural site for summer recreation for Little Rock's Black children, for whom no recreational facilities were available anywhere in the state. After securing a $25,000 grant from the Women's

Division, the council acquired an abandoned turkey farm on 120 acres of land a few miles away from downtown Little Rock and built Camp Aldersgate. Though it had been conceived originally as a rural sanctuary for Black children, the council stipulated from the beginning that it be open to persons of all races, especially for meetings and retreats during the off season. The local women's societies provided funds to hire a (white) director (Deaconess Margaret Marshall) and several African American assistants, of which Hoover was one. (The two young men hired to clean up the place and get buildings ready for human habitation both went on to become Methodist pastors.) For many years, it was the only place in Arkansas where white and Black people could safely meet.

Though interracial gatherings created backlash and the Little Rock Methodist Council often received threats, they were undeterred. Hoover said that Aldersgate was established by "a group of people who dared not accept the way it is as what must be," people who provided hope and a guide for future behavior. "We were doing a bold thing," she remembered later, "bringing together people across the lines of race. . . . Laywomen are justifiably proud of their involvement with the camp in its origin, and have continued to provide support during the myriad stages of change and development." The WD still owns the property, now worth millions of dollars, which, thanks to the division's excellent fiscal management, produces enough revenue to keep the camp well maintained and operative.[17] Multiracial collaborative efforts had been part of southern Methodist women's missionary work since the early twentieth century, a tradition that continued after the 1939 union. In 1951, Thelma Stevens, a white woman from Mississippi who headed the WD's Department of Christian Social Relations, convinced the WD to hire African American attorney Pauli Murray to do research on Jim Crow laws. The resulting publication was an eight hundred-page tome that NAACP attorney Thurgood Marshall referred to as "the Bible" of desegregation.[18] Stevens used *States' Laws on Race and Color* as a basis for developing a Charter of Racial Justice for the WD, which it adopted in 1952, two years before the *Brown* decision. The WD in turn persuaded the rest of the church to adopt it at the next General Conference. Hoover later recalled this controversial, even risky, decision with pride. Writing in 1990, she said that "in the last 30 years [the UMW] has developed at least three charters on race. The most recent charter focuses on institutional racism in church and society and acknowledges the globalization of racism. At least twice, [the General Conference] has made the WD charters its own. That is a miracle for which we can take some credit!"[19] Just because it was official policy for the church to begin dismantling segregation, however, did not mean that every entity supported that move or began to comply. In fact, there was a great deal of pushback against the charter in the Deep South.

Despite resistance, Stevens persisted in moving the division toward greater inclusivity. By this time, Theressa Hoover had appeared on Stevens's radar, and she persuaded the division to hire Hoover as a field secretary in 1948. For the next ten years, she travelled widely, visiting Methodist churches (some of which had never had a Black person inside before), schools, colleges, and camps and attending international meetings overseas. She travelled by bus (always sitting in the back), "train, and plane, preaching in local churches, teaching, interpreting, training, cultivating women for mission." Typically, she stayed in Black people's homes because hotels did not allow African Americans to stay there.[20]

One of the things Hoover learned during her ten years as a field worker was that pastors assigned to Black churches often did not know much about Methodism. "Some of them came from other denominations," Hoover remembered; "some of them come off the streets, some from other countries, particularly the Caribbean nations, where their history has been rooted in British Methodism, which is quite different from American Methodism." In other words, she was better educated about Methodism than many men of the cloth were, which is one reason that she considered herself equal to the clergy—and to men. She also learned how important Black women were to the survival of the Black church.[21]

Hoover took those observations with her to New York City when Thelma Stevens hired her in 1958 to work for the Department of Christian Social Relations, the most radical subunit of the WD. Hoover was promoted to secretary for legislative affairs and opened an office in Washington, DC, where she could keep tabs on legislation of interest to women. She traveled frequently between Washington and New York, rubbing shoulders with people who had considerable power not only nationally but also internationally.[22]

Hoover lauded the WD "as the first major employer of women in the church," one that "led the way for acceptance of women in other agencies, annual conferences and local churches." She also credited the women's missionary organizations for helping to win clergy rights for women in 1956.[23] Even though women could be ordained after 1956, resistance and the length of the ordination process ensured that they remained both tokenized and marginalized as clergy for years after that. Organized laywomen, Hoover noted regularly, were far more effective at bringing about social change than were clergy.

By the mid-1960s, with the successes of the civil rights movement, these women insisted that it was time—actually, long past time—for the Methodist Church to abandon its policy of racial segregation. The occasion presented itself when the Methodist Church and the Evangelical United Brethren began contemplating a merger of the two churches. Hoover served on the Structure Study Commission that hammered out the agreements between the two, and Hoover along with some other committee members insisted that no union would take place unless all parties agreed to end racial segregation in every institution supported by the church. Though the commission got its wish and United Methodists agreed to phase out racial segregation within the next few years, it was a painful and tumultuous transition in many parts of the country, particularly in the Deep South. Mrs. Glenn Laskey of Louisiana, the elected (volunteer) president of the WD, believed that there was no better person to preside over this transition than a southern Black woman with a track record of wise, measured, and courageous leadership. Laskey asked Hoover if she would take the recently vacated top staff position, at that time called the associate general secretary. When she accepted, Hoover made history by occupying the highest rank of that kind ever held by an African American woman in the United States.[24]

By all accounts, Hoover was a smashing success. A gifted administrator, she adeptly guided the process of merging white and Black conferences and in so doing ensured that Black members retained positions of responsibility. She also skillfully executed the merger of several women's missionary organizations into one umbrella group, the United Methodist Women (UMW), another process fraught with tension and discord because it required drawing up a new constitution and bylaws as well as deciding on a new name. She was a master at moving the process along despite differences of opinion. A lay organization numbering about one and a half million members organized through thirty-five thousand local chapters, the UMW became, upon its creation, the largest Protestant women's organization in America. In 1972, its annual budget was five million dollars. In effect, Hoover ran a giant corporation, and in that capacity she displayed excellent managerial skills. Thanks to the assistance of a small army of volunteer women at all levels of the organization, the WD operated with extremely low overhead. More than 90 percent of the funds collected went to the cause for which they were designated by the elected board, a far higher percentage than most other charitable organizations.[25] The record showed Methodist women had good business acumen, treated workers fairly, and could be trusted with decision-making roles. Never was there any hint of scandal, impropriety, misuse of funds, or abuse of power. That would have been entirely contrary to Hoover's feminist ethics.

HOOVER'S FEMINIST/WOMANIST THEOLOGY

In addition to modeling feminist-inspired leadership skills that inspired an almost worshipful awe in her coworkers, Hoover popularized concepts that would, in the hands of more systematic thinkers, be called womanist theology—an ethical worldview that combined elements of feminism and Black power. Feminist theology pivoted away from traditional male-dominated interpretations of the Bible that focused on "sins of the flesh" (brought into the world by Eve) to argue instead that sin and salvation were social and structural rather than personal. What most needed attention and fixing was the use and abuse of power, particularly male power over women (Hoover's chief priority), but also any kind of domination of others. While Hoover asserted that the ministry of Jesus had been "destabilizing, inclusive, and nonhierarchical," the patriarchal structures within Christianity that developed after his death used Scripture to subordinate women in a way that Jesus never intended.[26]

We see the elements of womanism in her writings from the late 1960s forward. In 1972, for example, she gave an invited lecture at Harvard's Divinity School entitled "Triple Jeopardy." While all women suffered oppression because of their gender, she told her audience, Black women also suffered because of their race (a phenomenon today called intersectionality), while the third leg of oppression for Black churchwomen resided in the church.[27] This lecture, later published in *response* magazine and thus made widely available, critiqued Black male theology and control in Black churches. Her ten years spent crisscrossing the country as a field worker had taught Hoover that Black women were the glue that kept churches alive and afloat. Based on those strengths, Hoover argued that Black churchwomen should challenge the assumptions of white churchwomen as well as the power of Black male clergy: "The Black churchwoman must come to the point of challenging both her sisters in other denominations and the clergy-male hierarchy in her own. She has given the most, and in my judgment, gotten the least. Her foresight, ingenuity and 'stick-to-it-ive-ness' have kept many Black churches open, many Black preachers fed, many parsonages livable."[28] Oppression was unjust no matter the sphere in which it operated, no matter the race or gender of the oppressor.

Just as Hoover was a bridge figure between Black and white Christians, her theological emphases represented overlapping strains of Wesleyanism, feminism, and womanism, the intersections of which she repeatedly emphasized in her speeches, interviews, and writings. The Venn diagram of those three strains would show in the center: the importance of the grassroots laity (in the case of Wesleyanism), optimism and hope, churchwomen's history (including that of ethnic minorities), holism, connectedness and community, environmentalism (ecotheology and ecofeminism), and a feminist ethic that took seriously women's experiences as a source of truth. Womanists also applauded Black women's nurturing traditions, which Hoover did less publicly than others, but she certainly appreciated the role of Black women in both church and community for the reasons she expressed above. The Black churchwoman, Hoover said in praise, "has borne her children in less than desirable conditions, managed her household often in the absence of a husband. She has gathered unto herself the children of the community . . . in short she has been their missionary, substitute mother, their teacher. Many leaders of the present-day Black church owe their commitment to the early influence of just such a Black woman."[29] Like Alice Walker, Hoover benefitted from such a group of people: her aunt had supported her and other Black Fayetteville residents while they attended high school in Texas. Without that opportunity, it is likely that Hoover never would have achieved a white-collar career. People in her position, she believed, who had, with much assistance, been fortunate enough to break free of the quadruple oppressions of race, class, gender, and a male-dominated church, had a Christian responsibility to educate themselves, through reading and study, about how structural oppression worked. Their eyes thus opened and their collective consciousnesses raised, the subsequent responsibility was to formulate pragmatic, concrete solutions that could overturn those systems of oppression.

As the elected leader of the WD, Hoover needed to appeal to her constituency. She therefore grounded her arguments in Christian beliefs, the Gospel texts, the life of Jesus, Wesley's deeds and words, and the official doctrines of The United Methodist Church. Saying that it was a Methodist's responsibility to work toward racial and gender equality in church and society, she established the credentials and the theological taproots that laid the groundwork for acceptance of her ideas. Jan Love, a mentee and CEO of the WD in the mid-2000s, told me in an interview that Hoover never lost support (or her job) because "she was Biblically grounded, theologically grounded, she kept the focus on God's reign in the world, and she had people inside her own organization who supported her." Drawing on traditions and texts shared by all Methodists gave her arguments authority in the eyes of her audience.

While Christianity's ethical traditions formed the bedrock of her arguments, Hoover was not bound by the past. Quite the opposite. She read contemporary Black audience magazines such as *Ebony* and was keen to learn new ways of thinking, which she did by reading the most current theological treatises as well as the *New York Times*. She encouraged all Methodist women to start the day as she did, with a Bible in one hand and a newspaper in the other. She was particularly informed by the works of contemporary feminist theologians and by the Black liberation theology stemming from the pen of another Arkansan and Philander Smith graduate, James Cone. Liberation theology and feminist theology both postulated the idea that theology is not an objective science, but that it is, rather, a product of culture, gender, and the individual thinker's experiences. Up to this point, said modern feminist theologians, the experiences of white Western men were mistakenly presumed to be representative of everyone else's.[30] As Hoover expressed this sentiment in 1971, "Theology has developed too much around a masculine understanding of the world. . . . Theology arises from experience, and is rooted in the histories and happenings of where we live." To counter masculinist hegemony, Hoover developed a theological view that expanded the meaning and accessibility of the Methodist heritage. She scolded male leaders for hindering women simply because of how society perceived them: "As the individual discovers her true abilities and gives commitment to the Lord of all life, she will find still more ways to work for a world where no human being is degraded, exploited, or restricted, NOT EVEN WOMAN." This was a matter of feminist principles, of course, but it was especially important to Methodists because women made up 55 percent of the membership.[31]

Womanists, under Alice Walker's definition, were not separatists, and Hoover did not condone separatism. Take, for example, her reaction to the *Black Manifesto*, a document written and endorsed by the Black Economic Development Conference but introduced publicly by James Forman, formerly the executive director of SNCC. In May 1969, Forman disrupted a Sunday service at Riverside Church in New York City, the symbolic home of liberal Protestantism, and, after demanding access to the pulpit, read the *Black Manifesto* that demanded that white churches and synagogues pay reparations for the sins of slavery and segregation. The $500 million, he told the startled audience, would be collected "by any means necessary." While many churches responded by donating money either to the Black Economic Development Conference or to more well-established and trusted Black organizations or institutions, Hoover responded by trashing his group's ideology, methods, and demands. Church Women United, she reported, "called a small consultation of Black churchwomen in September 1969" in New York "to consider their role and expectations in the aftermath of the Black Manifesto" and decided to stay put. She also denounced Black Methodists for Church Renewal, a caucus formed in 1968 upon the dissolution of the Central Jurisdiction, for allowing Black male clergy to dominate in numbers and in decision-making roles and for not putting any women into leadership positions.[32]

Above all else, she stressed that a sincere Christian needed to be open to new ideas before the dismantling of systems of hierarchy and oppression could begin. One cannot destroy structural racism and sexism if one is not first aware of how those structures operate, and Hoover proposed five ways to develop insight into those structures: learning history, travelling internationally, working in mission, keeping apprised of the news, and honing critical thinking skills.[33]

This emphasis on continuous learning about the world was consistent with the Wesleyan tradition that taught believers to stay engaged with their environment, no matter how evil, wrong-headed, or depraved it may appear. Unlike many evangelical religions, Methodists were taught not to isolate themselves from political and social changes for fear of corruption. Instead, the faithful should embrace people and parts of society that made them uncomfortable in order to transform them and to usher in the Kingdom of God. The church offered a sacred opportunity to "discover a variety of views of the world and to learn from the unexpected," Hoover wrote. "Properly engaged work in mission," she continued, "can be a lesson in theology, geopolitical understanding, economic awareness, global history and geography." Membership in the UMW thus assisted Methodist women's moral imperative to effect positive change in the world.[34]

Methodism had always foregrounded the responsibility of the converted to minister to and seek to liberate those suffering from exploitation and subjugation—be it slavery, poverty, gender, or any other kind of oppression. The women's missionary organizations focused especially on the most disempowered and voiceless ones, women and children. To better assist them, Methodist women needed to educate themselves about the poor conditions that women and children faced on an international scale. "Thus developed the strong linkage between education for mission and giving to support it all around the world," Hoover explained. A robust reading program had long been part of Methodist women's commitment to mission. Each year the staff published a list of dozens of books that members could choose from, and Hoover read many of them herself. Out of this study program emerged the liberalism that characterized Methodist women's outlook and led them to embrace progressive change movements.[35]

If the UMW reading list provided one source of inspiration for Hoover's philosophy, so too did her location in New York City, a feminist hotspot where many influential second-wave women's liberationists, including feminists of color, lived. As she stated in *With Unveiled Face*, the WD "understood at once what the secular feminists were struggling with and in revolt against. These intelligent, angry younger women articulated our frustrations also. Their analyses deepened our understanding of the systemic oppression of women. Their determination to revise patriarchal culture and politics energized us."[36] Likewise, she encouraged UMW units to adopt many of the movement's strategies such as "consciousness-raising" group meetings, in which women tried to understand themselves within a male-dominated society and church. She wanted to see the church as a whole, not just the women, return to its roots in small communities of reflection—a practice that the women's liberation movement emphasized as a route to broader feminist consciousness. "Testifying in a friendly and supportive atmosphere enables people to see that their experiences are often duplicated by others," she noted. Therefore, such an environment led to a spirit of liberation, which in turn could be the motivation for greater activism.[37]

This respect for "little people," that is, those on the bottom rung, is an area in which the new women's movement and traditional Wesleyanism overlapped:

they both valued the role of the grassroots populace to contribute and to make decisions. The liberation movements of the 1960s, including the Black freedom struggle, called this "participatory democracy." Hoover stressed that laypeople—male and female, Black and white—were as critical to the church's mission as were male clergy. All church members were people of God, she said repeatedly—perhaps keeping the lowly background of her own family in mind—reminding them that the Holy Spirit could be found in the disempowered as well: "We must use our strength to . . . offer 'free way' access to and through the church for lay participation in the affairs of the church. It is through such participation that we can help the church avoid the trauma of non-participation of its laity and the tragedy of its own non-involvement in the world."[38] Acknowledging and unveiling the role of laity meant appreciating the historical efforts of laywomen too.

To second-wave feminist Christian theologians, the erasure of women in the Judeo-Christian tradition and, for Methodists, in Wesleyanism, was yet another method of trivializing and marginalizing them. In making a case for developing a women's history program, Hoover quoted Peggy Ann Way, an ordained minister in the United Church of Christ: "I am not interested in church history as a source of authority for my ministry, but as a vehicle of disclosure, by which myths are lifted up to visibility and real persons appear in the historical record."[39] Whereas patriarchs had employed history as a source of repression and domination, women of faith used it to establish their authenticity as equal partners with men in the corporate body of the Church.

Hoover emphasized churchwomen's history and historical role models as sources of inspiration, pride, self-worth, self-esteem, and self-love, something that Black women too often lacked, given the withering disapproval suffered by so many on a daily basis in their interactions with white women and Black men. She devoured the books in women's history that began appearing from academic presses in the 1970s and wrote of them approvingly in her columns. She was largely responsible for launching a project to reclaim Methodist women's past and for recruiting the assistance of and collaboration with the Methodist General Commission on Archives and History in the effort. To that end, the commission convened the first-ever conference on Methodist women's history, held in Cincinnati in 1980.[40] The WD contributed funds and chose Hilah M. Thomas as the coordinator. Thomas conducted numerous oral histories with leading Methodist women. In addition, the new Committee on Women's Concerns encouraged churchwomen to write the histories of their work, especially if they were ethnic minorities. Out of this came several volumes chronicling the institutional record of women's work, written by leaders and participants themselves.[41]

Knowing their story enabled them to point with pride to past accomplishments and to validate their identity. Methodist women's organizations had perhaps "the longest continuing history of any women's groups in the country," Hoover pointed out as she also reminded the UMW of why it had come to be in the first place: "Concerns for health and educational needs of all women, as well as our own need to be witnesses to the faith, brought these organizations into being."[42] History justified continuation of that mission, she asserted. Among other things, it showed that, over the course of a century of existence, they had conscientiously managed and invested funds, destroying yet another myth about women's incompetence.[43] In the mid-1980s, the Methodist women's missionary associations celebrated one hundred years of existence, which provided the occasion Hoover needed to encourage every chapter of the organization—all thirty thousand of them—to write their own histories. It was important that they take time and effort to do this because, Hoover explained, "The community of faith is never left at the mercy of the present alone. The community of faith draws hope from its memory of God's work. In this form, hope is the antidote to rootlessness."[44] Not only did the Methodist missionary societies form the oldest continuously existing single-sex women's organizations in the country, but they had also been the most autonomous among Christian denominations. If the past was any guide, Methodist women could be trusted to hold power and to make decisions responsibly; thus, it should be self-evident that they could be trusted with greater decision-making roles within the contemporary church.[45]

As we have seen, Christian feminist theologians held that people on the bottom, including those who were the target of missionary activity, had much to teach privileged people living in the First World. Hoover stressed the reciprocal nature of mission work regularly, saying, "We are learning more about theological thought from sources other than the Western world. Theologies are being recorded from other continents, from women, from ethnic groups in this country and from peoples' movements struggling to free themselves from tyranny and oppression."[46] This appreciation for grassroots, indigenous theology accompanied changes to mission after World War II, when decolonization occurred and Western missionaries were either forced out or forced to reconceptualize their traditional roles in the receiving countries. For many, it caused shock and alarm, but for Hoover, it was cause for celebration because it indicated that missionary efforts had succeeded in their goals: "We rejoice that early missionaries developed programs and projects in many places around the world. We also rejoice to see places where the planted seeds have grown, sprouting new ones in the form of leaders and manageable program outreach."[47] Coming from a class of marginalized others herself, Hoover felt this more deeply than a white person would, and she could say with the voice of authority that missionaries should listen to the people they served and should avoid an attitude of imperiousness that portrayed Westerners as the saviors, the know-it-alls who were bringing spiritual as well as physical resources to the needy.

Telling missionaries to avoid the "God-complex," seeing themselves as the people who held the truth that was to be imparted to the heathen, is consistent with another common tenet of feminist theology: the stress on commonalities and cooperation among all living creatures rather than domination and conflict. Feminists hold that the hierarchies and disharmony among people of different classes, ethnicities, and denominations were male-imposed forms of conflict that hindered the unity of the body of Christ. They rejected the idea of God as separate from us and detached—a vengeful punisher. Such a view, they maintained, was a product of male hierarchical thinking. Instead, they emphasized connections based in mutually supportive relationships among God, oneself, others, and nature. Feminists and Wesleyans all stressed community-building, but where feminists differed from the male founder of Methodism was in rejecting the emphasis on dualism. Hoover's brand of proto-womanism wedded those ideas together: "Much of our training and experience has been focused on seeing our world divided into 'we' and 'they'" (or us and others). She continues, "My act of re-committing to the future is to break out of this violence of dualisms which leads to unjust systems." In her view, mutual respect for the full humanity of everyone within the body of Christ is what the church must strive for.[48]

Seeking an end to conflict led feminist Methodist women to put their energies into peace movements and ecumenism (working with other Christian denominations toward the goal of unity). Hoover believed so strongly in the church universal that she called herself an "ecumaniac." She served on the boards of a number of ecumenical organizations with strong social justice backgrounds, organizations that forged alliances among people committed to the transformation of society, committed, that is, to action in the public sphere rather than simply prayer: the YWCA, the National and World Councils of Churches, the Bossey Ecumenical Institute, the National Council of Negro Women, the World Federation of Methodist Women, and Church Women United.[49] Hoover regularly attended meetings of the World Federation of Methodist Women, which met in various places around the world every five years and which had as its goal "the visible unity of Christians in witness and mission." Working toward Christian unity, she pointed out, involved frequent disappointment and setbacks, but that was not a reason to give up on the ultimate objective. As she wrote in 1982, "We are a pilgrim people. We are in the process of becoming one visible sign of unity in the world. . . . Victory was not achieved yet; the process was plagued by failures but with each failure we start anew, recommitting ourselves to the hope that is within us."[50]

That she ends on a hopeful note is typical of feminist theology of the 1980s, which was marked by optimism. She expressed this "gospel of hope" (also referred to as the "theology of hope") regularly, stating that the necessary components of a meaningful life were "love, belief, HOPE!" And "We [United Methodist Women] believe that women should not only look to the future with hope, but that together we should help shape that future." Her Christmas columns in *response* often focused on the birth of the Christ child as context for the investment the UMW made in all children—sources of hope for the future and symbols for the potential good in all humans.[51]

The theology of hope included the vision for a liberated world, one in which not just each human being but all animals and the natural habitat they occupied would be treated with dignity and respect. Ecofeminists and eco-theologians (typically women) called for an end to environmental racism and human exploitation of the environment. Eradicating hierarchies of power was essential because all exploitation and tyranny must be stamped out before the Kingdom of God would appear on Earth. This included the exploitation of the natural world by humans, another manifestation of patriarchy. Neither feminists nor womanists adhered to the patriarchal view of humans as at the apex of God's creation. Ecofeminists, as they came to be called, argued that the way Christians had traditionally viewed the earth—as something to be dominated and controlled—was a manifestation of patriarchy.[52] Ecofeminists, like womanists, stressed that humans should be conservators and preservers of environmental resources rather than destroyers of worlds. The exploitation of the earth's resources for the benefit of those who *have* without showing real concern for those who *have not* was wasteful and unethical. Hoover even raised alarm bells about human-caused global warming back in the 1980s. She took issue with the old view that the earth existed to support human existence and that it had no value of its own, saying, "All the earth's people, especially Christians, are called to be responsible stewards of the earth's resources. 'The earth is the Lord's' takes on a new dimension of stewardship as we see populations grow and as we experience great potential for destruction and depletion of the natural resources."[53] Arising out of feminist theology's emphasis on the integrity of creation, of viewing human beings as one strand within a connected web of being, came a new ethic of population control as a moral choice, something that led her and others in the WD to call for an end to forced birth.

HOOVER'S FEMINIST THEOLOGY IN ACTION

In addition to identifying the structural bases of oppression, womanists insisted that, once identified, solutions for the eradication of oppression needed to be formulated and acted upon. Hoover, like all Methodist leaders, emphasized the idea that faith and love should be put into action, which meshed nicely with womanist principles. She regularly reminded *response* readers that "Christian values are not important when they are only 'held'; they must also be expressed in all of our life."[54] Many of the stands she took were quite controversial, for example, the hotly debated issue of women's access to family planning resources and to legal abortion. Thanks to Hoover and the WD, The United Methodist Church became one of the first mainline Christian denominations to go on record in support of reproductive freedom, or what it referred to as "responsible parenthood." Methodists and other Christian feminists had to develop this line of reasoning on their own because there is no tradition of "body rights" within Christianity. Therefore, Christian feminists reconfigured the old male-defined view of woman as "the weaker vessel" who, through the sin of Eve, was responsible for humans' fall from grace. They pointed out the inconsistency of condemning woman for Original Sin while simultaneously regarding her ability to bear children as blessed. They sought a desacralization of women's power to reproduce and to remove biology from the equation altogether. Women need not be biological mothers for their lives to have value in the eyes of God, they insisted.[55] After all, nuns had proven that centuries before.

Hoover and many of the Methodist staff women she worked with in New York lived the Protestant equivalent of a nun's life in that they were married to the cause and remained single their entire lives. Perhaps this was a sacrifice to their commitment to mission or perhaps it was because of their desire for romantic relationships with other women (as was certainly true of many nuns), or maybe a bit of both. Hoover's sexual orientation cannot be determined, but we do know that she believed she could do the Lord's work more effectively by nurturing large numbers of children (and mothers) through the vehicle of the church rather than by having biological children of her own. To feminist Methodists, quality of life was more important than quantity. Controlling reproduction, then, allowed women the space to choose to become mothers to society or to advance their own careers instead of becoming biological mothers themselves.

Within a year of taking over, Hoover led the WD to adopt a resolution calling for an end to uncontrolled overpopulation and forced sterilization and in favor of reproductive freedom and decriminalization of abortion. The women persuaded the Board of Christian Social Concerns of the United Methodist Church (the male version of the WD's Department of Christian Social Relations) to approve the resolution as well, and in 1971 the two agencies produced an educational pamphlet, *Abortion: A Human Choice*, to prepare the upcoming General Conference to adopt a similar resolution, which it did. As of 1972, therefore, the *Social Principles* of the *Book of Discipline* said that abortion did not belong in the criminal code and that it should be regulated no differently than any other medical procedure.[56]

Given the WD's long history of support for women's equality and its recent espousal of reproductive rights, it is clearly no coincidence that Sarah Weddington, the young attorney in Austin, Texas, who successfully litigated the case of *Roe v. Wade*, was the daughter of a Methodist clergyman whose wife was a member of the local UMW and that Weddington graduated from a small Methodist college in Texas. It's no accident, either, that the justice who wrote the majority opinion in that Supreme Court ruling, Henry Blackmun, was also Methodist. Clearly, Hoover's leadership of the WD had national impact.[57]

Following the legalization of abortion in 1973, the WD became a founding member of the Religious Coalition for Abortion Rights, a national body today known as the Religious Coalition for Reproductive Choice. Representing that group, Hoover testified before a House subcommittee in March 1976 about why mainline Protestant and Jewish groups opposed a constitutional amendment to prohibit abortion.[58] In 1975, the General Conference passed a resolution proclaiming that while all human life had sacred value, pregnancy was a unique situation in which two lives sometimes came into conflict and, in that case, the life of the woman must take precedence over the fetus. The WD also joined a historic legal battle against the infamous Hyde Amendment, which prevented Medicaid from paying for abortions, in the case of *McRae v. Califano.* Unfortunately, they lost when in 1980 the Supreme Court ruled that Hoover and Ellen Kirby (a staff member) did not have standing to sue because they were neither pregnant nor Medicaid recipients.[59]

Part of Hoover's agenda was to persuade not just the WD board but the General Conference to adopt feminist positions and policies. Hoover hired Ellen Kirby, who had a master's degree in theology from Union, precisely for this purpose. Kirby and Hoover convinced the 1968 General Conference to authorize an Ad Hoc Committee on Churchwomen's Liberation to compile data about discrimination against women in the United Methodist Church. The committee produced a report in 1972 that showed women were "grossly underrepresented in decision-making positions in the general church," to no one's surprise.[60] At the 1972 General Conference, the Ad Hoc Committee became the permanent Commission on the Status and Role of Women in Church and Society, charged with eliminating "sexism in all its manifestations from the total life of the United Methodist Church." This commission recommended the establishment of a variety of programs that would benefit women not just in the church but in the neighborhoods where they lived, including women's centers, counseling services on abortion (that helped women find safe, affordable abortions before and after it became legal), childcare, job and vocation counseling, groups to plan women's studies curricula in seminaries, and other aids to women students. With Hoover's encouragement, hundreds of local churches and conferences organized their own commissions although in some cases they were packed (or controlled) by the bishops, which blunted their impact.[61]

In addition to demanding that women be accorded greater representation in decision-making roles in the church, another thorny issue that Hoover and other Christian feminists grappled with was male-defined language. Hoover had long ago decried the fact that theology and church structures were "premised on a male understanding of life, the church, and its functions," and she pled "the men of God to provide an image of God inclusive of male and female."[62] The use of the ubiquitous "man" erased women from the liturgy, hymns, and gospel texts. To correct that, the WD persuaded the General Conference to establish the United Methodist Task Force on Inclusive Language and resolved "to move intentionally towards a church in which unhealthy distinctions are neither expressed nor implied in language and symbolism." They also pushed the National Council of Churches, on whose board she sat, to produce a guide to an inclusive language lectionary in the early 1980s as a model for members, although its use was voluntary. The United Methodist Church followed its guidelines, and the WD issued an even more comprehensive set of guidelines that removed other kinds of bias as well.[63]

The most sought-after goal of second-wave feminism was the ratification of the proposed Equal Rights Amendment. Again at the urging of Hoover and her staff of committed feminists, the WD executive committee unanimously approved support for ratification of the ERA in 1971, making it one of the first religious groups to do so. In 1972, following the ERA's passage by Congress, the General Conference voted almost unanimously in favor of a Resolution on Equal Rights for Women, which said in part, "The Gospel makes clear that Jesus regarded women, men and children equally. In contrast to the contemporary male-centered society, Jesus related to women with respect and sensitivity, as individual persons. . . . We urge all United Methodists to work through the appropriate structures and channels toward ratification of the Amendment by their respective states."[64] The ERA Support Project, a joint body combining the efforts of several church agencies, wrote and published a pamphlet, "The Church, Religion, and the Equal Rights Amendment," that educated readers and urged action on behalf of the amendment. The WD was a founding member and the only religious group on the Board of Directors of ERA America, the umbrella organization for all national organizations working for ERA, and *response* regularly carried articles educating readers on how they might persuade their legislators to vote in support of the amendment. As a result, the largest number of churchwomen working for ratification of the ERA were United Methodists, and at least four UMW women became chairpersons of their statewide coalitions. Unfortunately, all their efforts went down in flames when the time limit on the ERA's ratification ran out in 1982.[65]

Not only did Hoover view elimination of gender hierarchies as part of her missionary calling, but she also sought to end discrimination based on race. Among those antiracism initiatives was a program of racial reconciliation established by the national YWCA, where Hoover worked with another Black United Methodist and fellow New Yorker, Dorothy Height, president of the National Council of Negro Women. Height had overseen the implementation of the Y's Interracial Charter, adopted in 1946, and founded its Center for Racial Justice. She appointed Hoover as chair of the YWCA's national public affairs committee in the mid-sixties, during which time the YWCA sponsored a dozen or so voter registration projects in the South. Starting in 1973, Hoover led its task force on racial justice, just one more means by which she put her beliefs into action.[66]

Advocating policy positions that advanced the cause of women's equality was yet another way that UMW members could live out their faith in the world. Perhaps to allay criticism from more conservative elements that the WD was becoming too political, Hoover cited its own history for authority, saying,

> through the years, the Division has encouraged members of the organization to be concerned about and involved in the legislative process. From citizenship brunches of the '50s to legislative training events of the '70s and '80s, we have acquainted hundreds of women with political issues; and even helped many practice the art of involvement as they worked to elect the candidates of their choice. Many church women will find the Division's new political-skills emphasis an opportunity to extend the bounds of mission.[67]

Since she had been the legislative liaison for the division at one point, she could draw on her own experience: she had testified before Congressional committees and served as an observer at the United Nations, another international agency that the WD had long supported.

The WD had always had a "peace" division and thus was particularly interested in the goals of the UN. While all churches had been invited to send representatives to the 1945 charter meeting of the UN in San Francisco, and The Methodist Church along with other mainline denominations had done so, the WD had sent its own representatives and, once the UN began functioning in New York City, hired Margaret Bender as its own official observer. The WD loaned half a million dollars (from which it received no profit) to The Methodist Church for the construction of the twelve-story office building called the Church Center for the United Nations on the United Nations Plaza. A project managed jointly by the National Council of Churches, the Division of World Peace of the Board of Christian Social Concerns, and the WD, it was then and remains today an interdenominational hub for any religion or representatives from any country—particularly those not given recognition in the UN General Assembly—concerned with and attempting to influence decisions of the United Nations. Hoover took seriously the division's mission as peacekeepers and encouraged members of the UMW to become global citizens. "We must increasingly widen the angles of our vision to give the term 'neighbor' a new interpretation, to focus our energies in order to proclaim peace on earth," she said, striking a theme common to her columns that appeared around Christmastime. She was an active participant herself, frequently taking groups to the UN headquarters to sit in on the proceedings and to participate in study sessions.[68] The WD publicized and cheered on the UN's designation of International Women's Year in 1977 and the Year of the Child in 1979, printing pamphlets and writing columns for *response* that educated UMW members about ways they could participate.[69]

Unfortunately, these progressive positions began to hurt the UMW (and The United Methodist Church) as the country tilted to the right politically in the 1970s. As early as April 1972, Hoover reported that the UMW had lost more than 190,000 members although fundraising remained strong.[70] What Hoover bemoaned, however, was a phenomenon suffered by all the mainline denominations in the latter third of the twentieth century for a variety of reasons. For one thing, the church was no longer the central institution in most people's lives, and women were far more likely to work outside the home in 1990 than in the 1950s, meaning they had less time to devote to volunteer activities. The UMW was a particularly demanding taskmaster, requiring monthly local meetings, quarterly district meetings, and attendance at "schools of Christian mission" in the summer for continuing education, along with collecting money and writing reports. The schedule was simply too onerous for modern women.

But in some ways, the UMW and its leaders were victims of their own success. As they persuaded government to provide services for which they had demonstrated an unmet need, the missionary imperative of doing good works in the name of God declined in importance. Hoover credited Methodist women for their accomplishments: "Many of the helping agencies in society today are the direct result of activity engaged in and developed by women. This is particularly true of the social and public welfare systems in this country."[71] The expanded welfare state meant that people who were down on their luck could look to federal relief agencies for assistance instead of to private charities. Additionally, the UN picked up programs that had once been the work of foreign missionaries, and, as a result of changes in missiology, the division turned over older mission communities to the converted Christian indigenous people to run. In the 1950s, the WD pioneered a new model for college-educated missionaries to serve two-year terms, the US-2 program, which became the prototype for the Peace Corps established by President Kennedy in the early 1960s. Seldom did missionaries commit for life anymore, meaning that there were few incentives for churches to raise huge sums of money to support them. Hospitals, schools, and other institutions that had filled gaps in services a century before now had competition from state-supported and for-profit institutions. As the imperative waned, so did interest, particularly among young women.[72]

Retiring from the WD in 1990 after having dedicated forty-two years of her life to it, Hoover could point to an impressive record of accomplishments and multiple honors. *Ebony* listed her among the "100 most influential African-American women," and she was inducted into the Arkansas Black Hall of Fame. Moreover, she was the first laywoman to have a church named for her: Theressa Hoover United Methodist Church in Little Rock. The UMW created a permanent award in tribute to her, the Theressa Hoover Community Service and Global Citizenship Fund, in the amount of $100,000. It honored her commitment to global citizenship, ecumenism, international travel, and informal learning by supporting the recipient's voyage to a country or region other than her own. "The emphasis on travel and informal learning rather than a period of formal study through scholarship aid recognizes Ms. Hoover's strong belief in that form of learning for women and for laity in particular," read the acknowledgment.[73] There could be no more fitting tribute to someone who affirmed the layperson's ability to "do theology," who added her authority and voice to the chorus of those insisting upon the dignity and value of women's experiences, who asserted the need for liberation of women and all other oppressed groups, who advanced the fight for women's status within the church, in politics, in society, and in the world, who stressed the interconnectedness of relationships, inclusiveness, and pluralism, and who insisted that Christians be open-minded and empathetic rather than arrogant, imperialistic, or divisive—all with the hope that these values, if fully implemented, would eventually set everyone free.

NOTES

1. In 1939, when three branches of Methodism united, the women's missionary organizations were consolidated into two organizations: the Woman's Society of Christian Service and an auxiliary for working women, the Wesleyan Service Guild. The elected members of the *Woman's* Division of the Board of Missions governed both. Upon the merger with the Evangelical United Brethren in 1968, the formal name was changed to the *Women's* Division of the General Board of Global Ministries of the United Methodist Church. For consistency and ease of reading, the governing body for which Hoover worked will be referred to throughout as the Women's Division, the division, or the WD. In 1973, all previously existing women's missionary organizations merged into the United Methodist

Women, supervised by the Women's Division's elected board. Ellen Blue, *Women United for Change: 150 Years in Mission* (New York: United Methodist Women, 2019), 111–14.

2. Numbers are based on some guesswork due to irregular and inconsistent reporting. Hoover believed membership may have been as high as two million. In 1965, the Woman's Society of Christian Service reported a membership of 1.7 million, while the Methodist Church had 10.3 million members. Statistics for the United Methodist Church and the Evangelical United Brethren are available at http://www.gcah.org/history/united-methodist-membership-statistics.

3. Theressa Hoover, *With Unveiled Face: Centennial Reflections on Women and Men in the Community of the Church* (New York, 1983), 29–31; and Betty Thompson, "Women and Missions: The Struggle and the Structure—A Brief History of the 1964 Agreements," *Methodist History* 33, no. 2 (January 1995): 98–111. For a historical overview of women's foreign and domestic missionary work in the Methodist Episcopal Church, the Methodist Episcopal Church South, and the Evangelical United Brethren, see Blue, *Women United for Change.*

4. Although many historians have challenged the wave metaphor in feminist history, pointing to the many years of women's activism between the so-called waves, "second wave" remains a common and useful designation for the feminist movement of the 1950s–1970s. Online biographies of Hoover include Rebecca Haden, "Theressa Hoover (1925–2013)," in *The Encyclopedia of Arkansas*, https://encyclopediaofarkansas.net/entries/theressa-hoover-4006/; and Linda Bloom, "Remembering Theressa Hoover, Woman of Firsts," United Methodist News Service, January 9, 2014, http://methodistmission200.org/hoover-theressa/ (accessed June 7, 2019). *response* magazine deviated from the standard and did not capitalize the first letter in its title.

5. Interviews I have conducted with those who knew and worked with Hoover have confirmed Sohl's appraisal of her, e.g., Barbara Campbell, telephone interview with author, June 1, 2019; and Joyce Sohl, remarks at Theressa Hoover's service (copy in possession of the author).

6. Bloom, "Remembering Theressa Hoover."

7. *response*, June 1970; Wesley Pippert, *Faith at the Top* (Elgin, IL: David C. Cook, 1973), 108; and NBC *Today* show tape, June 28, 1974, General Commission on Archives and History (GCAH), United Methodist Archives and History Center, Drew University, Madison, NJ. Hoover gave the Fondren lecture at Perkins and the Lentz lecture at Harvard.

8. Jan Love, interview with author, January 17, 2022, via Zoom. Love worked closely with Hoover in the 1970s, and Hoover recruited her to serve as the CEO of the WD in 2004. Love is currently a dean at Emory University. Emilie Townes notes that Walker first used the term "womanism" in several places in the 1970s, but elaborated on it in her book *In Search of Our Mothers' Gardens: Womanist Prose* (New York: Harcourt Brace Jovanovich, 1983), xi–xii. See Emilie M. Townes, "Womanist Theology," in *Encyclopedia of Women and Religion in North America*, ed. Rosemary Skinner Keller and Rosemary Radford Ruether (Bloomington: Indiana University Press, 2006), 1165. The term "womanist theology" was first used by Delores S. Williams in "Womanist Theology: Black Women's Voices," *Christianity and Crisis* 47 (March 2, 1987): 66–70. See also Rosemary Radford Ruether, "Feminist Voices," in *Christian Social Teachings: A Reader in Christian Social Ethics from the Bible to the Present*, ed. George W. Forell, rev. and updated by James M. Childs, 298-323, 2nd ed. (Minneapolis: 1517 Media, Fortress Press, 2013), https://doi.org/10.2307/j.ctt22nm868; Jacquelyn Grant,

White Women's Christ and Black Women's Jesus: Feminist Christology and Womanist Response (Atlanta: Scholars Press, 1989); Emilie M. Townes, ed., *A Troubling in My Soul: Womanist Perspectives on Evil and Suffering* (Maryknoll, NY: Orbis, 1993), 2; and Kimberlé Crenshaw, "Mapping the Margins: Intersectionality, Identity Politics, and Violence Against Women of Color," *Stanford Law Review* 43, no. 6 (July 1991): 1241–99.

9. The United States proved to be particularly fertile territory for Methodism. On the eve of the Civil War, it was the largest Protestant denomination in the nation. Though over 75 percent of Methodists worldwide lived in the United States, they were not all part of the same church, which fractured into several branches. It split over the issue of slavery in 1846 when white southern Methodists seceded from the Methodist Episcopal Church (MEC) to form the Methodist Episcopal Church, South (MECS). African Americans, who were especially drawn to Methodism's emphasis on spiritualism combined with outreach to the poor and marginalized, formed their own denominations unaffiliated with the MEC or the MECS: the Christian Methodist Episcopal Church, the African Methodist Episcopal Church, and AME Zion. In 1939, the MEC and MECS voted to join with the Methodist Protestant Church to become The Methodist Church. Black Methodist congregations (affiliated with the MEC but not the other denominations) were placed into a segregated nationwide administrative district called the Central Jurisdiction, a sprawling, difficult-to-govern territory with too few resources. See Nancy Britton, *Two Centuries of Methodism in Arkansas, 1800–2000* (Little Rock: August House, 2000), 198–99, 217–21; and Blue, *Women United for Change*, 72.

10. *response*, September 1990.

11. See Willard B. Gatewood, "School Desegregation in Fayetteville: A Forty-Year Perspective," in *Civil Obedience: An Oral History of School Desegregation in Fayetteville, Arkansas, 1954–1965*, ed. Julianne Lewis Adams and Thomas A. DeBlack (Fayetteville: University of Arkansas Press, 1994), 3; Pippert, *Faith*, 115; and Betty Thompson, "Theressa Hoover: A Woman for All Seasons," *response*, October 1990.

12. Gatewood, in "School Desegregation," supports the claim that Fayetteville was more moderate than most places in Arkansas. He credits the small size of the Black population (four hundred people out of a population of eighteen thousand in the 1950s) with reducing white fears of a "takeover" and ensuring that whites and Blacks knew each other as individuals. In addition, the University of Arkansas, the first state university in the South to admit African Americans (in 1948), had brought in faculty from outside the South "who gave expression to attitudes and values that made Fayetteville more cosmopolitan and racially tolerant than many towns of comparable size in the state. . . . Finally," he continued, "in the 1950s, the business leadership in Fayetteville exhibited a degree of pragmatic enlightenment that often did not exist in other parts of Arkansas." Leaders "saw the link between good schools and economic development," which they were keenly interested in (5–6). Four days after the *Brown* decision, the Fayetteville school board voted unanimously to integrate Fayetteville Senior High School (7). See also United Methodist News Service, October 4, 1990; George Daniels, *Turning Corners: Reflections of African Americans in the United Methodist Church from 1961–1993* (Dayton, OH: United Methodist Church, General Council on Ministries, 1996), 45–46; Pippert, *Faith*, 116; and Cherisse Jones-Branch, "Segregation and Desegregation," *Encyclopedia of Arkansas*, last updated September 12, 2022, http://www.encyclopediaofarkansas.net/encyclopedia/entry-detail.aspx?search=1&entryID=3079.

13. Philander Smith students led or participated in several waves of sit-ins in Little Rock (the only ones in Arkansas) beginning in March 1960. See Jones-Branch, "Segregation and Desegregation"; Randy Finley, "Crossing the White Line: SNCC in Three Delta Towns, 1963–1967," *Arkansas Historical Quarterly* 65, no. 2 (2006): 118–19; John A. Kirk, "Capitol Offenses: Desegregating the Seat of Arkansas Government, 1964–1965," *Arkansas Historical Quarterly* 72, no. 2 (2013): 95–119, http://www.jstor.org/stable/24477433; and Sarah Riva, "Desegregating Downtown Little Rock: The Field Reports of SNCC's Bill Hansen, October 23 to December 3, 1962," *Arkansas Historical Quarterly* 71, no. 3 (2012): 264–82. Hoover earned an MA in human relations and social policy from New York University in 1962. See Pippert, *Faith*, 118.

14. Britton, *Methodism in Arkansas*, 14.

15. Sara M. Evans, *Journeys That Opened Up the World: Women, Student Christian Movements, and Social Justice, 1955–1975* (New Brunswick, NJ: Rutgers University Press, 2004), 1, 6–7.

16. See Daniels, *Turning Corners*, 46; Britton, *Methodism in Arkansas*, 238, 243; and Ben F. Johnson, III, *Arkansas in Modern America, 1930–1999* (Fayetteville: University of Arkansas Press, 2000), 66.

17. The National Urban League cosponsored the project. Theressa Hoover, interview by Tammie Dillon, March 21, 1996, UALR Seminar in Public History (HIST 7391) Files on Camp Aldersgate, UALR.MS.0229, Butler Center, Central Arkansas Library System; Hoover, "Responsively Yours," *response*, April 1988, 28; and Ernestine Henderson, "An Experience at Aldersgate," *Methodist Woman*, July 1949, 30–31. Henderson (later McKinney) was president of the Little Rock Methodist Council. She and Mrs. E. D. (Sarah) Galloway, another council president, negotiated the contract for the camp. Walter Vernon, *Methodism in Arkansas, 1816–1976* (Little Rock: Joint Committee for the History of Arkansas Methodism, 1976), 221; and Nancy Britton, *Camp Aldersgate: A Brief History* (Little Rock: Camp Aldersgate, 1997).

18. MECS women's outreach to African American women in the South began in the early twentieth century. For overviews of that work, see John Patrick McDowell, *The Social Gospel in the South: The Woman's Home Mission Movement in the Methodist Episcopal Church, South, 1886–1939* (Baton Rouge: Louisiana State University Press, 1982); Blue, *Women United for Change*, especially 81–84; and *States' Laws on Race and Color, and Appendices: Containing International Documents, Federal Laws and Regulations, Local Ordinances and Charts* (Cincinnati: Women's Division of Christian Service, Board of Missions and Church Extension, Methodist Church, 1950). The publication assisted Marshall as he drafted arguments for the *Brown v. Board of Education* lawsuit. Pauli Murray, *Pauli Murray: The Autobiography of a Black Activist, Feminist, Lawyer, Priest, and Poet* (Knoxville: University of Tennessee Press, 1987), 284–87.

19. *response*, March 1990.

20. Thompson, "Theressa Hoover," 6; and Pippert, *Faith*, 117.

21. Daniels, *Turning Corners*, 45–48. The idea that there is little distinction between clergy and laypeople is common to Protestantism and was especially important in the Wesleyan tradition, so this is not an idea Hoover invented, but it is one that held particular significance for her as a high-profile lay leader.

22. *response*, January 1969; and Campbell interview.

23. *response*, March 1990.

24. Hoover, *With Unveiled Face*, 32–33. The study commission was also called the Ad Hoc Committee on EUB Union.

25. Pippert, *Faith*, 121–22; and *response*, March 1978, September 1973, October 1971, and October 1983. The annual budget of the Women's Division, including a table or chart of how monies were spent, was published yearly in *response*. See for example *response*, May 1980, 51. The organization had a national fiscal officer and tens of millions of dollars in investments managed by staff as well as the board.

26. Sallie McFague, "Models of God," in *The Cambridge Companion to Feminist Theology*, ed. Susan Frank Parsons (Cambridge, UK: Cambridge University Press, 2002), 236.

27. Theressa Hoover, "Black Women and the Churches: Triple Jeopardy," in *Sexist Religion and Women in the Church: No More Silence*, ed. Alice L. Hageman in collaboration with The Women's Caucus of Harvard Divinity School (New York: Association Press, 1974), 75.

28. Hoover, "Black Women and the Churches," 75.

29. Hoover, "Black Women and the Churches," 75.

30. For more on this topic, see Rosemary Radford Ruether, *Sexism and God-Talk: Towards a Feminist Theology* (London: SCM, 1983).

31. James H. Cone, *Black Theology and Black Power* (New York: Seabury Press, 1969); *response*, January 1972; and Hoover in *Christian Ministry*, no. 2 (May 1971): 3.

32. David P. Cline, *From Reconciliation to Revolution: The Student Interracial Ministry, Liberal Christianity, and the Civil Rights Movement* (Chapel Hill: University of North Carolina Press, 2016), 133, 146, 186–89, 191. The July-August 1969 issue of *response* contains Hoover's denunciation of Forman's words and actions. See also Hoover, "Triple Jeopardy"; and *response*, May 1973, 19–20.

33. *response*, September 1982.

34. Both quotes from *response*, March 1988.

35. *response*, March 1969.

36. Hoover, *With Unveiled Face*, 34.

37. Elaine Magalis, *Conduct Becoming to a Woman: Bolted Doors and Burgeoning Missions*, rev. ed. (New York: Women's Division, General Board of Global Ministries, United Methodist Church, 2003), 167; and Hoover, *Christian Ministry*, 3.

38. *response*, May 1969; and Hoover, *Christian Ministry*, 3.

39. Sarah Bentley Doely, ed., *Women's Liberation and the Church: The New Demand for Freedom in the Life of the Christian Church* (New York: Association Press, 1970), 86; and *response*, May 1971.

40. *response*, June 1982. Proceedings were subsequently published in *Women in New Worlds: Historical Perspectives on the Wesleyan Tradition*, 2 vols., ed. Rosemary Skinner Keller, Louise L. Queen, and Hilah F. Thomas (Nashville: Abingdon, 1982).

41. Ellen Kirby, "The Evolution of a Focus: Women's Concerns in the Women's Division, 1970–1980," Women's Division, General Board of Global Ministries, the United Methodist Church, 1983, 34–35; and "Growing Interest in History," *response*, April 1980.

42. *response*, January 1978.

43. See for example *response*, June 1982.

44. I have seen hundreds of histories of local church missionary societies scattered around various Methodist conference archives. Quote is from *response*, April 1982, 11–12.

45. *response*, October 1983.

46. *response*, October 1982.

47. *response*, November 1990.

48. Quote is from *response*, November 1990, 11. See also Hoover's columns in *response*, June 1979, September 1982, and April 1984.

49. Methodist women were the majority membership and the energizing force for Church Women United, founded as an interracial ecumenical Christian organization in 1941; see https://www.churchwomenunited.net/. Founded in 1946, The Ecumenical Institute at Bossey (in Geneva, Switzerland) is now part of the University of Geneva; https://institute.oikoumene.org/en. The World Federation of Methodist Women's charter of assent, signed by twenty-seven countries in 1939, was the official beginning of this organization, although its antecedents stretched back to the 1920s; see World Federation of Methodist and Uniting Church Women, World Federation PowerPoint Presentation, updated March 12, 2022, https://wfmucw.org/about/history.

50. *response*, October 1982.

51. *response*, March 1971 and September 1990.

52. Grace Jantzen, *God's World, God's Body* (Philadelphia: Westminster Press, 1984); Sallie McFague, *The Body of God: An Ecological Theology* (Minneapolis: Fortress Press, 1993); and Natalie K. Watson, *Feminist Theology* (Grand Rapids, MI: William B. Eerdmans Publishing Company, 2003), 50–51.

53. *response*, April 1990.

54. Pippert, *Faith*, 108; and Thompson, "Theressa Hoover," 19.

55. Elizabeth A. Clark and Herbert Richardson, eds., *Women and Religion: The Original Sourcebook of Women in Christian Thought*, rev. ed. (New York: HarperCollins, 1996), 288–90.

56. *Abortion: A Human Choice* (Washington, DC: Division of General Welfare, Department of Population Problems, Board of Christian Social Concerns of the United Methodist Church, May 1971). Three female OB/GYNs assisted in drafting the resolution: Dr. Louise Branscomb from Alabama, Dr. Kathryn Wilcox, and Dr. Leigh Roberts. For the 1975 resolution, see Appendix H in Hoover, *With Unveiled Face. response* issues that concentrated on the abortion controversy include those of July/August 1972, April 1975, September 1975, November 1978, and January 1981. See also Ashley Boggan Dreff, "Methodists and the New Morality: A History of Twentieth-Century Methodist Sexual Ethics" (PhD diss., Drew University, 2017), 260–61; and Ashley Boggan Dreff, *Nevertheless: American Methodists and Women's Rights* (Nashville: Wesley's Foundery Books, 2020), chapter 4.

57. Janet Allured, *Remapping Second-Wave Feminism: The Long Women's Rights Movement in Louisiana, 1950–1997* (Athens: University of Georgia Press, 2016), chapter 5.

58. "Statement of the Religious Coalition for Abortion Rights before the Subcommittee on Civil and Constitutional Rights of the Committee of the Judiciary U.S. House of Representatives" (March 24, 1976), Folder "Religious Coalition for Abortion Rights 1979," Women's Division (2593-7-6:1), GCAH.

59. See Kirby, "Evolution of a Focus," 29; *response*, February 1990, 16; and Theressa Hoover, "The Other Side," in *What about Abortion?* (Willmore, KY: Good News, 1977), 9–13.

60. Norma Taylor Mitchell, a participant who wrote about it almost concurrently, described the new group of women as "radical feminists," a different breed from the "social feminists" they replaced. Mitchell, "From Social to Radical Feminism: A Survey of Emerging Diversity in Methodist Women's Organizations, 1869–1974," *Methodist History* 13, no. 3 (April 1975): 21–44.

61. See Kirby, "Evolution of a Focus," 5; Hoover, *With Unveiled Face*, 35–36; and Magalis, *Conduct*, 167.

62. Hoover, *Christian Ministry*.

63. For the Women's Division's role in the NCC, see Hartmann, *Other Feminists*, chapter 4; *response*, March 1970; Carolyn Henninger Oehler, *The Journey Is Our Home: A History of the General Commission on the Status and Role of Women*, 1995, rev. and updated, http://www.kyumc.org/files/oldfileslibrary/Thejourneyhome.pdf; Magalis, *Conduct*, 167; *Journal of the 1976 General Conference*, 1836; *response*, January 1976; and Task Force on Language Guidelines, "Words That Hurt, Words That Heal: Language about God and People," A Churchwide Study from the 1988 General Conference of the United Methodist Church, 1990.

64. *response*, July–August 1976.

65. ERA Support Project, a joint project of the Women's Division of the Board of Global Ministries and the Board of Church and Society of the United Methodist Church, "The Church, Religion, and the Equal Rights Amendment," n.d., c. 1975.

66. Hoover served as a member of the executive council of the National Council of Negro Women. See Pippert, *Faith*, 107; Evans, *Journeys*, 3–7; and Dorothy Height, *Open Wide the Freedom Gates* (New York: Public Affairs, 2003).

67. *New World Outlook*, April–May 1984, 14.

68. The observer at the San Francisco Conference was Dorothy McConnell, https://www.unitedmethodistwomen.org/ccun. See Campbell interview; *response*, December 1985 and February 1989; and A. Lanethea Mathews-Gardner, "From Ladies' Aid to NGO: Transformations in Methodist Women's Organizing in Postwar America," in *Breaking the Wave: Women, Their Organizations, and Feminism, 1945–1985*, ed. Kathleen A. Laughlin and Jacqueline L. Castledine (New York: Routledge, 2011), 99–112.

69. Pippert, *Faith*, 110; and *response*, April 1970, January 1972, and March 1979.

70. *response*, July–August 1978 and June 1980. By the 1980s, the UMW was down to 1.2 million members.

71. *response*, February 1982.

72. Alison Collis Greene, *No Depression in Heaven: The Great Depression, the New Deal, and the Transformation of Religion in the Delta* (New York: Oxford University Press, 2016), 6; and Hoover, *response*, June 1980.

73. *response*, January 1991.

SELECTED BIBLIOGRAPHY

Abortion: A Human Choice. Washington, DC: Division of General Welfare, Department of Population Problems, Board of Christian Social Concerns of the United Methodist Church, 1971.

Allured, Janet. *Remapping Second-Wave Feminism: The Long Women's Rights Movement in Louisiana, 1950–1997*. Athens: University of Georgia Press, 2016.

Annual Reports of the Woman's Division of Christian Service of the Board of Missions and Church Extension of the Methodist Church, 1940–1964.

Bloom, Linda. "Theressa Hoover." *Methodist Mission Bicentennial*. Accessed October 7, 2020. http://methodistmission200.org/hoover-theressa/.

Britton, Nancy. *Two Centuries of Methodism in Arkansas, 1800–2000*. Little Rock: August House Publishers, 2000.

Campbell, Barbara. Telephone interview with the author, June 1, 2019.

Clark, Elizabeth A., and Herbert Richardson, eds. *Women and Religion: The Original Sourcebook of Women in Christian Thought*. Rev. ed. New York: HarperCollins, 1996.

Collier-Thomas, Bettye. *Jesus, Jobs, and Justice: African American Women and Religion*. New York: Alfred A. Knopf, 2010.

Daniels, George M. *Turning Corners: Reflections of African Americans in the United Methodist Church from 1961–1993*. Dayton, OH: United Methodist Church, General Council on Ministries, 1996.

Doely, Sarah Bentley, ed. *Women's Liberation and the Church: The New Demand for Freedom in the Life of the Christian Church*. New York: Association Press, 1970.

Dreff, Ashley Boggan. "Methodists and the New Morality: A History of Twentieth-Century Methodist Sexual Ethics." PhD diss., Drew University, 2017.

ERA Support Project. "The Church, Religion, and the Equal Rights Amendment." Joint project of the Women's Division of the Board of Global Ministries and the Board of Church and Society of the United Methodist Church, n.d., c. 1975.

Grant, Jacquelyn. "Black Theology and the Black Woman." In *Black Theology: A Documentary History, 1966–1979*, edited by Gayraud S. Wilmore and James H. Cone, 418–43. Maryknoll, NY: Orbis Books, 1979.

Greene, Alison Collis. *No Depression in Heaven: The Great Depression, the New Deal, and the Transformation of Religion in the Delta*. New York: Oxford University Press, 2016.

Haden, Rebecca. "Theressa Hoover (1925–2013)." *The Encyclopedia of Arkansas*. Last modified February 23, 2018. https://encyclopediaofarkansas.net/entries/theressa-hoover-4006/.

Hartmann, Susan M. *The Other Feminists: Activists in the Liberal Establishment*. New Haven, CT: Yale University Press, 1998.

Height, Dorothy. *Open Wide the Freedom Gates*. New York: Public Affairs, 2003.

Hoover, Theressa. "Black Women and the Churches: Triple Jeopardy." In *Sexist Religion and Women in the Church: No More Silence*, edited by Alice L. Hageman in collaboration with the Women's Caucus of Harvard Divinity School, 63–76. New York: Association Press, 1974.

Hoover, Theressa. "The Other Side." In *What about Abortion?*, 9–13. Willmore, KY: Good News, 1977.

Jantzen, Grace. *God's World, God's Body*. Philadelphia: Westminster Press, 1984.

Kirby, Ellen. "The Evolution of a Focus: Women's Concerns in the Women's Division, 1970–1980." In *Journal of the Women's Division*. New York: Women's Division, General Board of Global Ministries, The United Methodist Church, April 1983, Appendix G.

Magalis, Elaine. *Conduct Becoming to a Woman: Bolted Doors and Burgeoning Missions*. New York: Women's Division, General Board of Global Ministries, United Methodist Church, 2003.

Manis, Andrew M. "'City Mothers': Dorothy Tilly, Georgia Methodist Women, and Black Civil Rights." In *Before Brown: Civil Rights and White Backlash in the Modern South*, edited by Glenn Feldman, 125–56. Tuscaloosa: University of Alabama Press, 2004.

McDowell, John Patrick. *The Social Gospel in the South: The Woman's Home Mission Movement in the Methodist Episcopal Church, South, 1886–1939*. Baton Rouge: Louisiana State University Press, 1982.

McFague, Sallie. *The Body of God: An Ecological Theology*. Minneapolis: Fortress Press, 1993.

Mitchell, Norma Taylor. "From Social to Radical Feminism: A Survey of Emerging Diversity in Methodist Women's Organizations, 1869–1974." *Methodist History* 13, no. 3 (April 1975): 21–44.

Murray, Pauli. *States' Laws on Race and Color, and Appendices: Containing International Documents, Federal Laws and Regulations, Local Ordinances and Charts*. Cincinnati: Women's Division of Christian Service, Board of Missions and Church Extension, Methodist Church, 1950.

NBC *Today* show videotape, June 28, 1974.

Oehler, Carolyn Henninger. *The Journey Is Our Home: A History of the General Commission on the Status and Role of Women*. New York: General Commission on the Status and Role of Women of the United Methodist Church, 2005. https://www.kyumc.org/files/oldfiles library/Thejourneyhome.pdf.

Pippert, Wesley. *Faith at the Top*. Elgin, IL: David C. Cook, 1973.

response. Magazine published by Division of Education and Cultivation, Board of Global Ministries of the United Methodist Church, 1969–.

Sohl, Joyce. Remarks at Theressa Hoover's memorial service. Copy in possession of the author.

"Statement of the Religious Coalition for Abortion Rights before the Subcommittee on Civil and Constitutional Rights of the Committee of the Judiciary U.S. House of Representatives," March 24, 1976. Folder "Religious Coalition for Abortion Rights 1979," Women's Division (2593-7-6:1), General Commission on Archives and History.

Task Force on Language Guidelines. "Words That Hurt, Words That Heal: Language about God and People." A Churchwide Study from the 1988 General Conference of the United Methodist Church, 1990.

Thompson, Betty Jane. "Theressa Hoover: A Woman for All Seasons." *response*, October 1990, 5–7, 19.

Vernon, Walter N. *Methodism in Arkansas, 1816–1976*. Little Rock: Joint Committee for the History of Arkansas Methodism, 1976.

Watson, Natalie K. *Feminist Theology*. Grand Rapids, MI: William B. Eerdmans Publishing Company, 2003.

Chapter 8

THE LIFE AND THOUGHT OF ANNA ARNOLD HEDGEMAN

A Pragmatic Christian Feminist

HETTIE V. WILLIAMS

Anna Arnold Hedgeman (1899–1990), activist, politician, educator, and writer, is one of the most important, yet least known, women who were instrumental in the historical development of the Black freedom struggle in the twentieth century. Her life of activism spanned nearly the entire century and encompassed more than six decades of social justice work. She is often only mentioned in passing in the scholarly literature concerning the civil rights era, with the exception of Jennifer Scanlon's biography *Until There Is Justice: The Life of Anna Arnold Hedgeman*, yet she was integral in advancing the major movements of the twentieth century including the civil rights movement and the women's liberation movement.[1] A self-defined feminist and social justice advocate who was the only woman on the committee to organize the March on Washington in 1963 and a cofounder of the National Organization for Women (NOW), she lived an extraordinary life of activism that also included membership in the National Association for the Advancement of Colored People (NAACP) and the Young Women's Christian Association (YWCA). Further, she worked with trade unions, with A. Philip Randolph and the Fair Employment Practices Committee, and with other associations concerned with human liberation during the rise of the civil rights movement. This chapter traces the intellectual development of Hedgeman's ideas and her activism as a pragmatic Christian feminist and pluralist-interracialist within the larger framework of the long Black freedom struggle.

Though defining herself specifically as a feminist, Hedgeman is part of a long tradition of Black proto-womanist and -feminist thinkers in the Methodist tradition, including Maria W. Stewart, Jarena Lee, Zilpha Elaw, Julia A. J. Foote, and

Florence Spearing Randolph.[2] Stewart, for example, is noted for her concern for women's rights and for inaugurating an intersectional approach to Black empowerment in her writings and speeches as early as 1831. Advancing a belief in Black women's activism as mothers, teachers, and leaders of the community, her writings reveal both a recognition of the interlocking nature of race, gender, and class oppression and an awareness of sexual politics.[3] Similarly, Elaw's writings reflect a concern for women's empowerment and Black freedom. Foote, a notable figure in the Wesleyan-Holiness movement, applied an intersectional approach in her writings and was the first woman to be ordained a deacon in the African Methodist Episcopal Zion Church. Randolph, likely the more recognizable figure in this tradition, wrote and preached sermons illustrating a concern for women's rights, having supported suffrage, temperance, and racial justice. Hedgeman's two autobiographical works sit squarely in this tradition. It is important to note, however, that Hedgeman's protest epistemology is shaped by and connected with 1960s liberalism, which includes a concern for the individual rights of women, such as reproduction.

In the development of the early civil rights movement in the North, Hedgeman was a paramount figure. Scanlon describes her as an "exceptional woman" who played a "central role" in the Black freedom struggle and "a critical advocate for civil rights legislation in the 1960s and 1970s."[4] Some of the major associations beyond the YWCA that Hedgeman became affiliated with, according to Scanlon, include the NAACP, National Urban League, American Missionary Association, National Council of Churches, United Nations Association, and NOW (as a cofounder and first executive vice president). Hedgeman was also a public policy professional working with federal agencies including the Emergency Relief Bureau (Department of Welfare), National Office of Civil Defense, National Council for a Fair Employment Practices Commission (as executive director), the Federal Security Agency, and the State Department, as well as serving on Harry S. Truman's New York presidential election campaign in 1948.[5] She eventually became the first Black woman to serve in a mayoral cabinet in New York.[6] Hedgeman was particularly influential as executive director of several YWCAs in the Midwest and Northeast from 1924 to 1939 and as a policy official working with the Democratic Party. Her tenure as executive director during this time included working with or overseeing YWCAs in Jersey City, Harlem, Philadelphia, and Springfield, Ohio. Hedgeman's personal biography and the development of her ideas about interracial cooperation as a national figure active in communities in New Jersey and New York are important to understanding the role of Black women and the civil rights movement in the North.[7] Her privileged upbringing and Christian education in the Midwest shaped her ideas on human liberation and Black empowerment. Hedgeman's activism with the YWCA, her role as a policymaker, and her position as a member of the National Committee for a Permanent Fair Employment Practices Commission into the mid-1940s are aspects of her role in the Black freedom struggle that this chapter explores.

Anna Arnold was born on July 5, 1899, in Marshalltown, Iowa, to William James Arnold II and Marie Ellen (Parker) Arnold. The family subsequently moved to Anoka, Minnesota, which she described in her 1964 memoir, *The Trumpet Sounds*, as "a small comfortable Midwestern town with the traditional main street."[8] In that book, she characterizes her childhood as idyllic, where she saw "no poverty" and lived in a large house with "space where children could run and play. . . . There were trees to climb and a small garden plot to tend. It was no accident that we had space in which to grow and were surrounded by growing things. My father planned it that way." Her father was a college graduate who instilled in his children a strong academic work ethic. "He was of the first generation of Negro college graduates immediately following the Civil War era," she writes in her second memoir, with a "fanatical desire for education."[9] Hedgeman, who played the piano and spent much of her free time studying, had a penchant for intellectual pursuits early on as a self-described "plain and a bit solemn" child, unlike her "two beautiful sisters" who had fair complexions and one of whom had blonde hair.[10] The only Black family in Anoka at that time, the Arnolds lived a community populated primarily by families of Norwegian, Swedish, Irish, and German ancestry.[11] She describes her family as living in "the heart of an Irish neighborhood" next to the Doyle family, whom she loved "as much as any neighbors" that she ever had.[12] The Arnold children attended a white Methodist church where her father served on the Board of Trustees (her father had a very light complexion, and Hedgeman implies in her memoirs that he may have passed, however inadvertently). This was an upbringing within which Hedgeman later realized when active in civil rights demonstrations that she "had not realized that a man could need bread and not be able to get it."[13]

The community she grew up in, as a whole, was deeply religious, according to Hedgeman in her second memoir, *The Gift of Chaos*, and the pursuit of education was important to most families: "Four ideas dominated our family life and for that matter the life of a great many people in our community—education, religion, character, and service to mankind."[14] In Anoka, she writes, there was a "stress on the development of God-given talent for service to the world." Her family, with the exception of her mother, who was Catholic, was staunchly Methodist, and Hedgeman declares in her memoirs that she "inherited the Methodist Church from her two grandfathers [and] her father." She also notes that "under her father's influence," her mother eventually became a Methodist. Not surprisingly, then, Hedgeman's personal, educational, and intellectual development was strongly influenced by the Methodist Church.

Upon her graduation from high school in 1918, her father chose for her undergraduate education a Methodist college in St. Paul, Minnesota, called Hamline University: "Qualified and concerned professors made education at Hamline University, St. Paul, Minnesota a stimulating and enriching adventure. In a basic sense, Hamline was an extension of my home experience. Daily chapel (not convocation) was a unifying dimension where theology and the disciplines of the academic program presented us with new ideas, choices, and suggestions for exploration." There were no Black teachers or professors in Hedgeman's formative educational experience though she was aware of what she called her "African Heritage."[15] She claims that "the color problem had been minimal" in these early years. In fact, Hedgeman's first prolonged encounter with Black youth and the Black community beyond her own family occurred on the eve of her entrance to Hamline when her Aunt Mayme took her to meet some "young Negro people" in St. Paul, where she experienced the "emotional shock" of hearing shouting during a Black church service.[16] The first Black student at Hamline and first Black student to graduate from there, Hedgeman earned a BA in English in 1922 and, upon graduation, found work at Rust College in Holly Springs, Mississippi, where she taught English and history from 1922 to 1924.[17] It was there in the Deep South that she became more intimately aware of Black oppression, but her professional development occurred primarily working with the YWCA, with which she had developed a relationship as an undergraduate by working as a volunteer with a local chapter.

Her spiritual awakening as a young Methodist in Anoka and then her professional development with the YWCA shaped her protest ethic, which was grounded primarily in Methodist theology, fused with ideas about women's empowerment and Black liberation ideologies. The Methodist focus on works of mercy through social action is evident in her thought and social justice endeavors, whereas the YWCA's platform of social feminism impacted her thinking on women's empowerment and human liberation. In fact, Methodism and feminism were both integral to her interracialist philosophy of human liberation. And yet, while the Methodist Church and the YWCA were the most important institutional resources of identity-making in Hedgeman's life, these institutions remained divided by race during the height of her activism, which led Hedgeman to a more pronounced Black consciousness. Her lived experience of racism and sexism, coupled with her religious background, heavily informed her development as a public intellectual; however, her newfound Black consciousness became juxtaposed with—not superimposed over—Methodism and feminism as the guiding principles of her protest ethic.[18] This intersectional approach to empowerment is illustrated most distinctly in *The Trumpet Sounds*, in which she clearly and repeatedly expresses concerns about both racial oppression and sexism.[19] Although she flirted with Black power ideologies, she consistently embraced an interracialist approach to human liberation that was juxtaposed with an intersectional approach to Black women's empowerment.

MEMOIRS OF A PUBLIC INTELLECTUAL

Hedgeman's life and work illustrate the Black freedom struggle in the North from the perspective of a Black woman and public intellectual. It is pertinent to state here that Hedgeman's protest ethic, although heavily influenced by Methodism, was also partly a feminist approach to empowerment as revealed in her two memoirs, public addresses, essays, and private correspondence. Both *The Trumpet Sounds* and *The Gift of Chaos*, which she published thirteen years later, illuminate the external forces that helped shape her ideas on human liberation. *The Trumpet Sounds* had the subtitle *A Memoir of Negro Leadership* because with this text she delivered a history of Black leadership that showcased the major organizations and leaders most active in the early civil rights movement. Casting herself as one of the central characters in this narrative, she provided only minimal details on her personal life overall. With phrases such as "on a personal level" in the fleeting instances when she actually shares any private details of her life, she reminds her readers that she may be overlooked in this history. Given that she published two memoirs within a dozen years, she seemed to realize that the only way to ensure her life history would be recorded was to write it herself. To date, there remains only one scholarly discussion of her life (Scanlon's), despite her countless contributions to the early Black freedom struggle in the North.

African American women have forged a strong tradition of self-life-writing exemplified in autobiography and memoir; it also appears at times as a type of *scriptotherapy*, a form particularly evident in the genre of Black women's slave narratives that should be understood as an oppositional way of knowing within the larger historical context of Black intellectualism.[20] Joanne M. Braxton argues that Black women have been "knowers" who have "not been known."[21] These women turned to self-life-writing, she writes, as a response to enslavement, sexual violence, and Jim Crowism and to become known through literary acts of self-articulation.[22] The process of enslavement led to the loss of African languages in the New World as well as ownership of the body for the enslaved population. This attempt to become known through literary processes, Braxton writes, inaugurates a tradition of Black women's self-life-writing that is defined by a reclamation of words, language, the body, and image. For these women, the ownership of words is an act of self-liberation. Braxton posits that these Black women writers, "through the juxtaposition of oral and literary forms," functioned as a type of "outraged" mother voice that spoke for and to the Black masses.[23] This outraged mother is defined by Braxton as "a variation of the articulate hero archetype" evident in the autobiographical writings of Black men.[24]

These outraged mothers wrote about the violence of racial oppression and sexual assault as a form of re-memory/reenactment that seeks public validation for suffering through testimony.[25] Trauma, though, does not overtake agency or action in Black women's self-life-writing, given that a core theme in Black autobiographical writing specifically is action, not contemplation.[26] Thus, a unique tradition of Black women's self-life-writing was born, defined by the trope of a Black mother who seeks redress and action through the written word, a tradition that is intrinsic to understanding Black women's intellectualism. This is illustrated in both literary and oral traditions from the era of enslavement to the autobiographical writings or participant histories of civil rights activists such as the writings of Hedgeman. Ma Rainey's lesbian song of self-affirmation "Prove It on Me" is as autobiographical in nature as Anne Moody's participant history *Coming of Age in Mississippi*. These women, who speak in mother tongues that fuse the personal and the political, fashioned a tradition of Black women's self-life-writing that, in Alice A. Deck's words, "challenges ways of knowing" often defined by the voices of (white) men.[27] This continues to be evident in self-life-writing about the civil rights era such as the memoir and autobiography written by Hedgeman.

There is a perennial debate about the uses of self-life-writing in understanding history, and this argument is especially pronounced in discussions of this genre in the civil rights literature. According to Kathryn L. Nasstrom, some civil rights era activists such as Student Nonviolent Coordinating Committee (SNCC) member Joyce Ladner, Ralph Abernathy of the Southern Christian Leadership Conference (SCLC), and Casey Hayden have accused historians of inaccurately presenting the movement in their writings on the civil rights era. Moreover, she writes, historians have repeatedly cautioned against the use of self-life-writings such as autobiographies when examining the movement, and even writers of participant histories have gone so far as to imply that their histories of the movement are more "accurate" and "truer to the experience." Nasstrom contends, however, that "the relationship between memoir and history is fundamentally more dialogic than adversarial" and that "autobiography is a distinctive form of historical writing on the movement, able to do work that scholarly writing has not done." These writers, several of whom are Black women, are engaged in what Nasstrom calls "helping to define the public memory of a movement" through self-life-writing, which they consider to be "ongoing."[28] Civil rights activist Hedgeman was involved in such practice when she produced her two memoirs at the height of the movement.

Hedgeman's memoir *The Trumpet Sounds,* published in 1964, a year after she helped organize the March on Washington, covers her early childhood, formal education, work with the YWCA and Democratic Party, and involvement in the committee to organize the March on Washington in 1963. *The Gift of Chaos: Decades of American Discontent,* published in 1977, is a participant history and combines a memoir of her life to that point with a detailed account of Black leadership that concentrates primarily on the years after the march through the mid-1970s. Understood together, these texts might be taken as parts one and two of an extended form of self-life-writing as a record of Hedgeman's life as an activist from the Harlem Renaissance era through the March on Washington.

The Trumpet Sounds was Hedgeman's first major book-length attempt to insert herself into the narrative of the Black freedom struggle. This text reveals her unwavering commitment to Christian fellowship and Black consciousness; her feminist sensibilities are also ever-present in the narrative. The title is taken from the traditional African American spiritual "Steal Away," and Hedgeman's commitment to social justice and interracial cooperation across denominations is revealed as heavily influenced by Methodism and feminism. On the dedication page of the first edition, Hedgeman states, "To my husband Merritt, who has never permitted the fact that I am a woman to color his judgement of me or his support of my work."[29] In the telling of her early years, Hedgeman states unequivocally that her "love of God and the Church" was a "comfortable and natural" aspect of her desire to "live as simply as Jesus lived" through her own efforts. Her education at Hamline only reinforced her Christian values further. The first part of the text is taken up primarily with her formative development in Anoka, Minnesota, and her education. After graduating from Hamline in 1922, she tells how she went to the Deep South to work at an all-Black school—Rust College—where she witnessed serious poverty and Jim Crow racism. Her decision to work with the YWCA was shaped by her embrace of Christian ethics and views on women's empowerment, coupled with the fact that as a Black woman in early twentieth-century America she had only limited choices. Hedgeman served in several administrative and executive positions with the YWCA from 1924 to 1934. While with the organization, she developed her skills as an organizer and advocate for workers. In 1926 New Jersey, where she served as executive director of the Jersey City YWCA, she disguised herself as another laundry worker to interview working-class women about their conditions. She eventually left New Jersey for New York to work in the Harlem YWCA during the height of the New Negro era in the 1930s. She eventually left the YWCA because she believed it could not live up to its commitment to build Christian fellowship between women and girls. By the mid-1940s, Hedgeman was working with labor leader A. Philip Randolph to organize the March on

Washington to demand fair employment practices. In 1954, she became the first Black woman to serve in a mayoral cabinet in New York City. She wrote *The Trumpet Sounds* in the 1960s when she had established herself as a voice working within and between multiple human rights organizations.

Hedgeman's role as director of ecumenical action with the National Council of Churches through the mid-1960s, as detailed in *The Trumpet Sounds*, reflects her continued adherence to Christianity as a guiding principle of her life. Written a year after the devastating bombing at the Sixteenth Street Baptist Church in Birmingham, Alabama, that killed four Black girls—Addie Mae Collins, Cynthia Wesley, Carole Robertson, and Carol Denise McNair—the book begins with a depiction of the scene in the church after the bomb blast. Hedgeman arrived on the scene to survey the carnage following the blast and likens the brutal murder of the four to the crucifixion of Christ. She evocatively uses the metaphor of the crucifixion to describe the broken glass and shattered windows including that of the stained glass image of Christ amid the rubble of the church: "The dynamite had wrecked his portrait. His face was gone, his heart was ripped out, and his vital organs were torn from his body."[30]

She goes on to extend the metaphor to encompass the history and experience of African Americans: "The African slaves understood this Crucifixion story. . . . They understood His crucifixion because they themselves were living it out as slaves in a strange land, stripped of their clothing, their dreams, their family and tribal relationships, their language, their direction of their own bodies and their opportunity for fulfillment."[31] For Hedgeman, the crucifixion was the "full meaning of the demonstrations" that were taking place in the streets, as led by African American freedom fighters, and she postulated that perhaps the death of the "four crucified children" might lead to the promise of the Resurrection "in our living." She utilizes biblical imagery, metaphor, and Christian ethics to narrate her story as a key figure in the Black freedom struggle. Her strident Black consciousness is juxtaposed with an unwavering commitment to Christian social ethics and interracial cooperation. Hedgeman continues describing the events surrounding the church bombing by noting that she was glad that the opening prayer was read by "a white minister" as this meant that "Negroes could still listen to a white minister."[32] This is Hedgeman revealing her concern about the breakdown of interracial cooperation amid the backdrop of continued violence perpetrated by white supremacists against African Americans. Hedgeman reveals herself to be, in this text, a pragmatic political pluralist who continued to believe in interracial cooperation as a strategy to secure Black liberation.

In *The Trumpet Sounds*, Hedgeman also reveals on many occasions her commitment to women's empowerment. She voiced her concerns about women staffers while working with Randolph to secure a Fair Employment Practices

Commission law and while contemplating the decision to join the mayoral cabinet of Robert Wagner in New York. While working with the Wagner campaign for mayor, she made it clear that political campaigns should not be segregated and that she expected to be an "assistant to the campaign manager" and not a part of any women's division because organizing women into a distinct division "separates them from the mainstream of political campaigns." Hedgeman recalls the incident regarding her participation in the Wagner campaign in such a way:

> In New York City they [women] are expected to have teas, fashion shows, coffee klatches and cocktail sips and sell roses. None of these activities is unimportant, but I have no interest in them and I like to make my own choice of where to use my contribution. To startle some of the men a bit, I said very simply: "I hate all segregation." It worked, and when Mr. Wagner introduced his campaign leaders, I was introduced as an assistant campaign manager.[33]

By examining Hedgeman's public career coupled with an analysis of her self-life writings, we come to see that she is likely one of the more significant public intellectuals and thinkers in the history of the Black freedom struggle. It is important to note here that African American women have continuously been left out of the major volumes on American intellectual history; this is an act of erasure and a projection of white supremacist thinking that routinely reduces Black women to the category of nonthinkers. As an activist, strategist, and thinker, Hedgeman is credited with advancing ideas of interracial cooperation that ultimately sustained a level of cross-racial cooperation that helped to make possible mass demonstrations such as the March on Washington, leading to policy changes such as laws about equal employment opportunity and voting rights. Hedgeman also engaged in cross-class interactions with Blacks and whites in both local and national civil rights associations, such as the NAACP and National Urban League as well as Christian associations like the YWCA that she was a member of. The term "intersectionality" as I am using it in this chapter refers to both a theoretical and methodological tool to discuss the interconnections among gender, race, and class within the larger framework of the Black freedom struggle. Ann Garry defines it as the "idea that various forms of oppression interact with one another in multiple complex ways."[34] The variables of oppression and privilege by race, class, gender, or other aspects of human identity such as nationality or sexual orientation, as Garry explains, do not function independently in the lives of individuals or in social institutions; rather, each is shaped by and works through the others.[35] This concept functions as a method in that Hedgeman, like many other Black women, embraced an intersectional approach to empowerment in her writings, speeches, and public statements including within the context of her social group affiliations.

Hedgeman is part of the long tradition of Black women's intellectualism described in the chapters in this book, one that is deep and broad. Historically, Mia Bay and her coauthors note that Black women have rarely worked out of "the academy or research institutes," and "Black women's intellectual history can never be explained by way of a mere genealogy of ideas."[36] Given that Black women have been routinely closed out of prominent academies and institutions on the account of race and gender, according to Bay and her coauthors, their ideas have often been "produced in dialogue with lived experience" as shaped by their social condition.[37] More restrictive definitions of the term "intellectual" as one who makes her living through an activity of the mind and produces written work attached to academies or research institutes are inadequate when defining many Black women intellectuals who may have been self-taught and/or preoccupied with concerns of race and gender. Terms such as "organic intellectual," "activist intellectual," and "public intellectual" tend to be more applicable when considering these Black women intellectuals.[38] A more broadly construed definition of the term "intellectual" allows for a discussion of activist public intellectuals such as Hedgeman in the struggle for Black equality. David Hollinger has argued that American intellectual history concerns people who "made a living by arguing," whereas Antonio Gramsci contended that there is no such thing as a "non-intellectual."[39] In other words, for Hollinger intellectuals are those who typically possess a classical education and are associated with academic life or a life in letters. This term "intellectual" is more broadly construed by Gramsci to suggest that everyone has the capacity to think and individuals such as Hedgeman can be understood as an intellectual given this understanding of the term.

Historians Paula Giddings, Deborah Gray White, Evelyn Brooks Higginbotham, Nell Painter, Hazel Carby, Anthea Butler, Mia Bay, and Bettye Collier-Thomas, among others, have assiduously documented in their writings the lives of Black women in the historical record. Their books feature histories of Black women in the era of their enslavement, in the context of religion or religiosity or the Black church, and in the Black women's club movement, as well as intellectual biographies of women such as Ida B. Wells and Sojourner Truth. In analyses covering a broad range of subjects, scholars have also demonstrated the trajectory of Black women's ideas about empowerment with writings that have cogently revealed the importance of intersectionality in the history of these women's thought.[40]

Hedgeman became part of the tradition of Black women intellectuals by embracing an intersectional approach to empowerment while advancing a pragmatic feminist theology. Though she was among the Black women who placed morality and justice in the realm of public policy as a part of the larger progressive ethos among Christian reformers influenced by the social gospel—a movement that sought to apply Christian ethics to social problems with the ultimate goal of transforming the society—she became increasingly more pragmatic in her thinking regarding Black freedom. This became particularly significant in the twentieth-century phase of the Black freedom struggle as she adopted a broad perspective regarding political liberalism and worked within government as a member of the Democratic Party. As a practitioner of Christian activism, Hedgeman took up the intellectual position and language of New Deal liberalism and later 1960s liberalism that emphasized individual rights.[41] Hedgeman, though she remained a staunch Methodist and feminist, came to embrace New Deal liberalism and later sixties liberalism as Black activists began to rely more heavily on secular associations, legal remedies, and social science data to make claims about Black equality. Though she moved between religious and secular associations, the practice of Methodism remained the guiding principle in her protest ethic expressed through her social activism.

Methodism, founded by the ardent abolitionist John Wesley, has a complex history regarding race relations in the US. David N. Field has identified what he defines as the "historic Methodist praxis" predicated on Wesley's stated mission for the faith "as spreading scriptural holiness."[42] Wesley's theology is rooted in concepts of holiness such as love, justice, mercy, truth, and social holiness as expressed through evangelism. According to Field, there is a relationship between social justice and the larger mission of the Church that he describes as a "praxis of justice, mercy, and truth," which he sees as integral to holiness. This is often expressed through such actions as works of mercy expected of all Methodists. Hedgeman's family lived in an all-white midwestern community and attended a white Methodist church although Methodism, as was the case with other religious denominations in America in the first part of the twentieth century, remained generally a segregated church. That said, Hedgeman's thoughts on human liberation were shaped by the core tenets of Methodism as well as her upbringing and later exposure to Black communities in the American South and Harlem. Hedgeman clung to interracialism in practice though she espoused a more ardent concern for Black equality as her protest ethic evolved.

I use the phrase "pluralist-interracialist" to define the complex dimensions of Hedgeman's thought to reveal a more nuanced interpretation of intellectuals in the Black freedom struggle. Many Black activists such as California newswoman Charlotta Bass or labor activist Ernest Thompson did not pledge their allegiance to one organization, nor did they completely abandon interracial cooperation. Bass was a member of both the NAACP and Garvey's Universal Negro Improvement Association. Similarly, Thompson worked with whites in major labor unions but turned towards political pluralism by becoming a cofounder of the National Negro Labor Council. Hedgeman once declared her disdain for white people, becoming a nationalist while working within the confines of the YWCA and continuing to work among whites in national Christian organizations. While pluralists such as Bass, Thompson, and Hedgeman embraced the value of independent Black organizations, coupled with a belief in the necessity of Black leadership, interracialists cling to the value of interracial cooperation as a strategy to secure equal rights. The pluralist-interracialist defines an individual who might work outward from a Black-centered worldview or protest ethic while upholding the value of cooperation with other races to actualize the goals of Black equality. Hedgeman on more than one occasion in her autobiographical writings claims a worldview that gravitates towards Black nationalism, stating that she did not talk to white people for five years while working primarily in Harlem; but her *actions* indicate that over the course of her lifetime she continued to engage in interracial cooperation as a strategy before, during, and after she parted with the YWCA movement. As a pragmatic Christian feminist, she may have embraced nationalist tendencies at the height of the Harlem Renaissance but remained, at the time, with the YWCA although deeply disillusioned about interracial cooperation. Her support of African American studies later in life might, at best, be understood as a form of cultural nationalism; however, cultural nationalists are not necessarily territorial nationalists (separatists). Her decisions to join first the Truman campaign and then the Truman administration as a bureaucrat with the Federal Security Agency are the acts of a pragmatist, also evidenced by her role in the administration of New York Mayor Robert Wagner Jr. in the 1950s.

HEDGEMAN'S ROLE IN THE "LONG CIVIL RIGHTS MOVEMENT"

It is necessary at this point to situate Hedgeman within the historiography of the Black freedom struggle, which Jacqueline Dowd Hall has "termed the long civil rights movement."[43] Though there exists a short, more well-known narrative of the civil rights movement in US history, that period is now more commonly understood to be a part of a larger struggle that extends before the 1950s and after the 1960s and includes the fight for Black equality in both the North and South. Short narrative approaches, Hall writes, routinely address the following topics: *Brown v. Board of Education* in 1954, the mass public protests that followed, the passage of key civil rights legislation during the 1960s, and the assassination of Martin Luther King Jr. in 1968.[44] Historians such as Hall, Jeanne Theoharis, Komozi Woodward, Matthew Countrymen, and Robert

Self have abandoned this notion of a "short civil rights movement," rejecting the popular retelling of events and embracing the view of a Black freedom struggle that began decades before the turbulent 1950s and 1960s.[45] Hall has argued that a short narrative "distorts and suppresses as much as it reveals."[46] In contrast, the history of the long movement begins before the *Brown* decision and continues after the assassination of King. This long narrative understanding emerged as the dominant conceptual framework for understanding the civil rights movement with the publication of Theoharis and Woodward's *Freedom North: Black Freedom Outside of the South.*

This conceptualization of the civil rights era as a long movement does have its critics.[47] Challengers include scholars such as Steven F. Lawson, Clarence Lang, and Charles Eagles. Lawson cautions against the artificial extension of the short traditional timeline, while Cha-Jua and Lang argue that a long movement is an "overly elastic" chronological framing of the movement that has not been consistently applied by the adherents to such an approach.[48] Hedgeman is a historical figure who allows for the application of Lawson's understanding of the "short movement with long origins."[49] Lang has also argued that the overemphasis on similarities across regions is problematic, but that exploring Black social movements "north of Dixie" allows scholars to "observe regional particularities" while "highlighting the significance of difference" in the development of Black social movements.[50]

Hedgeman is an important transitional figure and link between the early and later phases of the Black freedom struggle, as evidenced by her associations with Black labor-left coalition politics of the 1930s and '40s and liberal politics of the '50s, culminating in her activities as coorganizer of the March on Washington in 1963.[51] Her activism can be understood within the framework of the civil rights movement in the North, particularly in the Northeast, as illustrated by her civil rights work in New Jersey and New York.[52] Routinely moving within and between multiple organizations to advance human freedom, Hedgeman was among the core personalities responsible for laying the foundation of the Black freedom struggle in the North that centered largely on the demand for fair employment practices.[53]

The basis of the modern Black freedom struggle at the local and national levels was structured around the demand for fair labor and employment practices as a result of Black labor-left interracial cooperation.[54] The National Council for a Permanent Fair Employment Practices Committee was made possible through interracial cooperation. In total, according to Hedgeman, fifty-seven national labor, religious, philanthropic, and civil rights organizations convened to support the Fair Employment Practices (FEP) law, including individuals from various ethnoracial groups: Catholic, Protestant, and Jewish groups joined together with labor organizations such as the Congress of Industrial Organizations and

American Federation of Labor to defend the FEP bill.[55] Eleanor Roosevelt maintained her support of a fair employment law after leaving the White House, and George Hunton of the National Catholic Interracial Council spoke at public hearings in support of the law. Rabbi Stephen Wise and Bishop G. Bromley Oxnam of the Methodist Church also defended the idea of an FEP law at public hearings. Some prominent Black attorneys, Hedgman reports, offered their services to the council (pro bono), including Charles Hamilton Houston; William H. Hastie; Spottswood Robinson, who eventually became dean of Howard University School of Law; and George Johnson, working alongside white liberals in the US Congress interested in the passage of an FEP law. Congressional support, she notes, included both Democratic and Republican members such as Charles La Follette, a representative from Indiana; William L. Dawson from Illinois; Senator Dennis Chavez from New Mexico; Helen Gahagan Douglas, a representative from California; and Frances Bolton, a representative from Ohio. Ruth Haefner loaded copies of the bill into her car to rally white churchwomen, Hedgeman remembers, and Daisy Bates in Little Rock, Arkansas, became an important voice at the local level in support of the idea of the law. The fact that New Jersey passed its FEP law only a month after New York did suggests that Hedgeman—active in both states at the time—helped shape both. She spearheaded the national campaign for a federal FEP law alongside labor leader A. Philip Randolph that led to ground-breaking legislation in nearly every northern state by the mid-1940s.[56] This is illustrated by the state FEP laws that were passed across the nation as a result of the national council that had been created to secure such laws as well as the agencies later developed to enforce these laws in states like New York and New Jersey.[57]

Hedgeman was also part of a multifaceted northern civil rights movement that fought various forms of discrimination. Throughout the North, Thomas Sugrue writes, segregation persisted in schools and residential areas despite laws forbidding such practices.[58] Separate schools and separation within schools were common in the North both before and after 1954. There are even documented cases, he notes, indicating that some school districts in the North gerrymandered school attendance zones to maintain segregation. Chicago schools remained notoriously segregated by race well into the 1960s, while Long Island schools, according to Sugrue, "sent all Black students regardless of their race to a single all-Black school." In some cases in the North, he writes, Black students were forced to eat their lunch in segregated cafeterias and occupy separate playgrounds.[59] Students in Asbury Park were segregated within the school buildings, according to Jack Washington, while students in Trenton were segregated within the school system by grade level.[60] Residential segregation was maintained in the North through practices such as blockbusting, redlining, and restrictive covenants that have been well documented by historians and sociologists.[61] Sugrue stated that residential segregation was "mandated in Federal mortgage programs supervised by the Home Owners' Loan Corporation, the Federal Housing Administration, and Veterans Administration" from the 1920s to the '40s.[62]

State governments in the North and South maintained segregation across the nation as a whole. It would be wrong to assume that segregation by practice or custom was the only type of segregation that appeared outside of the South in the twentieth century. Federally sanctioned discriminatory practices worked in tandem with local practices deployed throughout the North in both public and private contexts. In cities such as Chicago, Detroit, St. Louis, and Los Angeles, practices of segregation through restrictive covenants at the local level were consistently challenged by Black communities, culminating in the 1948 Supreme Court decision in *Shelley v. Kraemer* that declared such covenants unenforceable.[63] In response to segregation in public facilities, Black communities in the North organized "wade-ins" at public beaches, including those in cities such as Chicago and Asbury Park, and sit-ins at segregated lunch counters; further, these communities refused to purchase products from stores that did not hire Blacks.[64] Historian Stanley Keith Arnold has noted that the Black community in Philadelphia created coalitions through organizations such as the Fellowship House, Philadelphia Housing Association, and Fellowship Commission to secure civil rights at the state, local, and national levels.[65] He further argues that Martin Luther King Jr. first learned of the Indian principle of *satyagraha* at a Fellowship House Sunday forum. Sugrue notes that mothers from Trenton to Harlem led a series of protests against public schools in both states in the early 1950s.[66] Jeanne Theoharis counters what she calls the "southernization" of Rosa Parks's story in *The Rebellious Life of Mrs. Rosa Parks*.[67] She notes that Parks spent forty years of her life fighting for Black equality in Detroit, having been forced out of Montgomery, Alabama, after the bus boycott in 1956 due to death threats.[68] In Detroit, according to Theoharis, Parks was involved in campaigns against discrimination in housing, schools, and public accommodations more generally.

CONCLUSION: WRITING HERSELF INTO HISTORY

Anna Arnold Hedgeman, who began her life in an all-white town in Minnesota, lived in a New York nursing home after her husband's death in 1987 and died at ninety years of age in Harlem Hospital on January 17, 1990. Her life spanned nearly the entire history of the Black freedom struggle in the twentieth century from her trade union activism in the 1920s, to her work with the NAACP during the height of the New Negro Era, to her work as a politician and a co-organizer of the March on Washington in 1963. As a Black feminist, Hedgeman was aware that her work could be forgotten, as she suggests in the pages of her books, so she wrote things down. She wrote herself into the history of the Black freedom struggle, the women's liberation movement, and the history of American religion as an ardent Methodist. Her long life can also be used to highlight the complexities of Black civil rights activism. Though a member of the YWCA while describing herself as a Black nationalist who refused to speak to white people for several years, she never completely abandoned the idea of interracial cooperation that was expected of someone of her Methodist faith.

Hedgeman's life tells us a lot about the history of Black women's intellectual traditions, the long Black freedom struggle, and women's history as well as American religious studies. Ironically, although Hedgeman was college-educated and received an honorary doctorate from Hamline University in 1948, she along with many other Black women is not routinely classified as an American intellectual. She herself would have likely rejected the term as applied to her life and work. She sought coalitions across race, gender, and class lines to ensure a more just society for all, exemplified in her work with the YWCA in Jersey City, Harlem, and Philadelphia. Though she became disillusioned about the possibility of white redemption from racism, she never lost her faith in the possibility of human liberation through a strategy of interracial coalition building. For Hedgeman, the Civil Rights Act of 1964 would not have been possible without interracial cooperation, though she understood why Black civil rights activists needed to take the lead on pushing for such initiatives. Furthermore, Hedgeman helped build these coalitions largely at first through religious associations such as the YWCA and the National Council of Churches. Her Methodism was the most important ideological component of her protest ethic; in fact, she was first and foremost a Methodist, which is clear throughout her life of activism and writings. In many respects, the civil rights movement was a type of religious revival with churchwomen like Hedgeman at the center. The study of her life allows us to revisit the role of religion in the modern Black freedom struggle and in twentieth-century social movements more generally.

The notion of Hedgeman as a pluralist-interracialist allows us to develop a more nuanced interpretation of key figures in the Black freedom struggle. Given the multidimensional character of Black oppression, Black civil rights activists often straddled a variety of associations and groups created to advance human freedom. Hedgeman joined the YWCA to help improve the plight of Black women and continued to work with this association despite her disillusionment over issues related to race and class while espousing Black nationalist views. Through her activism and experiences in the YWCA, she increasingly gravitated to a pluralist position while continuing to champion interracial cooperation; Jennifer Scanlon credits Hedgeman with single-handedly securing the cooperation of more than thirty thousand Protestant church members, many of whom were white, in the March on Washington in 1963.[69] This mass civil rights demonstration was an interracial event that involved more than 250,000 people. African Americans such as Hedgeman thought carefully about the possibility of securing their rights in education, employment, public housing, and other sectors of American life. This took sensitivity and compromise in terms of ideological stances and membership in human rights associations as Hedgeman suggests in her books. Historians of the Black freedom struggle must begin to examine more deeply the nature of Black power ideologies and strategies as revealed in Hedgeman's life and activism. This then will help collapse the more rigid categories of integrationist/separatist while allowing scholars to utilize more accurate labels such as pluralist-interracialist or pluralist-separatist.

Hedgeman was also aware that white women, especially those she encountered in the YWCA movement, were oftentimes disingenuous about advancing Black freedom claims, as she found out when she traveled as an executive for the YWCA and was forced to stay in segregated lodgings or when, as a member, she spoke out in support of Black women's participation in boycotts against segregation. She came to believe that white women will more often than not place the interests of their race over matters of gender equity, and she witnessed this as an administrator with the YWCA. Her experiences with that organization might also help us to understand the reasons behind the breakdown of interracial cooperation in the women's liberation movement over matters of race and class. Historian Brittney Cooper commented at a recent meeting of the Aspen Ideas Festival on the tension between feminists across racial lines: "The thing that unites white women and Black men is that they both understand freedom to be having access to what white men have. . . . And what they [white women] want is for their gender to not keep them from ruling the world the way white men do."[70] Thus, race often supersedes gender in the lives and activism of white women. Hedgeman experienced this firsthand and though she never gave up interracial cooperation as a strategy to secure human equality and became a cofounder of the National Organization for Women, her protest ethic was centered not only on Methodism and feminism but on Black social justice claims. Hedgeman's life reveals to us a great deal about multiple aspects of twentieth-century history and society. Her image hangs in the National Portrait Gallery for a reason.

NOTES

1. Jennifer Scanlon, *Until There Is Justice: The Life of Anna Arnold Hedgeman* (New York: Oxford University Press, 2016), 2.

2. See Marilyn Richardson, *Maria W. Stewart, America's First Black Woman Political Writer: Essays and Speeches* (Bloomington: Indiana University Press, 1997); Zilpha Elaw,

Memoirs of the Life, Religious Experience, Ministerial Travels, and Labours of Mrs. Zilpha Elaw, an American Female of Colour; Together with Some Account of the Great Religious Revivals in America [Written by Herself], in *Sisters of the Spirit: Three Black Women's Autobiographies of the Nineteenth Century*, ed. William L. Andrews (Bloomington: Indiana University Press, 1986), 49–160; Jarena Lee, *The Life and Religious Experience of Jarena Lee, a Colored Lady, Giving an Account of Her Call to Preach the Gospel*, rev. and corrected, in Andrews, *Sisters of the Spirit*, 25–48; Julia A. J. Foote, *A Brand Plucked by the Fire: An Autobiographical Sketch by Mrs. Julia A. J. Foote*, in Andrews, *Sisters of the Spirit*, 161–234; and Bettye Collier-Thomas, "Minister and Feminist Reformer: The Life of Florence Spearing Randolph," in *This Far by Faith: Readings in African-American Religious History*, ed. Judith Weisenfeld and Richard Newman (New York: Routledge, 1996), 177–85.

3. Patricia Hill Collins, *Black Feminist Thought: Knowledge, Consciousness, and the Politics of Empowerment* (New York: Routledge, 2000), 23.

4. Scanlon, *Until There Is Justice*, 2.

5. Julie A. Gallagher, *Black Women & Politics in New York City* (Urbana: University of Illinois Press, 2012), 106–7.

6. Gallagher, *Black Women & Politics*, 107–8.

7. Scanlon, *Until There Is Justice*, 3.

8. Anna Arnold Hedgeman, *The Trumpet Sounds: A Memoir of Negro Leadership* (New York: Holt, Rinehart, Winston, 1964), 7.

9. Hedgeman, *The Gift of Chaos: Decades of American Discontent* (New York: Oxford University Press, 1977), 4.

10. Hedgeman, *Gift of Chaos*, 8; and Hedgeman, *Trumpet Sounds*, 9.

11. Hedgeman, *Trumpet Sounds*, 1.

12. Hedgeman, *Trumpet Sounds*, 11.

13. Hedgeman, *Trumpet Sounds*, 1.

14. Hedgeman, *Gift of Chaos*, 5.

15. Hedgeman, *Gift of Chaos*, 6.

16. Hedgeman, *Gift of Chaos*, 12.

17. Hedgeman, *Trumpet Sounds*, 18.

18. The term "experience" here is defined as the process through which an individual interacts with the material world and the translation of these interactions, by said individual, into subjective reality.

19. Hedgeman, *Trumpet Sounds*, 18.

20. Suzette A. Henke, *Shattered Subjects: Trauma and Testimony in Women's Life-Writing* (New York: St. Martin's Press, 2000), xii.

21. Joanne M. Braxton, *Black Women Writing Autobiography: A Tradition within a Tradition* (Philadelphia: Temple University Press, 1989), 1.

22. Braxton, *Black Women Writing Autobiography*, 2.

23. Braxton, *Black Women Writing Autobiography*, 5, 3.

24. Braxton, *Black Women Writing Autobiography*, 10.

25. Henke, *Shattered Subjects*, xi–xii.

26. Braxton, *Black Women Writing Autobiography*, 5.

27. Alice A. Deck, "Autobiography as Activism: Three Black Women of the Sixties," *African American Review* 36, no. 3 (Fall 2002): 507.

28. Kathryn L. Nasstrom, "Between Memory and History: Autobiographies of the Civil Rights Movement and the Writing of Civil Rights History," *Journal of Southern History* 74, no. 2 (May 2008): 325-28, 333, 335.

29. Hedgeman, *Trumpet Sounds*, 1.

30. Hedgeman, *Trumpet Sounds*, 4.

31. Hedgeman, *Trumpet Sounds*, 4.

32. Hedgeman, *Trumpet Sounds*, 6.

33. Hedgeman, *Trumpet Sounds*, 112.

34. Ann Garry, "Intersectionality, Metaphors, and the Multiplicity of Gender," *Hypatia* 26, no. 4 (Fall 2011): 826. See also Kimberlé Williams Crenshaw, "Mapping the Margins: Intersectionality, Identity Politics, and Violence Against Women of Color," in *Critical Race Theory: The Key Writings That Formed the Movement*, ed. Kimberlé Williams Crenshaw et al. (New York: New Press, 1995), 357–83. Crenshaw has been credited with coining the phrase "intersectionality" in 1989, although historians such as Catherine Clinton, Elizabeth Fox Genovese, and Deborah Gray White were utilizing a methodology that can only be described as an intersectional approach to understanding race, gender, and class in US history before the publication of the Crenshaw essay. Kathleen Brown among others later deploys a similar approach in her study of colonial Virginia. The sociologist Patricia Hill Collins also plays an important role in the development of this approach.

35. Garry, "Intersectionality," 827.

36. Mia Bay et al., Introduction, in *Toward an Intellectual History of Black Women*, ed. Mia Bay et al. (Chapel Hill: University of North Carolina Press, 2015), 1, 5.

37. Bay et al., Introduction, 4.

38. The phrase "organic intellectual" is borrowed here from the writings of the Italian neo-Marxist Antonio Gramsci, who states that "all men are intellectuals." See Antonio Gramsci, "The Intellectuals," in *An Anthology of Western Marxism from Lukacs and Gramsci to Socialist Feminism*, ed. Roger S. Gottlieb (New York: Oxford University Press, 1989), 115. Gramsci further contends in the same section of his *Prison Notebooks* that the category of intellectual is multiple and that everyone has the capacity to think; therefore, there are only categories of intellectuals, and "nonintellectuals do not exist" (115). In the tradition of African American history, the phrase "activist intellectual" has been utilized by scholars of the Black experience to connote the dialogic relationship among lived experience, the formation of ideas, and the production of knowledge. As Bay et al. contend: "The result is intellectual history 'Black woman-style,' an approach that understands ideas as necessarily produced in dialogue with lived experience and always inflected by the social facts of race, class, and gender" (Introduction, 4). Jürgen Habermas has defined the public intellectual as one who makes "public use of reason"; quoted in Arlette Frund, "Phillis Wheatley, a Public Intellectual," in Bay et al., *Toward an Intellectual History of Black Women*, 35. Frund defines the term "intellectual" as an "individual who engages in an activity of the mind, produces written work, and participates in public debates" (35).

39. David Hollinger, "American Intellectual History, 1907–2007," *OAH Magazine of History* 21, no. 2 (April 2007): 17; and Gramsci, "Intellectuals," 115.

40. In *When and Where I Enter: The Impact of Race and Sex in America* (New York: William Morrow, 1984), Paula Giddings focuses on women such as Ida B. Wells and Anna Julia Cooper to provide the first historical survey of how Black women, through their reform

activism, confronted the dilemma of race and sex. Deborah Gray White's *Ar'nt I a Woman: Female Slaves in the Plantation South* (New York: W. W. Norton, 1985) is one of the first historical surveys of Black women in slavery. Hazel Carby's *Reconstructing Womanhood: The Emergence of the Afro-American Woman Novelist* (New York: Oxford University Press, 1987) focuses on nineteenth-century Black women writers who helped to shape the emerging field of Black women's intellectual history that arose from literary studies and cultural studies in the 1980s. See also Darlene Clark Hine, *We Specialize in the Wholly Impossible: A Reader in Black Women's History* (Lehi, UT: Carlson Publishing, 1995); Evelyn Brooks Higginbotham, *Righteous Discontent: The Women's Movement in the Black Baptist Church, 1860–1920* (Cambridge, MA: Harvard University Press, 1993); Nell Irvin Painter, *Sojourner Truth: A Life, a Symbol* (New York: W. W. Norton, 1999); Anthea Butler, *Women in the Church of God and Christ: Making a Sanctified World* (Chapel Hill: University of North Carolina Press, 2007); and Mia Bay, *To Tell the Truth Freely: The Life of Ida B. Wells* (New York: Hill and Wang, 2009). For works on Black women preachers and religion, see Chanta M. Haywood, *Prophesying Daughters: Black Women Preachers and the Word, 1823–1913* (Columbia: University of Missouri Press, 2003); Jualynne E. Dodson, *Engendering Church: Women, Power, and the AME Church* (New York: Rowman & Littlefield, 2002); Bettye Collier-Thomas, *Jesus, Jobs, and Justice: African American Women and Religion* (New York: Alfred A. Knopf, 2011); and Bettye Collier-Thomas, *Black Women's Christian Activism: Seeking Social Justice in a Northern Suburb* (New York: New York University Press, 2016).

41. There is a difference between New Deal liberalism and 1960s liberalism (with roots in the mid-1950s). Franklin D. Roosevelt's liberalism is rooted in Progressive reform efforts to utilize government action as a means to ameliorate or control social problems through regulation. 1960s liberalism emphasizes individual rights and freedoms (civil rights) that is counter, in its broadest sense, to the civic righteousness that some Black Christian women promulgated through the 1940s. Hedgeman is a cofounder of the National Organization for Women (NOW), which goes on to advocate for women's right to an abortion.

42. David N. Field, "Holiness, Social Justice, and the Mission of the Church: John Wesley's Insights in Contemporary Context," *Holiness: The Journal of Wesley House Cambridge* 1, no. 2 (2015): 177.

43. Jacqueline Dowd Hall, "The Long Civil Rights Movement and the Political Uses of the Past," *Journal of American History* 91, no. 4 (March 2005): 1235. The phrase "Long Civil Rights Movement" was coined by Hall in this essay and has since become the basis for an expansive large-scale collaborative digitization initiative among the University of North Carolina Press, the Southern Oral History Program, the Center for Civil Rights in the University of North Carolina School of Law, and the University of North Carolina Library called "The Long Civil Rights Movement Project" that is helping to popularize the long movement approach. See http://sohp.org/research/the-long-civil-rights-movement-initiative/ for the Southern Oral History Project interviews.

44. Hall, "Long Civil Rights Movement," 1234.

45. Hall, "Long Civil Rights Movement," 1235. For examples of the extended narrative approach, see also Jeanne Theoharis and Komozi Woodward, eds., *Freedom North: Black Freedom Outside of the South, 1940–1980* (New York: Palgrave Macmillan, 2003); Thomas Sugrue, *The Forgotten Civil Rights Movement in the North* (Princeton, NJ: Princeton University Press, 2008); and Danielle McGuire, *At the Dark End of the Street: Black Women,*

Rape, and Resistance: A New History of the Civil Rights Movement from Rosa Parks to the Rise of Black Power (New York: Alfred A. Knopf, 2010).

46. Hall, "Long Civil Rights Movement," 1233.

47. See Charles Eagles, "Toward New Histories of the Civil Rights Era," *Journal of Southern History* 66, no. 4 (November 2000): 815–48; Sundiata Keita Cha-Jua and Clarence Lang, "The Long Movement as Vampire: Temporal and Spatial Fallacies in Recent Black Freedom Studies," *Journal of African American History* 92, no. 2 (Spring 2007): 265–88; Steven F. Lawson, "The Long Origins of the Short Civil Rights Movement," in *Freedom Rights: New Perspectives on the Civil Rights Movement*, ed. Danielle L. McGuire and John Dittmer (Lexington: University Press of Kentucky, 2011), 9–37; and Clarence Lang, "Locating the Civil Rights Movement: An Essay on the Deep South, Midwest, and Border South in Black Freedom Studies," *Journal of Social History* 47, no. 2 (Winter 2013): 371–400, for some of the more ardent criticisms of the long movement approach.

48. Lawson, "Long Origins"; and Cha-Jua and Lang, "Long Movement."

49. Lawson, "Long Origins."

50. Lang, "Locating the Civil Rights Movement," 390.

51. Scanlon, *Until There Is Justice*, 3.

52. Gallagher, *Black Women & Politics*, 106.

53. Anthony S. Chen, "The Party of Lincoln and the Politics of State Employment Practices Legislation in the North 1945–1964," *American Journal of Sociology* 112, no. 6 (May 2007): 1714–17.

54. Chen, "Party of Lincoln," 1717.

55. Hedgeman, *Trumpet Sounds*, 88–91.

56. Hedgeman, *Trumpet Sounds*, 86.

57. See Martha Biondi, *To Stand and Fight: The Struggle for Civil Rights in Postwar New York City* (Cambridge, MA: Harvard University Press, 2003). Many scholars, including Biondi in her text on the early Black freedom struggle in New York, have failed to adequately discuss the relationship between northern states such as New Jersey and New York in the early Black freedom struggle in the North. Biondi reduces Hedgeman's role to a few lines in her text, which is surprising given Hedgeman's pivotal activism in the development of the civil rights movement in New York.

58. Thomas Sugrue, "Northern Lights: The Black Freedom Struggle Outside the South," *Organization of American Historians Magazine of History* 26, no. 1 (January 2012): 12–14.

59. Sugrue, "Northern Lights," 13–14.

60. Jack Washington, *The Quest for Equality: Trenton's Black Community: 1890–1965* (Trenton, NJ: Africa World Press and Red Sea Press, 1993), 104–5.

61. For definitive discussions of the discriminatory practices deployed by the state in northern contexts, see Arnold Hirsch, *Making the Second Ghetto: Race and Housing in Chicago, 1940–1960* (Chicago: University of Chicago Press, 1983); Kenneth T. Jackson, *Crabgrass Frontier: The Suburbanization of the United States* (New York: Oxford University Press, 1985); Joe Trotter, *Black Milwaukee: The Making of an Industrial Proletariat, 1915–1945* (Urbana: University of Illinois Press, 1985); Peter Gottlieb, *Making Their Own Way: Southern Blacks' Migration to Pittsburgh, 1916–1930* (Urbana: University of Illinois Press, 1987); Douglas Massey and Nancy Denton, *American Apartheid: Segregation and the Making of the Underclass* (Cambridge, MA: Harvard University Press, 1993); and Thomas Sugrue, *The*

Origins of the Urban Crisis: Race and Inequality in Postwar Detroit (Princeton, NJ: Princeton University Press, 1996).

62. Sugrue, "Northern Lights," 13.

63. Sugrue, "Northern Lights," 13.

64. Haley Leuthart, "Wading-In at Rainbow Beach," *OAH Magazine of History* 26, no. 1 (January 2012): 12.

65. Stanley Keith Arnold, *Building the Beloved Community: Philadelphia's Interracial Civil Rights Organizations and Race Relations, 1930–1970* (Jackson: University Press of Mississippi, 2014), 3–5.

66. Sugrue, "Northern Lights," 14.

67. Jeanne Theoharis, *The Rebellious Life of Mrs. Rosa Parks* (Boston: Beacon Press, 2014), xii.

68. Theoharis, *Rebellious Life*, ix.

69. Scanlon, *Until There Is Justice*, 158. Another scholar posits that number was forty thousand; see S. Smith, "The Untold Story of the March on Washington," *Diverse: Issues in Higher Education* 30, no. 15 (2013): 20.

70. Brittney Cooper, "Good Feminist, Bad Feminist—Who Gets to Decide?," Panel, Aspen Ideas Festival, June 21–30, 2018, https://www.aspenideas.org/sessions/good-feminist-bad-feminist-who-gets-to-decide.

SELECTED BIBLIOGRAPHY

Arnold, Stanley Keith. *Building the Beloved Community: Philadelphia's Interracial Civil Rights Organizations and Race Relations, 1930–1970*. Jackson: University Press of Mississippi, 2014.

Bay, Mia. *To Tell the Truth Freely: The Life of Ida B. Wells*. New York: Hill and Wang, 2009.

Bay, Mia, Farah J. Griffin, Martha S. Jones, and Barbara D. Savage. Introduction. In *Toward an Intellectual History of Black Women*, edited by Mia Bay, Farah J. Griffin, Martha S. Jones, and Barbara D. Savage. Chapel Hill: University of North Carolina Press, 2015.

Biondi, Martha. *To Stand and Fight: The Struggle for Civil Rights in Postwar New York City*. Cambridge, MA: Harvard University Press, 2003.

Braxton, Joanne M. *Black Women Writing Autobiography: A Tradition within a Tradition*. Philadelphia: Temple University Press, 1989.

Butler, Anthea. *Women in the Church of God and Christ: Making a Sanctified World*. Chapel Hill: University of North Carolina Press, 2007.

Carby, Hazel. *Reconstructing Womanhood: The Emergence of the Afro-American Woman Novelist*. New York: Oxford University Press, 1987.

Cha-Jua, Sundiata Keita, and Clarence Lang. "The Long Movement as Vampire: Temporal and Spatial Fallacies in Recent Black Freedom Studies." *Journal of African American History* 92, no. 2 (Spring 2007): 265–88. https://doi.org/10.1086/JAAHv92n2p265.

Chen, Anthony S. "The Party of Lincoln and the Politics of State Employment Practices Legislation in the North 1945–1964." *American Journal of Sociology* 112, no. 6 (May 2007): 1713–74. https://doi.org/10.1086/512709.

Collier-Thomas, Bettye. *Black Women's Christian Activism: Seeking Social Justice in a Northern Suburb*. New York: New York University Press, 2016.

Collier-Thomas, Bettye. *Jesus, Jobs, and Justice: African American Women and Religion*. New York: Alfred A. Knopf, 2011.

Collier-Thomas, Bettye. "Minister and Feminist Reformer: The Life of Florence Spearing Randolph." In *This Far by Faith: Readings in African-American Religious History*, edited by Judith Weisenfeld and Richard Newman, 177–85. New York: Routledge, 1996.

Cooper, Brittney. "Good Feminist, Bad Feminist—Who Gets to Decide?" Panelist, Aspen Ideas Festival, June 21–30, 2018. https://www.aspenideas.org/sessions/good-feminist-bad-feminist-who-gets-to-decide.

Crenshaw, Kimberlé Williams. "Mapping the Margins: Intersectionality, Identity Politics, and Violence Against Women of Color." In *Critical Race Theory: The Key Writings That Formed the Movement*, edited by Kimberlé Williams Crenshaw, Neil Gotanda, Gary Peller, and Kendall Thomas, 357–83. New York: New Press, 1995.

Deck, Alice. Review of *Autobiography as Activism: Three Black Women of the Sixties* by Margo V. Perkins. *African American Review* 36, no. 3 (Autumn 2002): 505–7. https://doi.org/10.2307/1512220.

Dodson, Jualynne E. *Engendering Church: Women, Power, and the AME Church*. New York: Rowman & Littlefield, 2002.

Dudziak, Mary L. *Cold War Civil Rights: Race and the Image of American Democracy*. Princeton, NJ: Princeton University Press, 2002.

Eagles, Charles. "Toward New Histories of the Civil Rights Era." *Journal of Southern History* 66, no. 4 (November 2000): 815–48. https://doi.org/10.2307/2588012.

Elaw, Zilpha. *Memoirs of the Life, Religious Experience, Ministerial Travels, and Labours of Mrs. Zilpha Elaw, an American Female of Colour; Together with Some Account of the Great Religious Revivals in America [Written by Herself]*. In *Sisters of the Spirit: Three Black Women's Autobiographies of the Nineteenth Century*, edited by William L. Andrews, 49–160. Bloomington: Indiana University Press, 1986.

Field, David N. "Holiness, Social Justice, and the Mission of the Church: John Wesley's Insights in Contemporary Context." *Holiness: The Journal of Wesley House Cambridge* 1, no. 2 (2015): 177–98. https://doi.org/10.2478/holiness-2015-0005.

Foote, Julia A. J. "A Brand Plucked by the Fire: An Autobiographical Sketch by Mrs. Julia A. J. Foote." In *Sisters of the Spirit: Three Black Women's Autobiographies of the Nineteenth Century*, edited by William L. Andrews, 161–234. Bloomington: Indiana University Press, 1986.

Frund, Arlette. "Phillis Wheatley, a Public Intellectual." In *Toward an Intellectual History of Black Women*, edited by Mia Bay, Farah J. Griffin, Martha S. Jones, and Barbara D. Savage. Chapel Hill: University of North Carolina Press, 2015.

Gallagher, Julie A. *Black Women & Politics in New York City*. Urbana: University of Illinois Press, 2011.

Garry, Ann. "Intersectionality, Metaphors, and the Multiplicity of Gender." *Hypatia* 26, no. 4 (Fall 2011): 826–50. https://doi.org/10.1111/j.1527-2001.2011.01194.x.

Giddings, Paula. *When and Where I Enter: The Impact of Black Women on Race and Sex in America*. New York: William Morrow, 1984.

Gottlieb, Peter. *Making Their Own Way: Southern Blacks' Migration to Pittsburgh, 1916–1930*. Urbana: University of Illinois Press, 1987.

Gramsci, Antonio. "The Intellectuals." In *An Anthology of Western Marxism from Lukacs and Gramsci to Socialist Feminism*, edited by Roger Gottlieb, 113–19. New York: Oxford University Press, 1989.

Greenberg, Cheryl. *Or Does It Explode? Black Harlem in the Great Depression*. New York: Oxford University Press, 1997.

Hall, Jacquelyn Dowd. "The Long Civil Rights Movement and the Political Uses of the Past." *Journal of American History* 91, no. 4 (March 2005): 1233–63. https://doi.org/10.2307/3660172.

Haywood, Chanta M. *Prophesying Daughters: Black Women Preachers and the Word, 1823–1913*. Columbia: University of Missouri Press, 2003.

Hedgeman, Anna Arnold. *The Gift of Chaos: Decades of American Discontent*. New York: Oxford University Press, 1977.

Hedgeman, Anna Arnold. "The Role of the Negro Woman." *Journal of Educational Sociology* 17, no. 8 (April 1944): 463–72.

Hedgeman, Anna Arnold. *The Trumpet Sounds: A Memoir of Negro Leadership*. New York: Holt, Rinehart, Winston, 1964.

Henke, Suzette A. *Shattered Subjects: Trauma and Testimony in Women's Life-Writing*. New York: St. Martin's Press, 2000.

Higginbotham, Evelyn Brooks. *Righteous Discontent: The Women's Movement in the Black Baptist Church, 1860–1920*. Cambridge, MA: Harvard University Press, 1993.

Hine, Darlene Clark. *Black Women in America*. New York: Oxford University Press, 2005.

Hine, Darlene Clark. *We Specialize in the Wholly Impossible: A Reader in Black Women's History*. Brooklyn: Carlson Publishing, 1995.

Hirsch, Arnold. *Making the Second Ghetto: Race and Housing in Chicago, 1940–1960*. Chicago: University of Chicago Press, 1983.

Hollinger, David. "American Intellectual History, 1907–2007." *OAH Magazine of History* 21, no. 2 (April 2007): 14–17.

Horne, Gerald. *W. E. B. Du Bois and the Afro-American Response to the Cold War, 1944–1963*. New York: State University of New York Press, 1986.

Jackson, Kenneth T. *Crabgrass Frontier: The Suburbanization of the United States*. New York: Oxford University Press, 1985.

Kirby, John B. *Black Americans in the Roosevelt Era: Liberalism and Race*. Knoxville: University of Tennessee Press, 1980.

Lang, Clarence. "Locating the Civil Rights Movement: An Essay on the Deep South, Midwest, and Border South in Black Freedom Studies." *Journal of Social History* 47, no. 2 (Winter 2013): 371–400. http://www.jstor.org/stable/43305919.

Lawson, Steven F. "The Long Origins of the Short Civil Rights Movement." In *Freedom Rights: New Perspectives on the Civil Rights Movement*, edited by Danielle L. McGuire and John Dittmer, 9–27. Lexington: University Press of Kentucky, 2011.

Lee, Jarena. *The Life and Religious Experience of Jarena Lee, a Colored Lady, Giving an Account of Her Call to Preach the Gospel*, rev. and corrected. In *Sisters of the Spirit: Three Black Women's Autobiographies of the Nineteenth Century*, edited by William L. Andrews, 25–48. Bloomington: Indiana University Press, 1986.

Leuthart, Haley. "Wading-In at Rainbow Beach." *OAH Magazine of History* 26, no. 1 (January 2012): 9–15.

Massey, Douglas, and Nancy Denton. *American Apartheid: Segregation and the Making of the Underclass*. Cambridge, MA: Harvard University Press, 1993.

McGuire, Danielle. *At the Dark End of the Street: Black Women, Rape, and Resistance—A New History of the Civil Rights Movement from Rosa Parks to the Rise of Black Power*. New York: Alfred A. Knopf, 2010.

Nasstrom, Kathryn L. "Between Memory and History: Autobiographies of the Civil Rights Movement and the Writing of Civil Rights History." *Journal of Southern History* 74, no. 2 (May 2008): 325–64. https://doi.org/10.2307/27650145.

Painter, Nell Irvin. *Sojourner Truth: A Life, a Symbol*. New York: W. W. Norton, 1999.

Scanlon, Jennifer. *Until There Is Justice: The Life of Anna Arnold Hedgeman*. New York: Oxford University Press, 2016.

Sitkoff, Harvard. *New Deal for Blacks: The Emergence of Civil Rights as a National Issue*. New York: Oxford University Press, 1981.

Sugrue, Thomas. *The Forgotten Civil Rights Movement in the North*. Princeton, NJ: Princeton University Press, 2008.

Sugrue, Thomas J. *The Origins of the Urban Crisis: Race and Inequality in Postwar Detroit*. Princeton, NJ: Princeton University Press, 1996.

Sullivan, Patricia. *Days of Hope: Race and Democracy in the New Deal Era*. Chapel Hill: University of North Carolina Press, 1996.

Sweet, John Wood. *Bodies Politic: Negotiating Race in the American North, 1730–1830*. Philadelphia: University of Pennsylvania Press, 2006.

Theoharis, Jeanne. *The Rebellious Life of Mrs. Rosa Parks*. Boston: Beacon Press, 2014.

Theoharis, Jeanne, and Komozi Woodard, eds. *Freedom North: Black Freedom Struggles Outside the South, 1940–1980*. New York: Palgrave Macmillan, 2003.

Trotter, Joe. *Black Milwaukee: The Making of an Industrial Proletariat, 1915–1945*. Urbana: University of Illinois Press, 1985.

Washington, Jack. *The Quest for Equality: Trenton's Black Community: 1890–1965*. Trenton, NJ: Africa World Press and Red Sea Press, 1993.

White, Deborah Gray. *Ar'nt I a Woman: Female Slaves in the Plantation South*. New York: W. W. Norton, 1985.

Chapter 9

"IT SINGS IN OUR BLOOD"

Pauli Murray's Re-Mattering of the World

DARCY METCALFE

INTRODUCTION: A LIFE "SUPERB IN LOVE AND LOGIC"

The Rev. Dr. Pauli Murray (1910–1985) lived a life of unwavering resistance to the categories of identity imposed upon her. This resistance is partially what makes it difficult for scholars to capture Murray in a way that accurately addresses her complexity. She has been categorized as a gender-fluid Black woman, a poet, lawyer, social activist, public intellectual, professor, priest, academic, political candidate, friend to Eleanor Roosevelt, and civil rights leader. More personally, Murray described herself as a "rebel, instigator, and survivor, at times a nettle in the body politic, an opener-of-doors, and always a devout child of God and friend of mankind."[1] Her spirit of resistance was consistently manifested in direct and strategic action, which sought to destabilize and end white male regimes of knowledge and power that imperil Black women in particular in the US. Murray's primary tools of resistance include her rigorous intellect, relentless pursuit of knowledge, and love for the written word. In her own words, "One person plus one typewriter constitutes a movement."[2]

Murray's fiery spirit of resistance was shaped, in part, from her personal experience of rejection and limited opportunity because of her gender and race. However, she relentlessly resisted the limitations placed upon her and was undeterred in pursuing what she identified as her purpose as a "child of destiny."[3] For example, after being denied entrance for graduate studies at the University of North Carolina because of her race, Murray refused to let this rejection stop her. Instead, she applied to Howard University School of Law and graduated top of her class in 1944. There, she noted that the "racial factor was removed in the intimate environment of a Negro law school dominated by men, and the factor of gender was fully exposed."[4] When a professor mocked

Murray's gender in front of her male classmates, she later explained that he "had just guaranteed that I would become the top student in his class." Entering with a class of thirty students, including one other woman who dropped out before the end of the first term, Murray's experience of sexism at Howard led her to create the term "Jane Crow," which reflects her assertion that the same legal arguments used to condemn race discrimination could be used to battle gender discrimination. As a Black feminist, Murray took an intersectional approach, which became a hallmark of her legal strategy long before Black feminist legal scholar Kimberlé Crenshaw more fully developed intersectionality theory in the late 1990s.[5] As intersectionality was the guiding principle that inflected all her work, it makes sense to "read" Murray through this critical lens.

Murray had ample opportunity to develop a Black feminist intersectional consciousness throughout her life. After graduating from Howard, she was denied entry to Harvard to pursue master's work in law because of her gender. She then applied to and was accepted at the University of California, Berkeley, earning a master's degree in law in 1945. Her pursuit of justice did not end there. Murray also earned a doctorate in juridical law from Yale Law School in 1965, was a professor in the American Studies department at Brandeis University from 1968 to 1973, and was a visiting lecturer for an academic year at Ghana School of Law in 1960. Among other pursuits, in 1966 she cofounded the National Organization for Women (NOW) and was commissioned by President Kennedy to serve on the Committee on Civil and Political Rights of the President's Commission on the Status of Women in 1961. Murray's legal scholarship contributed to landmark cases regarding the interpretation of the Fourteenth Amendment. In fact, Justice Ruth Bader Ginsburg relied heavily upon Murray's legal arguments in her groundbreaking application of the Fourteenth Amendment's Equal Protection Clause to gender. Evidence of Ginsburg's high esteem for Murray is apparent in her landmark Supreme Court brief for *Reed v. Reed*, in which she lists Murray as an author even though Murray had not directly participated in writing it.[6] In the 1950s, Murray's legal scholarship enabled Thurgood Marshall and his legal team to successfully challenge the constitutional validity of racial segregation in *Brown v. Board of Education*.[7] In short, Murray left an indelible mark upon US history and legal theory. However, until the last few decades, she has been largely relegated to a footnote in academic and public discourse. This glaring omission is finally being rectified.

This prominent legal scholar is also an exemplar of Black women's religious leadership, just as her forebears were, confronting and challenging the sexism and racism (in some cases) inherent in institutionalized religion governed by patriarchal social norms that rendered women subordinate to men. The trajectory of her life from childhood to adulthood demonstrates how her subversive leadership manifested itself. Though she was initially not recognized formally by institutional religion, it is apparent that her calling to religious leadership was present from her childhood and manifested itself through her words, actions, and deep commitment to social justice. And so, after an active legal career dedicated to dismantling systems of institutional sexism and racism, Murray entered General Theological Seminary in 1973, fully aware that the Episcopal Church did not yet permit women to be candidates for ordination. She commenced her studies determined to change the historical trajectory of the Episcopal Church, as she recognized that church institutions were not free of the deep-seated racism and sexism that pervades all realms of life in the US. In 1977, she became the first Black female priest ordained by the Episcopal Church. This drastic shift occurred, in part, because of her sustained efforts to manifest her vision of justice within the church. Her work as a public intellectual and social activist merged with her life of faith to bring about lasting changes in the Episcopal Church and beyond.

This chapter departs from much of the academic work that situates Murray's life and work primarily through the lenses of history, legal theory, gender studies, or religion. Instead, I employ theories of new materialisms as well as womanist and Black feminist methodologies to situate Murray's poetry as an indispensable mode of her ethical self-expression. Murray's poetry is an intriguing vantage point for discerning her ethical perspectives, as her interior and public lives coalesce to reveal a life uncommonly "superb in love and logic," as poet Robert Hayden writes of Frederick Douglass.[8] In Murray's poetry, her brilliant and penetrating logic as a public intellectual and legal theorist is inextricably entangled with a deeply rooted ethic of love. Murray's academic and legal writing, combined with her poetry, allows for a broad understanding of her foundational ethical perspectives, which are inseparable from her many roles, including that of public intellectual, activist, and person of faith. The work of women's studies scholar Patricia Bell-Scott and ethicist Christina Z. Peppard compellingly exemplify the multiple ways that Murray's poetry served public ethical functions and as a mode of activism. Specifically, Peppard highlights the public dynamic of Murray's poetry and the ways that it meaningfully "resonated with the deep grief, anguish, and frustration of many Americans."[9]

Murray's copious legal writings provide glimpses into the profundity of her logic. Her poetry, however, allows for a more intimate understanding of the passions that fueled her resilience and dreams for universal freedom and reconciliation. That is, her poems reveal a person who loved deeply while simultaneously navigating spaces of painful uncertainty within herself. Although the bulk of her career was dedicated to responding to social injustice as a lawyer, priest, and community organizer, Murray consistently referenced her writing as the accomplishment she cherished most in her countless accolades.[10] Bell-Scott explains the uncommonly situated nature of Murray's poetry: "Along with a brilliant record of activism, Murray left poetry that bridges the writers of the Harlem Renaissance and the Black cultural arts movement of the sixties. She showed us that a well-crafted essay could link history and theory to daily life."[11] The poet's work, then, offers a more intimate understanding of the complex ways her ethical ideals, religious commitments, and ontological perspectives informed one another and coalesced in thought and action, permitting an intimate view of her interior life. This chapter examines how her poetic work destabilizes racist and sexist ideologies, while also reconfiguring the material world and US history.

Numerous materialist themes proliferate throughout Murray's poetry as she consistently reflects upon the *intra*-connected nature of all material existence, both human and nonhuman (Karen Barad's concepts of *intra*-connected and *intra*-action will be discussed below). Murray's specific counternarrative approach in her poetry and legal work exemplifies a historical-materialist methodology. In other words, Murray repeatedly offers a counternarrative that meticulously traces the materialities by which race was historically constructed and employed in America, simultaneously mapping specific material/bodily effects of race upon all existence. Having intimately experienced the embodied nature of racism and sexism in ways that drastically shaped her perceptions of reality and history, Murray developed a heightened awareness of the material world and the multiform ways that it embodies and reflects prevailing destructive racist and sexist ideologies. Moreover, her Episcopal religious influences and commitments also deeply informed the ways in which she perceived the urgency of effecting social justice within the complexities of an *intra*-connected world. Based on her unique perception of reality, Murray used her poetry as a vehicle to articulate a beautiful, distinctive vision of what it means to be an ethical person in the becoming of a just world. Ironically, she also experienced her Black womanhood to be antithetical in nature. Lines from her 1943 poem "Dark Testament" exemplify this: "This is America, dual-brained creature / One hand thrusting us out to the stars, / One hand shoving us down in the gutter."[12] As a Black woman living in a society in which regard for an individual's humanity was socially and politically valued differently depending on constructed categorizations of gender, race, and class, Murray spent a lifetime firmly resisting these oppressive constructions of power. She believed that all people—regardless of skin tone or gender—are valued and vibrant "intra-actions" constituted ethically and purposely to move toward the good of "cosmic companionship" and universal flourishing.[13]

THEMES OF NEW MATERIALISMS

Murray's poetry reveals her conceptualization of matter as vibrant and agential in ways similar to new materialisms scholarship. A primary goal of new materialisms is to destabilize theories of human privilege by attending to the agency of all matter, both human and nonhuman. Murray employs poetry partially as a vehicle to grieve the countless ways that human hubris and unjust sociopolitical and economic structures have harmed all existence, while at the same time calling attention to the vibrancy and vitality of the most minute and/or underestimated elements of the material world. Through her careful attention to matter, Murray demonstrates how all matter "matters" and possesses "story." In "Dark Testament," "The Wanderer," and *States' Laws on Race and Color*, she poignantly and disturbingly underscores the strategic means by which the constructs of "race" gained vibrancy in the material world.[14] *States' Laws*, for example, is a remarkable compilation of state laws and local ordinances mandating racial segregation and of pre-*Brown v. Board of Education*-era civil rights legislation that Murray wrote, in part, to demonstrate how race was created through strategic reconfigurations and policing of the material world and how race continues to create real material effects.

Many contemporary scholars of new materialisms reject anthropocentric ontologies that place humanity as the pinnacle and center of all existence. Instead, new materialisms are posthumanist and present humans as one mattered phenomenon among many other material phenomena. Dominant Western philosophies regarding the nature of matter and the privilege of humans have often resulted in the conceptual and practical domination and destruction of Earth as well as "othered" bodies. For example, some scholars of new materialisms contend that classic Cartesian-Newtonian understandings of matter as fixed and mechanical have contributed to a "specifically modern attitude or ethos of subjectivist potency" that has resulted in great harm to all existence.[15] A more fruitful way to theorize new materialisms and thus employ them as a lens through which to read Murray's poetry comes from the feminist philosopher and physicist Karen Barad. Barad's posthumanist, agential realist theory uniquely attends to the smallest conceptions of mattered existence. By focusing on the vibrancy and relationality of all matter, Barad emphasizes an urgent need to reconfigure human perceptions of reality, especially at the most infinitesimal levels, in order for humans to respond ethically to the lively relationalities and flourishing of which humans are only a part. Such sustained attention to the smallest material details of everyday life allows for a broader understanding of how established geopolitical and socioeconomic structures meticulously work to ensure the embodiment of injustice within/upon "othered" bodies.

Although Barad and Murray are not contemporaries, do not specialize in the same fields of study, and do not share life experiences, Barad's work is a provocative perspective from which to read Murray's poetry because they both envision all existence as relational in nature (albeit in different ways). Because Murray and Barad have similar understandings of the material world as relational, they also both identify relational ethics as foundational to any meaningful human response to inequities and injustice. Thus, a Baradian lens properly situates Murray's poetry in a way that foregrounds her careful attention to and meticulous treatment of the material world and the harms of racism that have befallen even the most infinitesimal "elements" of existence. Murray's poetry offers this meticulous treatment of existence by offering an alternative historical narrative concerning race. She employs countermemory to methodologically ascribe vibrancy and expression to every element of the material world—as all existence is expressive and shares a story that contradicts dominant white narratives of history. For Murray, every particle of existence has been affected by the harms and cruelties of race, and all the world is crying out with countermemory.

MURRAY'S USE OF COUNTERMEMORY: RECONFIGURING HISTORY, TIME, AND MATTER

One methodological approach often employed in womanist scholarship is the use of countermemory—or counternarrative. Countermemories are remembrances and histories that destabilize dominant narratives of history and provide wholly different narratives' revelatory counters. As womanist ethicist Emilie M. Townes explains,

> Countermemory has the potential to challenge false generalizations and gross stereotypes often found in what passes for "history" in the United States. Countermemories can disrupt our status quo because they do not rest solely or wholly on objectivity or facts. They materialize from emotions and sights and sound and touch and smell. They come from the deepest part of who we are. Countermemories are dynamic and spark new configurations of meaning.[16]

Womanist scholars and theologians often approach African American women's literary work—both fiction and nonfiction—through the lens of countermemory. In like manner, Murray skillfully employs countermemory in her poetic works, especially in the timelessly prophetic poem "Dark Testament," which she wrote, in part, as a powerful indictment of the powers of white patriarchy. "Dark Testament" resonates with historical experiences of Black Americans and serves as an urgent and forceful plea to the white public to come to terms with the rootedness of racism in America history. Throughout the poem, Murray counters popular historical white narratives that position America as a beacon of freedom, liberty, and equality among nations. Instead of this morally admirable vision of US history, Murray offers a counternarrative that demonstrates why the US values of freedom, liberty, and equality remain unmet dreams, torn asunder by the realities of historically rooted racism.

Murray challenges Americans to recognize racism as a component of American life that is as foundational as the Constitution or the Declaration of Independence. However, unlike these historical documents, the vibrancy of racism within all spheres of life has led to the moral paralysis of a nation. After the assassination of Martin Luther King Jr. in 1968, this poem was read at a memorial service for him in Seattle, Washington, which was attended by nearly ten thousand people. In many ways, "Dark Testament" foresees the deeply painful but resiliently hopeful vision that shaped King's life. However, Murray wrote it twenty-five years before, in 1943, during a summer in which the US experienced widespread racial violence and riots. While composing "Dark Testament," Murray also wrote "Mr. Roosevelt Regrets"—a poem she sent directly to President Roosevelt—which was published in *The Crisis* in 1943.[17] The poem forcefully calls the president to account after his milquetoast response to the Detroit riots. After Murray describes the police violence inflicted upon a "Black boy," she asks what the "man next to God" had to say in response: "What'd the Top Man say, Black boy? / Mr. Roosevelt regrets . . ."

Murray's frustration and anger with white "apathy" toward racial violence continued to grow in the summer of 1943. "Dark Testament" was birthed from a collective Black anger that Murray embodied; she had originally entitled the poem "Dark Anger."[18] Murray challenges white apathy throughout "Dark Testament" and constructively employs her anger to awaken the moral consciousness of an apathetic white public. At this time, Murray was also grieving the execution of Odell Waller, a Black Virginia sharecropper who argued that he was acting in self-defense when he killed his white landlord during an argument in July 1940. Waller was quickly tried in Virginia and sentenced to death.

In 1940, Murray began working on an executive committee for the Workers' Defense League (WDL), a labor rights organization that was also active in civil rights cases. Undeterred by Waller's sentence, Murray toured the US with Waller's mother as the public voice of the WDL to raise public awareness and funds for his case, hoping to secure his freedom on appeal. Interestingly, the WDL challenged the verdict not on the basis of Waller's innocence, but on the grounds that poll taxes in the state of Virginia did not permit Waller to be tried by a jury of his peers. Because of poll taxes, only 26 percent of the adult population in Virginia was permitted to vote in 1940. And in rural Pittsylvania County, where Waller was tried, only 10 percent of the adult population was qualified to vote.[19] Murray even appealed to Eleanor Roosevelt, with whom she was developing a life-changing friendship. Roosevelt repeatedly pleaded with her husband to intervene, but Virginia's governor refused to issue a stay of execution.[20] Waller was executed in 1942, and Murray responded by writing a highly critical and uncompromising open letter to President Roosevelt on behalf of the WDL that was widely published and signed by several prominent Black leaders. She wrote: "Negroes are beginning to express a willingness and determination to die right here in America to attain a democracy which they have never had. . . . [Waller's execution] was a signal for the barbarous forces in this country to renew the unleashing of their hatred upon the Negro people."[21] Waller's death combined with the racial violence of the Harlem riots left Murray infuriated and in a state of deep anguish by the time she wrote "Dark Testament." She said that writing this poem was a type of religious undertaking for her: "I wrote as one possessed, pouring all my pain and bitterness into 'Dark Testament.' When the poem was completed, I felt as if a demon had been exorcised and a terrible fever inside me had been broken."[22] "Dark Testament" presents a direct counternarrative to dominant historical narratives that uphold an illusion of America as "one nation indivisible with liberty and justice for *all*."

The poem begins with the unified voice of every person who has dreamed of freedom throughout history and kept hold of the dream while never realizing it. As it continues, the narrative voice is narrowed to the experience of persons specifically categorized as "Black." This dream transcends all time, evidenced in the poem's chilling recall of the violence that has relentlessly confronted the countless dreamers: "Freedom is a dream / Haunting as amber wine / Or worlds remembered out of time."[23] The poem also describes the dream of freedom as transcendent yet immanent and as haunting as "worlds remembered out of time." In these first lines, time is suspended in a way that purposely situates the reader in an otherworldly space—a dreamworld entangled throughout every time, all people, and all materiality. The dream encapsulates a hope of universal freedom that persists despite the cruel passages of time and the volume of suffering and injustice heaped upon the dreamers. This purposeful poetic move also captures the disoriented state of the dreamer.

Following the opening passage, the primary narrative voice shifts more specifically to the millions of African people who were captured and forced into the early colonies. The poem artfully evokes the disoriented state of time and being for an entire people who were savagely stolen from their lives and homes and endured the brutal atrocities of the Middle Passage before being sold into slavery. Arriving in a new land where they were regarded as less than human, Africans were stripped of their previous identities, given new (white) names, and forced to adhere to whites' religions, which Murray poetically describes thus: "Trade a king's freedom for a barrel of molasses, / Trade a queen's freedom for a red bandanna, / . . . Sell a man's brain for a handful of greenbacks, / Mark him up in Congress—he's three-fifths human."[24]

The speaker disturbingly articulates how Black bodies have been strategically reconfigured by white patriarchy, dehumanized as a commodity or production to be bought and sold for purposes of white pleasure and economic gain. Any noble concept of universal human freedom that the US Constitution declares is forsaken and traded for a barrel of molasses, a red bandanna, and a Black man's brain for cash. The high regard for human equality professed by the Declaration of Independence appears to be only a cruel fiction. The speaker then alludes to the Three-Fifths Compromise of 1787 in which Congress voted to count three out of every five people held in slavery as human in order to determine the number of seats a state would be assigned in the Congress. This compromise allowed southern states to gain congressional and electoral votes without the legal necessity of counting people held in slavery as full human beings of equal status.

Here, as elsewhere, Murray reveals in poetic fashion the malicious fluidity and negotiability of a Black person's legal status as "human" in America. According to a historical-materialist perspective on state and federal law, a Black person's legal status as human exists in a state of negotiable fluidity, according to how the recognition or negation of human status either benefits or limits the parameters of white power and greed. In terms of quantum mechanics, white legislative powers have strategically relegated a Black person's humanity to a superposition of states. Murray demonstrates how, legally, the Black body has historically existed in a state of indeterminacy, in states of "human" or "nonhuman" according to the measuring apparatus and determinations of white legislators.

Through "Dark Testament," Murray immediately and purposely situates the reader within a thick, descriptive ontological space of hopeless desperation in which time is suspended and the countless injustices of the past are revealed as veritably dynamic and expressive in what Barad calls the "thick-now of the present."[25] Her poetic approach to time works against classic Newtonian perceptions of space and time, which claim that space is distinct from the body and time passes uniformly without regard to whether anything happens in the world. In Newtonian theory, time and space exist independently of any observer and are measurable but wholly imperceptible. Murray's poetry disrupts such understanding of time and space with her distinctly materialist approach and presents instead a historical-materialist counternarrative that reveals how time, space, and being are in themselves materializations that appear to be specifically political. Her use of countermemory also reveals memory and history as distinctly material and vital to the present and future flourishing of the world. In this sense, memory and history are not pronouncements of the past that are closed-ended. Womanist scholars recognize that the dominant US historical narratives as open-ended productions of knowledge must be challenged.

Townes references W. E. B. Du Bois in asserting that the "propaganda" of history "paints perfect men and noble nations, but it does not tell the truth."[26] The womanist notion of countermemory seeks to rectify the untruths of history. In this sense, history and memory are materialities unrestrained by time and capable of enacting real material effects in the present; they are materialities that suspend concepts of linear time, are vital in the present, and are consequential for the future.

Murray's unique treatment of time is notably similar to the understanding of time exemplified in lines from the diary of her maternal grandfather, Robert Fitzgerald. She places his words in the first lines of her family memoir *Proud Shoes*: "The past is key of the present and the mirror of the future, therefore let us adopt as a rule, to judge the future by the history of the past, and having key of past experience, let us open the door to present success and future happiness."[27] In positioning this quote at the beginning of her family's history, Murray situates readers conceptually in time and history before they actually read the first words of the story. Barad's unique understanding of time is a useful heuristic here, for it allows us to appreciate how Murray used her poetry to envision time as being as open-ended instead of linear and bounded. Specifically, Barad employs the work of German philosopher Walter Benjamin to clarify her own substantive departures from classic understandings of time, being, and space. In his philosophy of history, Benjamin used the German term *Jetztzeit* to refer to what Barad calls the "thick-now of the present." *Jetztzeit* and Barad's "thick-now of the present" are notions of time that rupture linear conceptions and position the present as a continuous unfolding of the past into the future.[28] What is particularly notable about "the thick-now of the present" is that the past is never left behind, as reflected in Murray's grandfather's statement. The past, present, and future are inextricably entangled and bound together. Time unfolds upon itself, and the past is never left behind—never closed-ended.

"IT SINGS IN OUR BLOOD": MURRAY'S PORTRAYALS OF MATERIAL VIBRANCY

As I've discussed above, "Dark Testament" performs a counternarrative function, illustrating the vibrancy of the material world in direct opposition to popular narratives of American history. Specifically, Murray undermines historical myths of white superiority that subtended the institution of slavery and later Jim Crow segregation by creatively examining ordinary materialities—such as the soil of the earth and decaying human bones—thus uncovering the truths of equality imparted by these overlooked materialities. The poem also holds the slave song and the Constitution as equally vital to the telling of US history: "*In coffin and outhouse all men are equal, / And the same red earth is fed / By the white bones of Tom Jefferson / And the white bones of Nat Turner*" (italics in the original).[29] No matter what historical efforts have been taken to enslave and segregate Black people and perpetuate the racialized myths of Black inferiority, the poem's speaker portrays a material world whose very composition appears in direct opposition to such racialized myths. "Dark Testament" also reminds the reader that death is the enduring great equalizer of all people. "All men are equal," whether Black or white—and the outhouse, coffin, and soil of the earth testify to this truth.

In *States' Laws on Race and Color*, Murray delineates states' laws that segregated Black bodies in every realm of daily life, including in the "coffin" and "outhouse." During slavery and the Jim Crow era, Black communities were forced by states' laws to bury loved ones in "colored" or "Negro" cemeteries and to use clearly marked segregated public restroom facilities. This portion of "Dark Testament" directly reflects upon these laws while noting that all of the material world reverberates with a story of equality that stands in direct opposition to them. The soil of the earth and the bones of dead people function as distinctly vibrant material bearers of truth. Moreover, a constructed wooden box (which once was a tree and before that a sapling—both fed by the soil) is materially identified as "coffin" in one moment and "outhouse" in another. Although the materiality of the wood is reconfigured—and perpetually reconfigured—the poem demonstrates how the wood (the material) consistently bears witness to a similar story of human equality. Similarly, the decomposing "materials" of a venerable president of the United States and a famous American slave rebel now equally nourish the soil of Virginia; from president and rebel to worm food, materiality is always in flux and yet perpetually gives witness to the resounding persistence of human/material equality. The poem continues, reminding readers of the impossibility of muting the story of racialized oppression and brutality in America's history and references the many attempts to "tear" this story from the history books. However, the story continues to rise up because it is written in the material composition of our faces "Twenty million times over! / *It sings in our blood / It cries from the housetops / It mourns with the wind in the forests*" (italics in the original).[30]

Even though white narratives of American history have often sought to bury or understate the horrors of slavery, the speaker proclaims that the truths of history are already materialized in the faces of twenty million Americans. The human body itself is the primary "Dark Testament," the perpetual material proof of the history of slavery and racialized injustice. This testament *is* the "life-pulse" the speaker identifies, the story that "sings in our blood."[31] Murray's own body, and the bodies of millions of Americans of various skin tones, are the incontrovertible material evidence of a history that cannot be hidden. It is written in our faces, "Twenty million times over." The counternarrative she articulates is expressly evident in the materialities that are American bodies.

Murray intimately experienced embodied racism. Her own family history was a prime example of how the story that "sings in our blood" is embodied throughout the material world. In her memoirs *Proud Shoes* and *Song in a Weary Throat*, for example, Murray recounts how her maternal grandmother, Cornelia Smith Fitzgerald, was conceived in North Carolina as the result of the brutal rape of Cornelia's enslaved mother by her white captor. Cornelia's mother and Murray's great-grandmother, Harriet Smith, was an enslaved woman who was also part Cherokee. Harriet was repeatedly raped by James Sidney Smith, a white Episcopal lawyer and her owner according to the state of North Carolina. Smith's sister, Mary Ruffin Smith, was eventually given ownership of Cornelia and raised the girl in her home. Through recounting her family history, Murray presents a historical-materialist reconfiguration of human bodies as she maps the many ways that her own body and the bodies of the members of her family manifestly embody and comprise the "Dark Testament." Throughout her memoirs and poetry, Murray references the frequent occurrence of the rape of enslaved women in the South. Even after the Emancipation Proclamation and the end of federally legalized chattel slavery, the rape of Black women continued, as white men desperately sought to reassert the power they egregiously claimed over Black women's bodies. The horrors of rape are repeatedly exposed throughout Murray's family tree and evidenced in her own light skin tone.

Murray's careful attention to the materiality of the human body foresees what epidemiologist Nancy Krieger calls the "embodiment of race." Krieger seeks to understand scientifically how racism and powers of whiteness operate as primary determinants of disparities in public healthcare. Legal scholar Dorothy Roberts reports how Krieger explained embodiment theory to her: "Embodiment gives you a frame to allow you to appreciate what the connections are, but recognizes society as the key driver. That's the profound difference of having an embodiment approach versus one that sees innate biology as the key driver which just happens to get expressed. My focus is on how inequity becomes embodied and harms health."[32] As her poetry and legal work demonstrate, Murray sought a similar understanding of the effects of racism years before embodiment theory came to be a recognized academic endeavor; that is, she wanted to comprehend how social and political constructions of race affect and inform material/bodily becomings. Racialized injustice literally gets "under the skin" and "in the blood." This image occurs repeatedly in "Dark Testament," as she also works to unsettle popular historical narratives, writing, "Ours is no bedtime story children beg to hear, / No heroes rode down the night to warn our Sleeping villages. / Ours is a tale of blood streaking the Atlantic."[33]

Christiana Peppard notes how these lines of the poem directly counter a popular nineteenth-century poem by Henry Wadsworth Longfellow, "Paul Revere's Ride."[34] In it, Revere is portrayed as a hero who rides through the night to warn colonial villagers of an impending British attack so that they might prepare to fight. The poem begins: "Listen, my children, and you shall hear / Of the midnight ride of Paul Revere."[35] Told to generations of American schoolchildren, the poem has been passed down in US history as an exemplar of the valor and values that define the American ideal of freedom. Murray directly uproots the deeply embedded "truth" of this narrative and unsettles its grandeur by offering a counternarrative resurrected from the countless forgotten graves of slaves—from the ocean floor of the Middle Passage to the bottomlands of the Mississippi Delta. No child wants to hear this story—no brave heroes tried "to warn our Sleeping villages. / Ours is a tale of blood streaking the Atlantic."[36]

Throughout her poetry, legal analysis of state laws, and memoirs, Murray gives sustained attention to the materiality of blood. She maps the ways in which blood has been reconfigured as an implement to substantiate racialized myths of Black inferiority. In fact, she repeatedly singles out blood as a key material element of concern throughout her poetry because she was acutely aware of the multiple ways conceptions of the word have been employed and constantly reconfigured in race-based legal strategies. In *States' Laws on Race and Color*, for example, Murray details how states' laws historically defined "Negro" by contrivances of "blood quotas." In her home state of North Carolina, the miscegenation laws defined "Negro" thus: "Every person who has one-eighth Negro blood in his veins is within the prohibited degree set out in this section."[37] Many states retained a similar one-eighth quota as a means to politically categorize bodies as "negro" or "mulatto." Mississippi further complicated its definition of "negro" and "colored":

> Article 14, section 263 of the Constitution of Mississippi which prohibits marriage of a white person with a Negro or mulatto, or a person having one-eighth or more Negro blood, does not determine the status of a person as to whether he is white or colored under Art. 8, section 207 of the Constitution which provides for separate schools for children of the white and colored races. The word "white" under Section 207 means a member of the Caucasian race and the word "colored" includes not only Negroes but persons of mixed blood having any appreciable amount of Negro blood.[38]

States' Laws strategically tracks how difference is created and employed through such legislative means.

In race science, state definitions of "blood" served as implements of whiteness and have been historically manipulated in various eras and locales as mediums of bodily inscription. There are varieties of "blood quota" parameters throughout *States' Laws,* which highlight the strategic fluidity in the laws of the states. Such denotative indeterminacies of what qualifies as a "Negro blood quota" allowed for structures of power to vary application across different locales. White legislative powers sought to control and survey Black people differently in different contexts—and the states' laws were constructed to permit such flexibility. Most egregiously, the fluidity of what qualified as a "Negro blood quota" allowed for flexibility in how each state determined and substantiated the myth of "race" itself. For Murray, blood is one of the many materialities that actively embody truths of history that stand in direct opposition to white legislative implements.

"Dark Testament" demonstrates that the veracity of American history is unequivocally manifest in millions of vital materialities that are vibrant and expressive by nature: blood, buried bones, soil, red clay, forests, wind, faces, and the millions of bodies of flesh and bone. They are all brimming with vitality and story. While white narratives of history often serve as materialities purposed to praise white morality, Murray asserts that the material world is vibrant countermemory that, instead, elucidates the suffering of those who exist at the margins of society. She relies upon the material world to reframe a nation's story as it dynamically "mourns with the wind in the forests," "sings in our blood," and "is written in our faces."[39] For Murray, the story is not simply "told" or "revealed by" the material world. Instead, the story *is* the material world—the story is entangled within the most incremental elements of existence and reverberates throughout the vast incomprehensible whole. Reality is the embodied story. In this sense, the material world (all existence) is an *intra-active* whole—a term introduced by Barad—entangled in an open-ended becoming, as opposed to traditional understandings of material existence as compositions of *inter-active* individuated objects that are mechanical and function according to systematic laws of nature.[40] "Dark Testament" destabilizes classic philosophies of the material world throughout. The material world is not mechanical and fixed. It is quite the opposite. Instead, the smallest most neglected materialities are vibrant, calling out and *intra-actively* expressive with story.

Barad's understanding of the material is useful for framing Murray's portrayal of the material world as *intra-active*. In *Meeting the Universe Halfway,* Barad introduces the idea of the material as *intra-active* instead of *inter-active* through conceptions of quantum theory that were formulated by physicist Niels Bohr. The *inter-active/intra-active* distinction is vital to Barad's perspective of material entities as emerging from the *intra-action* of materiality within a whole (phenomena) rather than the *inter-action* of already determinate/individuated entities. In this sense, reality is composed not of "things-in-themselves" but of "things-in-phenomena." This distinction allows Barad to articulate and investigate the "ontological inseparability" of all that exists. She identifies localized material separability (or what we may identify as individuated objects) as "exteriority-within-phenomena."[41]

A similar distinction is also discernible in Murray's poetry and memoirs as she references a more theological idea of *intra-action* that she at times refers to as "cosmic companionship."[42] Murray references Martin Luther King Jr.'s use of this phrase as reflective of her own understanding of the *intra-active* relationality of existence. One example of King's idea of cosmic companionships is in a sermon he delivered on Christmas day in 1967. On this day, King stood before his congregation at Ebenezer Baptist Church in Atlanta and gave his final Christmas sermon before his assassination. "It really boils down to this: that all life is interrelated," he said. "We are all caught in an inescapable network of mutuality, tied into a single garment of destiny. Whatever affects one directly, affects all indirectly. We are made to live together because of the interrelated structure of reality."[43] Murray shared King's vision of "cosmic companionship" and recognized the God she professed in her Episcopal faith as the overarching "higher force" that connected and energized endeavors toward universal justice and flourishing throughout millennia.[44] However, I contend that Murray's poetry reflects more of a Baradian understanding of the *intra-active* nature of existence rather than the "interrelated" structure of reality that King envisioned. It is likely that this nuanced difference is observable in Murray's poetry because of her intimate experience with and resistance to a life lived in rigidly bounded categorizations. As her poetry reflects, Murray intimately understood the fluid and entangled nature of the material world as well as the limits and harms of mechanical and strictly bounded understanding of existence.

Based on this understanding from gender identification to race and class, she strongly resisted the many legal and social categorizations imposed upon her body and the material world she inhabited. For example, from early childhood, Murray expressed that she felt she was a male living inside a female body and, in adulthood, she was only attracted to heterosexual women.[45] In Murray's lifetime, there was no terminology to express variety or fluidity of gender identity. If she were alive today, Brittney Cooper speculates, Murray might identify as transgender.[46] Race was another example of an imposed bodily categorization for Murray. During young adulthood, Murray's race was consistently categorized as either "colored" or "Negro" by the state. These legal categorizations of race did not remotely reflect the complexities she identified in the ancestries of most Americans. For example, Murray had a light skin tone and descended from what she called a "Euro-African-American" mix of white antislavery Quakers, Episcopalian slave owners, mixed-race slaves, freedmen farmers, and Cherokee Indians.[47] Murray consistently resisted categorizations of her body and world because of their dehumanizing effects and because of the cruel objectives of such categorizations to limit individuals and/or cause harm. Countless social and legal boundaries were imposed upon Murray merely by virtue of her existence, and she strategically resisted them all. Through her disquieted resolve and strong aversion to the boundaries imposed upon her body and world, Murray developed a unique recognition and appreciation for material fluidity and the *intra-active* nature of existence.

MURRAY'S "ENTREATY"

This appreciation is expressed in another poem, "The Wanderer," in which the material world is portrayed as "vibrant and expressive."[48] Ultimately, in this poem, love is the vital force of material vibrancy and the impetus of life-giving material reconfigurations. Before we turn to the contents of the poem, it is important to situate the composition of this poem within the context of Murray's life. She wrote this poem in March 1940, in the same month that she was released from inpatient psychiatric treatment in New York City. Shortly before being admitted for treatment, a longtime friend and love interest had moved away, leaving Murray devastated and heartbroken. Murray desperately sought to persuade her friend to stay and set out in male attire, hitchhiking from New York to Massachusetts, determined to meet with her. However, at some point in the trip, Rosenberg reports, Murray was picked up by Rhode Island State Police for hitchhiking.[49] After being detained, Murray confided to a sympathetic woman officer that she was a "homosexual" who was taking hormones, although there is no evidence that Murray was ever successful in acquiring these. For years prior to this event, Murray had desperately sought hormone treatments that she hoped would allow her to express her identity more fully as male. Rosenberg attributes Murray's "homosexual" self-reference in the officer's account of the detainment as a term Murray sometimes used as the only "available descriptor that people would accept." The officer did not arrest Murray, but instead escorted her to the New York City Police Department, where they admitted her for psychiatric care at Bellevue Hospital. At Bellevue, a psychiatrist diagnosed Murray with schizophrenia because the doctor believed Murray suffered from a primary delusion: that she was a woman who believed she was a man.[50] A friend of Murray's checked her out of Bellevue and subsequently admitted her to a private psychiatric facility, Dr. Rogers Hospital in New York. Murray's friend brought a typewriter to her room, and during her stay at this hospital, Murray itemized reasons for her "nervous collapse." She identified the primary contributor as her repeated misfortune of falling in love with women without having any "opportunity to express such an attraction in normal ways," which was as a heterosexual male in love with a heterosexual female.[51]

Throughout her life, Murray frequently fell in love with heterosexual women and entered into relationships of unrequited love that later abruptly ended. The end of these relationships often left Murray devastated and grieving the loss of love and the unmet desire for acceptance for which she longed. Although "The Wanderer" is a poem about the desire to love and be loved, it is not merely romantic love to which Murray refers. Instead, she envisions love as the vital force that initiates, sustains, and is capable of reconfiguring/transforming all existence for universal good. Through her portrayal of the material world in this poem, Murray envisions love as the vibrant and reverberating force of life that is expressive in all things. "The Wanderer" longs for a place to belong but, finding no place of belonging, holds on to hope and the reassurances of love's limitless capabilities that are perpetually witnessed in the material world. "The Wanderer" lends a frame by which one can appreciate the profoundly expansive vision of Murray's ideal and ethic of love. Similar poetic renderings of time and matter already addressed in this chapter are also present throughout this poem. Only recently have Murray's writings and struggles related to her sexual identity become resources of interest and recognized as essential to framing social justice struggles related to LGBTQ+ lives. Sadly, in Murray's time her struggle was often discounted as a psychiatric condition, as this part of her life was not accepted or understood by many—even those closest to her. Although this poem was overlooked in its time, I implore readers to reserve space for this poem as a work of public intellectualism that resonates with and offers a multitude of wisdoms for our times—times in which people who identity as LGBTQ+ continue to fight for basic civil rights alongside social and political space in which all people are valued and loved. Murray was ahead of her time in countless ways, and her profound understanding of queer identities is no exception.

The title of this poem mirrors the title of an Old English poem estimated to be written in the tenth century. Murray's familiarity with this classic poem is evinced in its thematic parallels with her own poem. The main themes of the Old English poem recount the story of a solitary warrior who wanders in a foreign land after being ousted and rejected by his homeland. He is an outsider by all counts, and he daily grieves his existence in exile. By the end of the poem, the wanderer concludes that true meaning and ultimate peace cannot be attained through the limited nature of human wisdom, but is, instead, something of God, eternal—beyond the bounds of human time and existence. Similarly, the speaker in Murray's poem is a "lonely wanderer," a "patient seeker" in exile who cries after her "lost desire."[52] Murray divides the poem into three sections: I. *The Query*, II. *The Answer*, and III. *The Entreaty*. *The Query* portrays a wanderer looking for "young love from the hills."[53] The wanderer searches everywhere in the city for a friend to go "along these many streets," and ultimately asks, "Must love be desolate this long night?" *The Answer* section of the poem responds to *The Query* with a devastating reply, that although people gather and move together, "Through clash of metallic laughter, / And though the streets swell with man-juices, / Yet each lies down alone at last / Crying after his lost desire."[54]

I imagine this hopeless answer is partially what grieved Murray so during her stay at Bellevue and Rogers hospitals in March 1940. She mourned not only her loss of love but also the countless ways she had never found belonging or space to unreservedly offer the love contained and restrained within her.

The third section of this poem, *The Entreaty*, is most profound in scope and vision, as Murray maps love as a vital force throughout the material world and throughout time. Once again, she disrupts concepts of linear time, portraying love and *The Entreaty* to love as simultaneously transcending and emanating from time and space. *The Entreaty* begins with the desire of love singing out in the exquisite beauty and staggering mysteries of the cosmos, and then abruptly shifts and carefully observes the "tremulous whispers," "elemental throat gurgles," and "silent agonies" of the desire of love in every "helpless, inarticulate small thing," proclaiming that she has seen this love "In every helpless, inarticulate small thing, / In every trodden, meek, despised creature; . . . / And in the blood and weeping of the first lifebeat. / I have felt you in the life-pulse and sweep."[55]

The Entreaty reveals that everything begs to be loved, and when this entreaty to love is left unmet, it ultimately has devastating effects on all matter of existence. "The Wanderer" imagines what will happen if the entreaty is refused by humanity: "If you turn back / The squirrels will not gather nuts, / The sparrows will scorn their crumbs, / Crickets will forget their chirping—."[56]

The vitality of life will cease and the flourishing of all that exists will quickly dissipate if humanity chooses to recoil from the entreaty to "cosmic companionship." The "life-pulse and sweep" of existence will surrender its vitality in a state of forlorn grief. The poem concludes with a heartfelt plea that reveals "The Wanderer's" own commitment to love, which also insists on a vision of universal justice and reconciliation despite all the sufferings and injustice the narrator has witnessed and experienced. As such, "The Wanderer" extends an entreaty to the reader—an entreaty to love all that begs to be loved: "Do not send me away, my beloved. / Come with me and we will go singing / All our days, brimming with laughter, / Touched with the sun."[57]

These last lines have particular religious meaning; indeed, Murray's religious commitments and theological influences are especially discernible throughout "The Wanderer." Employing imagery and phrases directly from the Song of

Solomon, the Psalms, and *Treatise of the Love of God* by Francis de Sales, she elucidates the exact nature of the love she desires and envisions.[58] Her thick descriptive poetic approach purposely situates the reader as both transcending and existing within time and space as the narrator investigates the essential nature of *The Entreaty* by closely observing the vital nature of all materiality. The poem exemplifies the *intra-active* nature of existence as a vast and cosmic whole. Ultimately, Murray's entreaty is the fundamental human desire to love and be loved. This poem, then, is an entreaty to a life of love. According to Murray's Episcopal faith, God *is* Love, and Love *is* the material manifestation of God.[59] She writes that she has felt *The Entreaty* in "The comrade's handclasp and the compassion / Of the Nazarene."[60] The compassion of the Nazarene refers to the compassion of Jesus, which according to Christian theology (and as described by de Sales) is also the Love of God. The compassion of Jesus was God/Love in human form. Therefore, human commitment to and action in love for universal humanity and all material existence *are* God/Love made manifest—an inseparable entangled vibrancy of materiality that moves by nature towards justice and flourishing for all. Murray's poem portrays *The Entreaty* as an entangled and relational call to humanity that begs for a response of love as an individual commitment and action towards the good of all existence. Her specific entreaty to love calls upon all people to recognize the value and significance of all existence—both human and nonhuman. The response of love she hopes for entails an individual commitment to act and live in such a way that ethically contributes to and participates in the *intra-active* flourishing of the becoming of all that is.

The very last words of *The Entreaty* come directly from Francis de Sales's *Treatise on the Love of God*. In them, Murray urges her reader not to turn from love and not to send her away, but to come with her and be "Touched with the sun." These last four words of the poem are taken from Book II of the *Treatise* in which de Sales describes his ontological understanding of the material/bodily transformations/reconfigurations of love through an analogy of a honeycomb "touched with the sun." He writes, "As we see a honeycomb touched with the sun's ardent rays go out of itself, and *forsake its form*, to flow out towards that side where the rays touch it, so the soul of this lover flowed out towards where the voice of her well-beloved was heard, *going out of herself and passing the limits of her natural being*, to follow Him that spoke unto her" (emphasis added).[61] These final words contain particular meaning when one reflects upon the circumstances of Murray's life when she wrote this poem. In March 1940, as she sat in Bellevue and Rogers hospitals, it seems she desired nothing more than to "pass the limits of her natural being." She was in a state of deep grief and agonized that the women she loved could not accept who she knew herself to be. She decried the limits of "race," "gender," and "class" that had restrained her existence in innumerable ways since birth. Desperately seeking to "forsake the form" that she had been perpetually limited to and constrained within, she yearned to soar beyond the limits and boundaries that were consistently forced upon her body, mind, dreams, and even her loves. In the poem's last lines, "The Wanderer" reveals that "to be touched with the sun" or to be "touched with love" is the ultimate answer to humanity's most pressing queries. Only love can lead to the envisioned freedom, and only love is the impetus capable of transforming all forms of being into wholeness.

For Murray and de Sales, love entails an ontological transformation of one's own form—we are literally forever changed by love. Like de Sales, the poet proposes that love calls humanity to radical reconfigurations of fundamental perceptions of reality itself. When one is "touched with the sun," the understanding of what/who "matters" is radically reconfigured. Any plausible response to effectively meet this entreaty demands individuals to "forsake their forms" and go beyond the limits of what dominant epistemologies have espoused as hierarchically "natural being." Ultimately, Murray is calling for a response that reconfigures the material world in a way that disavows white theoretical ontologies that seek to deny the vitality and significance of "othered" bodies, both human and nonhuman. In this sense, women of color, forgotten children, LGBTQ+ communities, the poor—the majority of the world's populace must not continue suffering the indignities, perils, and horrors of their ascribed "nonexistence," as matter that does not matter. And the most vulnerable individuals are not the only materialities at stake in Murray's plea to love. The good and flourishing of the world, the cosmos, and all that exists depend upon how humanity chooses to ultimately respond to *The Entreaty*.

CONCLUSION: RELATIONAL MATERIALITY DEMANDS RELATIONAL ETHICS

As demonstrated throughout this chapter, Murray's poetry often works to drastically shift perspectives concerning the nature of reality as she portrays the material world as specifically *intra-active* and relational. Ultimately, her unique understanding of the material world contributed to how she envisioned addressing and ending the "problem" of race in America in any lasting and meaningful way. And once again, I turn to Barad's work as a helpful lens by which one may discern Murray's ruminations concerning the relational nature of existence. By examining the fundamental inseparability of all materiality, Barad presents a relational ontology that repudiates any idea that humans can exist as outside observers in any material context. Instead, all existence is relational and dynamic, and humans are a part of that which possesses distinct ethical capabilities. Barad's relational ontology demands a similarly relational ethic rooted in an understanding of all existence as entanglement. She writes:

> Matter itself is always already open to, or rather entangled with, the "Other." . . . The other is not just in one's skin, but one's bones, in one's belly, in one's heart, in one's nucleus, in one's past and future. . . . Ethics is therefore not about right response to a radially exterior/ized other, but about responsibility and accountability for the lively relationalities of the becoming of which we are a part.[62]

In a world of entanglement that is relational by nature, a relational ethic is indispensable. Barad contends that neglect of relational ontologies and relational ethics has caused great harm to both humans and all material existence. Therefore, she presents an ethic that begins with a foundational understanding of all materiality as entanglement. This implies that no one and nothing are exteriorized or truly "other." Instead, humans are responsible and accountable for the relational becoming of which we are only a part. Barad writes, "We have to meet the universe halfway. To move toward what may come to be in ways that are accountable for our part in the world's differential becoming. All real living is meeting. And each meeting matters."[63]

Within her own frame of thought, Murray also recognized that relational ethics are indispensable to any hope of addressing and ending America's ugly history with race. For Murray, lasting justice and equity in an ultimate sense can only be realized through mutuality and relationship. In hoping for making specific "meetings matter" in the world, she writes,

> Almost from birth I had been conditioned by religious training to believe that love was more powerful than hate—not a passive, submissive love but a vigorous love which resisted injustice without stooping to the level of hating the oppressor. Applying this belief to the racial problem in the United States, I held to the conviction that once discriminatory laws and systemic practices were removed, the ultimate resolution of racism would come through one-to-one interracial relationships creating a climate of acceptance.[64]

For Murray, meaningful change can only be realized through relationships grounded in a "vigorous love that resists injustice." It is primarily through this grounding in love and "mattered meetings" of people that Murray envisioned the harms of race ceasing and the opportunities arising for reconciliation to begin. What is most dangerous is when humans embrace any ontology that places a singular human group as a separate unentangled entity from the whole.

Her vision of human equality and dignity is partially what drew Murray to life as a public intellectual and activist as well as to service as a priest in the Episcopal Church. As a priest, she was able to "minister the sacrament of One in whom there is no north or south, no Black or white, no male or female—only the spirit of love and reconciliation drawing us all toward the goal of human wholeness."[65] In this spirit of love and reconciliation, she was able to find reprieve from a deeply divided and segregated world that "revolved on color and variations of color."[66] More directly, she mapped the harms that have resulted from philosophies of separability or supremacy in human groups in *States' Laws on Race and Color*. In it, she strategically tracks historical legislative measures that state governments have employed for the purpose of imposing white male self-proclaimed separability and preeminence above all others. In that treatise, Murray details how the white males who governed the states had legislated distinctive material measures to inscribe difference upon Black populations, such as demarcating ground where Black people were to bury their dead, separate from white people; creating separate "White" and "Colored" toilets, sinks, and drinking fountains; instituting laws detailing the thickness and specified material of walls installed between "Colored" and "White" restroom facilities; declaring that books used by Black schoolchildren could not be borrowed or used by white schoolchildren; and so on. But for Murray, any supposition of separability from other humans is patently false. Her legal writing details whites' suppositions of separability and superiority while her historical-materialist narratives offer a direct counter. What Murray's historical-materialist narrative reveals is that, ultimately, the cruelties of white patriarchy do not simply deny Black flourishing; they also deny the flourishing of the becoming of *all* that is—including the goodness that is possible for white people.

The Rev. Dr. Murray arduously worked as a social advocate and lawyer to destabilize and destroy the rooted social and political constructions of race and gender and expended great effort in educating herself and thoroughly mastering the legislative means by which race was constructed. Ultimately, however, it was clear for Murray that the best hope for making true difference in the world's becoming was in the relationships yet to come. Social and political constructions of oppression must be destroyed; at the same time, the lasting effects of justice can only be realized through human commitment to sustained, ethical, up-building relationships with one another universally and with all that exists. She applauded the many courageous and sustained efforts that contributed to the eventual dismantling of systems of legalized segregation and for all the people whose efforts laid the groundwork for sweeping changes in federal laws regarding discrimination. However, Murray also grieved that the "desegregation of hearts and minds was light years away from the pronouncements of the Supreme Court and the Congress."[67] Lasting change to human hearts and minds requires sustained relationships, grounded in a "vigorous love that resists injustice." Only through such relational ethics can humans achieve just and drastic reconfigurations of the world that uphold the distinctively *intra-connected* nature of all that exists. Within this relational dynamic, Murray reminds us that "each meeting matters." As Barad explains: "Meeting each moment, being alive to the possibilities of becoming, is an ethical call, an invitation that is written into the very matter of all being and becoming. We need to meet the universe halfway, to take responsibility for the role that we play in the world's differential becoming."[68] This is the nature of *The Entreaty* that Murray extends to the reader even now, undeterred by the passing of time and death. All material existence continues to cry out in the thick-now of the present, and the "Dark Testament" still speaks.

NOTES

1. Quoted in Patricia Bell-Scott, "Introduction," in *Song in a Weary Throat: Memoir of An American Pilgrimage* by Pauli Murray (New York: Liveright, 1987), xiv.

2. Murray, *Song in a Weary Throat*, 314.

3. Murray, *Song in a Weary Throat*, 91.

4. Murray, *Song in a Weary Throat*, 237.

5. Kimberlé Crenshaw, "Demarginalizing the Intersection of Race and Sex: A Black Feminist Critique of Antidiscrimination Doctrine, Feminist Theory, and Antiracist Politics," *University of Chicago Legal Forum* no. 1 (1989): article 8, 139–67, http://chicagounbound.uchicago.edu/uclf/vol1989/iss1/8.

6. US Reports: *Reed v. Reed*, 404 US 71 (1971), https://supreme.justia.com/cases/federal/us/404/71/.

7. US Reports: *Brown v. Board of Education of Topeka*, 347 US 483 (1954), https://supreme.justia.com/cases/federal/us/347/483/.

8. Robert Hayden, "Frederick Douglass," Poetry Foundation, accessed May 18, 2020, https://www.poetryfoundation.org/poems/46460/frederick-douglass.

9. Christiana Z. Peppard, "Poetry, Ethics, and the Legacy of Pauli Murray," *Journal of the Society of Christian Ethics* 30, no. 1 (Spring-Summer 2010): 21–43.

10. Murray, *Song in a Weary Throat*, 229–35.

11. Patricia Bell-Scott, "'To Write Like Never Before': Pauli Murray's Enduring Yearning," *Journal of Women's History* 14, no. 2 (Summer 2002): 60.

12. Murray, "Dark Testament," *Dark Testament and Other Poems* (New York: Liveright, 2018), 15.

13. Murray, *Song in a Weary Throat*, 300.

14. Murray, *Dark Testament and Other Poems*, 1–20, 88–92; and Pauli Murray, *States' Laws on Race and Color* (Athens: University of Georgia Press, 2016).

15. Diana Coole and Samantha Frost, "Introducing the New Materialisms," in *New Materialisms: Ontology, Agency, and Politics*, ed. Diana Coole and Samantha Frost (Durham, NC: Duke University Press, 2010), 8.

16. Emilie M. Townes, *Womanist Ethics and the Cultural Production of Evil* (New York: Palgrave Macmillan, 2006), 45–46.

17. Murray, "Mr. Roosevelt Regrets," *Dark Testament and Other Poems*, 27. The multiple ellipses in the poem are Murray's. *The Crisis* is a magazine of the NAACP, accessed July 13, 2020, https://www.thecrisismagazine.com/.

18. Rosalind Rosenberg, *Jane Crow: The Life of Pauli Murray* (Oxford, UK: Oxford University Press, 2017), 130.

19. Rosenberg, *Jane Crow*, 98.

20. Patricia Bell-Scott, *The Firebrand and the First Lady: Portrait of a Friendship—Pauli Murray, Eleanor Roosevelt, and the Struggle for Social Justice* (New York: Vintage Books, 2016), 72–77.

21. Murray, *Song in a Weary Throat*, 225–26.

22. Murray, *Song in a Weary Throat*, 277.

23. Murray, "Dark Testament," 3.

24. Murray, "Dark Testament," 12.

25. Karen Barad, "TransMaterialities: Trans*/Matter/Realities and Queer Political Imaginings," *GLQ* 21, no. 2–3 (2015): 388.

26. Emilie M. Townes, "And Still We Struggled to Be Counted," *Reflections: A Magazine of Theological and Ethical Inquiry from Yale Divinity School*, Spring 2013, https://reflections.yale.edu/article/future-race/and-still-we-struggle-be-counted. See also W. E. B. Du Bois, "The Propaganda of History," in *Black Reconstruction in America: An Essay Toward the History of the Part Which Black Folk Played in the Attempt to Reconstruct Democracy in America* (New York: Russell & Russell, 1966), 722.

27. Pauli Murray, *Proud Shoes: The Story of an American Family* (Boston: Beacon Press, 1956), unnumbered introductory page.

28. Karen Barad, "What Flashes Up: Theological-Political-Scientific Fragments," in *Entangled Worlds: Religion, Science, and New Materialisms*, ed. Catherine Keller and Mary-Jane Rubenstein (New York: Fordham University Press, 2017), 33.

29. Murray, "Dark Testament," 16.

30. Murray, "Dark Testament," 17.

31. Murray, "Dark Testament," 17.

32. Quoted in Dorothy Roberts, *Fatal Invention: How Science, Politics, and Big Business Re-Create Race in the Twenty-First Century* (New York: New Press, 2011), 130.

33. Murray, "Dark Testament," 8.

34. Peppard, "Poetry, Ethics," 28.

35. Henry Wadsworth Longfellow, "Paul Revere's Ride," Poets.org, accessed March 4, 2020, https://poets.org/poem/paul-reveres-ride.

36. Murray, "Dark Testament," 8.

37. Murray, *States' Laws on Race and Color*, 329.

38. Murray, *States' Laws on Race and Color*, 237.

39. Murray, "Dark Testament," 16–17.

40. Karen Barad, *Meeting the Universe Halfway: Quantum Physics and the Entanglement of Matter and Meaning* (Durham, NC: Duke University Press, 2007).

41. Barad, *Meeting the Universe Halfway*, 140, 128, 140.

42. Murray, *Song in a Weary Throat*, 300.

43. Martin Luther King Jr., "A Christmas Sermon on Peace," *Beacon Broadside*, accessed May 19, 2020, https://www.beaconbroadside.com/broadside/2017/12/martin-luther-king-jrs-christmas-sermon-peace-still-prophetic-50-years-later.html.

44. Murray, *Song in a Weary Throat*, 300.

45. Rosenberg, *Jane Crow*, 2.

46. Brittney Cooper, "Black, Queer, Feminist, Erased from History: Meet the Most Important Legal Scholar You've Likely Never Heard Of; Ruth Bader Ginsburg Is This Supreme Court's Liberal Hero, But Her Work Sits on the Shoulders of Dr. Pauli Murray," *Salon*, February 18, 2015, https://www.salon.com/2015/02/18/Black_queer_feminist_erased_from_history_meet_the_most_important_legal_scholar_youve_likely_never_heard_of/.

47. Rosenberg, *Jane Crow*, 3.

48. Murray, "The Wanderer," *Dark Testament and Other Poems*, 88–92.

49. Rosenberg, *Jane Crow*, 80.

50. Rosenberg, *Jane Crow*, 81.

51. Pauli Murray, "Summary of Symptoms of Upset," March 8, 1940, Pauli Murray Papers, Schlesinger Library, Radcliffe Institute for Advanced Study, Harvard University, Box 4, Folder 71; and Rosenberg, *Jane Crow*, 81.

52. Murray, "Wanderer," 89.

53. Murray, "Wanderer," 88.

54. Murray, "Wanderer," 89

55. Murray, "Wanderer," 90–91.

56. Murray, "Wanderer," 92.

57. Murray, "Wanderer," 92.

58. St. Francis de Sales, *Treatise on the Love of God* (New York: Cosimo Classics, 2007).

59. 1 John 4:7–9, New Revised Standard Version.

60. Murray, "III. *The Entreaty*," *Dark Testament and Other Poems*, 91.

61. de Sales, *Treatise*, 266.

62. Barad, *Meeting the Universe*, 393.

63. Barad, *Meeting the Universe*, 353.

64. Murray, *Song in a Weary Throat*, 511.

65. Murray, *Song in a Weary Throat*, 569.

66. Murray, *Proud Shoes*, 270.

67. Murray, *Song in a Weary Throat*, 513.

68. Barad, *Meeting the Universe*, 396.

SELECTED BIBLIOGRAPHY

1 John 4:7–9. New Revised Standard Version.

Barad, Karen. *Meeting the Universe Halfway: Quantum Physics and the Entanglement of Matter and Meaning*. Durham, NC: Duke University Press, 2007.

Barad, Karen. "TransMaterialities: Trans*/Matter/Realities and Queer Political Imaginings." *GLQ* 21, no. 2–3 (2015): 387–422.

Barad, Karen. "What Flashes Up: Theological-Political-Scientific Fragments." In *Entangled Worlds: Religion, Science, and New Materialisms*, edited by Catherine Keller and Mary-Jane Rubenstein, 21–88. New York: Fordham University Press, 2017.

Bell-Scott, Patricia. *The Firebrand and the First Lady: Portrait of a Friendship—Pauli Murray, Eleanor Roosevelt, and the Struggle for Social Justice*. New York: Vintage Books, 2016.

Bell-Scott, Patricia. "Introduction." In *Song in a Weary Throat: Memoir of an American Pilgrimage* by Pauli Murray. New York: Liveright, 1987.

Bell-Scott, Patricia. '"To Write like Never Before': Pauli Murray's Enduring Yearning." *Journal of Women's History* 14, no. 2 (Summer 2002): 58–61.

Coole, Diana, and Samantha Frost. "Introducing the New Materialisms." In *New Materialisms: Ontology, Agency, and Politics*, edited by Diana Coole and Samantha Frost, 1–43. Durham, NC: Duke University Press, 2010.

Cooper, Brittney. "Black, Queer, Feminist, Erased from History: Meet the Most Important Legal Scholar You've Likely Never Heard Of; Ruth Bader Ginsburg Is This Supreme Court's Liberal Hero, But Her Work Sits on the Shoulders of Dr. Pauli Murray." *Salon*, February 18, 2015. https://www.salon.com/2015/02/18/Black_queer_feminist_erased_from_history_meet_the_most_important_legal_scholar_youve_likely_never_heard_of/.

Crenshaw, Kimberlé. "Demarginalizing the Intersection of Race and Sex: A Black Feminist Critique of Antidiscrimination Doctrine, Feminist Theory and Antiracist Politics." *University of Chicago Legal Forum* no. 1 (1989): Article 8. http://chicagounbound.uchicago.edu/uclf/vol1989/iss1/8.

The Crisis. Official magazine of the NAACP. https://www.thecrisismagazine.com/.

de Sales, Francis. *Treatise on the Love of God*. New York: Cosimo Classics, 2007.

Du Bois, W. E. B. "The Propaganda of History." In *Black Reconstruction in America: An Essay Toward the History of the Part Which Black Folk Played in the Attempt to Reconstruct Democracy in America*. New York: Russell & Russell, 1966.

Hayden, Robert. "Frederick Douglass." *Poetry Foundation*. Accessed May 18, 2020. https://www.poetryfoundation.org/poems/46460/frederick-douglass.

King, Martin Luther, Jr. "A Christmas Sermon on Peace." *Beacon Broadside*. Accessed May 19, 2020. https://www.beaconbroadside.com/broadside/2017/12/martin-luther-king-jrs-christmas-sermon-peace-still-prophetic-50-years-later.html.

Longfellow, Henry Wadsworth. "Paul Revere's Ride." Poets.org. Accessed May 19, 2020. https://poets.org/poem/paul-reveres-ride.

Murray, Pauli. *Dark Testament and Other Poems*. New York: Liveright, 1970.

Murray, Pauli. *Proud Shoes: The Story of an American Family*. Boston: Beacon Press, 1956.

Murray, Pauli. *Song in a Weary Throat: Memoir of an American Pilgrimage*. New York: Liveright, 1987.

Murray, Pauli. *States' Laws on Race and Color*. Athens: University of Georgia Press, 2016.

Murray, Pauli. "Summary of Symptoms of Upset." March 8, 1940. Pauli Murray Papers, Schlesinger Library, Radcliffe Institute for Advanced Study, Harvard University, Box 4, Folder 71.

Peppard, Christiana Z. "Poetry, Ethics, and the Legacy of Pauli Murray." *Journal of the Society of Christian Ethics* 30, no. 1 (Spring-Summer 2010): 21–43. https://www.pdcnet.org/jsce/content/jsce_2010_0030_0001_0021_0043.

Roberts, Dorothy. *Fatal Invention: How Science, Politics, and Big Business Re-Create Race in the Twenty-First Century*. New York: New Press, 2011.

Rosenberg, Rosalind. *Jane Crow: The Life of Pauli Murray*. Oxford, UK: Oxford University Press, 2017.

Townes, Emilie M. "And Still We Struggled to Be Counted." *Reflections: A Magazine of Theological and Ethical Inquiry from Yale Divinity School*, Spring 2013. https://reflections.yale.edu/article/future-race/and-still-we-struggle-be-counted.

Townes, Emilie M. *Womanist Ethics and the Cultural Production of Evil*. New York: Palgrave Macmillan, 2006.

US Reports: *Brown v. Board of Education of Topeka*, 347 US 483 (1954). https://supreme.justia.com/cases/federal/us/347/483/.

US Reports: *Reed v. Reed*, 404 US 71 (1971). https://supreme.justia.com/cases/federal/us/404/71/.

TWENTY-FIRST CENTURY

Chapter 10

SANDY SPEAKS

The Digital Resurrection of Sandra Bland's Religious History

PHILLIP LUKE SINITIERE

IN HER OWN WORDS

Sandra Bland's death in Texas in July 2015 sparked national outrage about anti-Black state violence. While the medical examiner ruled her death in Waller County Jail a suicide by asphyxiation, her family disputed the claim that Bland took her own life. The dashcam footage of her arrest and apprehension—and Texas Department of Public Safety officer Brian Encinia dragging her out of her car while screaming, "I will light you up!"—went viral. It mobilized a Black Lives Matter-era response of activism locally in Waller County and throughout the country that included marches, vigils, petitions, hashtags, and legislation that aimed to hold law enforcement accountable for violence against Black people, especially Black women. The Sandra Bland Movement, as the collective response became known, sought to keep her case in the public eye. Activists worked to provide educational support, foster aesthetic creativity, and produce documentary films to honor her memory. Her family gave media interviews, delivered speeches, and assisted activists in stirring political pressure for change.[1] In May 2019, the release of Bland's own cellphone footage of her arrest demonstrated even more clearly Encinia's hostile actions towards her. It brought renewed attention to the case and generated calls for a new investigation into her arrest, apprehension, and death.[2]

Since Bland's death in 2015, the ongoing rehearsal of the dashcam footage and her violent arrest reproduces painful, traumatic images that have largely dominated how she is remembered. The full Texas Department of Public Safety video of the traffic stop arrest is forty-nine minutes long.[3] By contrast, Bland recorded more than one hundred minutes of *Sandy Speaks*. Why does the dash-cam footage receive the lion's share of attention in discussions about Sandra

Bland? When we say #SandyStillSpeaks, do we know what she said? Why don't we listen more to Bland in her own words? While it acknowledges that the July 2015 traffic stop video is a central aspect of understanding her story, this chapter finds Bland beyond the dashcam in her *Sandy Speaks* videos.

Working from the standpoint of Black women's intellectual history that centers Black women's ideas and intellectual production, this chapter explores the rich religious content of Bland's video blogs known as *Sandy Speaks*—recorded between January and April 2015 and posted to Facebook. It presents Bland as a public religious intellectual who threaded her spiritual sensibility with social activism. Now archived on YouTube and thus widely accessible, the *Sandy Speaks* videos offer additional content from which to remember Bland. The videos provide one avenue through which to reconstruct the final months of her life and thought. They document how, over time during the first half of 2015, she started to clarify her life's mission of enacting social change by creating justice-oriented community activism and public engagement spurred by her Christian faith. Though the activist herself is dead, the concept of digital resurrection shows how Sandy still leads the movement that bears her name.

Particulars about historiography and disciplinary frameworks are helpful ground to cover at the outset of this chapter. A quick discussion of these features will position my scholarship and relate it more fully to the shape of this collection. I write this chapter positioned as a privileged white male scholar of American religion and African American history. From this vantage point, I do not presume to offer *the* story of Sandra Bland, but one account from one perspective that recognizes the likelihood of potential blind spots and omissions with respect to gender, race, and class, along with other identity markers. There is much historical excavation and analysis that remains for developing a fuller understanding of Bland's life and death that time, distance, and other scholars of diverse backgrounds will deliver. Drawing on the words of anti-racist activist Tim Wise, naming my positionality is one way to "speak treason fluently" against whiteness.[4] I offer these reflections on Sandra Bland's history as both an observer of and participant in direct action protests associated with the Sandra Bland Movement in Waller County. I currently reside in northwest Houston, about a half-hour's drive from Bland's arrest site and Waller County Jail. A former Waller County resident, I am familiar with the area and was active in environmental justice concerns prior to my involvement with the Bland actions.[5] As I wrote on *Black Perspectives* in August 2015, I joined the protests and Waller County Jail prayer vigil as an act of solidarity and as a way to embody both intellectual and political commitments to anti-racism and social justice. A large number of female activists championed the campaigns and organized the protests, individuals I called Sandy's "sister comrades." I followed their lead.[6] I did not show up in Waller County intending to write about my experiences or to produce scholarship. However, once an opportunity presented itself, I consulted with activists. Upon receiving permission to commence with research and share stories, I shifted my mindset to one of both activist engagement and historical documentation. Since that time, invitations to write on aspects of Bland continue to materialize, of which this chapter is a part.[7]

RECORDING A LIFE

Sandra Bland is the subject of a growing body of scholarship. Her name often appears in the litany of African Americans killed by state violence that several historical accounts of the Black Lives Matter movement examine.[8] In addition, scholarly evaluation from the fields of law, discourse analysis, feminist studies, media studies, philosophy, psychology, aesthetics, and religion explore various dimensions of Bland's experience and the social and political dynamics of her encounter with law enforcement.[9] In this chapter, the excavation of Bland's religious perspectives from the public record of her *Sandy Speaks* videos draws on conventions of Black intellectual history. One consideration in the field expands intellectual identity beyond the walls of the academy to center the intellectual production of working-class people and movements. Sandra Bland was not a university intellectual but an organic one whose ideas drew exclusively from everyday experiences, not archives or other institutional repositories.[10] Another question in producing scholarship in the Black intellectual tradition is the availability of and access to primary source material and additional avenues of documentation. Outside of memories of her that family members share, the *Sandy Speaks* videos are the only records that contain a range of Bland's religious thought over time. Their presence on digital platforms, both in origin and delivery, exemplifies Manning Marable's suggestion to use the unique primary sources that new media provides in the production of what he calls "living Black history."[11] While Marable's cross-disciplinary proposal emerged nearly a decade before the rise of the Black Lives Matter era, applying his methodology today allows scholars to draw on a wide variety of print, visual, and digital source materials to offer an abundance of meaning and interpretation. "Living Black history" is tailor-made for twenty-first century study. Further, the orality of Bland's religious discourse is a form of what LeRhonda Manigault-Bryant terms Black women's "testimony," verbal transmission and public expression in which religious traditions, ideas, or practices reside in both form and substance.[12] From the standpoint of Black women's intellectual history, then, Bland may be construed as an everyday thinker, an activist whose spiritual sensibilities informed her political expressions on social media. The *Sandy Speaks* videos display Bland's intellectual production and document a distinct space of Black feminist public intellectual culture in which she connected religious perspectives, political activism, and social change.[13]

On the evening of January 14, 2015, Sandra Bland tapped record on her phone to capture the first minutes of what would become her series of *Sandy Speaks* video blogs. Recorded at home, on location at a mall, coffee shop, or museum, or in her car, over the course of several months throughout nearly two dozen videos, each began with her greeting "my beautiful kings and queens" and ended with "Sandy speaks." Contextually, the first episode presented a vision for what she hoped the videos would accomplish; subsequently, the messages throughout February, March, and April 2015 changed based on news headlines, local events in Chicago, Black History Month, recent films or popular culture, Black women's hair and the politics of beauty, Black Lives Matter (BLM), racial justice, or whatever spiritual message was occupying her mind. Sandy recorded her final vlog on April 10, in which she addressed critics who claimed her messages intended to stir racial animosity instead of racial unity. This topic, ironically, has served as something of a flashpoint for legacy and is in fact one of the organizing threads that ties together all her videos.

In her inaugural January video, Bland spoke softly, as if feeling her way into an audience. Her thoughts were wide-ranging and did not reflect the thematic focus that would characterize her subsequent messages. Yet, Bland's voice gained strength and gravity. She exhibited confidence about the divine source of what she had to deliver. She described "a seed that I feel like God has truly planted in my life, work that he has said for me to do, a message that he has for me to get out." Using the biblical image associated with expansion, she noted that the idea for the *Sandy Speaks* vlog is to tackle current events like police brutality, interact with young people on their experiences, and "educate these kids." She elaborated on what she identified as the spiritual origins of her work: "It's time for me to do God's work at the end of the day because He. . . ." Her voice drifted off. After a brief moment of gathering her thoughts, she continued, "I know everybody don't believe in God, which is fine, but I want you to know on *Sandy Speaks* I'm talking about God because for me he has truly opened my eyes and showed me there's something out there that we can do." The potential of using her phone as a transformative political tool also animated the urgency of her message. "This thing that I'm holding in my hand, this telephone, this camera, it is quite powerful, social media is powerful," she said. "We can do something with this if we want to change; we can really truly make it happen."[14] In retrospect, Bland's phone became a central instrument in documenting her experiences. Not only did her footage of her own arrest literally offer a new vantage point to understand her experience, but the act of documenting her life and thought through *Sandy Speaks* videos extends her voice in perpetuity. This is significant because the dashcam footage of her arrest and apprehension is not the final image of her life that we see. Unlike many other BLM-era deaths at the hands of police, Bland still speaks.

ACTIVISM AND FAITH

The African Methodist Episcopal (AME) Church of which Sandy was a part likely helped her to link Christian faith with social activism. She had been active at DuPage AME Church since her teenage years, where she also participated in the choir. DuPage AME's pastors emphasized spiritual leadership in sermons and teachings and also had training in social outreach and the field of social work. The spiritual orientation of *Sandy Speaks* and the spiritual categories and religious language through which she presented her social engagement suggest that her church's teachings produced activist fruit documented throughout her vlogs. This makes it all the more tragic—and ironic—that her apprehension and arrest in Waller County literally took place in front of Good Hope AME Church. It is also highly appropriate, however, that a makeshift memorial at Sandy's arrest site remains in front of the church. It serves as a powerful symbolic reminder of Bland's Methodist roots and what Rosetta Ross terms the "ordinary and superlative" testimony of Black religious women's civil rights work and public performance.[15] As I discuss more fully below, for many Black women the memorial site remains not just a space of tragedy; it is a space of resistance and resilience. People pilgrimage to the Sandra Bland Parkway to pay their respects, often recording a short video of their thoughts about Bland's life, thus testifying to her ongoing significance and inspiration.

On Martin Luther King Day in January 2015, Bland put her theory about using social media for public good into practice. Out running errands, she overheard a white woman at a Chicago DMV express frustration that public services were closed that day. "Why do they need one more day?" the woman asked as she angrily huffed and got back in her car. Bland challenged and dismantled the woman's racist vexation about national recognition of a prominent Black American. "The weight behind those words is just very interesting when you think about how big of a deal that 'one more day' is," Bland commented.[16] After nearly two decades of calling for federal recognition of the civil rights icon following his death in 1968, the nation first celebrated Martin Luther King Day in 1986. Aware of the fierce resistance to commemorating King's birthday—North Carolina Senator Jesse Helms denounced it over claims King was a communist and Arizona refused to recognize the federal holiday until 1992, for example—Bland's frustration with the woman's comment about "one more day" alluded to the long history behind this achievement.[17]

In hindsight, her message about technology's democratizing potential—in other words the power of the phone on which Bland speculated in the first *Sandy Speaks* video—reflects popular perspectives of the current epoch while it demonstrates the intellectual production she hoped to create through such a public platform. Yet the prophetic significance of her first message bears heavily in retrospect because the collective impact of her videos has changed history. Uniquely, as it turned out, the perpetual availability of them online meant that activists who played her videos at protest marches ensured that through a digital resurrection she led the movement that bears her name. In ways that she called for in the first *Sandy Speaks* videos, Bland literally spoke at protest actions that bore her name. Her digital afterlife continues to create space for authentic, meaningful social engagement and an ordinary yet superlative nature.[18] While the concept of digital resurrection may evoke comparisons to the use of holograms that celebrate noted figures in popular culture, the performative entertainment value of such retrievals contrasts with Bland's figurative reappearance (or, rather, reappearances on multiple videos) because she lives online in direct relation to the state violence that surrounded the circumstances of her death. While there was a performative dimension to her making *Sandy Speaks* videos insofar as she meant them for social media, my concept of digital resurrection positions the videos as activist tools and tools of activism instead of an entertainment context determined by the flow of capital and practices of consumption.

February's videos reeled off selected facts about Black History Month, discourse that revealed an excitement about new discoveries she was then making about the African American past. Seeing the movie *Selma* over the Christmas holiday in late 2014—the movie debuted on December 25 that year—seemed to have catalyzed Bland's emphasis on history and inspired a maturing historical consciousness.[19] Given this interest, Bland's January MLK *Sandy Speaks* episodes reflected deeper meaning. They weren't just about honoring MLK: they manifested Bland's practice of "living Black history." Videos in February also featured a more explicit focus on spiritual themes. Not only did she talk about God's work in her life and thought; she exhibited spiritual practices like prayer and performed such meditations on camera for her audience by enunciating petitions to God on her behalf and for her listeners.

An evolving focus on Black history formed a great deal of *Sandy Speaks* content for February. In two videos she discussed *Selma* and its depiction of the activism that took place in the modern civil rights movement. Her discussion of the film pivoted off *American Sniper*, one of the leading movies in early 2015. Sandy found it problematic that a movie celebrating the War on Terror and glorifying American imperialist violence received such expansive box office praise. She called *Selma* an "Oscar-worthy movie in my book" and wanted listeners to understand the history and legacy of civil rights. "I feel it needs to be a part of our American history classes' curriculum," she said. "Stop pushing it to the wayside. Stop acting like it didn't happen. Civil rights . . . was a war right here at home . . . it still goes on right now. We are still in that fight today so please don't think it's over because it's not, it's really not."[20] Her commentary the following day continued harkening back to a history that demanded further recognition: the history of white supremacist violence with "your grandmother and your grandfather having to fight and walk the front line being bit by dogs, sprayed by water hoses, maced [and] crosses burned on their front lawn in the name of their American freedom." It is past time to honor civil rights heroes who died for freedom and equality, Sandy continued, in the same way that the nation currently frames patriotic celebrations of service members who fight abroad.[21]

In addition to sharing assorted facts about important moments in Black history such as Carter G. Woodson's founding of Negro History Week in 1926 and the Million Man March in 1995, Sandy emphasized the "seed planted in me to preserve our Black history" was to clarify the centrality of Black history in the American story. Beyond just learning facts, names, and dates, she encouraged her listeners to take advantage of educational opportunities to learn and grasp history's importance. "So, what are you going to do out there to make your stamp? What are you going to do to change not just Black history, but American history this week?" she asked on February 15.[22] She had earlier said, "We like to categorize and say oh it's Black History Month, it's Black this, it's Black that. No, this is American history. Black history is American history, it's a part of America."[23] Bland called for people to put knowledge into practice. Using her platform as an organic working-class Black feminist intellectual, her videos aimed to challenge and to change society.

This is the same message she echoed in subsequent *Sandy Speaks* episodes recorded the day she visited the DuSable Museum of African American History in Chicago with her church. An important cultural space for the city's Black heritage, the DuSable Museum has long inspired visitors since its 1961 founding. Its design aimed to spotlight overlooked chapters in American history and mobilize historical knowledge for meaningful social change.[24] Bland excitedly said that the visit "shed light on how deep Black history is in America. I will say as a Chicagoan myself there were some things I found out that I never even knew after living here my whole life."[25] The video included references to Chicago's role in the Great Migration and the city's history of jazz, among other topics. The new insight she gained revolutionized how she was beginning to understand the foundations of American society and the transatlantic connections between Africa and America. Bland's wider conception of American history shifted how she communicated the national narrative: "Without Black people there would be no America. Let's just make it plain: without us there is no you." She proposed future trips to the DuSable Museum that would invite busloads of young people to learn about Black history, "so that we can spread this knowledge and really truly do something to make a change. Y'all, I'm so tired of sitting idly by . . . we have to get this message out here. The only thing that is going to save us is us. With freedom there comes responsibility and we as a culture, we are responsible for ourselves. We have a job to do. So my kings and queens, let's get to work. I'm ready, what about you?" Transferring historical knowledge into political action became a staple of *Sandy Speaks*. The videos reveal how over time she clarified her political vision by connecting personal transformation to the cultivation of community, a historical practice in the work of Black feminist intellectuals.

If learning Black history and sharing it were part of Bland's political calculus, then her conception and practice of prayer rooted the social aspect of her vision of a just society. An early *Sandy Speaks* episode, which Bland recorded on her way to a Sunday service, centered the practice of prayer. For Bland, the simple act of verbalizing a desire for societal change counted as prayer as much as a silent petition with eyes closed and head bowed did: "On my way to church this morning, I'm going to make sure I'm doing my part. I'm going to pray for my country. I'm going to pray for my people. I'm going to pray for you if you're watching this."[26] Prayer was not a meditative practice for individual wants and desires; she used it to include her listeners and the wider communities of which she was a part. In her March 1, 2015, episode, for example, Bland opened up about the depression she was then experiencing and asked for prayer even as she promised to pray for those listening.[27] Several days later, she returned to the topic of depression, spiritualized its manifestation as "nothing but the devil," and rehearsed a sample prayer designed to create peace of mind in the midst of feeling down and hopeless. "God, block these feelings of depression," Bland pleaded. "Take them away because I've still got work to do. There is a job you have placed over my life."[28]

On other occasions, Bland verbalized more traditionally religious prayers, such as one on February 6, 2015. In this vlog, she voiced a specific prayer, the only video in which she paused, bowed her head, and closed her eyes. "God put it on my heart to pray for you guys, so that is what I'm going to do. Short, sweet, to the point," she told her audience. She continued:

> Lord, Father, we come before you this morning, first of all thanking you, God, thanking you for giving us life. Thanking you for giving us breath. Thanking you for giving us the opportunity to move around and do everything that we need to do. But in all of that Lord still praise your name, God. We ask that you just watch over us on today. Watch over us as we go off to work and we work on establishing our kingdoms and

> our queendoms. Lord, we just ask that you bless our lives. Give us the opportunity to do something great, be an impact to someone else that we can even if it's with something as small as a smile. Father I pray for everyone watching this video right now that they have a blessed day, they make the most out of their day, that they can have safe traveling mercies to and from work. Father, all these things we ask in your son Jesus' name, Amen.[29]

Bland's prayer was capacious enough to include a broad cross-section of her listeners while it was specific enough to address her own fears, concerns, and plans. In traditional Christian form, gratitude defined the prayer's opening followed by a request for divine guidance. Then she moved into a petition about opportunity for social transformation as well as for impactful plans and actions to promote a more just community. By praying for herself, she was praying for others, and by praying for others, she was supporting herself. Aware of Black history's civil rights rhythms in which activists used prayer as a centering practice for political engagement, Bland used the platform she had and deployed the tools at her disposal to connect meaningful meditations to social change. Her practice of prayer expressed what Manigault-Bryant termed testimony—the public transmission of religious sensibilities designed to both create meaning in the world and transform it.

In early 2015, an opportunity presented itself for Bland to apply her philosophy of political change through her media platform. It was another way she could use her phone to, as she put it in the inaugural *Sandy Speaks* vlog, change history. The Jackie Robinson Little League controversy in Chicago became a particularly meaningful social justice campaign in which Bland became involved and for which she used her online presence. In 2014, the all-Black youth baseball team made it to the Little League World Series in Pennsylvania. Although they lost in the final game, the Jackie Robinson players were the nation's top team. Allegations swirled that they had out-of-district and therefore ineligible players, and after two investigations Little League officials stripped the team of its championship designation. Some believed racism triggered the investigations and lay at the heart of publicly dismantling the success of the young Black baseball players.[30] In late March, she created a petition and went to local Chicago-area coffee shops, malls, and retail spaces seeking signatures in support of reversing the ruling. Her stated support of young people across her videos, and her connection of faith with activism, drove her direct-action efforts to create social transformation. She also praised the inspirational speech she heard from rapper Common, who spoke at an event in early 2015 at St. Sabina parish in Chicago. St. Sabina's is the church of Father Michael Pfleger, the white radical priest well known for his stylistic sermons and justice-based activism. Being in such creative, insurgent, and spiritual spaces moved Bland to act. Even though she obtained only twenty of the five hundred planned signatures on the petition, her digital efforts on *Sandy Speaks* functioned as leverage to foster transformation across the community.[31]

Bland's final videos in April 2015 also deserve mention. Incensed by the death of Walter Scott on April 4, 2015—Officer Michael Slager pulled Scott over and eventually shot him in the back as Scott darted from the scene after which Slager attempted to plant evidence to cover up the murder, the video of which went viral—*Sandy Speaks* addressed clearly and passionately the epidemic of police violence, the nature of structural inequality, the need to dismantle whiteness, and the possibility of Black-white unity despite society's acrimonious conditions. In a "message to my white people" on April 8 and another on April 10, Bland identified economic privilege, color blindness, and whiteness's social power as impediments to understanding the difficulties of being Black in the United States.[32] "But some of us are really doing as much as we can" to change society, she passionately stated, so "we can't help but get pissed off when we see situations where it's clear the Black life didn't matter." To clarify, she explained:

> I'm not calling all white people racist because y'all not . . . but for the ones who want to [say] all lives matter, show me in American history where all lives have mattered. Show me where there has been liberty and justice for all like that f****** Pledge of Allegiance we love to say. Excuse my French because *Sandy Speaks* don't usually cuss. . . . White people, if all lives mattered would there need to be a hashtag for Black lives mattering? Think about that. Just truly think about that."[33]

At the end of the day, Bland's commitment to racial unity emanated from an unashamed willingness to tell the hard truth about problematic race relations in the United States, support innovative efforts to instigate social transformation, unapologetically embrace her Blackness, and unflinchingly root her social justice in religious faith, prayer, and purposeful activism.

Although Sandra Bland's case is of recent origin, its expansive digital documentation and the new media age in which we are currently living present the possibility to begin to reflect on the influence of her ideas. *Awaken the Voice* is a documentary produced by activist Hannah Bonner and codirected by former Prairie View A&M University (PVAMU) students Kayla Gilchrist and Jazmine Salsman that features commentary from Black female PVAMU students who participated in many facets of the Sandra Bland Movement. The film explores Bland's ideas, her work across social platforms, and the impact of her legacy. "Just because she passed doesn't mean that she's not a part of our community," 2017 PVAMU grad Mirissa Tucker says at the documentary's beginning. "I think remembering the people who came before us and the people who fought for us is a way to pay homage and also a way to remember what we're continuing to do."[34] Tucker's observation powerfully summarizes how the film's orientation identifies the impact of Bland's creativity as a Black feminist public intellectual. The women discuss how they transformed the shock and dismay over Bland's death into empowerment, bravery, boldness, and community responsibility. They marched, they spoke at rallies and on college campuses, and they creatively deployed social media to effect political change on behalf of both themselves and African-descended people more broadly. Inspired by *Sandy Speaks*, the common thread of faith and activism emboldened Black female PVAMU activists to work in Bland's name for greater justice and equity. Bland's inspirational testimony through *Sandy Speaks* impacted the world while she was still alive, and *Awaken the Voice* demonstrates that her digital resurrection continues to amplify marginalized voices and foster purposeful change.

There is a profound interrelation between Bland's intentions behind *Sandy Speaks* to flesh out social justice practices and the ways that her inspiration led Sandra Bland Movement activists at PVAMU to amplify their voices. In a September 2019 meditation on power, Bonner commented on the richness of Bland's powerful public voice and the ways that she made sure it accompanied her into different spaces of activism and worship. "Beyond all the work that we did to make sure that her death was not erased," Bonner stated, "there was a more personal commitment that I made to her than simply to sit vigil in rural Texas." Consonant with Bonner's Christian practice of serving and centering the marginalized and erased in society, her intention to literally amplify Bland's voice from *Sandy Speaks* extended the power of her digital resurrection. "The commitment was that wherever my voice was heard, her voice would be heard," continued Bonner. "That meant that every microphone that heard my voice, heard her voice—as I held the speaker of my phone up to the microphone. Whether a pulpit, a conference, or a protest—if I had the mic, then she had the mic. She spoke in the midst of sermons, at a planning meeting for the World Methodist Conference, at trainings for the Forum for Theological Exploration, and City Council Meetings. It wasn't always easy, it wasn't always welcome—but it was always just, and it was always necessary."[35]

The motivations, desires, deep religious faith, passionate activism, and fearlessness appear across the one hundred-plus minutes of the *Sandy Speaks* episodes. Through the videos, her digital resurrection not only keeps her ideas alive, but it also allows her to figuratively lead the ongoing political movement that bears her name. Reading Bland's life through the lens of Black intellectual history develops a richer understanding of her social and political meaning as a Black feminist public intellectual who used her digital platform to mobilize efforts for societal change along the lines of racial and economic justice. The intersections among

Black history, theological ideas, and contemporary culture that exist throughout the *Sandy Speaks* videos invite enriching comparisons to womanist scholars and theologians like Brenda Salter McNeil and Kelly Brown Douglas, for example. Douglas's insightful 2015 book, *Stand Your Ground: Black Bodies and the Justice of God*, brought theological and critical commentary on Black life in the wake of Trayvon Martin's murder, and her 2021 book, *Resurrection Hope*, presented urgent interventions in response to more recent murders of Black people at the hands of state officials.[36] McNeil's writings have challenged degraded dimensions of white supremacist Christianity while calling for justice and repair with the hopes of forging more honest and therefore ethical Christian community.[37] Importantly, their work, like Sandy's did, accents deeper religious reflection with a public dimension that calls for social change. Their writings draw on historical and religious ideas to radically transform the present. Her performance of intellectual labor through *Sandy Speaks*, along with the videos' perpetual availability online that future generations will continue to watch, find inspiration from, and interpret, ensures that although she has died, her legacy as a Black feminist intellectual and as a social justice saint will live on beyond the dashcam.

NOTES

1. For an overview of the case in cinematic form, see the documentary *Say Her Name: The Life and Death of Sandra Bland* (Home Box Office, 2018). For another perspective on the work that family and allies carried out on behalf of Sandra Bland's case between 2015 and 2019, see Phillip Luke Sinitiere, "Sandy Still Speaks: Remembering Sandra Bland," *The North Star*, July 13, 2019, https://thenorthstar.com/articles/sandy-still-speaks-remembering-sandra-bland.

2. Alex Samuels, "Lawmaker Grills Department of Public Safety over Disclosure of Sandra Bland Cellphone Video," *Texas Tribune*, May 24, 2019, https://www.texastribune.org/2019/05/24/sandra-bland-hearing-texas-house-committee/.

3. Sandra Bland Traffic Stop, Texas Department of Public Safety, July 22, 2015, https://www.youtube.com/watch?v=CaWo9Ymr2BA.

4. Tim Wise, *Speaking Treason Fluently: Anti-Racist Reflections from an Angry White Male* (Berkeley: Soft Skull Press, 2008), 3, 7.

5. Phillip Luke Sinitiere, "From Standing Rock to Waller County: Repression, Resistance, and Environmental Justice," *Black Perspectives*, December 18, 2016, https://www.aaihs.org/from-standing-rock-to-waller-county-repression-resistance-and-environmental-justice/.

6. Phillip Luke Sinitiere, "What Is Happening in Waller County? Sandra Bland and the Sister Comrades Who #SayHerName," *Black Perspectives*, August 12, 2015, https://www.aaihs.org/what-is-happening-in-waller-county-sandra-bland-and-the-sister-comrades-who-sayhername/.

7. The original *Black Perspectives* blog post in note 6 turned out to be the basis for a book chapter in a volume on contemporary civil rights. Additional *Black Perspectives*

posts I published on Sandra Bland produced an invitation to write about the Sandra Bland Movement and art for *Souls*. I discuss this work below.

8. On books that place Sandra Bland in the context of Black Lives Matter, see Keeanga-Yamahtta Taylor, *From #BlackLivesMatter to Black Liberation* (Chicago: Haymarket, 2016); Marc Lamont Hill, *Nobody: Casualties of America's War on the Vulnerable, from Ferguson to Flint* (New York: Atria, 2016); Eddie S. Glaude, *Democracy in Black: How Race Still Enslaves the American Soul* (New York: Crown, 2016); Wesley Lowery, *"They Can't Kill Us All": Ferguson, Baltimore, and a New Era in America's Racial Justice Movement* (New York: Little, Brown, 2016); Chris Lebron, *The Making of Black Lives Matter: A Brief History of an Idea* (New York: Oxford University Press, 2017); Barbara Ransby, *Making All Black Lives Matter: Reimagining Freedom in the Twenty-First Century* (Berkeley: University of California Press, 2018); and Jennifer E. Cobbina, *Hands Up, Don't Shoot: Why the Protests in Ferguson and Baltimore Matter and How They Changed America* (New York: New York University Press, 2019).

9. See Josh Bowers, "Annoy No Cop," University of Virginia School of Law, Public Law and Legal Theory Research Paper Series, March 2017; Belen V. Lowrey-Kinberg and Grace Sullivan Buker, "'I'm Giving You a Lawful Order': Dialogic Legitimacy in Sandra Bland's Traffic Stop," *Law and Society Review* 51, no. 2 (2017): 379–412; Ashley B. Reid, "The Sandra Bland Story: How Social Media Has Exposed the Harsh Reality of Police Brutality" (MA thesis, Bowie State University, 2016); Brian Pitman et al., "Social Media Users' Interpretations of the Sandra Bland Arrest Video," *Race and Justice* (2017): 1–19; Victoria D. Gillon, "The Killing of an 'Angry Black Woman': Sandra Bland and the Politics of Respectability," Augustana College, Augustana Digital Commons, 2016, https://digitalcommons.augustana.edu/mabryaward/3/; Andrea J. Ritchie, *Invisible No More: Police Violence against Black Women and Women of Color* (Boston: Beacon Press, 2017), 101, 220; Theresa M. Senft, "Skin of the Selfie" (Unabridged Version, 2015), 1–21, http://www.academia.edu/15941920/The_Skin_of_the_Selfie_Unabridged_Version [an abridged version of Senft's paper appeared in *Ego Update: The Future of Digital Identity*, ed. Alain Bieber (Düsseldorf: NRW Forum, 2015)]; Lebron, *Making of Black Lives Matter*, 70–72, 154–55; Phillip Luke Sinitiere, "A Literary Libation on Sandra Bland Parkway," in *Our Voices, Our Stories: An Anthology of Writings Advancing, Celebrating, Embracing, and Empowering Girls and Women of Color*, ed. Donnamaria Culbreth (Jersey City, NJ: Complexity Publishing, 2019), 175; Phillip Luke Sinitiere, "The Aesthetic Insurgency of Sandra Bland's Afterlife," *Souls: A Critical Journal of Black Politics, Culture and Society* 20, no. 1 (2018): 122–47; and Phillip Luke Sinitiere, "Religion and the Black Freedom Struggle for Sandra Bland," in *"The Seedtime, the Work, and the Harvest": New Perspectives on the Black Freedom Struggle in America*, ed. Reginald K. Ellis, Jeffrey Littlejohn, and Peter Levy (Gainesville: University Press of Florida, 2018), 197–226.

10. Keisha N. Blain, Christopher Cameron, and Ashley D. Farmer, "Introduction: The Contours of Black Intellectual History," in *New Perspectives on the Black Intellectual Tradition*, ed. Keisha N. Blain, Christopher Cameron, and Ashley D. Farmer (Evanston, IL: Northwestern University Press, 2018), 4.

11. Manning Marable, *Living Black History: How Reimagining the African-American Past Can Remake America's Racial Future* (New York: Basic Books, 2006), 21–22.

12. LeRhonda S. Manigault-Bryant, "'I Had a Praying Grandmother': Religion, Prophetic Witness, and Black Women's Herstories," in Blain et al., *New Perspectives on the Black Intellectual Tradition*, 115–30.

13. Mia Bay et al., "Introduction: Toward an Intellectual History of Black Women," in *Toward an Intellectual History of Black Women*, ed. Mia Bay et al. (Chapel Hill: University of North Carolina Press, 2015), 3–9.

14. Bland, *Sandy Speaks*, January 15, 2015, https://www.youtube.com/watch?v=f5VhTY3_FC8. On the meaningful pause in Bland's first video and its implications for her religious sensibility, see Hannah Bonner, "The Prophetic Preaching of Sandra Bland," *Sojourners*, September 16, 2015, https://sojo.net/articles/faith-action/prophetic-preaching-sandra-bland.

15. On Bland's early role at DuPage AME Church, see Debbie Nathan, "What Happened to Sandra Bland?," *The Nation*, April 21, 2016, https://www.thenation.com/article/what-happened-to-sandra-bland/. The ministerial staff page at DuPage AME's website documents each pastor's training and specialty areas; see http://www.dupageamec.org/ministerial-staff/, accessed January 5, 2022. On the public performance of Bland's "ordinary and superlative" work, see Rosetta E. Ross, *Witnessing & Testifying: Black Women, Religion, and Civil Rights* (Minneapolis: Fortress Press, 2003), xiii.

16. Sandra Bland Movement activist and Methodist minister Rev. Hannah Bonner first posted the MLK *Sandy Speaks* video on January 18, 2016, to Instagram. Due to the length of the video, Bonner posted the message in eight parts: Part 1, https://www.instagram.com/p/BAqywaPKgqx/; Part 2, https://www.instagram.com/p/BAr5Hj-qgnk/; Part 3, https://www.instagram.com/p/BAr_HUjKgnO/; Part 4, https://www.instagram.com/p/BAsMFr9qgk1/; Part 5, https://www.instagram.com/p/BAsatxvqgll/; Part 6, https://www.instagram.com/p/BAsqz9dKgjW/; Part 7, https://www.instagram.com/p/BAsq-MYqgjr/; and Part 8, https://www.instagram.com/p/BAs4Jsuqgor/. For Bonner's role in the Sandra Bland Movement, see Sinitiere, "Religion and the Black Freedom Struggle for Sandra Bland."

17. On the history of the King holiday, see Frances Romero, "A Brief History of Martin Luther King Jr. Day," *Time*, January 18, 2010, http://content.time.com/time/nation/article/0,8599,1872501,00.html; and Nicole Crawford-Tichawonna, "Years of Persistence Led to Holiday Honoring King," *USA Today*, January 12, 2018, https://www.usatoday.com/story/news/nation-now/2018/01/12/king-holiday-origin/1006109001/.

18. Sinitiere, "Religion and the Black Freedom Struggle"; and Ross, *Witnessing & Testifying*.

19. On *Selma*'s impact on Bland, see Nathan, "What Happened to Sandra Bland?"

20. Bland, *Sandy Speaks*, February 5, 2015, https://www.youtube.com/watch?v=wOxWPXdFyYo&t=0s.

21. Bland, *Sandy Speaks*, February 6, 2015, https://www.youtube.com/watch?v=vnDWUP7Y8Xo&t=0s.

22. Bland, *Sandy Speaks*, February 15, 2015, https://www.youtube.com/watch?v=fTXAngT8qXw&t=0s.

23. Bland, *Sandy Speaks*, February 7, 2015, https://www.youtube.com/watch?v=KfrZM2Qjvtc&t=0s.

24. On the educational and political significance of the DuSable Museum's history, see Ian Rocksborough-Smith, *Black Public History in Chicago: Civil Rights Activism from World War II to the Cold War* (Urbana: University of Illinois Press, 2018), 49–73.

25. Bland, *Sandy Speaks*, February 21, 2015 (Part 2), https://www.youtube.com/watch?v=cv6lZCB73SU&t=0s.

26. This *Sandy Speaks* episode on prayer is another unreleased video that Hannah Bonner posted to her Instagram on February 1, 2016. The quote is from Part 4 of the episode:

https://www.instagram.com/p/BBQXrFfKgqO/. See also Part 1, https://www.instagram.com/p/BBPLyosKggN/; Part 2, https://www.instagram.com/p/BBPvPTiKgnj/; and Part 3, https://www.instagram.com/p/BBQKJ_kKggM/.

27. Bland, *Sandy Speaks*, March 1, 2015, https://www.youtube.com/watch?v=WJw3_cvrcwE.

28. Bland, *Sandy Speaks*, March 4, 2015, https://www.youtube.com/watch?v=UONMFvm1JBA&t=0s.

29. Bland, *Sandy Speaks*, February 6, 2015, https://www.youtube.com/watch?v=vnDWUP7Y8Xo&t=0s.

30. Michelle Manchir and Christy Gutowski, "Little League: Jackie Robinson West Didn't Cheat," *Chicago Tribune*, December 16, 2014, https://www.chicagotribune.com/news/ct-jackie-robinson-west-residency-met-20141216-story.html; and Michelle Manchir, Lolly Bowean, and Lexy Gross, "Jackie Robinson West Stripped of Little League Championship," *Chicago Tribune*, February 11, 2015, https://www.chicagotribune.com/business/chi-jackie-robinson-west-little-league-20150211-story.html#page=1.

31. For Bland's efforts on behalf of the Jackie Robinson team, see Bland, *Sandy Speaks*, February 15, 2015, https://www.youtube.com/watch?v=fTXAngT8qXw&t=0s; Bland, *Sandy Speaks*, March 22, 2015 (Part 2), https://www.youtube.com/watch?v=uJ__WydVrYk; Bland, *Sandy Speaks*, March 22, 2015 (Part 3), https://www.youtube.com/watch?v=_EV9xjrb1qI&t=0s; and Bland, *Sandy Speaks*, March 28, https://www.youtube.com/watch?v=l6T6s3aQhAY.

32. Bland, *Sandy Speaks*, April 8, 2015, https://www.youtube.com/watch?v=CIKeZgC8lQ4&t=0s.

33. Bland, *Sandy Speaks*, April 10, 2015, https://www.youtube.com/watch?v=YsTgyabGtL4.

34. "Awaken the Voice," Amplify the Shout, YouTube, July 13, 2017, https://www.youtube.com/watch?v=a5dvOSdSbVA.

35. Hannah Bonner, "Power Exists to Be Given Away—Reminders from Movement Living," Hannah Adair Bonner (blog), September 24, 2019, https://hannahadairbonner.com/2019/09/24/power-exists-to-be-given-away-reminders-from-movement-living/. For the rationale behind Bonner's theological and spiritual practice of amplification, see Bonner, *The Shout: Finding the Prophetic Voice in Unexpected Places* (Nashville: Abingdon, 2016).

36. Kelly Brown Douglas, *Stand Your Ground: Black Bodies and the Justice of God* (New York: Orbis, 2015); and Douglas, *Resurrection Hope: A Future Where Black Lives Matter* (New York: Orbis, 2021).

37. Brenda Salter McNeil, *Roadmap to Reconciliation 2.0: Moving Communities into Unity, Wholeness, and Justice* (Downers Grove, IL: InterVarsity Press, 2020); and Brenda Salter McNeil, *Becoming Brave: Finding the Courage to Pursue Racial Justice Now* (Grand Rapids, MI: Brazos, 2020).

SELECTED BIBLIOGRAPHY

"Awaken the Voice." Amplify the Shout. YouTube, July 13, 2017. https://www.youtube.com/watch?v=a5dvOSdSbVA.

Bay, Mia, Farah J. Griffin, Martha S. Jones, and Barbara D. Savage. "Introduction: Toward an Intellectual History of Black Women." In *Toward an Intellectual History of Black Women*, edited by Mia Bay, Farah J. Griffin, Martha S. Jones, and Barbara D. Savage, 3–9. Chapel Hill: University of North Carolina Press, 2015.

Blain, Keisha N., Christopher Cameron, and Ashley D. Farmer. "Introduction: The Contours of Black Intellectual History." In *New Perspectives on the Black Intellectual Tradition*, edited by Keisha N. Blain, Christopher Cameron, and Ashley D. Farmer, 3–16. Evanston, IL: Northwestern University Press, 2018.

Bland, Sandra. "MLK Message." *Sandy Speaks*, January 8, 2016. Posted by Hannah Bonner, Instagram: Part 1, https://www.instagram.com/p/BAqywaPKgqx/; Part 2, https://www.instagram.com/p/BAr5Hj-qgnk/; Part 3, https://www.instagram.com/p/BAr_HUjKgnO/; Part 4, https://www.instagram.com/p/BAsMFr9qgk1/; Part 5, https://www.instagram.com/p/BAsatxvqgll/; Part 6, https://www.instagram.com/p/BAsqz9dKgjW/; Part 7, https://www.instagram.com/p/BAsq-MYqgjr/; and Part 8, https://www.instagram.com/p/BAs4Jsuqgor/.

Bland, Sandra. "Prayer Episode." *Sandy Speaks*, February 1, 2016. Posted by Hannah Bonner, Instagram: Part 1, https://www.instagram.com/p/BBPLyosKggN/; Part 2, https://www.instagram.com/p/BBPvPTiKgnj/; Part 3, https://www.instagram.com/p/BBQKJ_kKggM/; and Part 4, https://www.instagram.com/p/BBQXrFfKgqO/.

Bland, Sandra. *Sandy Speaks*, January 15, 2015. https://www.youtube.com/watch?v=f5VhTY3_FC8.

Bland, Sandra. *Sandy Speaks*, February 5, 2015. https://www.youtube.com/watch?v=wOxWPXdFyYo&t=0s.

Bland, Sandra. *Sandy Speaks*, February 6, 2015. https://www.youtube.com/watch?v=vnDWUP7Y8Xo&t=0s.

Bland, Sandra. *Sandy Speaks*, February 7, 2015. https://www.youtube.com/watch?v=KfrZM2Qjvtc&t=0s.

Bland, Sandra. *Sandy Speaks*, February 15, 2015. https://www.youtube.com/watch?v=fTXAngT8qXw&t=0s.

Bland, Sandra. *Sandy Speaks*, February 21, 2015 (Part 2). https://www.youtube.com/watch?v=cv6lZCB73SU&t=0s.

Bland, Sandra. *Sandy Speaks*, March 1, 2015. https://www.youtube.com/watch?v=WJw3_cvrcwE.

Bland, Sandra. *Sandy Speaks*, March 4, 2015. https://www.youtube.com/watch?v=UONMFvm1JBA&t=0s.

Bland, Sandra. *Sandy Speaks*, March 22, 2015 (Part 2). https://www.youtube.com/watch?v=uJ__WydVrYk.

Bland, Sandra. *Sandy Speaks*, March 22, 2015 (Part 3). https://www.youtube.com/watch?v=_EV9xjrb1qI&t=0s.

Bland, Sandra. *Sandy Speaks*, March 28, 2015. https://www.youtube.com/watch?v=l6T6s3aQhAY.

Bland, Sandra. *Sandy Speaks*, April 8, 2015. https://www.youtube.com/watch?v=CIKeZgC8lQ4&t=0s.

Bland, Sandra. *Sandy Speaks*, April 10, 2015. https://www.youtube.com/watch?v=YsTgyabGtL4.

Bonner, Hannah. "Power Exists to Be Given Away—Reminders from Movement Living." Hannah Adair Bonner (blog), September 24, 2019. https://hannahadairbonner.com/2019/09/24/power-exists-to-be-given-away-reminders-from-movement-living/.

Bonner, Hannah. "The Prophetic Preaching of Sandra Bland." *Sojourners*, September 16, 2015. https://sojo.net/articles/faith-action/prophetic-preaching-sandra-bland.

Bonner, Hannah. *The Shout: Finding the Prophetic Voice in Unexpected Places*. Nashville: Abingdon, 2016.

Bowers, Josh. "Annoy No Cop." University of Virginia School of Law, Public Law and Legal Theory Research Paper Series, March 2017.

Cobbina, Jennifer E. *Hands Up, Don't Shoot: Why the Protests in Ferguson and Baltimore Matter and How They Changed America*. New York: New York University Press, 2019.

Crawford-Tichawonna, Nicole. "Years of Persistence Led to Holiday Honoring King." *USA Today*, January 12, 2018. https://www.usatoday.com/story/news/nation-now/2018/01/12/king-holiday-origin/1006109001/.

Douglas, Kelly Brown. *Resurrection Hope: A Future Where Black Lives Matter*. Maryknoll, NY: Orbis, 2021.

Douglas, Kelly Brown. *Stand Your Ground: Black Bodies and the Justice of God*. Maryknoll, NY: Orbis, 2015.

DuPage African Methodist Episcopal Church. Accessed January 5, 2022. http://www.dupageamec.org/ministerial-staff/.

Gillon, Victoria D. "The Killing of an 'Angry Black Woman': Sandra Bland and the Politics of Respectability." Augustana College, Augustana Digital Commons, 2016. https://digitalcommons.augustana.edu/mabryaward/3/.

Glaude, Eddie S. *Democracy in Black: How Race Still Enslaves the American Soul*. New York: Crown, 2016.

Hill, Marc Lamont. *Nobody: Casualties of America's War on the Vulnerable, from Ferguson to Flint*. New York: Atria, 2016.

Lebron, Chris. *The Making of Black Lives Matter: A Brief History of an Idea*. New York: Oxford University Press, 2017.

Lowery, Wesley. *"They Can't Kill Us All": Ferguson, Baltimore, and a New Era in America's Racial Justice Movement*. New York: Little, Brown, 2016.

Lowrey-Kinberg, Belen V., and Grace Sullivan Buker. "'I'm Giving You a Lawful Order': Dialogic Legitimacy in Sandra Bland's Traffic Stop." *Law and Society Review* 51, no. 2 (2017): 379–412.

Manchir, Michelle, and Christy Gutowski. "Little League: Jackie Robinson West Didn't Cheat." *Chicago Tribune*, December 16, 2014. https://www.chicagotribune.com/news/ct-jackie-robinson-west-residency-met-20141216-story.html.

Manchir, Michelle, Christy Gutowski, Lolly Bowean, and Lexy Gross. "Jackie Robinson West Stripped of Little League Championship." *Chicago Tribune*, February 11, 2015. https://www.chicagotribune.com/business/chi-jackie-robinson-west-little-league-20150211-story.html#page=1.

Manigault-Bryant, LeRhonda. "'I Had a Praying Grandmother': Religion, Prophetic Witness, and Black Women's Herstories." In *New Perspectives on the Black Intellectual Tradition*, edited by Keisha N. Blain, Christopher Cameron, and Ashley D. Farmer, 115–30. Evanston, IL: Northwestern University Press, 2018.

Marable, Marable. *Living Black History: How Reimagining the African-American Past Can Remake America's Racial Future*. New York: Basic Books, 2006.

McNeil, Brenda Salter. *Becoming Brave: Finding the Courage to Pursue Racial Justice Now*. Grand Rapids, MI: Brazos, 2020.

McNeil, Brenda Salter. *Roadmap to Reconciliation 2.0: Moving Communities into Unity, Wholeness, and Justice*. Downers Grove, IL: InterVarsity Press, 2020.

Nathan, Debbie. "What Happened to Sandra Bland?" *The Nation*, April 21, 2016. https://www.thenation.com/article/what-happened-to-sandra-bland/.

Pitman, Brian, Asha M. Ralph, Jocelyn Camacho, and Elizabeth Monk-Turner. "Social Media Users' Interpretations of the Sandra Bland Arrest Video." *Race and Justice* (2017): 1–19.

Ransby, Barbara. *Making All Black Lives Matter: Reimagining Freedom in the Twenty-First Century*. Berkeley: University of California Press, 2018.

Reid, Ashley B. "The Sandra Bland Story: How Social Media Has Exposed the Harsh Reality of Police Brutality." MA thesis, Bowie State University, 2016.

Ritchie, Andrea J. *Invisible No More: Police Violence against Black Women and Women of Color*. Boston: Beacon Press, 2017.

Rocksborough-Smith, Ian. *Black Public History in Chicago: Civil Rights Activism from World War II to the Cold War*. Urbana: University of Illinois Press, 2018.

Romero, Frances. "A Brief History of Martin Luther King Jr. Day." *Time*, January 18, 2010. http://content.time.com/time/nation/article/0,8599,1872501,00.html.

Ross, Rosetta E. *Witnessing & Testifying: Black Women, Religion, and Civil Rights*. Minneapolis: Fortress Press, 2003.

Samuels, Alex. "Lawmaker Grills Department of Public Safety over Disclosure of Sandra Bland Cellphone Video." *Texas Tribune*, May 24, 2019. https://www.texastribune.org/2019/05/24/sandra-bland-hearing-texas-house-committee/.

Sandra Bland Traffic Stop, Texas Department of Public Safety, July 22, 2015. https://www.youtube.com/watch?v=CaW09Ymr2BA.

Say Her Name: The Life and Death of Sandra Bland. Home Box Office, 2018.

Senft, Theresa M. "Skin of the Selfie." Unabridged Version, 2015, 1–21. http://www.academia.edu/15941920/The_Skin_of_the_Selfie_Unabridged_Version.

Sinitiere, Phillip Luke. "The Aesthetic Insurgency of Sandra Bland's Afterlife." *Souls: A Critical Journal of Black Politics, Culture and Society* 20, no. 1 (2018): 122–47.

Sinitiere, Phillip Luke. "From Standing Rock to Waller County: Repression, Resistance, and Environmental Justice." *Black Perspectives*, December 18, 2016. https://www.aaihs.org/from-standing-rock-to-waller-county-repression-resistance-and-environmental-justice/.

Sinitiere, Phillip Luke. "A Literary Libation on Sandra Bland Parkway." In *Our Voices, Our Stories: An Anthology of Writings Advancing, Celebrating, Embracing, and Empowering Girls and Women of Color*, edited by Donnamaria Culbreth, 175. Jersey City, NJ: Complexity Publishing, 2019.

Sinitiere, Phillip Luke. "Religion and the Black Freedom Struggle for Sandra Bland." In *"The Seedtime, the Work, and the Harvest": New Perspectives on the Black Freedom Struggle in America*, edited by Reginald K. Ellis, Jeffrey Littlejohn, and Peter Levy, 197–226. Gainesville: University Press of Florida, 2018.

Sinitiere, Phillip Luke. "Sandy Still Speaks: Remembering Sandra Bland." *The North Star*, July 13, 2019. https://thenorthstar.com/articles/sandy-still-speaks-remembering-sandra-bland.

Sinitiere, Phillip Luke. "What Is Happening in Waller County? Sandra Bland and the Sister Comrades Who #SayHerName." *Black Perspectives*, August 12, 2015. https://www.aaihs.org/what-is-happening-in-waller-county-sandra-bland-and-the-sister-comrades-who-sayhername/.

Taylor, Keeanga-Yamahtta. *From #BlackLivesMatter to Black Liberation*. Chicago: Haymarket, 2016.

Wise, Tim. *Speaking Treason Fluently: Anti-Racist Reflections from an Angry White Male*. Berkeley: Soft Skull Press, 2008.

Chapter 11

"BLACK FEMINIST LOVE EVANGELIST" AND "PRAYER POET PRIESTESS"

Alexis Pauline Gumbs

LAURA L. SULLIVAN

> Black feminism is this radiant practice of loving beyond, beyond, beyond, beyond across difference, being transformed by love, which means, yeah, everyone's here, and we're everywhere.
> —Alexis Pauline Gumbs[1]

"BRILLIANCE REMASTERED"

A self-proclaimed "Black Feminist Love Evangelist" and "Prayer Poet Priestess," Alexis Pauline Gumbs is a Black feminist who operates in multiple modalities. Inspired by the Kitchen Table: Women of Color Press, Gumbs founded her own outlet called Broken Beautiful Press in 2002. After studying English, Women's Studies, and Africana Studies and obtaining her PhD from Duke University in 2010, Gumbs eschewed the pursuit of a traditional tenure-track academic job. Instead, as she continued to participate in community organizing, to write poetry, and to publish in academic venues, she vigorously promoted Black feminist thinking and pedagogy on- and offline and developed a mentorship service for scholars of color under the rubric of "Brilliance Remastered." Reflecting the healing and spiritual orientation of the enterprise, the tagline was "take your degree home whole and keep your soul." Since 2010, Gumbs has offered webinars organized around Black feminist writing and themes that connect social dynamics to individual ones, intimate experiences that bridge political, spiritual, and emotional work. Her political and literary efforts have always been intertwined, and frequently her cultural productions are offered as timely, emotionally resonant responses to important issues and events. For example, in the wake of the violent murders at an Orlando nightclub frequented by members of the LGBTQ+ community in July 2016, Gumbs wrote a poem called "Pulse." She posted a video of herself reading the poem a few days after the mass shooting in which fifty people were killed, explaining that the poem is "for our loved ones in Orlando, who we didn't get to meet."[2] On Facebook, the video of Gumbs reading "Pulse" has been viewed over 73,000 times.[3]

Gumbs has recently branched out to publish a triptych of novel-length works, each inspired by a particular Black feminist scholar. Her first book, *Spill: Scenes of Black Feminist Fugitivity*, mobilizes phrases and concepts from the work of Hortense Spillers and features "scenes of Black women's lives mostly from the slavery era till now."[4] Her second book, *M Archive: After the End of the World*, draws upon the work of M. Jacqui Alexander.[5] The writings of Caribbean philosopher Sylvia Wynter provide the foundation for Gumbs's third book, *Dub: Finding Ceremony*.[6] Each book demonstrates, in Petal Samuel's words, how "Black women's speculative fiction is a precious . . . archive of intersectional theory."[7] Also a visual artist, Gumbs makes collages of important Black women and Black feminists (including some men). Honoring people such as organizer Fannie Lou Hamer and science fiction writer Octavia Butler, these collages are celebrations and objects of meditation as much as they are works of art.[8] As many of these examples illustrate, much of Gumbs's work—whether in textual, virtual, or ritual form—is a "validation ceremony" for Black women, as Toni Cade Bambara characterizes Julie Dash's visionary 1991 film, *Daughters of the Dust*.[9]

BLACK FEMINISM AND OR AS SPIRITUAL PRACTICE

Black feminism is foundational to Gumbs's spirituality. Gumbs "honors the lives and creative works of Black feminist geniuses as sacred texts for all people" and "believes that . . . access to the intersectional, holistic brilliance of the Black feminist tradition is as crucial as learning how to read."[10] Ultimately, Gumbs proclaims: "Black feminism is my primary spiritual practice."[11] "Informed by many other spiritual traditions," her practice, she says, "comes from a deep place of faith and incorporates breathing, meditation, movement, many forms of prayer and ritual, and ancestor reverence." Connecting her spiritual practices to her community outreach and virtual offerings, Gumbs explains that the "container for the ceremonies [she] facilitate[s] is called Eternal Summer of the Black Feminist Mind." She views her own spiritual focus as an intergenerational inheritance, noting that "the ancestors who inspired me to engage this practice identified as Black feminists," citing examples such as Audre Lorde and June Jordan. Reflecting her understanding of the power of words and vocalizations, Gumbs explains, "When I say, 'I am a Black feminist,' I am saying a prayer that includes and cites them. I am quoting them with my life." Gumbs describes how her spiritual practices also align with and draw from traditional African religions and epistemologies: "The ancestor reverence that I practice is informed by New World Ifa/Yoruba practices and exists alongside the Ifa/Yoruba practices that we hold sacred in our household. I also see Black feminist historical figures and writers as representations of key energetic forces in the universe in a manner similar to the way that Yoruba practitioners understand the Orisha." Gumbs's spirituality, she explains, "is also very grounded in nature" and in this way "is also in alignment with the practices of Black feminists, who have historically advocated for the planet without being called 'environmentalists.'"

An especially salient aspect of Gumbs's spirituality involves lifting up the beliefs, values, words, and texts of Black women. For Gumbs, "Black feminism is the practice of believing and acting on [an understanding that] Black women are inherently valuable."[12] Gumbs expresses faith in this reality, "even when it is [based upon] pure faith/evidence of things unseen in . . . daily life and in our current society." She elaborates: "So, specifically I chant quotes from the ancestors who inform my Black feminist practice. I make intentional spaces to share food and poetry with other Black women and other people whose lives are informed by Black feminist possibility. I read the sacred texts created in the past and being created now by Black feminists. I exercise devotion." Referencing the profound gifts she has received from "this love practice called Black feminism," Gumbs specifies, "My relationships with other Black women and women of color are sourced by it. My relationship with other Black folks, other queer folks, plants, animals, the river, everything." One of the most crucial benefits of this practice has been "permission and tangible faith in loving myself, which is what the intersecting oppressions that sustain capitalism try to steal from me every day." Quoting June Jordan's declaration, "Love is lifeforce!," Gumbs says she "cannot imagine [her] life without this love." She underscores that while her Black feminist spirituality involves daily and individual practices and benefits, it also has a communal dimension, as reflected in the group rituals, classes, and workshops she leads.

Gumbs follows in the tradition of spiritually informed Black women writers and thinkers highlighted in Akasha Gloria Hull's groundbreaking book, *Soul Talk: The New Spirituality of African American Women*, in which she writes that, like Toni Cade Bambara, Gumbs ascribes to a "metaphysics that is highly intellectual and occult, as well as revolutionary and Black."[13] Hull points out that while "many people talk about their spirituality and never indicate any awareness that it is socially embedded or could be used in a socially responsive way to fight societal ills," for Black women "that is rarely the case." Hull describes the sensibility conveyed in Bambara's 1982 novel *The Salt Eaters*, the understanding that "spiritual wisdom is first and foremost a force for transforming social and political ills" that "wear the very specific faces of racism, poverty, gender inequality, rampant capitalism, ignorance, and so forth," a perspective that pervades all of Gumbs's textual productions and collective endeavors.[14]

ALTERNATIVE TEMPORALITIES AND ANCESTORS

In an episode of the podcast *How to Survive the End of the World*, hosts and sisters adrienne maree brown and Autumn Brown and guest interviewee Gumbs discuss the historical period when important Black feminist organizations were created, the challenges they faced, and the evolution of their methods and practices.[15] Specifically drawing on what Combahee River Collective member Hull describes in *Soul Talk*, Gumbs explains that Black feminists in the 1970s who "were coming out of Left movements" and "Civil Rights Movements" "were in the streets . . . organizing" and also confronting extreme and pervasive anti-Black violence, including a series of murders involving protestors, Black children, and Black women. Gumbs echoes Hull when she explains that these conditions led the "Black feminists [to] know that they had to go much deeper with their work—that they couldn't just keep responding to everything that was happening, because it was literally killing them." The solutions they came upon were unconventional by the standards of mid-century organizing and activism: "They had to do spiritual work. They had to listen on another level; they had to be more intergenerational. They had to create practices that were generative, and not only responsive."

Gumbs and the Brown sisters observe that they were all born in the late 1970s and 1980s—around the time these Black feminist organizations were forming and then dissolving; thus, they view themselves as the inheritors of this intergenerational legacy. Their Black feminist foremothers came to believe in a spiritual power and understood that they were working for a liberation that was not to come during their own lifetimes. In this way, Gumbs explains, she and the Brown sisters were born in the "energy" and "trust" of these insights. In an interview in *Ms. Magazine*, Gumbs shares that she "feel[s] like [she] just was born in a beautiful context of Black women's writing and creative energy."[16] The connection of all three leaders to their predecessors is part of a larger spiritual phenomenon: as Charlene Carruthers, cofounder of the Black Youth Project explains, "The hyper-visibility of Black women, lesbian, gay, bisexual, transgender, and queer leaders in today's struggle for Black liberation is not by happenstance. We were conjured through generations of magic."[17] Thus,

Carruthers, too, shares that she and other Black champions of social justice are following in the wake created for them, answering a spiritual-political calling from their ancestors.[18]

As Gumbs ponders the hopelessness with which the Black feminists of the late 1970s and 1980s had to contend, she describes the energy in which they operated and imagines them saying to themselves:

> You know what? The transformation we need in this world is not going to be linear; it's actually going to be beyond our lifetimes. And it actually is connected way before our lifetimes. And we are grounding in a power that is not similar to the power that we've seen before. You know, we're gonna believe in that. And we're gonna reach beyond, what we can see directly in front of us in the streets. And we trust that that energy is gonna come back.[19]

Such a philosophy resonates with Gumbs, who recalls that as a high school student she contemplated her own experience of and relation to temporality and realized that

> If I'm present, everyone is here. Like if I'm present, I have access to everyone and every moment that's ever existed. I don't know which one of those moments I'm gonna need to connect to in order to be fully present to this moment, but I know that I have to be open to the fact that there's a simultaneity of time. . . . It's not linear, in the sense that I cannot be separated from that love that has generated me.

It is the permanent, nonlinear, transcendent nature of love that enables this generative practice and connection, she says: "And Black feminism is this radiant practice of loving beyond, beyond, beyond, beyond across difference, being transformed by love, which means, yeah, everyone's here, and we're everywhere."

What, specifically, does a practice based on this understanding look like? According to Hull, Gumbs's epistemological approach, like another of her Black feminist mentors, Alexis De Veaux, considers the interconnection of transformation on the "spiritual, political, social, and emotional levels."[20] In speculative fashion, Black feminists often base their actions on a belief in the value and possibility of Black life and liberation, *despite* the pervasiveness of anti-Blackness and Black social death, and sometimes that faith is in physical, energetic dimensions—dimensions that can be understood as "mystical" but also as material and that include alternative temporal understandings and experiences. For example, Gumbs activates this perspective in what she calls the Black Feminist Breathing Chorus.

adrienne maree brown describes her participation in this chorus, when she connected to the spirit of Harriet Tubman at a meeting for Black Organizing for Leadership and Dignity (BOLD), in which Gumbs led the group in breathing and chanting "Black feminist words . . . together." brown says her group was given the words "My people are free" spoken by Tubman to chant, and that she wouldn't have imagined how this experience would be like a form of time travel, "how it really felt like a transporting into a different time, place, and understanding of how reality works."[21]

To develop a method of breathing that would help someone, as Gumbs describes it, "to be able to make a decision, right, in this present moment, informed by all other moments but really breathing into this moment," she invented the practice that evolved into the Black Feminist Breathing Project:

> I actually had a desire for my breathing to be in chorus with everyone who's ever loved Black women. With everyone who's ever decided that the freedom of Black women could be palpable and possible. I wanted to be breathing in chorus, and I knew that that would be how I could breathe beyond just responding to violence, or the violence that has shaped my experience. . . . Harriet Tubman said "My people are free" in the middle of slavery. And I can have access to that moment. She said that—I'm saying that. We're saying that, together. We have access to more than just the power of our individual lives, more than just the power of what linear facts we think have made up our day. We actually have access to *incredible power*, and power that people have used to do things that are miraculous. I mean, Harriet Tubman is only one of more than twenty folks we draw on in Black Feminist Breathing when we call them into our bodies.[22] (italics in the original)

This articulation has many implications for how we conceive of, design, and enact resistance. Love is a catalyst for a model that goes "beyond just responding to violence" and oppression, Gumbs continues. Moreover, every powerful declaration and vision of a world other than the current one and every decision to act based on that not-yet-realized vision—these are always available to us. The power of the miraculous, which exists outside of linearity, is available and, in this case, through the particular and *embodied* practice of Black Feminist Breathing. As Ashon T. Crawley asserts in *Blackpentecostal Breath: The Aesthetics of Possibility*, "Breathing is a resource from which to perform the resistance that is prior to power."[23] Gumbs's Black feminist exercises demonstrate how "the case of breathing," as Crawley explains, "is an ongoing openness to life that is always and exorbitantly social." In this spirit, Gumbs gathered twenty-one Black feminists to perform a ritual on the banks of the Combahee River on the 150th anniversary of the revolt led by Harriet Tubman in that place; they experienced the embodied, spiritual, and social practice of the Black Feminist Breathing exercise in an applied, collective context.[24]

Another instantiation of Gumbs's "worship" of and spiritual connection to Black feminist foremothers can be seen in the blog collection called *In Your Hands: Letters from My Chosen Ancestors*.[25] "One January," Gumbs says, she "found [herself] receiving urgent love letters from the internalized voices of the likes of Audre Lorde, Ella Baker, June Jordan and Toni Cade Bambara every morning."[26] She describes the process in more detail:

> I did this every morning. Listening first for who wanted to speak, or sometimes it would be announced the day before. And I would hold the pen and just listen and listen for what any mother warrior had to say, knowing that my ego is less important than my purpose, knowing that even if it wasn't what I wanted to hear it was what I needed somehow. Listening like the eager student that these ancestors deserve. I have learned that as often as my ancestors are affirming and supportive they can also be disruptive, changing my whole idea of what I need to do in a day, inserting themselves in ways that alter timelines and boundaries I set up. I should not be surprised. My ancestors were not well-behaved women.[27]

The "letters" Gumbs received from her Black feminist ancestors included ones from Nayo Watkins, Fannie Lou Hamer, Pat Parker, and Claudia Jones. The letters are gorgeous, fascinating documents that provide precise, detailed guidance to Gumbs.

For instance, Ella Baker tells Gumbs: "You are right to be obsessed with both the old and the dead because that is where you will get your grounding and context. You are right when you remember that you are not the one inventing this" and advises her to "never forget who your people are and what they deserve, which is all of who you are."[28] In a different register, Fannie Lou Hamer ends her letter with the proclamation: "There is more love here than anything. Eat it up while it's hot."[29] And "ancestor-trickster Octavia [Butler]" came to Gumbs and had the last word, telling her: "What your life and work will be will exceed your expectations, your invitations, your affinity. Life is stranger than anything you would want to imagine, and that's the good news. Wake up to the reality that survival is a sharp thing, full of edges and decisions and sacrifice."[30] The letters are an offering to the readers; as Gumbs explains, "My ancestors are socialist, so of course they would ask me to share these intimate insights and gifts with you."[31]

Gumbs situates the podcast she created that draws on the ancestors' letters of "In Your Hands" as an explicit alternative to Sunday services in the Christian tradition, telling us it "features music from Mahalia Jackson, Sweet Honey in the Rock, and more" and describing it in the following terms: "Because it takes a whole month to prepare for the day of the dead. Because some of us have to create eclectic Sunday morning rituals to hear our own truth. Because I want you to have this for when you need it. . . . I hope this piece grounds you and reminds you where you are from. You can save it for Sunday or you can listen right now."[32] The letters from Gumbs's "chosen ancestors"—Black feminist writers, teachers, artists, and organizers—are channeled spiritual messages of inspiration and revolutionary instruction.

The Black feminist spiritual practices in which Gumbs engages are also grounded in the material world. For not only does her love for Black feminists and writers involve a deep appreciation of their textual production and a concomitant commitment to bring their texts more notoriety—through, for example, a lending library known as the Black Feminist Bookmobile—it also manifests in a great compassion for these women's often challenging negotiations of the material conditions of their lives, dynamics Gumbs publicly exposes and critiques. In her contribution to *The Feminist Wire*'s forum honoring June Jordan, Gumbs notes that often Jordan "couldn't pay her phone bill."[33] Gumbs puts us into the scene of her own discovery of this disconcerting reality, as she is "sitting hungry and enthralled in the Black Feminist poet, educator, [and] revolutionary's papers in the Schlessinger [*sic*] Archives at Harvard" and holding "the disconnection notices in [her] own hands."

Similarly, in discussing the "survival of Black feminist intellectuals," Gumbs insists we acknowledge that—as she learned when reading the writer's archival papers—Audre Lorde "was denied medical leave" and "had to turn down prestigious fellowships . . . that required residency in places too cold for her to live" when she was battling cancer.[34] Pointing to the contradictions between commodified celebrations of famous Black feminists and the lack of material support for their lives and work, Gumbs notes that while the "English Department at Hunter . . . recently honored Lorde with a conference 20 years after her death," this same department "rejected her proposals [toward] the end of her life" that would have allowed her "to teach on a limited residency basis," "to teach poetry[-]intensive classes for students during warm weather in New York," and "to live in warmer climates during the winter" to address "her health needs." Lamenting this past treatment of beloved Black feminist ancestors such as Lorde, Gumbs also connects such practices to the academy's entrenched racism and to its hypocrisy. She asks us to contemplate, "If Audre Lorde's proposal to teach in a way that allowed her to survive can be denied by the City University of New York, even as she was simultaneously selected as the New York State Poet Laureate, what does that teach us about the value of our bodies in the spaces that tokenize our minds?" To counter the oppressiveness of academia and the isolation it fosters, Gumbs's epistemologies and practices emphasize *relationality*, a topic to which I now turn.

RELATIONALITY: COLLECTIVITY AND COLLABORATION

As Celeste Henery documents, Black women in the diaspora such as Gumbs exhibit a "praxis . . . of love."[35] Specifically, she writes, they draw upon the "generative possibilities" of love "as a framework for the communion pursued in Black life out of the ruptures torn by the life-depleting forces of heteropatriarchal racism and capitalism."[36] Gumbs's view of Black feminism, expressed in the podcast with the Brown sisters, as "a rigorous love practice that is profoundly inclusive" also reflects Henery's point that, for Black women's diaspora, "love holds the promise for what has been lost and what still needs to be."[37] In a similar register, Gumbs declares that "the logical endpoint of loving ourselves, and of loving Black women, means we have to dismantle everything that's not loving to people" and "even [going] beyond our species, beyond the life forms that we even recognize at this point."[38] So, she sums up, "it's a rigorous love practice and it radiates"; her activism and community outreach efforts embody this dynamic.

The Mobile Homecoming Project is exemplary in this regard. A joint undertaking by Gumbs and her partner, Julia Roxanne Wallace, the Mobile Homecoming Project began in 2009.[39] Commencing in 2010, Gumbs and Wallace in an RV "travel[ed] the country collecting oral histories of queer Black same-gender-loving elders, learning about the people who have been integral in transforming the Black queer movement since the 1980s or earlier, piecing together an intergenerational connection," according to Elsa Barkley Brown.[40] As Gumbs and Wallace explain, they were "queer Black feminist researchers and artists seeking a way to amplify Black feminist practices in the Black LGBTQ community across generations" and were "looking for Black queer rituals." They discovered kindred queer archival efforts and documented various examples of queer elders' "community building practice" and creation of "sacred ritual space." Gumbs and Wallace explain that "[their] journey" was "about passing on the legacies of Black queer visionaries to generate and affirm new life." The continuation of the project has involved hosting Mobile Homecoming retreats to provide "safe space for intergenerational groups of queer Black folks."[41]

Gumbs advises us to "think about the question, concept, and project of family outside of the terms set by white supremacy and patriarchy."[42] She offered a chance to reflect on and transform mother-daughter relationships in her "Visionary Daughtering Webinar" that drew upon the relationship of Assata Shakur with her daughter, Kakuya.[43] In an equally innovative vein, Gumbs defines "sistering" as the "queer belief that we can reach each other across everything" and "the decision that we can make the world better for each other."[44] In a blog post, Gumbs explains that she and the participants in the Sistorian webinar celebrated and interrogated "sistering as an intentional practice."[45] Here are some lines from a poem the participants wrote titled "Sister Is a Verb *After Toni Cade Bambara*":

> sistering is a technology we are supposed to forget
> sistering is deep love
> sistering is about showing up
> sistering is about showing out sometimes too
> sistering is conscious
> sistering affirms
> sistering is about telling Black women they are beautiful
> (there are enough compliments and adoration to go around)
> sistering is salvation earned and gifted
> sistering is transformative generosity

Another "validation ceremony" for Black women, the poem's connotations of "sistering" counter stereotypes at the intersection of race and gender and offer empowerment and healing.

Invoking the insights of Hortense Spillers, Gumbs proclaims that "Black people are inventing a whole different type of life,"[46] an imperative she has clearly taken to heart. She has created curricula, experiences, and collaborations that not only change lives but also model other types of social relations and formations. Heeding Spillers's understanding that Black people "cannot own anything, even our bodies and even our loved ones," Gumbs asks, "What is [Black] relationality made of?" Pointing to the central paradox of Black identity, she asserts, "It's not made out of property, but we've been made into property." Invoking "Black social life and Black community," Gumbs sums up and advocates Spillers's conception of Black relationality, in which relationships are "built on choice," "built on shared ritual practice," and "built on creativity . . . that can't be necessarily owned." Thus, it's no coincidence that Gumbs's Black feminist workshops, retreats, and webinars all emphasize building relationships and developing and enacting collective rituals. And all are highly creative in conception as well as execution.

These qualities are evident in Gumbs's experiential online seminars, which are occasions for learning; self-reflection; personal, emotional, and spiritual growth; and connection. Seminars are organized around a central theme, such as "The Evidence Intensive: Futurists Beyond Fear."[47] Each webinar uses the texts of one or more Black feminists as organizing principles and inspiration for group exercises and writing, such as "Free Enterprise . . . Towards an Autonomous Sustainable Writing Life," based upon Michelle Cliff's 1993 novel *Free Enterprise*.[48] (While early intensives focused on other Black feminist writers, more recent ones have drawn upon Gumbs's own writings.) The name for these virtual workshops—"intensives"—is apt, as they are opportunities for participants to dive deeply into emotional, spiritual, and political thinking, visions, challenges, and solutions.

For example, in January 2017, Gumbs led a three-day webinar she called "Dig: The Womanist Archeologies [*sic*] Intensive," which was "for anyone interested in deepening their knowledge of womanist practice, expanding their idea of the archive, and finding ways to research and listen without reproducing patriarchal and capitalist values."[49] The intensive drew "on Alice Walker's work, her concept of work, her digging for Zora [Neale Hurston,] and her poetic invention of womanism" and "look[ed] at Walker's work itself as a planting, excavating and harvesting ground for generations of long-memoried, ready-to-be nourished seekers." Employing writing by several Black women authors and scholars, the online seminar was set up to be "a place where we [could] reconceptualize mothers, gardens, and the dirt that has (not yet) been done." Each intensive is also a spiritual experience. Virtual meetings begin with dedications, in which the participants share the name(s) of the person or people to whom they are dedicating their practice on that day, including ancestors, relatives, and important friends and colleagues, and why. And Gumbs leads the group in taking deep breaths together to open and close each session, as well as to bookend intermittent meditative segments.

RELATIONALITY: "WRITING WITH"

One of the primary ways that Gumbs expresses relationality is in a process that I think of as a spiritual "writing with." We learn from Hull that "Poet Dolores Kendrick and novelist Alice Walker composed literary works through contact with otherworldly ideas and voices," "assisted by ancestral Black women from the realm of spirit."[50] "The invocative and evocative medium was voice," Hull explains, "harking back to the African concept of *nommo*, which is 'the power of the word and the receiving ear.' Writers are, in critical respects, listeners" "poised to hear" and "in the position to pass on whatever comes to them."[51] Gumbs works within this tradition. Calling *M Archive: After the End of the World* an "ancestral listening text," Gumbs describes her writing process as literally "a trip," "a listening process" that involves her "get[ting] up every morning and be[ing] available and get[ting] out of [her] own way."[52] It's a process in which "you just open yourself up and listen." Inspired by the experience of

Lucille Clifton—whose adventures in receiving ancestral communications are described by Hull—Gumbs says she "had this experience of sitting and listening" and getting to "be with some of [her] favorite scholars."[53] *M Archive* came from engagement with M. Jacqui Alexander's *Pedagogies of Crossing: Meditations on Feminism, Sexual Politics, Memory, and the Sacred*, which Gumbs describes as itself "an ancestrally cowritten text."[54] Gumbs explains that "as [she] sat there and listened, these scenes came through."[55] She was unsure if they were from the near or far future, but as she experienced some visual echo of each channeled scene later in her day, repeatedly, she "knew [this book] was not about [her] telling people what [she] knew" and understood the process and the writing it enabled as "collective." In this way, Gumbs echoes "what Toni [Cade Bambara] says about how she created the novel" *The Salt Eaters*, which "emphasizes that she was writing from a spiritual dimension outside her normal, everyday, rational self" and that she didn't know "at all some of the things she [had] written," including principles of science and physics.[56] Like Bambara, who "wrote *The Salt Eaters* in an altered state . . . that connected her to the universe of spirit," Gumbs has written the books in her triptych during meditations, in her case specifically using words from Black women writers as mechanisms to call in scenes of life from other times.[57] Gumbs calls *M Archive* "speculative documentary work" that "is written from and with the perspective of a researcher, a post-scientist sorting artifacts after the end of the world."[58] The book has been "written in collaboration with the survivors, the far-into-the-future witnesses to the realities we are making possible or impossible with our present apocalypse."

The process of "writing with" these Black women writers has deeply affected Gumbs, who explains that, in using the work of Spillers, Alexander, and Wynter, "I wanted to be transformed by their work, beyond explanation and beyond the idea of mastery, and it has changed my entire life. I knew that I wanted to take on their work in an intimate way."[59] This method of writing reflects Gumbs's commitment to a particular politics of citation and is also an explicit instantiation of her spiritual practice. As she elaborates: "Part of the performance of *M Archive* is citing one Black feminist theorist over and over on every single page of a book that's hundreds of pages long. This is part of my prayer, my gratitude, my libation—and my reminder that I don't think Black feminist theorists have been cited enough or given the credit that they deserve." In this way, according to Henery, Gumbs follows in a diasporic tradition in which "Black women write themselves into communion with other Black women and in whose lives they experience parts of themselves."[60]

Each session of Gumbs's Black feminist, online, multiday intensives ends with writing a group poem based on a prompt, a riff on a Black woman's writing that relates to the webinar's theme. During these experiences of "writing with," the collective energy of the group and the way it is open to receiving what comes through produces powerful work, a transformative, beautiful Black feminist spiritual creative practice. After each session, the collaboratively written poem serves as the invocation at the start of the next day's session. After Gumbs reads the poem aloud, participants take turns choosing one or two lines from the poem to use in conjunction with their dedication(s) for the day. It is such a beautiful experience to hear the new poem, to feel its energy and impact, and to hear people's explanations for the lines they choose and their relationship to their dedications. This is Gumbs's Black feminist love in action.

Gumbs's personal "writing with" process involves an intergenerational dimension across time and space. Just as Gumbs draws on Black feminist theorists and mentors in her speculative documentary fiction, it is fitting that many other people—teachers, students, writers, and artists—take up and use her texts as the basis for other creative work, from dance, to plays, to performances. For example, an event at Duke University in January 2017 based on Gumbs's book *Spill: Scenes of Black Feminist Fugitivity* took "place on the day of the General Strike and the day before the Women's March on Washington," provided "interactive protest prompts," featured Gumbs "present[ing] a commanding collection of scenes depicting fugitive Black women and girls seeking freedom from gendered violence and racism," and showcased the performances of "Ritual performance artist and cultural strategist" Ebony Noelle Golden.[61] Thus, just as Gumbs uses the words, thoughts, and analyses of Black women theorists to produce new ideas, stories, and genres, artists inspired by Gumbs's work are using it to present new types of creative work, including performance.

RELATIONALITY: ACCOUNTABILITY

In her visionary, influential book, *Ghostly Matters: Haunting and the Sociological Imagination*, Avery Gordon endorses and articulates "a form of historical accounting [whose] purpose [as] an alternative diagnostics is to link the politics of accounting, in all its intricate political-economic dimensions, to a potent imagination of what has been done and what is to be done otherwise."[62] These values of "an alternative diagnostics" apply to the ancestor- and community-accountable work—in its activist and academic varieties and hybrids thereof—that Gumbs creates, encourages, and facilitates. Specifically, her politics of accountability follows a long tradition of Black feminism and the diaspora. Patricia Hill Collins and Sirma Bilge explain that, from the "particular epistemological stance" of Black feminism, "Experience and embodied knowledge are valorized, as is the theme of responsibility and accountability that accompanies such knowledge."[63] This is a sentiment that motivates Gumbs and that she promotes in her teaching and leading. She tells *Left of Black* host and professor Mark Anthony Neal that she has been particularly inspired by Alexis De Veaux—poet, playwright, novelist, and scholar who wrote the definitive biography of Audre Lorde and who, along "with Cheryll Greene and other editors at *Essence*," worked to "develop . . . a Black feminist diasporic accountability" by publishing unique and important pieces such as a conversation between Lorde and James Baldwin.[64]

Like her activist, artistic, and academic Black feminist work, the web-based intensives Gumbs offers illustrate her commitment to accountability. For example, she explains that an intensive offered in 2016, "Breathe Underwater: A Baptismal Intensive for Ancestor-Accountable Artists, Activists, and Scholars," was based on "a curriculum informed by June Jordan's *Who Look at Me*, M. Jacqui Alexander's *Pedagogies of Crossing*, and M. NourbeSe Philip's *Zong*" and involved using guided meditations and writing exercises to "immerse participants in the peace, urgency and depth of ancestral accountability" and to "provide tangible ways to root . . . action steps, creative decisions and intellectual offerings in a profound connection to legacy and power."[65] As part of an endeavor she calls "The School of Our Lorde," Gumbs says she led a "summer series called The Summer of Our Lorde," Audre Lorde's last name substituting for the Christian "Lord" and making clear Gumbs's spiritual veneration of Black feminists/feminism. The summer effort, according to Mark Anthony Neal, involved "partner[ing] with a different community organization in Durham [North Carolina]" for each of three months.[66] And in 2013, Gumbs cofacilitated a retreat called "Guardian Dead: Ancestor-Led Intellectual Practice," which she described as "a 4-day gathering for community accountable intellectuals looking for ways to deepen the ancestral accountability and presence of their scholarly and community-based creative practices."[67]

Yet, for Gumbs, it has been important to take Black feminist knowledge beyond the academy. "Black feminist intellectual legacy," Gumbs insists, does not "need . . . to be siloed within the university. There's no need for it to be only legible and accessible within the academic marketplace. It has always belonged to all of us."[68] Thus, in outreach to her community in Durham, Gumbs has always worked to ensure that "babies, grandparents, people of all ages, people who work in community organizations or the grocery store, in public schools, in all sorts of sectors in our community, are part of this practice of continuing to learn from and create from the legacy of Black feminism." And accountability to the Black community (and various constituencies within that larger community) also includes healing from the damage of living in a white supremacist society. That is, Gumbs's effort to "spread the gospel" of Black feminism—including sharing, writing about, and celebrating Black women's literature and artistic productions—reflects a conscious desire for Black women and all Black people, as Hull describes it, to "become visible in all our glory to ourselves and to the blind, negating white world."[69]

Black feminist spiritual methods and rituals are being mobilized by Gumbs and her coconspirators as practices and energies that counter instances of all forms of domination, including white supremacy.[70] This Facebook post's description of an event from May 5, 2019, demonstrates the practice:

> Yesterday at the UNC Institute of Arts and Humanities while white supremacists gathered outside and progressive activists created a sound barrier with freedom chants, Black Feminist Bookmobile held a Black Feminist Breathing and Movement Ceremony called "And a People to Believe in It," in honor of Pauli Murray (who was denied an education at UNC which her racist rapist slaveholding ancestors founded) and Bayard Rustin who was chased by two cars of racist men and forced to work 22 days on a chain gang for the crime of not moving to the back of the bus in Chapel Hill. We led students, faculty, staff, and visitors (including the highest ranking administrator in the humanities at UNC) in a sonic embodied interactive Black feminist recoding of impulse.[71]

Gumbs ends the post with the hashtag "#onancestralassignment," underscoring her commitment to answer the spiritual calling to enact a collaborative Black feminist practice that responds creatively, vibrationally, and decisively in moments of trauma and oppression.

CONCLUSION: SIGNIFICANCE OF GUMBS AS BLACK FEMINIST PUBLIC INTELLECTUAL

Gumbs insists that Black feminists can "teach us the answer to every question that our species can possibly create."[72] Her deep faith in Black feminism is based upon her belief that it offers humanity lessons that could help us, as she explains, to "continue to exist on this planet," including the insights made possible by investigating our rich interrelatedness, as well as the understanding that liberation does not require us to give up pieces of "all of who we are." Other Black feminist lessons that Gumbs cites include how to resist binary identities, how to consider harm in its multiple manifestations, and "how to be inventive, and incorporate pleasure and critique and creativity into the same moments." Hull, too, emphasizes the connection among spirituality, political stances, and creativity when she describes how Black women writers and artists "routinely" practice "living . . . in the multidimensionality that is the true state of the universe."[73] Gumbs, like the artists profiled by Hull, embraces what Hull calls this "multidimensionality that most adults prefer to suppress."

Petal Samuel describes how "forms of [Black] speculation have become the bases of innovative methodologies that open up new paths for thinking about Black histories and futures," a trend that includes Gumbs's triptych of speculative works and facilitated experiential events.[74] We might think of Gumbs as a Black feminist practitioner of Astro-Blackness. In Anderson and Jennings's book on Afrofuturism 2.0, Rev. Andrew Rollins defines Astro-Blackness as an "Afrofuturistic concept in which a person's Black state of consciousness, released from the confining and crippling slave or colonial mentality, becomes aware of the multitude and varied possibilities and probabilities within the universe."[75] Such a change in consciousness facilitates belief in—and practices to manifest—what Anderson and Jennings call the "bright Black future."[76] Like the Black science fiction writers who exemplify Astro-Blackness, Gumbs is one of those Anderson and Jennings call the "galactic griots, sharing their data with every turn of a phrase" and bringing messages about "transcendence and becoming a complete and whole individual." As Gumbs puts it in an interview, "We can honor Blackness as what it is, the unstoppable energy of the universe being its beautiful, Black, blinged-out self."[77]

Drawing up what Gumbs calls this "unstoppable [Black] energy of the universe" as well as the understanding of "collective dreaming as a community resource," Gumbs and Almah LaVon Rice-Faina led "Dark Sciences: A People of Color Dream Retreat" in the summer of 2015, providing a "queer-Black-feminist imagined collective dreaming house for people of color."[78] Recognizing that, in the words of Almah Rice-Faina, "Queer Black feminist imagination has birthed worlds upon worlds," they designed a retreat that Gumbs says "employ[ed] [the] concept of dream work as a link between our ancestors, our communities, and the cosmos."[79] Asked by interviewer Tala Khanmalek "Why is it important for people to dream together?," Gumbs discusses the benefits of recognizing "how interconnected we are in our dreams."[80] Sometimes people of color "dream about each other" and sometimes these "dreams are in conversation," Gumbs notes, declaring that "In chorus [these] dreams have whole new meanings and a lot of power." Gumbs connects this power of dreaming to resistance, pointing out that "Capitalism treats our dreams (the dreams of multiply structurally oppressed people) as nightmares to repress." Ultimately, Gumbs connects this intentional, collective dreaming practice to a Black feminist legacy and imperative: "For generations Black feminists have had to support each other in working to create a drastically more loving world in the face of complete denial of our value, our thought processes, our existence, our labor, our loved ones, EVERYTHING." As a result, Gumbs concludes, "the space of dreams, shared and individual, has been an important counter-space and resource."

Gumbs "evangelizes" about her love of Black feminists and feminism, and she encourages us to love these people and their brilliance, too. And Gumbs herself is a Black feminist whose way of being and sharing is based on a Black feminist spiritually inflected love, which Hull explains is characterized by "an inclusiveness, understanding, and empathy that radiates, magnetizes, actualizes whatever can be benefitted by it."[81] In the tradition of the Black women Hull writes about, she says that Gumbs is "propelled by the transcendent truth of a deep spirituality" and in the midst of great awareness of the pervasive oppressiveness of society, "consciously working to choose love and relationality."[82]

As this discussion of Alexis Pauline Gumbs has illustrated, her varied and typically unconventional methods of writing, organizing, and leading provide an expansive vision of what comprises Black feminist practice. Collages, dream retreats, rituals, oracle readings, community reading groups and potlucks, online intensives, collaborative writing experiences, and occasions for collective breathing and chanting the words of Black feminists—these are just some of the activities in which Gumbs engages. They call our attention to possibilities of ancestral connection and communication on vibrational levels. Embodied and creative, collective and experiential, epistemological and ontological—the practices and experiences that Gumbs designs provide and create what Hull calls "portals that initiate new modes of thought and behavior."[83] As Samuel explains, Gumbs's work addresses "the ongoing necessity . . . of modes of Black innovation, creativity, and improvisation in the face of ongoing social, economic, and intellectual oppression."[84] Moreover, Gumbs is not only an evangelist who "spreads the gospel" of Black feminism and feminists; she is also, as I have attempted to show, one of the most important Black feminist public intellectuals, artists, and organizers of our day.

NOTES

1. Gumbs in adrienne maree brown and Autumn Brown, hosts, "A Breathing Chorus with Alexis Pauline Gumbs," *How to Survive the End of the World*, podcast, December 19, 2017, http://www.endoftheworldshow.org/blog/2017/12/19/a-breathing-chorus-with-alexis-pauline-gumbs.

2. Alexis Pauline Gumbs, "Pulse," *Vimeo*, video, 4:36, 2016, http://vimeo.com/170498649.

3. Gumbs, "Pulse," Facebook, June 13, 2016, http://www.facebook.com/alexis.gumbs/videos/10102465290584702/.

4. Gumbs, *Spill: Scenes of Black Feminist Fugitivity* (Durham, NC: Duke University Press, 2016). See also Gumbs, cited in Janell Hobson, "Black Feminist in Public: Alexis Pauline Gumbs," *Ms.*, January 1, 2019, http://msmagazine.com/2019/01/01/Black-feminist-public-alexis-pauline-gumbs/.

5. Gumbs, *M Archive: After the End of the World* (Durham, NC: Duke University Press, 2018).

6. Gumbs, *Dub: Finding Ceremony* (Durham, NC: Duke University Press, 2020).

7. Petal Samuel, "Black Speculation, Black Freedom," *Public Books*, August 20, 2019, http://www.publicbooks.org/top-10–2019-Black-speculation-Black-freedom/.

8. Exemplary collages, along with more information about the history, purpose, and nature of the chorus, can be viewed here: "Black Feminist Breathing Chorus," https://sangodare.podia.com/breathingchorus.

9. Toni Cade Bambara, Preface to *Daughters of the Dust: The Making of an African-American Woman's Film* by Julie Dash (New York: New Press, 1992), xv.

10. "Divine Memory and the Laurie Carlos Oracle: An Engagement with Alexis Pauline Gumbs," University of Minnesota Website, 2017, http://cla.umn.edu/gwss/events/divine-memory-and-laurie-carlos-oracle-engagement-alexis-pauline-gumbs.

11. Quoted in Lisa Factora-Borchers et al., "Undivided State: A Conversation on Feminism and Spirituality," *Bitch Media*, December 12, 2017, http://www.bitchmedia.org/article/undivided-state/conversation-feminism-and-spirituality.

12. Quoted in Factora-Borchers et al., "Undivided State."

13. Akasha Gloria Hull, *Soul Talk: The New Spirituality of African American Women* (Rochester, VT: Inner Traditions, 2001), 14.

14. Hull, *Soul Talk*, 30. See Toni Cade Bambara, *The Salt Eaters* (London: Women's Press, 1982).

15. Gumbs in brown and Brown, "Breathing Chorus."

16. Quoted in Hobson, "Black Feminist in Public." Gumbs elaborates on the Black feminist energy surrounding her birth and early life: "When I was conceived, my mom was working for *Essence* magazine; I was born the year Alice Walker's *The Color Purple* came out, and I was raised in a household where the poetry and novels and the choreopoem of Black women were valued. The works of Angela Davis, Toni Morrison, Alice Walker, Ntozake Shange and Nikki Giovanni were present for me always, and that obviously had a major influence on who I am."

17. Charlene A. Carruthers, *Unapologetic: A Black, Queer, and Feminist Mandate for Radical Movements* (Boston: Beacon Press, 2018), 59.

18. See also Christina Sharpe, *In the Wake: On Blackness and Being* (Durham, NC: Duke University Press, 2016). Here, I am invoking the language of Sharpe, who proposes that "we think the metaphor of the wake in the entirety of its meanings" (17), which include "the keeping watch with the dead, the path of a ship, a consequence of something, in the line of flight and/or sight, awakening, and consciousness" (17–18). To "make the wake and *wake work* our analytic, we might continue to imagine new ways to live in the wake of slavery, in slavery's afterlives, to survive (and more) the afterlife of property" (18). Gumbs, the Brown sisters, and other young Black feminists undertake this "wake work" that Sharpe describes, promoting "a mode of inhabiting *and* rupturing this episteme with [their] known lived and un/imaginable lives" (18; emphasis in the original).

19. Gumbs in brown and Brown, "Breathing Chorus."

20. Hull, *Soul Talk*, 83.

21. brown in brown and Brown, "Breathing Chorus."

22. Gumbs in brown and Brown, "Breathing Chorus." Some other examples of people whose words are used for these meditations and chants are Anna Julia Cooper, Pat Parker, and Zora Neale Hurston. To view the full archive of the Black Feminist Breathing Chorus, see http://blackfeministbreathing.tumblr.com/archive.

23. Ashon T. Crawley, *Blackpentecostal Breath: The Aesthetics of Possibility* (New York: Fordham University Press, 2017), 48.

24. Gumbs, "Prophecy in the Present Tense: Harriet Tubman, the Combahee Pilgrimage, and Dreams Coming True," *Meridians: feminism, race, transnationalism* 12, no. 2 (2014): 142–52.

25. Gumbs, *In Your Hands: Letters from My Chosen Ancestors* (blog), 2009, http://motherourselves.wordpress.com.

26. Gumbs, "When Goddesses Change," *The Hooded Utilitarian*, July 7, 2014, http://www.hoodedutilitarian.com/2014/07/when-goddesses-change/.

27. Gumbs, "About," *In Your Hands.*

28. Gumbs, "Ella Baker," *In Your Hands: Letters from My Chosen Ancestors* (blog), January 22, 2009, http://motherourselves.wordpress.com/2009/01/22/ella-baker.

29. Gumbs, "Fannie Lou Hamer," *In Your Hands: Letters from My Chosen Ancestors* (blog), January 22, 2009, http://motherourselves.wordpress.com/2009/01/22/fannie-lou-hamer/.

30. Gumbs, "When Goddesses Change."

31. Gumbs, *In Your Hands.*

32. Gumbs, *In Your Hands.*

33. Gumbs, "Off-the-Hook Black Feminist Mentorship: An Anti-Capitalist Re-evaluation," *The Feminist Wire*, December 21, 2011, http://thefeministwire.com/2011/12/off-the-hook-Black-feminist-mentorship-an-anti-capitalist-re-evaluation/.

34. Gumbs, "The Shape of My Impact," *The Feminist Wire*, October 29, 2012. http://thefeministwire.com/2012/10/the-shape-of-my-impact/.

35. Celeste Henery, "And So I Write You: Practices in Black Women's Diaspora," *Meridians: feminism, race, transnationalism* 15, no. 2 (2017): 435.

36. Henery, "And So I Write You," 437.

37. Gumbs in brown and Brown, "Breathing Chorus"; and Henery, "And So I Write You," 437.

38. Gumbs in brown and Brown, "Breathing Chorus."

39. Janell Hobson, *Body as Evidence: Mediating Race, Globalizing Gender* (Albany: SUNY Press, 2012), 106.

40. Elsa Barkley Brown, "African American Political Culture Workshop Invites You to . . . ," *Elsa Barkley Brown* (blog), http://www.barkleyb.com/mobile-homecoming-project.html.

41. Alexis Pauline Gumbs and Julia Roxanne Wallace, "Something Else to Be: Generations of Black Queer Brilliance and the Mobile Homecoming Experiential Archive," in *No Tea, No Shade: New Writings in Black Queer Studies*, ed. E. Patrick Johnson (Durham, NC: Duke University Press, 2016), 382, 389, 388.

42. Gumbs, "M/other Ourselves: A Black Queer Feminist Genealogy for Radical Mothering," in *Revolutionary Mothering: Love on the Front Lines*, ed. Alexis Pauline Gumbs, China Martens, and Mai'a Williams (Oakland, CA: PM Press, 2016), 29.

43. Gumbs, "Kakuya Collective: A Visionary Daughtering Webinar," *brokenbeautiful press* (blog), November 2, 2016, http://brokenbeautiful.wordpress.com/2016/11/02/kakuya-collective-a-visionary-daughtering-webinar/.

44. Gumbs, "BlueBellow: A New Work of Underwater Afrofuturism by Alexis Pauline Gumbs," *Eternal Summer of the Black Feminist Mind* (blog), January 17, 2017, http://blackfeministmind.wordpress.com/2017/01/17/bluebellow-a-new-work-of-underwater-afrofuturism-by-alexis-pauline-gumbs/.

45. Gumbs, "Sister Is a Verb: Clarifications from the Sistorians," *Brilliance Remastered* (blog), September 20, 2013, http://brillianceremastered.alexispauline.com/2013/09/20/sister-is-a-verb-clarifications-from-the-sistorians/.

46. Joy KMT, "We Stay in Love with Our Freedom: A Conversation with Alexis Pauline Gumbs," *Los Angeles Review of Books*, February 4, 2018, http://lareviewofbooks.org/article/we-stay-in-love-with-our-freedom-a-conversation-with-alexis-pauline-gumbs/.

47. Gumbs, "The Evidence Intensive: Futurists Beyond Fear," *Brilliance Remastered* (blog), November 30, 2016, http://brillianceremastered.alexispauline.com/2016/11/30/the-evidence-intensive-futurists-beyond-fear/.

48. Gumbs, "Free Enterprise: 3-Day Intensive Towards an Autonomous Sustainable Writing Life (After Michelle Cliff)," *Brilliance Remastered* (blog), July 1, 2016, http://brillianceremastered.alexispauline.com/2016/07/01/free-enterprise-3-day-intensive-towards-an-autonomous-sustainable-writing-life-after-michelle-cliff/. See Michelle Cliff, *Free Enterprise* (New York: Penguin/Dutton, 1993).

49. Gumbs, "Dig: The Womanist Archeologies Intensive," *Brilliance Remastered* (blog), December 29, 2016, http://brillianceremastered.alexispauline.com/2016/12/29/dig-the-womanist-archeologies-intensive/.

50. Hull, *Soul Talk*, 108, 109.

51. Hull, *Soul Talk*, 126.

52. Gumbs in adrienne maree brown and Autumn Brown, hosts, "Live Show, U of M," *How to Survive the End of the World*, podcast, June 19, 2019, http://www.endoftheworldshow.org/blog/2019/6/19/live-show-u-of-m.

53. Hull, *Soul Talk*, 54–67; and Gumbs in brown and Brown, "Live Show."

54. M. Jacqui Alexander, *Pedagogies of Crossing: Meditations on Feminism, Sexual Politics, Memory, and the Sacred* (Durham, NC: Duke University Press, 2005); and Gumbs, *M Archive*, ix.

55. Gumbs in brown and Brown, "Live Show."

56. Quoted in Hull, *Soul Talk*, 134, 137.

57. Hull, *Soul Talk*, 137.

58. Gumbs, *M Archive*, xi.

59. Hobson, "Black Feminist in Public."

60. Henery, "And So I Write You," 439.

61. "Spill: Black Feminist Fugitivity Conversation and Performance," Duke University, Gender, Sexuality, & Feminist Studies, accessed May 24, 2020, http://gendersexualityfeminist.duke.edu/events/spill-Black-feminist-fugitivity-conversation-and-performance.

62. Avery Gordon, *Ghostly Matters: Haunting and the Sociological Imagination* (Minneapolis: University of Minnesota Press, 2008), 18.

63. Patricia Hill Collins and Sirma Bilge, *Intersectionality* (Cambridge, UK: Polity Press, 2016), 82.

64. Mark Anthony Neal, "Left of Black with T. J. Anderson and Alexis Pauline Gumbs," *Left of Black*, Season 1, Episode 14, YouTube video, 36:35, December 20, 2010, http://www.youtube.com/watch?v=hektAuRlcWA.

65. Gumbs, "Breathe Underwater: A Baptismal Intensive for Ancestor-Accountable Artists, Activists, and Scholars," *Brilliance Remastered* (blog), July 13, 2016, http://alexispauline.com/brillianceremastered/2016/07/13/breathe-underwater-a-baptismal-intensive-for-ancestor-accountable-artists-activists-and-scholars/. See also June Jordan, *Who Look at*

Me (New York: Crowell, 1969); and M. NourbeSe Philip, *ZONG!* (Middletown, CT: Wesleyan University Press, 2011).

66. Gumbs in Neal, "Left of Black."

67. Gumbs, "Guardian Dead: Ancestor-Led Intellectual Practice Dec. 5–8, 2013," *Brilliance Remastered* (blog), June 11, 2013, https://brillianceremastered.alexispauline.com/2013/06/11/guardian-dead-ancestral-led-intellectual-practice-in-person-gathering/.

68. Quoted in Hobson, "Black Feminist in Public."

69. Hull, *Soul Talk*, 32.

70. "Co-conspirators" is a concept promoted in progressive organizing circles. Brittany Packett Cunningham explains how the term differs from "allies": "CO-CONSPIRATORS know they are not free until everyone is free & act like it. They don't just disrupt, they build. Not episodic actions, but ever-evolving mindsets and lifestyles. They seek permission from the most oppressed & listen more than they speak." Cunningham (@MsPackyetti), "CO-CONSPIRATORS know they are not free," Twitter, May 26, 2020, 11:33 a.m., https://twitter.com/MsPackyetti/status/1265320050094997508.

71. Gumbs, "Yesterday at the UNC," Facebook, May 5, 2019, http://www.facebook.com/photo.php?fbid=10104426073225572.

72. Gumbs in brown and Brown, "Breathing Chorus."

73. Hull, *Soul Talk*, 155.

74. Samuel, "Black Speculation."

75. Quoted in Reynaldo Anderson and John Jennings, *Afrofuturism 2.0: The Rise of Astro-Blackness* (Lanham, MD: Lexington Books, 2018), vii.

76. Anderson and Jennings, *Afrofuturism 2.0*, 22.

77. Gumbs in Cantrice Penn, "Dark Sciences: A People of Color Dream Retreat—An Interview with Alexis Pauline Gumbs and Almah LaVon Rice-Faina," *Lumen*, July 21, 2015, https://web.archive.org/web/20170728020457/http://www.lumenmag.net/blog/dark-sciences.

78. Gumbs quoted in Penn, "Dark Sciences"; and Tala Khanmalek, "Collective Dreaming: An Interview with Alexis Pauline Gumbs," *The Feminist Wire*, August 10, 2015, http://thefeministwire.com/2015/08/collective-dreaming-an-interview-with-alexis-pauline-gumbs-and-almah-lavon/.

79. Rice-Faina and Gumbs quoted in Penn, "Dark Sciences."

80. Khanmalek, "Collective Dreaming."

81. Hull, *Soul Talk*, 97.

82. Hull, *Soul Talk*, 100.

83. Hull, *Soul Talk*, 46.

84. Samuel, "Black Speculation."

SELECTED BIBLIOGRAPHY

Alexander, M. Jacqui. *Pedagogies of Crossing: Meditations on Feminism, Sexual Politics, Memory, and the Sacred.* Durham, NC: Duke University Press, 2005.

Anderson, Reynaldo, and John Jennings. *Afrofuturism 2.0: The Rise of Astro-Blackness.* Lanham, MD: Lexington Books, 2018.

Bambara, Toni Cade. Preface to *Daughters of the Dust: The Making of an African-American Woman's Film*, by Julie Dash. New York: New Press, 1992.

Bambara, Toni Cade. *The Salt Eaters*. London: Women's Press, 1982.

Barkley Brown, Elsa. "African American Political Culture Workshop Invites You to. . . ." *Elsa Barkley Brown* (blog), 2011. http://www.barkleyb.com/mobile-homecoming-project.html.

"Black Feminist Breathing Chorus." Accessed November 25, 2022. https://sangodare.podia.com/breathingchorus.

brown, adrienne maree, and Autumn Brown. "A Breathing Chorus with Alexis Pauline Gumbs." *How to Survive the End of the World*. Podcast. December 19, 2017. http://www.endoftheworldshow.org/blog/2017/12/19/a-breathing-chorus-with-alexis-pauline-gumbs.

brown, adrienne maree, and Autumn Brown. "Live Show, U of M." *How to Survive the End of the World*. Podcast. June 19, 2019. http://www.endoftheworldshow.org/blog/2019/6/19/live-show-u-of-m.

Carruthers, Charlene A. *Unapologetic: A Black, Queer, and Feminist Mandate for Radical Movements*. Boston: Beacon Press, 2018.

Collins, Patricia Hill, and Sirma Bilge. *Intersectionality*. Cambridge, UK: Polity Press, 2016.

Crawley, Ashon T. *Blackpentecostal Breath: The Aesthetics of Possibility*. New York: Fordham University Press, 2017.

Cunningham, Brittany Packnett (@MsPackyetti). "CO-CONSPIRATORS know they are not free." Twitter, May 26, 2020, 11:33 a.m. https://twitter.com/MsPackyetti/status/1265320050094997508.

Factora-Borchers, Lisa, Alexis Pauline Gumbs, Nyasha Junior, Krista Riley, Danya Ruttenberg, and zaynab shahar. "Undivided State: A Conversation on Feminism and Spirituality." *Bitch Media*, December 12, 2017. http://www.bitchmedia.org/article/undivided-state/conversation-feminism-and-spirituality.

Gordon, Avery. *Ghostly Matters: Haunting and the Sociological Imagination*. 1997. Minneapolis: University of Minnesota Press, 2008.

Gumbs, Alexis Pauline. "About." *In Your Hands: Letters from My Chosen Ancestors* (blog), 2009. http://motherourselves.wordpress.com/about/.

Gumbs, Alexis Pauline. "BlueBellow: A New Work of Underwater Afrofuturism by Alexis Pauline Gumbs." *Eternal Summer of the Black Feminist Mind* (blog), January 17, 2017. http://blackfeministmind.wordpress.com/2017/01/17/bluebellow-a-new-work-of-underwater-afrofuturism-by-alexis-pauline-gumbs/

Gumbs, Alexis Pauline. "Breathe Underwater: A Baptismal Intensive for Ancestor-Accountable Artists, Activists, and Scholars." *Brilliance Remastered* (blog), July 13, 2016. http://alexispauline.com/brillianceremastered/2016/07/13/breathe-underwater-a-baptismal-intensive-for-ancestor- accountable-artists-activists-and-scholars/.

Gumbs, Alexis Pauline. "Dig: The Womanist Archaeologies Intensive." *Brilliance Remastered* (blog), December 29, 2016. http://brillianceremastered.alexispauline.com/2016/12/29/dig-the-womanist-archeologies-intensive/.

Gumbs, Alexis Pauline. "Ella Baker." *In Your Hands: Letters from My Chosen Ancestors* (blog), January 22, 2009. http://motherourselves.wordpress.com/2009/01/22/ella-baker.

Gumbs, Alexis Pauline. "The Evidence Intensive: Futurists Beyond Fear." *Brilliance Remastered* (blog), November 30, 2016. http://brillianceremastered.alexispauline.com/2016/11/30/the-evidence-intensive-futurists-beyond-fear/.

Gumbs, Alexis Pauline. "Fannie Lou Hamer." *In Your Hands: Letters from My Chosen Ancestors* (blog), January 22, 2009. http://motherourselves.wordpress.com/2009/01/22/fannie-lou-hamer.

Gumbs, Alexis Pauline. "Free Enterprise: 3-Day Intensive Towards an Autonomous Sustainable Writing Life (After Michelle Cliff)." *Brilliance Remastered* (blog), July 1, 2016. http://brillianceremastered.alexispauline.com/2016/07/01/free-enterprise-3-day-intensive-towards-an-autonomous-sustainable-writing-life-after-michelle-cliff/.

Gumbs, Alexis Pauline. "Guardian Dead: Ancestor-Led Intellectual Practice Dec. 5–8, 2013." *Brilliance Remastered* (blog), June 11, 2013. https://brillianceremastered.alexispauline.com/2013/06/11/guardian-dead-ancestral-led-intellectual-practice-in-person-gathering/.

Gumbs, Alexis Pauline. *In Your Hands: Letters from My Chosen Ancestors* (blog), 2009. http://motherourselves.wordpress.com.

Gumbs, Alexis Pauline. "Kakuya Collective: A Visionary Daughtering Webinar." *brokenbeautiful press* (blog), November 2, 2016. http://brokenbeautiful.wordpress.com/2016/11/02/kakuya-collective-a-visionary-daughtering-webinar/.

Gumbs, Alexis Pauline. "M/other Ourselves: A Black Queer Feminist Genealogy for Radical Mothering." In *Revolutionary Mothering: Love on the Front Lines*, edited by Alexis Pauline Gumbs, China Martens, and Mai'a Williams, 19–31. Oakland, CA: PM Press, 2016.

Gumbs, Alexis Pauline. "Off-the-Hook Black Feminist Mentorship: An Anti-Capitalist Re-evaluation." *The Feminist Wire*, December 21, 2011. http://thefeministwire.com/2011/12/off-the-hook-Black-feminist-mentorship-an-anti-capitalist-re-evaluation/.

Gumbs, Alexis Pauline. "Prophecy in the Present Tense: Harriet Tubman, the Combahee Pilgrimage, and Dreams Coming True." *Meridians: feminism, race, transnationalism* 12, no. 2 (2014): 142–52.

Gumbs, Alexis Pauline. "Pulse." Facebook, June 13, 2016. http://www.facebook.com/alexis.gumbs/videos/10102465290584702/.

Gumbs, Alexis Pauline. "Pulse." *Vimeo*, video, 4:36, n.d. (2016). http://vimeo.com/170498649.

Gumbs, Alexis Pauline. "The Shape of My Impact." *The Feminist Wire*, October 29, 2012. http://thefeministwire.com/2012/10/the-shape-of-my-impact/.

Gumbs, Alexis Pauline. "Sister Is a Verb: Clarifications from the Sistorians." *Brilliance Remastered* (blog), September 20, 2013. http://brillianceremastered.alexispauline.com/2013/09/20/sister-is-a-verb-clarifications-from-the-sistorians/.

Gumbs, Alexis Pauline. *Spill: Scenes of Black Feminist Fugitivity*. Durham, NC: Duke University Press, 2016.

Gumbs, Alexis Pauline. "When Goddesses Change." *The Hooded Utilitarian*, July 7, 2014. http://www.hoodedutilitarian.com/2014/07/when-goddesses-change/.

Gumbs, Alexis Pauline. "Yesterday at the UNC." Facebook, May 5, 2019. http://www.facebook.com/photo.php?fbid=10104426073225572.

Gumbs, Alexis Pauline, and Julia Roxanne Wallace. "Something Else to Be: Generations of Black Queer Brilliance and the Mobile Homecoming Experiential Archive." In *No Tea, No Shade: New Writings in Black Queer Studies*, edited by E. Patrick Johnson, 380–93. Durham, NC: Duke University Press, 2016.

Henery, Celeste. "And So I Write You: Practices in Black Women's Diaspora." *Meridians: feminism, race, transnationalism* 15, no. 2 (2017): 435–63.

Hobson, Janell. "Black Feminist in Public: Alexis Pauline Gumbs." *Ms.*, January 1, 2019. http://msmagazine.com/2019/01/01/Black-feminist-public-alexis-pauline-gumbs/.

Hobson, Janell. *Body as Evidence: Mediating Race, Globalizing Gender*. Albany: SUNY Press, 2012.

Hull, Akasha Gloria. *Soul Talk: The New Spirituality of African American Women*. Rochester, VT: Inner Traditions, 2001.

Jordan, June. *Who Look at Me*. New York: Crowell, 1969.

Khanmalek, Tala. "Collective Dreaming: An Interview with Alexis Pauline Gumbs." *The Feminist Wire*, August 10, 2015. http://thefeministwire.com/2015/08/collective-dreaming-an-interview-with-alexis-pauline-gumbs-and-almah-lavon/.

KMT, Joy. "We Stay in Love with Our Freedom: A Conversation with Alexis Pauline Gumbs." *Los Angeles Review of Books*, February 4, 2018. http://lareviewofbooks.org/article/we-stay-in-love-with-our-freedom-a-conversation-with-alexis-pauline-gumbs/.

Neal, Mark Anthony. "Left of Black with T. J. Anderson and Alexis Pauline Gumbs." *Left of Black*, Season 1, Episode 14. YouTube video, 36:35. December 20, 2010. http://www.youtube.com/watch?v=hektAuRlcWA.

Penn, Cantrice. "Dark Sciences: A People of Color Dream Retreat—An Interview with Alexis Pauline Gumbs and Almah LaVon Rice-Faina." *Lumen*, July 21, 2015. https://web.archive.org/web/20170728020457/, http://www.lumenmag.net/blog/dark-sciences.

Philip, M. NourbeSe. *ZONG!* Middletown, CT: Wesleyan University Press, 2011.

"Spill: Black Feminist Fugitivity Conversation and Performance." Duke University, Gender, Sexuality, & Feminist Studies. Accessed May 24, 2020. http://gendersexualityfeminist.duke.edu/events/spill-Black-feminist-fugitivity-conversation-and-performance.

Chapter 12

"LOVE WINS" AND BLACK LIVES MATTER

The Spiritual Underpinnings of Patrisse Cullors's Crusade for Justice

JAMI L. CARLACIO

> We don't deserve to be killed with impunity. We need to love ourselves and fight for a world where Black lives matter. Black people, I love you. I love us. We matter. Our lives matter.
> —Alicia Garza[1]

> Love is at the very heart of Black life and resistance.
> —Nicole Jackson[2]

THE BIRTH OF A MOVEMENT: CIVIL RIGHTS, CARCERAL JUSTICE, AND BLACK LOVE IN THE TWENTY-FIRST CENTURY

The acquittal of Trayvon Martin's slayer George Zimmerman on July 13, 2013, sparked a cascade of outrage and activism in the assertion of African Americans' dignity and indeed the fight for their very lives in the twenty-first century. After #BlackLivesMatter (BLM) cofounder Patrisse Cullors (1984–), with her friends Alicia Garza and Opal Tometi, began a campaign on social media to proclaim what was historically a contested idea—that *Black lives matter*—the movement gained unstoppable force in 2014, when Michael Brown Jr. was gunned down in Ferguson, Missouri, and Cullors and her fellow activists arranged a Freedom Ride and rally there. The movement, which has become part of the larger Movement for Black Lives organization and the Black Lives Matter Global Foundation, has continued to raise awareness of and to organize large- and small-scale protests against the state-sanctioned violence perpetrated against Black and Indigenous peoples and those who identify as a person of color in the US. That said, in many ways complacency has often won the day. That is, outrage and the marshalling of forces against white-on-Black assaults, formal and informal education on structural racism and its effects, consciousness-raising, and the plethora of books, conferences, and other media that address racism and promote anti-racism are still not enough to stem the tide of racial injustice in the US. No small amount of effort has been expended by those whose pale skin color affords them untold privileges and by those for whom privilege is just a shibboleth and not a reality. Yes, there has been movement in the right direction—to a point. Racialized violence, the alarming carceral rates of Black men, and structural racism in general have ratcheted up in the early decades of the twenty-first century, reminding us that there is much work to be done.

Since that fateful summer day when Zimmerman was acquitted of his crime, literally thousands of Black lives have been stamped out prematurely, including Michael Brown, Freddie Gray, Eric Garner, Tamir Rice, Philando Castile, Ahmaud Arbery, Breonna Taylor, and George Floyd, whose names are most recognized by the general public due to media coverage of both the killing and the protests afterward. These African Americans are just a sample of the more than a thousand deaths, many of which were a result of skewed versions of white justice on Black bodies.[3] Clearly, there are countless thousands of reasons why Black lives matter. As womanist theologian Kelly Brown Douglas notes, "The repeated slaying of innocent Black bodies makes it clear that there is an urgent need for soul searching within this nation."[4] And yet, the violence perpetrated on African Americans has failed to quench their insatiable drive for justice and insistence on self-love. Indeed, love of self and race and the deep, abiding belief in the presence of healing ancestor spirits are the guiding principles in Cullors's crusade.

Cullors grew up in Van Nuys, California, living with her mother, two older brothers, and younger sister in Section 8 housing "where the paint is peeling and where there is a gate that does not close properly and an intercom system that never works."[5] Identifying herself as more organizer than activist, she began her journey at sixteen and "waded all the way in" by the time she was twenty, when with the help of her high school art teacher she spent a week at the Brotherhood Sisterhood social justice camp, "learn[ing] about not only systems of oppression, but more, how to be in courageous and compassionate relationships with people—all people. Campers are like me: poor, Queer and Black."[6] By the time #BlackLivesMatter was born in 2013, Cullors had been organizing for more than a decade; and since then, the BLM Network has become part of a wider global Movement for Black Lives (M4BL), expanding to include, as of this writing, chapters in the United States, United Kingdom, and Canada. The BLM Network "affirms the lives of Black queer and trans folks, disabled folks, undocumented folks, folks with records, women, and all Black lives along the gender spectrum. Our network centers those who have been marginalized within Black liberation movements."[7] In fact, valuing *all* Black lives inclusive of all intersectional identities is the cornerstone of the organization.

Recognized for her tireless work for Black justice and liberation, Cullors has won many awards. Since her honors are too numerous to mention them all, I highlight a selection here to offer a glimpse into the life of a committed social justice warrior.[8] In 2020, she was recognized as both one of the 100 Most Influential People and among 100 Women of the Year by *Time* magazine and honored with the Law and Policy Award for Public Service and Social Justice by Loyola Law School Center for Juvenile Law and Policy. In 2019, she was honored with the Champion for Justice and Peace Award from the Trayvon Martin Foundation, and in 2018, she was named one of 21 Leaders for the 21st Century by Women's eNews. She was awarded the Sydney [Australia] Peace Prize in 2017 "for building a powerful movement for racial equality, courageously reigniting a global conversation around state violence and racism, and for harnessing the potential of new platforms and power of people to inspire a bold movement for change at a time when peace is threatened by growing inequality and injustice."[9] The previous year, 2016, she and her BLM cofounders Alicia Garza and Opal Tometi were included among *Fortune* magazine's 50 Greatest Leaders; in the same year, she was named one of *Glamour* magazine's Women of the Year. Finally, in 2015 she was included among the new civil rights leaders in the twenty-first century alongside other social justice and race leaders Michelle Alexander, Ta-Nehisi Coates, Benjamin Crump, and Fania Davis.[10]

Cullors's 2017 memoir *When They Call You a Terrorist*, coauthored with journalist asha bandele, landed on the *New York Times* bestseller list and continues to be recognized with awards, including *Library Journal*'s Best Books in 2019, demonstrating the power of the word—notwithstanding her public speaking, organizing, and art-centered activism—to galvanize people to stand up for Black lives, disrupt the business-as-usual practices of law enforcement, and dismantle the prison industrial complex.[11] These and her other numerous awards are the result of love with a little bit of rage mixed in. In an interview with *OnBeing*'s Krista Tippett, she explains this:

> Rage and love [are] at the center of our work. . . . From the beginning, Alicia Garza's "Love Note" to Black people that ended with "Our lives matter, Black lives matter," . . . was from a place of rage, but also from a place of deep love for Black people. And . . . when we show up on the freeway, when we chain ourselves to each other, that's an act of love. That act of resistance is an act of love, that we will put our bodies on the line for our community and really for this country. In changing Black lives, we change all lives.[12]

Loving as an act of resistance has political overtones, to be sure, insofar as it is revolutionary, counterhegemonic, and radical. As bell hooks puts it, "all the great movements for social justice in our society have strongly emphasized a love ethic."[13] In her analysis of love-politics during what she refers to as "second-wave" Black feminism, Jennifer Nash takes her cue from June Jordan's (rhetorical) question posed in an address at Howard University: "Where is the love?"[14] Nash says she "reads Black feminist love-politics' insistence on transcending the self and producing new forms of political communities as a kind of affective politics . . . , [described as] how bodies are organized around intensities, longings, desires, temporalities, repulsions, curiosities, fatigues, optimism, and how these affects produce political movements (or sometimes inertia)."[15] Considering how Cullors describes love as one of the driving forces behind her commitment to justice for Black lives, Nash's ideas are helpful. Nash says she is less interested in Black feminism or feminist love as one of the sites of identity politics and more interested in how, pace Alice Walker's vision of womanist love, self-love "requires a particular orientation of self, and that ethical management of the self."[16] Black feminist love-politics is essentially counterhegemonic in that it asserts itself in the Black public sphere, akin to that described in the introduction to this book. In this way, love-politics—as a singular noun with a plurality of possibilities and instantiations—is radical and disruptive. This public sphere is not a site to expose injury to Black bodies so much as it is a site in which to assert that Black bodies are "sacred possibilities" that gesture toward a future whose horizon is hope.[17] The present cannot be undone nor can the past be changed, but there is always and already hope contained in the future. And so love, along with determination, commitment, and guts, fuels Cullors's work.

In a *Los Angeles Times* article on new civil rights leaders, she told reporters, "This post-racial Obama era has sort of bamboozled a lot of us into thinking that we've come much further than we actually have."[18] While some issues inspiring protest and change have remained the same—violation of voting rights, law enforcement misconduct, racial profiling—others, such as rights for gender nonconforming persons and disproportionate rates of imprisonment for persons of color and those suffering from mental illness, are taking center stage. These latter issues are particularly important to Cullors and are why she created the Coalition to End Sheriff Violence in 2011.[19] She and other volunteers stood outside of the Los Angeles County jails talking to formerly incarcerated people and their families and gradually built a movement to confront the culture of violence in them and to protect those most affected by it. Much has been accomplished by the coalition since then, including the creation of a Sheriff Civilian Oversight Commission in 2016, whose advisory board meets monthly and allows for public comment. In a 2018 editorial in the *Los Angeles*

Times, Cullors points out that carceral violence continues and that "there is much more work to do."[20] Given that the Los Angeles County jail system is the world's largest jailer and has housed anywhere from 14,212 to 18,687 inmates at any given time, 30 percent of whom are Black, this is a daunting task.[21]

This work takes place through Dignity and Power Now (DPN), a Los Angeles-based grassroots organization Cullors founded in 2012, whose mission is "to build a Black and Brown led abolitionist movement rooted in community power towards the goal of achieving transformative justice and healing justice for all incarcerated people, their families, and communities."[22] The organization "wages a fight for all lives because the prison industrial complex forms an imaginative limit on everyone's capacity to envision freedom and liberation."[23] The prison industrial complex derives its name from the military industrial complex, the unholy alliance of the nation's military and defense contractors in a mutually beneficial profit-centered relationship. In a similar way, the prison industrial complex signifies the relationship between the nation's carceral institutions and the private sector, in which businesses supply goods and services to prisons for profit, achieved by paying pennies on the dollar for inmates' labor. The prison industrial complex, simply put, sustains global capitalism. Some sobering statistics on the disproportionate rate of incarceration of Black people in the US will make clear what's wrong with this picture. The Pew Research Center reports that "in 2017, blacks represented 12% of the U.S. adult population but 33% of the sentenced prison population. Whites accounted for 64% of adults but 30% of prisoners. And while Hispanics represented 16% of the adult population, they accounted for 23% of inmates."[24] These numbers tell a story our siblings of color know all too well: the carceral system in the US is rigged and profits at the expense of their and non-Black persons' lives. As *The New Jim Crow* author Michelle Alexander notes, her work on the Racial Justice Project at the ACLU and experience thereafter led her to realize that "mass incarceration in the United States had . . . emerged as a stunningly comprehensive and well-disguised system of social control that functions in a manner strikingly similar to Jim Crow."[25] Likewise, Brown Douglas refers to the prison industrial complex as "the new slaveocracy."[26] Specifically, she traces the pandemic of white law enforcement's extermination of the Black body from the Stand Your Ground law (an extension of English Common Law that grants persons the right to defend their property), which "signals a social-cultural climate that makes the destruction of Black bodies inevitable and even permissible."[27] The prison industrial complex, then, "is the institutional manifestation of stand-your-ground culture. . . . This culture does its job when it removes the Black body from white space (a free space) and returns it to the Black space (an unfree space)."[28]

Cullors's work to dismantle the prison industrial complex and end the violence against Black and brown people has its roots in her childhood, which included many moments of horror in her family's encounters with the police. For example, even before she was ten years old, Cullors experienced the fear that racism visits on Black people. She recalls when her fourth-grade teacher gave her a copy of Mildred E. Taylor's book *The Gold Cadillac,* an account of the drive that Taylor and her father made through the Jim Crow South to Mississippi to visit her extended family.[29] Cullors writes, "The terror in it was palpable for me, the growing sense on every page that they might be killed; by the time I was nine, police had already raided our small apartment in search of one of my favorite uncles, my father Alton's brother," a drug user and dealer.[30] The police burst into her family's apartment in full riot gear, searching even her dresser drawers, as if that is where her uncle were hiding. The gold Cadillac for Cullors represented a reality she lived: fear of the white power structure and bona fide sanctioned institutionalized racism in the form of law enforcement.

It is not a surprise, then, to find that DPN and #BLM comprise the backbone of her activism and are vehicles through which she and other Black feminist and womanist public intellectuals live out their passion for Black justice, dignity, and healing.[31] In fact, most of Cullors's activism since creating the nonprofit organization revolves around dismantling the prison industrial complex. Inspired by one of the foremost critics of the complex, the Marxist and former Black Panther member Angela Davis, Cullors has called for the abolition of a system that claims, speciously, that locking up (a disproportionate number of) Black and brown people reduces crime.[32] The real crime is the logic that undergirds the prison industrial complex. Writing for the *Harvard Law Review,* Cullors argues that "only through an abolitionist struggle will we repair our communities and undermine the systems of oppression we know have facilitated devastation, from the transatlantic slave trade through the prison industrial complex."[33] In developing her ideas, she also draws on the work of West Indian philosopher and postcolonial theorist Frantz Fanon to frame the global context of this work as well as that of poet and prose writer Audre Lorde, whose queer, Black, and feminist identities provide a lens through which to testify to the importance of abolitionist theory and methods.

Restoring Black dignity and rights requires not just the abolition of the prison industrial complex but also reparations to the Black community. Historically, these have included land redistribution, financial restitution, political self-determination, and repatriation of land that had been stolen. Cullors explains that reparations "should include restoring a balance from within our communities and carrying our autonomous healing and reparatory work through the arts, culture, language, and emotional and mental health services. Reparations must also include pressure on state accountability as well as community-driven and -centered responses, nourished and sustained by the spiritual and ancestral tradition."[34] For Black people in the US, day-to-day living is exhausting; when one adds the efforts expended to fight injustice and attempts to dismantle the systems that sanction oppression, restoration is not just crucial: it is life-affirming and life-saving.

In her abolitionist journey, Cullors outlines twelve guiding principles, which include having courageous conversations, exercising the imagination and remaining flexible and open, forgiving "actively versus passively," refraining from abusive behavior toward others, maintaining accountability, and "valuing interpersonal relationships." Without structures for restorative justice, then freedom from trauma, alternatives to incarceration, and dialogue within and outside of justice-based groups cannot take place. She cites as one example her brother's situation. When he was released from prison while in the midst of a psychotic break, Cullors and her family attempted to engage social services but were unsuccessful, thus having to resort to help from the police, who were neither trained nor prepared to handle such a situation adequately or humanely. "Abolition authentically serves and protects our loved ones," she explains. "Abolition fights to ensure that all families have access to adequate and quality health services. Abolition means not having the police as first responders to mental and emotional health crises. Abolition advocates against imprisonment and policing."[35] Her brother's experience with law enforcement while suffering from an acute mental health episode is, in fact, one of the key reasons she has been tireless in advocating for carceral reform. Fully 38 percent of the inmate population in the Los Angeles County jail system suffer from some form of mental illness.[36] According to the Prison Policy Initiative, 37 percent of the state and federal prison population have been diagnosed with mental illness; the number in local jails is 44 percent. Worse, perhaps, is the fact that 25 percent of those incarcerated "experienc[e] serious psychological distress."[37] The statistics are sobering, and one wonders whether these numbers are even accurate, given that persons suffering from mental illness may be undiagnosed or that cases are not reported. Further, these statistics suggest that mental illness has been criminalized. This is not to say that crimes were not committed, but rather that prisons and jails are not the appropriate institutions for mental illness treatment. Other examples of situations requiring the use of abolitionist principles—holding people accountable, engaging community and sharing resources, and having difficult conversations—lead to transformative justice, which is also, importantly, "a cultural intervention" and reflects the health of human relationships.[38]

Abolition leads to liberation. Thus, if we view the movement from this perspective, we see how Cullors and other #BlackLivesMatter activists have adopted a theology of liberation, with a twist. Specifically, Cullors is guided by the many of the principles that undergirded the civil rights movement led by Martin Luther King Jr., namely nonviolence, social justice, love, and the basic freedoms guaranteed in the US Constitution. Yet, the BLMM uses disruption for transformation rather than politeness or political compromises that characterized some of the negotiations of earlier movements, including the civil rights movement; specifically, the BLMM disrupts everyday life. Protestors block traffic, for example, and refuse to allow business as usual. Contrary to what BLM detractors assert, these activists are not violent rioters. Rather, taking their justice claims to the streets means, literally, putting their bodies on the line. The response to injustice is not riot or violence; it is the twenty-first-century version of the sit-in.[39] This disruption is grounded in love mixed with rage, mentioned earlier; it is expressed in singing, music, and art; and it is grounded in hope for a better now and a better, safer future.

ART AS RESISTANCE

Art, in fact, is central to Cullors's activism. As a nonviolent form of protest, art has the power to shape perceptions; galvanize supporters; and demonstrate through visual, aural, and material media expressions of hope, anger, faith, and the demands of justice-seekers. For Cullors, art has the power to transform. Though she completed a master of fine arts degree from UCLA in 2019, art has been central to her activism and organizing since the early 2000s. Even before this, in middle school, it was through various modes—dance, especially—that she learned to express herself. The description on her website explains that "Using theatre techniques, performance, audio, and movement, [Cullors's] works render bare the narratives of state-induced trauma while lifting up a path towards healing. Her work ultimately asks the audience to identify themselves in relationship to various forms of violence, be it coded in silence behind jail walls or in the coming out stories of people of color. Wielding discomfort as her medium, art becomes an invitation to shed complicity and engage broader questions of systemic violence and spiritual rejuvenation."[40] In an interview with *Rolling Stone* magazine, she explains that "the way I understand my art and my politics is they are not different from each other, and that basically what I believe in and how I live is a part of how I understand politics and art. My art and my politics are based on my values and my principles and I'm often trying to make sense of it through the political arena or the artistic arena. And I'm also having a conversation about how anti-Black racism in particular is impacting our communities."[41] She continues, saying "We cannot forget that the work that we do as artists has to be deeply aligned with the movements that are calling for artists to be some of the visionaries in this process."

Two exemplars of her performative activism—much of which was catalyzed following the shooting of Michael Brown in Ferguson—are worth noting. In

"Where Will You Go?" she and six others spread out in the middle of the Third Street Promenade in Santa Monica, where live art is commonly performed, to demonstrate vividly "the impact law enforcement declaration has on Black bodies."[42] The performers adopted various positions including kneeling with head down and hands behind the head, standing with arms spread wide, standing with hands crossed behind the back signifying the presence of handcuffs, and lying face down mimicking the position of a dead body. Well received in that space, the performers moved a couple of blocks over to Santa Monica Place, a three-story mall, and were greeted "within seconds" by security telling them to stop. "It was brilliant," she tells *Field,* a journal of socially engaged criticism, since the very fact that the space was policed and the Black bodies were unwelcome underscores the point they were making.[43]

In another dramatic performance, Cullors draws attention to the traumatic experience with law enforcement that her brother endured, which I described earlier in the chapter. Commissioned by The Broad art museum as part of its special exhibition "Shirin Neshat: I Will Greet the Sun Again" in conjunction with "Allegories of Flight," Cullors's "Prayer to the Iyami" highlights the artist's efforts to liberate her brother from incarceration and the physical and verbal abuse that came along with it.[44] Bearing gigantic wings spanning twelve feet and comprised of her brother's clothing, Cullors walks around the room full of spectators—all of whom are standing—before situating herself in a nest of the same material. In the background, James Baldwin's voice is heard speaking of two "terrifying" realizations of the Black child born in America: that "he does not exist in it, no matter where he looks—by which I mean books, magazines, movies—there is no reflection of himself anywhere . . . or if . . . he finds anything which looks like him, he is authoritatively assured that he is a savage, or a comedian who has never contributed anything to civilization."[45] Cullors's voice follows, reading from the "Yes on R" ballot measure she introduced as part of her Reform LA County Jails work.[46] The performance dramatizes the plight not just of her brother but that of the Black body in general, imprisoned by legal and extralegal means. The wings are heavy, signaling, in Cullors's words, the "two decades' worth of weight . . . [of] the impact incarceration has had on my family, and specifically my brother, because of his mental illness. We were transforming that weight into this really gorgeous set of wings suggesting the image of a bird or any being who can fly. Wings often mean freedom."[47]

Cullors's interpretation is reminiscent of the role of freedom in Black folklore. Virginia Hamilton's "The People Could Fly" tells the story of Africans who knew magic, which enabled them to fly. Once captured from their native land and shackled to each other on slave ships crossing the Atlantic to the shores of the "land of slavery," these same Africans eventually forgot they could fly.[48] The tale, told in oral fashion, recounts how the "old man Toby," an other-worldly

African ancestor, would whisper magic words in the ear of those who had heretofore possessed the magic in their homeland, reminding them of their power. Soon, many of the enslaved, worked to the bone picking cotton and often nearly beaten to death by sadistic masters, flew away to "free-dom."[49] The story is significant on at least two levels. First, it gestures toward the value of ancestors and the importance of knowing where one comes from, which I discuss in more detail later in the chapter. The flight itself makes possible a return to the source of the magic. Second, the story speaks to the indelible spirit inherent in Africans and their descendants both then and today, Cullors's being just one example. Her physical, artistic renderings of the importance of Black lives is a contemporary manifestation of the power that Black people possess and express through varied art forms.

SPIRITUALITY AND LIBERATION

Just as art performs a transformative function in Cullors's social protest, the spiritual dimension is equally important. That is, she foregrounds the role of the spirit as the basis for hope and love in the struggle for life, that is, a life worth living. In an interview with Krista Tippett, host of NPR's *OnBeing*, she explains that at the very center of the Black person's being must lie hope and the firm belief in his or her inherent goodness. And this is spiritual. Thus, the philosophy that propels BLM and indeed all of Cullors's activism to reform the criminal justice system centers on a faith practice that reaches beyond the Western Judeo-Christian tradition or by the particular Christian ethic that defines the Black church. This is not to say that the Church is completely absent or that leadership in various faith communities is not instrumental in offering members solace and healing as well as a reminder of the history of struggle and liberation. This point is the subject of a 2016 forum entitled "Race, Religion, and Black Lives Matter." In it, Terrence L. Johnson explains that "from [the Black church's] conception, clergy weaved together religion and politics to create thick and thin versions of liberation theology," which was especially present during the civil rights movement. He recalls that members of many religious traditions found a space "to reflect on the religious and political concerns of ordinary Black folk."[50] As a result, he argues, "the BLM movement inherits its call to "(re)build the Black Liberation movement" from the Black Church's historical role in developing a theology of liberation based on social justice." Significantly, he points out that the emphasis that Black Lives Matter places on liberation—as opposed to rights—"reflects a core component of the church's legacy: Liberation does not always translate into the immediate acquisition of political rights, but it must be pursued without fear or trembling." Johnson acknowledges the waning of the Black church as an institution, but at the same time he insists that "the BLM movement is a natural extension of the Black Church's historical commitment to social transformation, liberation, and justice."

Cullors would not disagree with Johnson's description of liberation since the point of #BlackLivesMatter, as well as corollary organizations such as the Movement for Black Lives and Dignity and Power Now, is inspired by the deep need for self-love, the source of true liberation. And yet the Black church's patriarchal and heteronormative and sexist structures have left little space for a wider array of personal (and faith) expressions, which challenge this self-love. As the Black church scholar Kenneth D. Johnson points out, "some of the #BlackLivesMatter folks' aversion to the Black Church is their perception of the Church's conservative stance on issues of sexual conduct, sexual identity, and sexual presentation in daily life, specifically the status of gender nonconforming persons, transgender persons, and the presence of alternative sexual behaviors and expressions as a substitute for heterosexual conduct."[51] That said, Cullors does not completely discount the Black church nor, specifically, its faith leaders wholesale. In fact, in a conversation with Alexander, she recounts how Rev. Starsky Wilson, pastor of St. John's Church in St. Louis, offered to host six hundred protesters participating in the Black Lives Matter Ferguson Freedom Ride. The original host site fell through and as a result of fellow activist Cheeraz Gormon's email to her network in the St. Louis community, Wilson called Cullors and offered his church. She recalls, "I got a call-back from Starsky Wilson, who was so profound and this is like divine to me, and he says, 'I heard you're looking for somewhere to be when . . . you get here' and I said 'yes.'" She continues, explaining how she said to him that many of those on the ride were '"a bunch of queer and trans people . . . and if your church isn't into that then we can't utilize your space,"' to which he replied, "'everybody is welcome here.'"[52] Clearly, the Black church is committed to justice and liberation, but for some, like Cullors, the inspiration need not be God- or Christ-centered.

Black feminist liberation theologians focus on the practical considerations of living, which concerns the whole self: mind, body, and spirit. Any person, group, or institution that harms another based on an ideology of hate diminishes that self and thus must be challenged. This is what liberation theology in general does. It recognizes the social, economic, and political structures of marginalization and exclusion that function as barriers to fair wages and employment; to access to health care; to adequate and safe housing; and to personal safety, regardless of one's race, gender, class, physical condition, and sexual orientation or identity. Though some liberation theologies advocate preferential treatment for marginalized groups such as African Americans, the kind of liberation that Cullors and other BLM activists seek in the struggle for human rights and dignity is broad, inclusive.[53] It is not grounded in strict Christian dogma and biblical history, "where I can find no center for myself . . . what with its anti-woman origin story," reflects Cullors in an interview.[54] The religion of her childhood—Jehovah's Witness—was problematic for similar reasons. Her mother was excommunicated from the church for having children out of wedlock, and Cullors herself left the church, realizing, she says, she "couldn't be a Jehovah's Witness and also be queer, and also be political. Jehovah's Witnesses are taught not to be in the world. I mean, literally, we are taught not to vote. . . . There are hundreds of thousands of witnesses who are eligible to vote but don't because their religion is telling them not to be in the world. This didn't seem practical to me and the life that I live. It felt like it was taking my agency away to be in the world and change the world."

More important than its exclusionary tendencies, being a Jehovah's Witness "does not feel liberating or purposeful—beyond the purpose of shaving and scaring us. It doesn't provide me the feeling of connection and spirit I feel when reading Audre Lord, whose books I carry with me everywhere." For Cullors, Lorde's *Sister Outsider* inspires her to "becom[e] my truest self."[55] An outspoken lesbian feminist and civil rights activist, Lorde's work is particularly resonant with Cullors, who came out as queer when she was in high school. She recalls feeling liberated because she no longer had to pretend to be someone she was not, and this freedom, though not without cost, is part of what sustains her. Lorde's words, written in the early 1980s, could have been written by Cullors herself: "As Black women we have the right and responsibility to recognize each other without fear and to love where we choose. Both lesbian and heterosexual Black women today share a history of bonding and strength to which our sexual identities and other differences must not blind us."[56] It is worth repeating here that one of the key principles guiding BLM is its commitment to *all* persons, "affirm[ing] the lives of Black queer and trans folks, disabled folks, undocumented folks, folks with records, women, and all Black lives along the gender spectrum. Our network centers those who have been marginalized within Black liberation movements."[57]

Thus, a Black feminist theology of liberation takes on a new, broader resonance. For Cullors and others in the movement, working outside the framework of the Black church "hasn't stopped us from being deeply spiritual in this work. And I think, for us, that looks like healing justice work, the role of healing justice."[58] Cullors bases her understanding of healing justice on the work of Cara Page, who defines it as an intervention "on generational, individual, and collective trauma—from systemic violence, oppression, policing, and violence in all of our lives by centering our psychic, emotional, physical, spiritual, and environmental well-being for our collective liberation."[59] Cullors and other Black social justice organizers and activists have felt betrayed by the church because they are queer or because they are women. Criticized by Black feminists and womanist theologians for its chauvinism, the Black church has had to contend with diminishing numbers; for Black women like Cullors and other queer Black women, institutional spiritual support has had to come from somewhere else. She tells Tippett, "we have had to contend with that during this movement. How do we relate to the Black church and how do we understand ourselves in relationship to the Black church inside of this movement?"[60] The larger questions that animate her activism, she continues, are these: "How do we show up in this work as our whole selves? How do we be in it as our best selves? And how do we look at the work of healing? Her answer is that the spirit, in its richest sense, resides inside rather than beyond the self. At the same time, the spiritual life offers a way to be in relationship with "something that is bigger than us" that allows for the presence of dignity and the power to heal, not just the person but a society in which Black people have had to endure institutionally sanctioned violence for four centuries.[61] Cullors adds that "to live in their full dignity" is the goal of those organizing around #BLM. In reflecting on her life in her memoir, she realizes that "I do know that in my heart, the heart dedicated to Black liberation, I love people. Period. I love complicated, imperfect, beautiful people. People, I suppose, like me."[62]

Healing is a predominant theme that emerges repeatedly in #BlackLivesMatter activists' description of their spiritual practice, specifically the role that spirit and healing play in their activism: as Hebah Farrag says, "Black Lives Matter chapters and affiliated groups are expressing a type of spiritual practice that makes use of the language of health and wellness to impart meaning, heal grief and trauma, combat burn-out and encourage organizational efficiency."[63] To tap into the spiritual well-being and healing of the Black community, Cullors and other Black activists have turned to the West African Yoruba religious tradition of Ifá. Cullors explains, "In Ifá we believe that all living beings, all elements of nature, are inter-dependent and possessing of soul. Rocks. Flowers. Rivers. Clouds. Thunder. The wind. These energies are called Orisha and it is these Orisha with whom we are in direct contact, whether we know it or not." She continues, "we . . . believe that our Ancestors are always with us and must be honored and acknowledged. They are part of what both grounds and guides us."[64] Being in direct contact with one's African ancestry is of primary spiritual relevance insofar as it has "allowed ancestral connections to be reestablished, restored, and renewed for native-born Black North Americans in a context where racialized identity is multifunctional," explains Africana Studies scholar Tracey Hucks.[65] When organizers gather together to mourn and honor those whose lives were lost, Cullors says, they begin with prayer, often purifying the space—usually by building an altar—with burning sage, signaling that they "'will not forget [the dead]. This protest will keep you remembered.' And Sandra

Bland was a perfect example. When she was arguably killed inside a jail cell, we said, we will not forget your name, because so often the names are forgotten."[66] Ritual and remembrance are where the sacred and the spiritual meet. Just as the enslaved Africans needed to hear the "magic words" spoken by the ancestor Toby in the story "I'll Fly Away," the altar practices make possible deep healing and reinforce the presence of (self-)love in the Black community.

The act of memorializing Black lives is not just healing and sacred; it is also political and countercultural. By this I mean that for as long as people descended from Africa have lived in the US, their lives have been rendered expendable and forgettable in the context of white supremacy. Art, demonstrations, and other acts of political resistance speak truth to power and render the seemingly impossible (that Black lives matter) possible. This paradox is explained well in Biko Mandela Gray's article "Religion in/and Black Lives Matter: Celebrating the Impossible." In it, Gray discusses the role of faith, "expressed . . . through the language of impossibility," which demonstrates a "reverence for . . . 'a celebration of' the sacrality of a Blackness that has not been deemed sacred within the context of the United States."[67] Therein lies the impossibility. Gray argues further that "Black Lives Matter names Black life—that is to say, it names *Blackness*—as *sacred*. And . . . this sacredness manifests itself as an impossible vision and goal, steeped in impossible experiences of identification and radical compassion." Without delving too far into his complex analysis of the paradox, it is worth exploring briefly how he arrives at this conclusion and why it illuminates the work Cullors and others have done to counter the historical narrative that Black lives are un-noteworthy and therefore of no consequence. As the movement has demonstrated in the depth and breadth of its growth and power, sacralizing and memorializing Black death honor Black life. Briefly, Gray draws on the work of Minkah Makalani, who argues that '"Black Lives Matter' . . . presents us with the paradigmatic noncitizen that suggests the impossibility of conjoining blackness and citizenship.'" As a player in both Black and white public spheres, the BLM movement and its constitutive elements (people) actually challenge the normative stance in white supremacist culture in which Black lives are not sacred and do not matter. By "highlighting the *impossible experience* of Blackness and . . . celebrating Black life by expressing an *impossible vision of Black sociality*," Gray posits, "BLM offers a vision of Blackness as *irreducibly sacred*, as Blackness disrupts the normative significance of the contemporary world in order to establish 'the basis for a more general moral order' based upon love and care over against the violence of distinction-making constitution" (italics in the original).[68] By the latter, Gray is referring to a distinction between the sacred and the profane, one of which is accorded privilege by virtue of one's perception. In other words, privileging one automatically relegates the other to a less-important status. In white supremacist culture, Black lives are considered profane, yet this notion is countered by the very people whose lives have principally *not* mattered. By situating Black lives in the realm of the sacred, BLM activists and allies have literally and figuratively flipped the script. They have centered the lives and deaths of Black people, memorializing the latter and valuing the former.

Such interventions in the social, political, and even religious realm are not encountered without some—or significant—resistance and violence. Specifically, centering, sacralizing, and loving Black lives have fueled political opposition in the form of specious attempts to divert public attention from racial violence perpetrated on persons of color toward a culture of fear. For example, #BLM has been referred to as "Nothing more than an American-born terrorist group" by a North Carolina police chief and as "leftist terrorists" by David Duke, who was responding to President Donald Trump's tweet about "the violent alt-left" in a press conference after a man drove his car through a crowd of counter-protesters at a white supremacist rally in Charlottesville, Virginia, in 2017, killing a young woman named Heather Heyer and injuring nineteen others.[69] The white supremacist violence that occurred at the University of Virginia that day is just one instantiation of the terror that African Americans have experienced since the first fleet of European ships transported Africans kidnapped from their West African homes in the early seventeenth century to the West Indies and to the colonial settlement in Virginia.

Being referred to as a terrorist (or to #BLM as a terrorist organization) has had the opposite of the alt-right's intended effect. Cullors's memoir, *When They Call You a Terrorist*, gives voice to victims of state-sponsored violence that reaches before and beyond Trayvon Martin. Not only does Cullors expose the spurious rhetoric of terrorism, but she dismantles it by calling attention to the insidious effects of heteronormativity, sexism, racism, ableism, and a host of other "isms" under which so many Black and brown people suffer. In writing the book, Cullors offers readers a "view from below," an unfiltered perspective that exposes a world where the behavior of a mentally ill person is perceived as criminal and where gender expression, skin color, organized religion, and poverty are markers of shame and inferiority. She writes, "Literally breathing while Black became cause for arrest—or worse."[70] Cullors's memoir, speaking for many, calls out the real terrorists and diminishes the strength of the term's rhetorical effect, reductive as it is. In it, we find a Black female public intellectual of indomitable strength whose personal struggles fueled her, as she told one newspaper, to "reignite a whole entire new generation" and "not just inside the U.S. but across the globe, centering Black people and centering the fight against white supremacy."[71] Moreover, the memoir describes a woman who takes pride in who she is, in the realm of both the material and the spiritual. It is also a rallying cry for us to pay attention.

Pointing the arrow of terror in the direction where it really belongs is reminiscent of Martin Luther King Jr.'s rhetorical move to proclaim the value of extremism when accused of it by the white moderate clergy in Birmingham, Alabama, in 1963. In his letter, written while sitting in the city's jail, he responded to their criticisms that the protests he led to end segregation were "unwise and untimely." He explained, moreover, that his presence there was necessary and called for, because "freedom is never voluntarily given by the oppressor; it must be demanded by the oppressed." Further, he counters the white clergymen's accusation that the protests are extreme by saying "oppressed people cannot remain oppressed forever," expressing satisfaction that the nonviolent direction action campaign was labeled extreme.[72] However true this is, Cullors tells D'Shonda Brown of *Essence* magazine that she "relate[s] more to the Black Panther than I do to Martin Luther King, Jr. and the Civil Rights Movement, a movement that really looks at how we not only protect and defend Black people but how do we create a new infrastructure for Black people so that we can get our needs met? The Black Panthers did that."[73] Like King and his followers, who were deemed extremists on the nonviolent end of the spectrum, the Black Panthers were declared to be militant and dangerous extremists, particularly because they preferred violence to ensure their civil rights were protected. And while they may have earned that reputation, it has eclipsed the work they did in the name of carceral reform, countering police brutality, and attempting to secure justice for Black communities.

Cullors highlights the importance of Black persons' representation in film generally, and as exemplars of Black activism particularly, with the Warner Bros. 2021 documentary *Judas and the Black Messiah* being one of them. Based on the life of Chicago Black Panther leader Fred Hampton, the film earned six Oscar nominations, among other awards. Cullors, who was named one of twelve Women in Film Pathmakers by *Essence* magazine, recognizes that the work she performs on screen, behind the camera, or in the writers' room is just as important as what she does on a canvas, on her body, or on the street. In fact, she notes the relationship between more representations of Black activism on screen and movements such as Black Lives Matter: "I think that the movement has allowed for a Black renaissance to be present."[74] She is visibly part of this renaissance, having appeared in and worked as a consultant for the script of the film *Good Trouble*, a fictional account of the real-world drama in which Black people live, namely those who die as a result of police brutality. The film draws on the Black Lives Matter Movement as a template but, says Cullors, it goes beyond this to portray the conditions and consequences of the lives stamped out by white law enforcement.[75] Like others of her ilk, Cullors has ensured that the world knows that Black lives do matter. They always have.

Drawing on the ideas and words of astrophysicist Neil deGrasse Tyson, who explains that the universe is made out of stardust, and as members of this universe we are part of that stardust, Cullors writes, "he is telling the truth because I have seen it since I was a child, the magic, the stardust we are, in the lives of the people I come from."[76] She continues, "We are not terrorists. I am not a terrorist. I am Patrisse Marie Khan-Cullors Brignac. I am a survivor. I am stardust."[77] In identifying her ancestors as stardust, Cullors is referring to the resiliency of people with African ancestry who insist on life in a culture that devalues them, as well as to the longevity of this twenty-first century civil rights movement. Cullors deliberately reframes members of the movement as American citizens ("We the People") and as herself bearing her given name; her surname Cullors; her father's family surname, Brignac; and her partner's surname, Khan, as well as proclaiming herself a survivor and as the essence of the universe:

> I am the 13th-generation progeny of a people who survived the hulls of slave ships, survived the chains, the whips, the months laying [*sic*] in their own shit and piss. The human beings legislated as not human beings who watched their names, their languages, their Goddesses and Gods, the arc of their dances and beats of their songs, the majesty of their dreams, their very families snatched up and stolen, disassembled and discarded, and despite this built language and honored God and created movement and upheld love. What could they be but stardust, these people who refused to die, who refused to accept the idea that their lives did not matter, that their children's lives did not matter?[78]

Certainly Cullors's words are echoed in Gray's point that Black lives *im*possibly matter. Her life and work—her commitment to racial justice and to prison abolition, and to calling for people descended from Africa to resist the lie that they do not matter but instead to dig deep where self-love resides and bring it up and out—are a testament to the truth of these words.

CONCLUSION: THE MOVEMENT IS MORE THAN JUST A HASHTAG: IT'S PARTICIPATORY DEMOCRACY

It would not be an overstatement to suggest that a hashtag with an assertion of the value of Black lives on a social media platform was one of the catalysts that have dramatically impacted the landscape of ostensibly intransigent structural racism and state-sanctioned violence, but that is not the whole story. The hashtag phrase and the determination and commitment of its three Black feminist cofounders who mobilized African Americans and their allies on this latest leg of the journey for Black justice are merely the most recent of many iterations of African-descended persons' calling the US to account for the wrongful treatment of, and worse, extermination of Black lives. Since the earliest years of the nineteenth century, Black women activists and intellectuals have positioned themselves in the public sphere to call attention to systemic inequities, to fight for Black justice, and to raise up Black lives. And Cullors is one powerful and committed woman who has joined their ranks. Leveraging social media along with traditional outlets created the conditions not only for the success of nationwide protests, but for a global movement to develop and thrive. Using the popular social media platforms of Twitter, Facebook, YouTube, and Instagram, Cullors is followed by hundreds of thousands of people, while the #BlackLivesMatter Facebook page is followed by more than three-quarters of a million people. This does not include followers of local chapters. Cullors's carceral reform (abolition) efforts, including Power and Dignity Now and Reform LA Jails, also employ social media, whose thousands of followers can be mobilized at a moment's notice. Though not the only public sphere in which she works, Cullors and the organizations she has founded or leads can shape and control the discourse around, about, and for Black justice, as well as counter the discourse of hate that denies it.

Using these platforms to reach multiple publics based on any number of political, social, and other demographic factors has meant that the arena for public discourse and protest has widened unimaginably and has made possible unlimited opportunities for participation by diverse groups of people whose ability to do so is not confined by spatial or temporal considerations. Because of this, the rhetoric around race, violence, Black bodies in public spaces, and carceral injustice plays out on a terrain that is certainly contested but liberating at the same time because Black voices can no longer be silenced. #BlackLivesMatter has its share of detractors who promulgate racist rhetoric and attempt to cancel the movement; but recent history has proven, and specifically Cullors's own efforts have demonstrated, the power of solidarity. Though she is not alone in her efforts to make #BlackLivesMatter, Power and Dignity Now, or other causes promoting Black justice formidable forces, her tireless efforts as a public intellectual who is informed by the principles of healing justice and the spiritual power of her Black ancestors have positioned her among the many other Black women for whom "no" was and is just not an acceptable answer. Her commitment to end the oppression of African American people has put her in harm's way—she has received death threats via phone, mail, and social media—but her organizing and advocacy for the Black community are undergirded by a deep and abiding belief in the spirit that overrides any hesitation to act based on such threats.[79] "Part of our calling as people who do this work for Black lives," she asserts, "is to lift our people up, both in their living, but also in their death. . . . The need to lift our folks up feels so incredibly spirit-driven for me."[80]

NOTES

1. Alicia Garza, Facebook post, July 13, 2013, qtd. in Patrisse Khan-Cullors and asha bandele, *When They Call You a Terrorist* (New York: St. Martin's Press, 2017), 180–81.

2. Nicole Jackson, "Black Love as Activism," *Black Perspectives*, February 28, 2018, https://www.aaihs.org/Black-love-as-activism/.

3. There are many websites that catalog the deaths of Black women and men by white police officers. Some, like that of the *Washington Post*, have collated data from 2015 to 2020 on shooting deaths of Black people alone. Of those shot, more than 130 were unarmed. See Julie Tate, Jennifer Jenkins, and Steven Rich, "Fatal Force," *Washington Post*, updated June 3, 2021. https://www.washingtonpost.com/graphics/investigations/police-shootings-database/.

4. Kelly Brown Douglas, *Stand Your Ground: Black Bodies and the Justice of God* (Maryknoll, NY: Orbis Books, 2015), xiii.

5. Khan-Cullors and bandele, *Terrorist*, 9.

6. Cullors "identif[ies] as an organizer versus an activist because . . . [an] organizer is the person who gets the press together and who builds new leaders, the person who helps to build and launch campaigns, and is the person who decides what the targets will be and how we're going to change this world." Patrisse Cullors, https://patrissecullors.com/about/, accessed August 18, 2018. That said, she is referred to as both an activist and an organizer in print and digital media. I use both "activist" and "organizer" throughout this chapter. Khan-Cullors and bandele, *Terrorist*, 86–87.

7. "About," Black Lives Matter, accessed January 1, 2020, https://blacklivesmatter.com/about/.

8. For a complete list of awards, including those relating to her memoir, visit https://patrissecullors.com/awards/. In 2021, the Swedish Academy nominated BlackLivesMatter for the Nobel Peace Prize.

9. "2017 Black Lives Matter: Movement for Freedom, Justice, and Dignity for All Black Lives," Sydney Peace Foundation, University of Sydney, accessed November 25, 2022, http://sydneypeacefoundation.org.au/peace-prize-recipients/Black-lives-matter/.

10. For a full list, see Matt Pearce and Kurtis Lee, "The New Civil Rights Leaders: Emerging Voices in the 21st Century," *Los Angeles Times*, March 5, 2015, https://www.latimes.com/nation/la-na-civil-rights-leaders-br-20150304-htmlstory.html.

11. On the Women's eNews website celebrating her book during Black History Month in 2018, Cullors is quoted as saying, "I hope this book reinvigorates our work across the globe. I will continue to create, organize, and shut it down until all Black lives matter." Isokol, "For Black History Month: Meet '21 Leader for the 21st Century' Patrisse Cullors," *Women's eNews*, February 19, 2018, https://womensenews.org/2018/02/for-Black-history-month-meet-21-leader-for-the-21st-century-patrisse-cullors/.

12. Patrisse Cullors and Robert Ross, "The Spiritual Work of Black Lives Matter," Interview by Krista Tippett, *OnBeing*, NPR, February 18, 2016, https://onbeing.org/programs/patrisse-cullors-and-robert-ross-the-spiritual-work-of-Black-lives-matter-may2017/.

13. Quoted in Jennifer Nash, "Practicing Love: Black Feminism, Love-Politics, and Post-Intersectionality," *Meridians* 11, no. 2 (2011): 2.

14. Nash, "Practicing Love," 2.

15. Nash, "Practicing Love," 3.

16. Nash, "Practicing Love," 5, 10.

17. Nash is quoting June Jordan's concept of "sacred possibility," which can be decoupled from the "seductive hold" of power. See Nash, "Practicing Love," 16.

18. Pearce and Lee, "New Civil Rights Leaders."

19. "About Us," Dignity and Power Now, accessed November 25, 2022, http://dignityandpowernow.org/about-us.

20. Cullors, "Op-Ed: My Brother's Abuse in Jail Is a Reason I Co-Founded Black Lives Matter. We Need Reform in L.A.," *Los Angeles Times*, April 13, 2013, https://www.latimes.com/opinion/op-ed/la-oe-cullors-los-angeles-sheriff-jail-reform-20180413-story.html.

21. "Los Angeles County Jail System by the Numbers," *Los Angeles Almanac*, updated for 2021, http://www.laalmanac.com/crime/cr25b.php. The lower number represents the average daily inmate population in 2020 and the larger number represents the average daily inmate population in 2013. The proportion of Black inmates to that of the population in Los Angeles County—30 percent to 8 percent—is one of the chief concerns of Dignity and Power Now.

22. "About Us," Dignity and Power Now.

23. "Dignity and Power Now," Media Justice, updated 2021, https://mediajustice.org/network-directory/dignity-and-power-now/.

24. John Gramlich, "The Gap between the Number of Blacks and Whites in Prison Is Shrinking," Pew Research Center, Fact Tank, https://www.pewresearch.org/fact-tank/2019/04/30/shrinking-gap-between-number-of-blacks-and-whites-in-prison/. The title of this report may lead some to think the tide is turning positive for African Americans, but this is not the case. Black persons are incarcerated at six times the rate (number of incarcerated persons per 100,000 people) of white persons. A number of factors may account for the gap, including increased incarceration rates of whites for drug-related and sex offenses. See Keith Humphreys, "There's Been a Big Decline in the Black Incarceration Rate, and Almost Nobody's Paying Attention," *Washington Post*, February 10, 2016, https://www.washingtonpost.com/news/wonk/wp/2016/02/10/almost-nobody-is-paying-attention-to-this-massive-change-in-criminal-justice. In a study based on the 2010 US Census, the Prison Policy Initiative reported that, in hundreds of counties across the US, prisons house a disproportionate number of African Americans; in these cases, there are more Blacks in prison than free. See Peter Wagner and Daniel Kopf, "The Racial Geography of Mass Incarceration," Prison Policy Initiative, July 2015, https://www.prisonpolicy.org/racialgeography/report.html.

25. Alexander, *New Jim Crow*, 4.

26. Brown Douglas, *Stand Your Ground*, 80. Both Alexander's and Brown Douglas's thoroughly well-researched studies require an in-depth treatment that is beyond the scope of this chapter.

27. Brown Douglas, *Stand Your Ground*, xiii.

28. Brown Douglas, *Stand Your Ground*, 80.

29. Mildred E. Taylor, *The Gold Cadillac* (Logan, IA: Perfection Learning, 1998).

30. Khan-Cullors and bandele, *Terrorist*, 20.

31. In May 2021, Cullors transitioned from her role as executive director of the Black Lives Global Network Foundation to "support grassroots, art/culture work and policy work that invests in the future of Black lives." See "Black Lives Matter Global Network Foundation Announces Leadership Transition," Black Lives Matter, May 27, 2021, https://blacklivesmatter.com/Black-lives-matter-global-network-foundation-announces-leadership-transition/.

32. See Gramlich, "Gap Between." The Sentencing Project reports on the "racial disparity that pervades the US criminal justice system, and for African Americans in particular. . . . African Americans are more likely than white Americans to be arrested; once arrested, they are more likely to be convicted; and once convicted, they are more likely to experience lengthy prison sentences. Quoting a 2016 report from the Bureau of Labor Statistics (BLS), [it says] African-American adults are 5.9 times as likely to be incarcerated than whites and Hispanics are 3.1 times as likely." To dramatize the status of carceral injustice further, the Sentencing Project notes that Black men are six times as likely to be incarcerated as white men and Latinos are 2.5 times as likely. For Black men in their thirties, about one in every twelve is in prison or jail on any given day. See "Criminal Justice Facts," The Sentencing Project, updated 2022, https://www.sentencingproject.org/criminal-justice-facts/.

33. Cullors, "Abolition and Reparations: Histories of Resistance, Transformative Justice, and Accountability," *Harvard Law Review*, April 10, 2019, 1684, https://harvardlawreview.org/2019/04/abolition-and-reparations-histories-of-resistance-transformative-justice-and-accountability/.

34. Cullors, "Abolition and Reparations," 1687.

35. Cullors, "Abolition and Reparations," 1990.

36. "Los Angeles County Jail System by the Numbers."

37. "Mental Health: Policies and Practices Surrounding Mental Health," Prison Policy Initiative, accessed November 25, 2022, https://www.prisonpolicy.org/research/mental_health/. These statistics, from studies conducted in 2011–12, are explained more fully in Jennifer Bronson and Marcus Berzofsky, "Indicators of Mental Health Problems Reported by Prisoners and Jail Inmates, 2011–12," US Department of Justice, Office of Programs, Bureau of Justice Statistics, June 2017, https://www.bjs.gov/content/pub/pdf/imhprpji1112.pdf.

38. Cullors, "Abolition and Reparations," 1694.

39. For helpful commentary on the relationship between #BlackLivesMatter and the Black church as well as its relationship to the civil rights movement, see Barbara A. Holmes, *Joy Unspeakable: Contemplative Practices of the Black Church*, 2nd ed. (Minneapolis: Fortress Press, 2017), 141–62.

40. "Artist Portfolio," Patrisse Cullors, accessed January 1, 2021, https://patrissecullors.com/artist/.

41. Quoted in Reed Dunlea, "Black Lives Matter Co-Founder on Building a Movement through Art," *Rolling Stone*, June 23, 2020, https://www.rollingstone.com/culture/culture-features/Black-lives-matter-protest-art-patrisse-cullors-broad-museum-1019078/.

42. Quoted in Dunlea, "Black Lives Matter."

43. Grant Kester, "Interview with Patrisse Cullors," *Field* 14 (Fall 2019), http://field-journal.com/issue-14/interview-with-patrisse-cullors.

44. In the Yoruba tradition, Iyami Aje describes a woman of African descent with the supernatural ability to heal and destroy as well as the capacity for political organization

and empowerment. See Theresa N. Washington, *The Architects of Existence: Aje in Yoruba Cosmology, Ontology, and Orature* (n.p.: Oya's Tornado, 2014).

45. James Baldwin, qtd. in Harlem Youth Opportunities Limited, Inc., *Youth in the Ghetto* (New York, 1964), 503–4. See John Runcie, "The Black Culture Movement and the Black Community," *American Studies* 10, no. 2 (August 1976): 185–214. The excerpt, from a speech Baldwin delivered in 1963, appears in Runcie's essay, 185–86.

46. "Performance: Allegories of Flight," The Broad, 2021, https://www.thebroad.org/events/allegories-flight. Also available on YouTube: https://youtu.be/bco1o-TKNlg.

47. Patrisse Cullors, Interview with Delia Brown, *Art Forum*, May 12, 2020, https://www.artforum.com/interviews/patrisse-cullors-talks-about-decarceration-and-her-activist-art-83031.

48. Virginia Hamilton, "The People Could Fly," in *The People Could Fly: American Black Folktales* (New York: Knopf, 1985), 166–67.

49. Hamilton, "People Could Fly," 171–72.

50. Terrence L. Johnson, "Black Lives Matter and the Black Church," *Race, Religion, and Black Lives Matter* (blog), October 19, 2016, https://berkleycenter.georgetown.edu/events/race-religion-and-Black-lives-matter.

51. Kenneth D. Johnson, "#BlackLivesMatter as a Secular Black Political Theology: Ethical and Practical Implications of the First New Black Social Movement of the 21st Century," *Telos*, February 8, 2016, http://www.telospress.com/blacklivesmatter-as-a-secular-Black-political-theology-ethical-and-practical-implications-of-the-first-new-Black-social-movement-of-the-21st-century/.

52. "Spirit of Justice: A Conversation between Michelle Alexander and Patrisse Cullors," Union Theological Seminary (New York City), April 19, 2018, YouTube, https://youtu.be/g37Hze3dGTM.

53. A case in point is the early instantiation of Black liberation theology, first articulated by James Cone, who asserted that the Jesus who cared for the oppressed of society was Black and that any white-centered Christian theology elided people of color. See James Cone, *Black Theology and Black Power* (Maryknoll, NY: Orbis, 1997) and *A Black Theology of Liberation*, 40th anniversary ed. (Maryknoll, NY: Orbis, 2010).

54. Trent Kannegieter, "Activist, Friend, Comrade: Interview with Patrisse Cullors, Co-Founder of Black Lives Matter," *The Politic*, November 28, 2018, https://thepolitic.org/activist-friend-comrade-interview-with-patrisse-cullors-co-founder-of-Black-lives-matter/.

55. Khan-Cullors and bandele, *Terrorist*, 72.

56. Audre Lorde, "Scratching the Surface: Some Notes on Barriers to Women and Loving," in *Sister Outsider* (Trumansburg, NY: Crossing Press, 1984), 52.

57. "About," BlackLivesMatter, accessed November 25, 2022, https://blacklivesmatter.com/about/.

58. Cullors and Ross, "Spiritual Work of Black Lives Matter."

59. Patrisse Cullors and Cara Page, "What Is Healing Justice?," Video, *Good Morning America*, July 24, 2020, https://www.goodmorningamerica.com/culture/video/healing-justice-71932989. The BlackLivesMatter website includes a resource entitled "Healing Action Toolkit" and a downloadable document for readers wanting to read more about the principles of healing justice; see https://blacklivesmatter.com/resources/.

60. Cullors and Ross, "Spiritual Work of Black Lives Matter."

61. Quoted in Vincent Lloyd et al., "Religion, Secularism, and Black Lives Matter," *The Immanent Frame*, September 22, 2016, 224, https://tif.ssrc.org/2016/09/22/religion-secularism-and-Black-lives-matter/.

62. Khan-Cullors and bandele, *Terrorist*, 142.

63. Hebah Farrag, "The Role of the Spirit in #BlackLivesMatter Movement," Commentary, Center for Religion and Civic Culture, University of Southern California, June 24, 2015, https://crcc.usc.edu/the-role-of-the-spirit-in-blacklivesmatter-movement/. For extended treatment of the subject, see Farrag, "The Spirit in Black Lives Matter: New Spiritual Community in Black Radical Organizing," *Transition* 125 (2018): 76–88.

64. Khan-Cullors and bandele, *Terrorist*, 151.

65. Tracey Hucks, "African Americans in the U.S.A. Bring Something Different to Ifa: Indigenizing Yoruba Religious Cultures," in Tracey Hucks, *Yoruba Traditions and African American Religious Nationalism* (Albuquerque: University of New Mexico Press, 2012), 272.

66. Cullors and Ross, "Spiritual Work of Black Lives Matter." Phillip Luke Sinitiere's chapter in this volume, "Sandy Speaks," reflects this sentiment.

67. Biko Mandela Gray, "Religion in/and Black Lives Matter: Celebrating the Impossible," *Religion Compass* 13, no. 1 (January 2019): 2, https://doi.org/10.1111/rec3.12293. The words quoted in the larger quotation are those of Fred Moten, whose work Gray draws on.

68. Gray, "Religion in/and Black Lives Matter," 5.

69. "NC Police Chief Who Retired After Calling 'Black Lives Matter' a 'Terrorist Group' Speaks Out," Myfox8.com, updated October 25, 2015, https://myfox8.com/news/nc-police-chief-who-retired-after-calling-Black-lives-matter-a-terrorist-group-speaks-out/; and "Charlottesville: Trump Reverts to Blaming Both Sides Including 'Violent Alt-Left,'" *The Guardian*, US edition, August 15, 2017, https://www.theguardian.com/us-news/2017/aug/15/donald-trump-press-conference-far-right-defends-charlottesville. On August 12, 2017, white supremacists held a "Unite the Right" rally at the University of Virginia to protest the removal of a statue of Civil War general Robert E. Lee on campus. Counter-protesters also convened, raising the crescendo of the protest, which ended in violence. A Toledo, Ohio, man drove his car into the crowd, crashing into another car and killing a Charlottesville woman. Nineteen persons were also injured. There are many book-length accounts of the tragedy that speak to its causes and its aftermath. See, for example, Terry McAuliffe, *Beyond Charlottesville: Taking a Stand against White Supremacism* (New York: St. Martin's Press, 2019); and Hawes Spencer, *Summer of Hate: Charlottesville, USA* (Charlottesville: University of Virginia Press, 2018).

70. Khan-Cullors and bandele, *Terrorist*, 8.

71. Patrisse Cullors, qtd. in Jamiles Lartey, "'We've Ignited a Whole New Generation': Patrisse Khan-Cullors on the Resurgence of Black Activism," *The Guardian*, US edition, January 28, 2018, https://www.theguardian.com/us-news/2018/jan/28/patrisse-khan-cullors-Black-lives-matter-interview.

72. Martin Luther King Jr., "Letter from Birmingham Jail," April 16, 1963, The Martin Luther King, Jr. Research and Education Institute, Stanford University, https://kinginstitute.stanford.edu/encyclopedia/letter-birmingham-jail.

73. D'Shonda Brown, "Patrisse Cullors' [sic] Vision of Social Activism Is Coming to Life through Her Work in Film," *Essence*, updated March 15, 2021, https://www.essence.com/articles/patrisse-cullors-social-activism-vision/.

74. Brown, "Patrisse Cullors' [*sic*] Vision of Social Activism."

75. See Kaitlin Reilly, "Black Lives Matter's Patrisse Cullors Talks the Most Challenging *Good Trouble* Storyline," *Refinery 29*, March 27, 2019, Vice Media Group, https://www.refinery29.com/en-us/2019/03/228125/patrisse-cullors-good-trouble-Black-lives-matter.

76. Khan-Cullors and bandele, *Terrorist*, 4.

77. Khan-Cullors and bandele, *Terrorist*, 8.

78. Khan-Cullors and bandele, *Terrorist*, 4–5.

79. Cullors, "FBI Contacted Me Yesterday," Instagram, June 10, 2021, https://www.instagram.com/p/CP8crxQnzWw/. The full text of the post reads, "FBI contacted me yesterday. Another threat on my life. Separate from the threat I received last year. I receive death threats via email, phone calls, and via my social media. An abolitionist world means an end to white supremacist threats and violence." Besides these serious threats, Cullors has been the subject of criticism on the left and the right for mismanagement of funds in the #BLM coffers. See, for example, Snejana Farverov, "BLM Co-Founder Patrisse Cullors Says Her Mistakes with 'White Guilt Money' Were Weaponized against Her," *New York Post*, May 18, 2022, https://nypost.com/2022/05/18/blm-co-founder-patrisse-cullors-says-white-guilt-money-mistakes-weaponized-against-her/; and Ailsa Chang, "Secret $6 Million Home Has Allies and Critics Skeptical of BLM Foundation's Finances," *All Things Considered*, NPR, April 7, 2022, https://www.npr.org/2022/04/07/1091487910/blm-leaders-face-questions-after-allegedly-buying-a-mansion-with-donation-money.

80. Alejandra Molina, "Black Lives Matter Is 'a Spiritual Movement,' Says Co-Founder Patrisse Cullors," *Religion News Service*, June 15, 2020, https://religionnews.com/2020/06/15/why-Black-lives-matter-is-a-spiritual-movement-says-blm-co-founder-patrisse-cullors/.

SELECTED BIBLIOGRAPHY

Alexander, Michelle. *The New Jim Crow: Mass Incarceration in the Age of Colorblindness*. Rev. ed. New York: New Press, 2012.

Andrews, William, ed. *Sisters of the Spirit: Three Black Women's Autobiographies of the Nineteenth Century*. Bloomington: Indiana University Press, 1986.

Baldwin, James. Speech delivered in 1963. Cited in John Runcie, "The Black Culture Movement and the Black Community." *American Studies* 10, no. 2 (August 1976): 185–214.

Black Lives Matter. "About." Accessed June 15, 2020. https://blacklivesmatter.com/about/.

Black Lives Matter. "Black Lives Matter Global Network Foundation Announces Leadership Transition," May 27, 2021. https://blacklivesmatter.com/Black-lives-matter-global-network-foundation-announces-leadership-transition/.

Blain, Keisha. "Writing Black Women's Intellectual History." *Black Perspectives* (blog), November 21, 2016. https://www.aaihs.org/writing-Black-womens-intellectual-history/.

Broad, The. "Performance: Allegories of Flight." 2021. https://www.thebroad.org/events/allegories-flight.

Bronson, Jennifer, and Marcus Berzofsky. "Indicators of Mental Health Problems Reported by Prisoners and Jail Inmates, 2011–12." US Department of Justice, Bureau of Justice Statistics, June 2017. https://www.bjs.gov/content/pub/pdf/imhprpji1112.pdf.

Brown, D'Shonda. "Patrisse Cullors' [*sic*] Vision of Social Activism Is Coming to Life through Her Work in Film." *Essence*, March 15, 2021. https://www.essence.com/articles/patrisse-cullors-social-activism-vision/.

Chang, Ailsa. "Secret $6 Million Home Has Allies and Critics Skeptical of BLM Foundation's Finances." *All Things Considered*, NPR, April 7, 2022. https://www.npr.org/2022/04/07/1091487910/blm-leaders-face-questions-after-allegedly-buying-a-mansion-with-donation-money.

"Charlottesville: Trump Reverts to Blaming Both Sides Including 'Violent Alt-Left.'" *The Guardian*, US Edition, August 15, 2017. https://www.theguardian.com/us-news/2017/aug/15/donald-trump-press-conference-far-right-defends-charlottesville.

Combahee River Collective. "The Combahee River Collective Statement." Library of Congress Web Archive. https://www.loc.gov/item/lcwaN0028151/.

Cone, James. *Black Theology and Black Power*. Maryknoll, NY: Orbis, 1997. First published 1969 by Harper & Row.

Cone, James. *A Black Theology of Liberation*. 40th anniversary ed. Maryknoll, NY: Orbis, 2010. First published 1970 by J. B. Lippincott.

Crenshaw, Kimberlé. "Demarginalizing the Intersection of Race and Sex: A Black Feminist Critique of Antidiscrimination Doctrine, Feminist Theory and Antiracist Politics." *University of Chicago Legal Forum* 1 (1989): Article 8, 139–67. https://chicagounbound.uchicago.edu/uclf/vol1989/iss1/8.

Cullors, Patrisse. "Abolition and Reparations: Histories of Resistance, Transformative Justice, and Accountability." *Harvard Law Review*, April 10, 2019, 1684–94. https://harvardlawreview.org/2019/04/abolition-and-reparations-histories-of-resistance-transformative-justice-and-accountability/.

Cullors, Patrisse. Interview with Delia Brown. *Art Forum*, May 12, 2020. https://www.artforum.com/interviews/patrisse-cullors-talks-about-decarceration-and-her-activist-art-83031.

Cullors, Patrisse. "Op-Ed: My Brother's Abuse in Jail Is a Reason I Co-Founded Black Lives Matter. We Need Reform in L.A." *Los Angeles Times*, April 13, 2013. https://www.latimes.com/opinion/op-ed/la-oe-cullors-los-angeles-sheriff-jail-reform-20180413-story.html.

Cullors, Patrisse, and Cara Page. "What Is Healing Justice?" Video, *Good Morning America*, July 24, 2020. https://www.goodmorningamerica.com/culture/video/healing-justice-71932989.

Cullors, Patrisse, and Robert Ross. "The Spiritual Work of Black Lives Matter." Interview by Krista Tippett. *OnBeing*, NPR, February 18, 2016. https://onbeing.org/programs/patrisse-cullors-and-robert-ross-the-spiritual-work-of-Black-lives-matter-may2017/.

Dignity and Power Now. "About Us." Accessed June 10, 2020. http://dignityandpowernow.org/.

Douglas, Kelly Brown. *Stand Your Ground: Black Bodies and the Justice of God*. Maryknoll, NY: Orbis Books, 2015.

Dunlea, Reed. "Black Lives Matter Co-Founder on Building a Movement through Art." *Rolling Stone*, June 23, 2020. https://www.rollingstone.com/culture/culture-features/Black-lives-matter-protest-art-patrisse-cullors-broad-museum-1019078/.

Farrag, Hebah. "The Role of the Spirit in #BlackLivesMatter Movement." Commentary. Center for Religion and Civic Culture, University of Southern California, June 24, 2015. https://crcc.usc.edu/the-role-of-the-spirit-in-blacklivesmatter-movement/.

Farrag, Hebah. "The Spirit in Black Lives Matter: New Spiritual Community in Black Radical Organizing." *Transition* 125 (2018): 76–88.

Farverov, Snejana. "BLM Co-Founder Patrisse Cullors Says Her Mistakes with 'White Guilt Money' Were Weaponized against Her." *New York Post*, May 18, 2022. https://nypost.com/2022/05/18/blm-co-founder-patrisse-cullors-says-white-guilt-money-mistakes-weaponized-against-her/.

Gramlich, John. "The Gap between the Number of Blacks and Whites in Prison Is Shrinking." *Pew Research Center*, April 30, 2019. https://www.pewresearch.org/fact-tank/2019/04/30/shrinking-gap-between-number-of-blacks-and-whites-in-prison/.

Gray, Biko Mandela. "Religion in/and Black Lives Matter: Celebrating the Impossible." *Religion Compass* 13, no. 1 (January 2019): 1–9. https://doi.org/10.1111/rec3.12293.

Hamilton, Virginia. "The People Could Fly." In *The People Could Fly: American Black Folktales*, 166–72. New York: Knopf, 1985.

Holmes, Barbara A. *Joy Unspeakable: Contemplative Practices of the Black Church*. 2nd ed. Minneapolis: Fortress Press, 2017.

Hucks, Tracey. "'Afrikan Americans in the U.S.A. Bring Something Different to Ifa': Indigenizing Yoruba Religious Cultures." In Tracey Hucks, *Yoruba Traditions and African American Religious Nationalism*, 271-310. Albuquerque: University of New Mexico Press, 2012.

Humphreys, Keith. "There's Been a Big Decline in the Black Incarceration Rate, and Almost Nobody's Paying Attention." *Washington Post*, February 10, 2016. https://www.washingtonpost.com/news/wonk/wp/2016/02/10/almost-nobody-is-paying-attention-to-this-massive-change-in-criminal-justice.

Isokol. "For Black History Month: Meet '21 Leader for the 21st Century' Patrisse Cullors." *Women's eNews*, February 2018. https://womensenews.org/2018/02/for-Black-history-month-meet-21-leader-for-the-21st-century-patrisse-cullors/.

Jackson, Nicole. "Black Love as Activism." *Black Perspectives*, February 28, 2018. https://www.aaihs.org/Black-love-as-activism/.

Johnson, Terrence L. "Black Lives Matter and the Black Church." *Race, Religion, and Black Lives Matter* (blog), October 19, 2016. https://berkleycenter.georgetown.edu/events/race-religion-and-Black-lives-matter.

Kannegieter, Trent. "Activist, Friend, Comrade: Interview with Patrisse Cullors, Co-Founder of Black Lives Matter." *The Politic*, November 28, 2018. https://thepolitic.org/activist-friend-comrade-interview-with-patrisse-cullors-co-founder-of-Black-lives-matter/.

Kester, Grant. "Interview with Patrisse Cullors." *Field* 14 (Fall 2019). http://field-journal.com/issue-14/interview-with-patrisse-cullors.

Khan-Cullors, Patrisse, and asha bandele. *When They Call You a Terrorist*. New York: St. Martin's Press, 2017.

King, Martin Luther, Jr. "Letter from Birmingham Jail." April 16, 1963. The Martin Luther King, Jr. Research and Education Institute, Stanford University. https://kinginstitute.stanford.edu/encyclopedia/letter-birmingham-jail.

Lartey, Jamiles. "'We've Ignited a Whole New Generation': Patrisse Khan-Cullors on the Resurgence of Black Activism." *The Guardian* (US Edition), January 28, 2018. https://www.theguardian.com/us-news/2018/jan/28/patrisse-khan-cullors-Black-lives-matter-interview.

Lloyd, Vincent, Wel Alcenat, Ahmad Greene-Hayes, Su'ad Abdul Khabeer, Pamela R. Lightsey, Jennifer C. Nash, Jeremy Posadas, Melynda Price, Cheryl J. Sanders, Peter Slade,

Josef Sorett, and Terrance Wiley. "Religion, Secularism, and Black Lives Matter." *The Immanent Frame*, September 22, 2016. https://tif.ssrc.org/2016/09/22/religion-secularism-and-Black-lives-matter/.

Lorde, Audre. "Scratching the Surface: Some Notes on Barriers to Women and Loving." In *Sister Outsider*, 45–59. Trumansburg, NY: Crossing Press, 1984.

Los Angeles Almanac. "Los Angeles County Jail System by the Numbers." Updated 2021. http://www.laalmanac.com/crime/cr25b.php.

McAuliffe, Terry. *Beyond Charlottesville: Taking a Stand against White Supremacism*. New York: St. Martin's Press, 2019.

Media Justice. "Dignity and Power Now." Updated 2021. https://mediajustice.org/network-directory/dignity-and-power-now/.

Molina, Alejandra. "Black Lives Matter Is 'a Spiritual Movement,' Says Co-Founder Patrisse Cullors." *Religion News Service*, June 15, 2020. https://religionnews.com/2020/06/15/why-Black-lives-matter-is-a-spiritual-movement-says-blm-co-founder-patrisse-cullors/.

MyFox8. "NC Police Chief Who Retired After Calling 'Black Lives Matter' a 'Terrorist Group' Speaks Out." MyFox8, updated October 25, 2015. https://myfox8.com/news/nc-police-chief-who-retired-after-calling-Black-lives-matter-a-terrorist-group-speaks-out/.

Pearce, Matt, and Kurtis Lee. "The New Civil Rights Leaders: Emerging Voices in the 21st Century." *Los Angeles Times*, March 5, 2015. https://www.latimes.com/nation/la-na-civil-rights-leaders-br-20150304-htmlstory.html.

Prison Policy Initiative. "Mental Health: Policies and Practices Surrounding Mental Health." Updated June 15, 2021. https://www.prisonpolicy.org/research/mental_health/.

Reilly, Kaitlin. "Black Lives Matter's Patrisse Cullors Talks the Most Challenging *Good Trouble* Storyline." *Refinery 29*, March 27, 2019. Vice Media Group. https://www.refinery29.com/en-us/2019/03/228125/patrisse-cullors-good-trouble-Black-lives-matter.

Sentencing Project. "Criminal Justice Facts." Updated 2019. https://www.sentencingproject.org/criminal-justice-facts/.

Spencer, Hawes. *Summer of Hate: Charlottesville, USA*. Charlottesville: University of Virginia Press, 2018.

"Spirit of Justice: A Conversation between Michelle Alexander and Patrisse Cullors." Union Theological Seminary (New York City), April 19, 2018. YouTube. https://youtu.be/g37Hze3dGTM.

Sydney Peace Foundation. "2017 Black Lives Matter: Movement for Freedom, Justice, and Dignity for All Black Lives." University of Sydney. Accessed November 25, 2022. http://sydneypeacefoundation.org.au/peace-prize-recipients/Black-lives-matter/.

Tate, Julie, Jennifer Jenkins, and Steven Rich. "Fatal Force." *Washington Post*, updated June 3, 2021. https://www.washingtonpost.com/graphics/investigations/police-shootings-database/.

Taylor, Mildred E. *The Gold Cadillac*. Logan, IA: Perfection Learning, 1998.

Wagner, Peter, and Daniel Kopf. "The Racial Geography of Mass Incarceration." *Prison Policy Initiative*, July 2015. https://www.prisonpolicy.org/racialgeography/report.html.

Washington, Teresa N. *The Architects of Existence: Aje in Yoruba Cosmology, Ontology, and Orature*. n.p.: Oya's Tornado, 2014.

ABOUT THE CONTRIBUTORS

Janet Allured retired as Professor of History and Director of Women's Studies at McNeese State University and is now Adjunct Instructor at the University of Arkansas. She is coeditor of *Louisiana Women: Their Lives and Times*, Volume 1; *Louisiana Legacies: Readings in the History of the Pelican State*, with Michael Martin; and, also with Michael Martin, *Firsthand Louisiana: Primary Sources in the History of the State*. She is the author of *Remapping Second-Wave Feminism: The Long Women's Rights Movement in Louisiana, 1950–1997* (2016), of numerous articles, and of other publications. She serves on the editorial board of *Methodist History* and is working on a multivolume history of Methodist women and progressive reform, 1920–2000.

Lisa Pertillar Brevard is Associate Director of Walden University's School of Undergraduate Interdisciplinary Studies, where she has taught Creative Writing, Women's Literature and Social Change, Ethics, Interdisciplinary Studies, and Intercultural Communication. She has authored *We'll Understand It Better By and By: Pioneering African-American Gospel Music Composers*, to which she contributed the first annotated bibliography of African American gospel music. Her other publications include *A Biography of E. Azalia Smith Hackley, 1867–1922, African-American Singer and Social Activist*; *A Biography of Edwin Henry Hackley, 1859–1940, African-American Attorney and Activist*; and *Whoopi Goldberg on Stage and Screen*.

Jami L. Carlacio is a consultant on writing, gender equity, anti-bias, and white privilege. Prior to this, she taught writing at Yale University and Cornell University, as well as at colleges and universities in New York, Wisconsin, Indiana, and California. She left academe to pursue a master of divinity degree from Yale Divinity School (2017–2021), after which she worked as a chaplain resident in a trauma level II hospital. She has published book chapters and articles on the subjects of rhetoric, pedagogy, and technology, as well as on the rhetorical practices of Harriet Jacobs, Sojourner Truth, Maria Stewart, and Sarah Grimké. She has also contributed an encyclopedia article on African American women's autobiography. She is the editor of *The Fiction of Toni Morrison: Reading and Writing on Race, Culture, and Identity* (NCTE, 2007) and contributed a chapter on Morrison's novel *A Mercy* in the collection entitled *Toni Morrison:* Paradise, Love, A Mercy (Continuum, 2012).

Cheryl J. Fish is the author of *Off the Yoga Mat*, a debut novel featuring three coming-of-middle-age characters (Livingston Press, 2022). She is the author of *The Sauna Is Full of Maids*, poems and photographs celebrating Finnish sauna culture, the natural world, and friendships, and *Crater & Tower*, poems reflecting on trauma and ecology after the Mount St. Helens volcanic eruption and the terrorist attack of 9/11. Fish teaches at Borough of Manhattan Community College in New York City and has been a Fulbright professor. She is the author of *Black and White Women's Travel Narratives: Antebellum Explorations* (University Press of Florida, 2004) and editor, with Farah J. Griffin, of *A Stranger in the Village: Two Centuries of African-American Travel Writing* (Beacon Press, 1999). Fish has also published essays on environmental justice, art, and activism in the works of ethnic American women writers and on film and photography by indigenous Sami artists in journals and anthologies.

Angela Hornsby-Gutting is Associate Professor of History and Chair of the African and African American Studies Committee at Missouri State University. Her scholarship centers on race-based communal activism, African American youth culture, and gender constructions among Black men and women in the early twentieth-century United States. Hornsby-Gutting is author of *Black Manhood and Community Building in North Carolina, 1900–1930* (University Press of Florida, 2009) and "Woman's Work: Race, Foreign Missions, and Respectability in the National Training School for Women and Girls," *Journal of Women's History* 31, no. 1 (Spring 2019). Other articles and essays have appeared in the *Journal of Southern History*, the *Journal of Negro History*, and the *Blackwell Companion to African-American History*. She is currently completing a monograph on the National Training School for Women and Girls, founded and led by race activist and educator Nannie Helen Burroughs.

Jennifer McFarlane-Harris is Associate Professor of English and Cultural Studies at Seattle Pacific University. She received her PhD in English and Women's Studies from the University of Michigan. Her research explores the function of divinity in conversion narratives and theology-making as self-constitutive. McFarlane-Harris is coeditor of the anthology *Nineteenth-Century American Women Writers and Theologies of the Afterlife: A Step Closer* *to Heaven* (Routledge, 2021); author of the journal article "Pauline 'Adoption' Theology as Experiential Performance in the *Memoirs* of African American Itinerant Preacher Zilpha Elaw," *Performance, Religion and Spirituality* (2019); and coauthor of the essay "Nationalism, Racial Difference, and 'Egyptian' Meaning in Verdi's *Aida*" in *Blackness in Opera* (University of Illinois Press, 2012). She regularly presents conference papers on nineteenth-century American texts, Black women writers, and constructions of mixed-race identity in literature and film.

Neely McLaughlin is Associate Professor of English in the English and Communication Department at the University of Cincinnati, Blue Ash. Her research interests include the relationship between religious and political discourse in nineteenth- and twentieth-century America with particular attention to how this intersection relates to literary studies, diversity and inclusion, and rhetoric in the first- and second-year composition and rhetoric classroom. Her conference presentations include "The 'Little Woman' and the 'Great War': Reading the Ambivalent Activism of *Uncle Tom's Cabin*" (Midwest Modern Language Association, 2017); "Relatability vs. Difference: Intercultural Competence and *American Born Chinese*" (Children's Literature Association, 2016); and "*Uncle Tom's Cabin* vs. *Elsie Dinsmore*: Exploring Slavery and Christianity in Erstwhile Best-Sellers" (Midwest Popular Culture Conference, 2015).

Darcy Metcalfe is Associate Professor of Religious Studies at the University of Findlay. She received her PhD from the University of Iowa in 2021 and was awarded the prestigious Spriestersbach Prize for her dissertation. Her academic interests include the works of Pauli Murray, bioethics and racial health care disparities, and ethical complications of future genetic technologies. She is currently working on a project on the ethics of inheritable genetic modification in light of the history of US medical institutions and the care of Black women. Darcy is also an ordained minister in the PC(USA) and has served for many years on various committees and NGOs committed to social justice.

Phillip Luke Sinitiere is Scholar in Residence at the W. E. B. Du Bois Center at UMass Amherst. He is also Professor of History and Humanities at the College of Biblical Studies, a predominantly African American school located in Houston's Mahatma Gandhi District, and is a scholar of American religious history and African American studies. His books include *Salvation with a Smile: Joel Osteen, Lakewood Church, and American Christianity* (NYU Press, 2015); *Citizen of the World: The Late Career and Legacy of W. E. B. Du Bois* (Northwestern University Press, 2019); and *Race, Religion, and Black Lives Matter: Essays on a Moment and a Movement* (Vanderbilt University Press,

2021). His essays have appeared in journals such as the *History Teacher, Socialism and Democracy, Christian Scholar's Review, Souls, Phylon,* and the *Black Scholar.*

P. Jane Splawn is Professor of English and Foreign Languages at Livingstone College, where she teaches a range of courses from Shakespeare to Black Cinema, World Literature to Composition. She holds a PhD in English (Drama as a Genre) with a minor in Comparative Literature from the University of Wisconsin and a Master of Divinity and a Master of Sacred Theology from Yale Divinity School. She serves as past-president of the Women's Caucus of the African Literature Association. She has published in *Modern Drama, Feminist Theology,* and G. K. Hall's *African American Women Writers, 1910–1940.* Currently, she is completing manuscripts on Rosa Parks and Ruby McCollum and on Black women dramatists, 1975–1999.

Laura L. Sullivan is a doctoral student in the Department of Communication & Film Studies at the University of Memphis. Her research interests include temporality studies, critical race studies, and the politics of affect. She has published articles in *Callaloo: A Journal of African Diaspora Arts and Letters, Computers & Composition,* and *ephemera: theory & politics in organization.* In addition, she has contributed to edited volumes on the topics of the politics of the Internet, the film *The Watermelon Woman* (1996), the politics of gentrification, electronic pedagogy, and the affective dimension of activism. She has also been a grassroots organizer in dozens of campaigns of resistance to neoliberal urban policies.

Hettie V. Williams is Associate Professor of African American history in the Department of History and Anthropology at Monmouth University. She has taught survey courses in US history and world history and upper division courses on the history of African Americans. Her teaching and research interests include African American intellectual history, gender in US history, and race and ethnicity studies. She has published entries and essays in several encyclopedias and edited volumes and has coedited/authored five books including, with G. Reginald Daniel, *Race and the Obama Phenomenon: The Vision of a More Perfect Multiracial Union* (University Press of Mississippi, 2014). Her latest book is an edited volume entitled *Bury My Heart in a Free Land: Black Women Intellectuals in Modern U.S. History* (Praeger, 2017).

INDEX

abolition/abolitionists: American Anti-Slavery Society (1833–70), 18; Boston Female Anti-Slavery Society (BFASS), 67, 73, 75; conflict among, 73–74, 76; criticism of, 74–75; involvement in, 62, 64, 65, 72; Lee, support of, 53; movement, 62; press, 61–62, 64, 71, 77, 78; Prince, as abolitionist, 78; of prisons, 314. *See also* Cullors, Patrisse
Adams, Jane, 140
Allen, Richard, 42, 49, 53
ancestors: accountability to, 298–99; Black feminist, 293, 298, 302; Black woman-spirit, 175; Black women, 28; communication with, 277, 292, 301; community, 322; connection to, 326; dedication to 296; guide, 311; mother, 167, 175; spiritual calling, 177, 293. *See also* Cullors, Patrisse; Gumbs, Alexis Pauline
Africana womanism. *See* womanism
Alexander, Michelle, 21, 312
AME Church. *See* Bland, Sandra; Lee, Jarena
antislavery: American Anti-Slavery Society, 18, 20, 53; Boston Female Anti-Slavery Society, 74; Harper and, 97, 98, 101; Lee and, 53. *See also* Prince, Nancy
autobiography. *See* Harper, Frances Ellen Watkins; Hedgeman, Anna Arnold; Lee, Jarena; Prince, Nancy

Baker, Ella: ancestor, 292; civil rights activist, 120; Young Negroes' Cooperative League, 129
Barad, Karen: intra-connected and intra-action theories of, 240, 250–52, 255–56, 259; and matter, 241; ontology of, 256–57; relational(ity), 257. *See also* Murray, Pauli
Bethune, Mary McLeod, as founder of International Council of Women of the Darker Races, 172
Black Atlantic, 61, 72. *See also* Prince, Nancy
Black church: autonomy for Black members, 19; Black churchwomen, 121, 129, 190, 192; Black liberation theology, relationship to, 26, 319; Black Lives Matter, 319, 320, 321; Black women's involvement in, 17, 42–43, 121, 221; chauvinism of, 13; criticism of, 20, 320; education, 185; moral guidance of, 129; sexism in, 13, 22; womanist theology, relationship to, 27
Black feminists/feminism: activism, 3, 15, 16, 26, 27, 83, 271; consciousness, 159; creativity, 4, 8, 10, 106, 120, 217; liberation theology, 28, 320; Muslim women as, 32n43; producers of knowledge, 4, 7, 8, 9, 10, 14, 19, 62, 125, 221; public intellectuals, 10, 11, 14, 16; rhetoric of, 9, 120; spirituality of, 15, 120; standpoint, 4, 5. *See also* Gumbs, Alexis Pauline
Black freedom struggle. *See* Hedgeman, Anna Arnold
Black liberation theology (Black theology of liberation): Black feminist liberation theology, 320; Cone and, 5, 164–65,

Black liberation theology (*cont.*) 171, 185; womanist critique of, 6; womanist theology, relationship to, 165
Black Lives Matter (#BlackLivesMatter), 311; assertion of, 26, 27, 323; Bland and, 267, 269–70, 276; Cullors and, 312; Garza and, 310; Martin and, 28, 278, 310, 324; movement, 28, 319, 320, 325; *Resurrection Hope*, discussed in, 27, 278; spirituality of, 322; Stand Your Ground law, 314; Tometi and, 310. *See also* Cullors, Patrisse
Black public sphere. *See* public sphere
Black women's clubs, 6, 17, 21, 123, 165, 172, 175, 221
Bland, Sandra: African Methodist Episcopal Church (AME), 271; *American Sniper* (film), 272–73; *Awaken the Voice* (film), 276–77; Black History Month, 270, 272–73; *Black Perspectives* (blog), 268, 278n7; civil rights activism, 272, 273, 275; digital resurrection, 268, 272, 277; Martin Luther King Day, 271; organic public intellectual, 269, 270, 273, 277; Prairie View A&M University, 276; Sandra Bland Movement, 267–68, 272, 276–77; *Sandy Speaks* (videos), 267–78; *Say Her Name: The Life and Death of Sandra Bland* (film), 278n1; *Selma* (film), 272–73; Texas Department of Public Safety, 267; Waller County, 267–68, 271; Walter Scott, 276
body, Black female, 62–64, 69, 82–83
Boston Female Anti-Slavery Society (BFASS). *See* Prince, Nancy
Burroughs, Nannie Helen: Christian moralism, 120, 133; Christian womanhood, 124; civil rights activism, 120; Cooperative Industries, Inc., 129; cooperative movement, purpose of, 130, 131, 133n2; education, 124, 130, 133; Great Depression, 119, 123, 128; mass intelligence, purpose of, 130, 133; *Mission Herald*, 122–23; National Training School, 119–21, 124, 126, 129, 131, 133; *New Challenge*, 120, 130–32; public intellectual, religious, 120; race ideology, lessons in, 120; social activism and, 125; *When Truth Gets a Hearing*, 126–28; womanist theology, 120, 129; Women's Auxiliary of the National Baptist Convention, president of, 119; *The Worker*, 122, 130, 131

Cannon, Katie Geneva: Black feminist consciousness, 159; Black/womanist theology, 59, 164, 165; pebble ethics, 29, 35n72
Carby, Hazel, 10, 23, 73, 179, 221, 231
Chapman, Maria Weston, 74
Chomsky, Noam, 8
Christianity: activism, justification for, 16; Black people, impact on, 127; Black women's, 6; as civilizing agent, 64; discourse, 44, 53; doctrine of, 102; enslaved Africans' learning of, 151; guiding principle for Black women, 191, 219; interpretation of in scripture, 50, 52; political, 44, 53; practiced in churches, 49; rhetorical power of, 43; slavery, justification for, 5; syncretic, 76, 77, 173; whiteness (white supremacist), 43, 278; womanist theology, 6; women's equality, justification for, 198; women's subordination, justification for, 190, 198. *See also* Hackley, Madame Azalia; Lee, Jarena; Prince, Nancy
civil rights. *See* Bland, Sandra; Hedgeman, Anna Arnold; Murray, Pauli
Clifford, Carrie Williams: anti-lynching cause, 165; Black ancestral mother, 167, 175; "community mother," 166; female deities and motherhood, 174; Harlem Renaissance, 176; Jim Crow, 167, 169, 172, 173; literary theology of Black women, 165, 167, 176–77; marriage to William H. Clifford, 165; Ohio Federation of Colored Women's Clubs, 165, 175; proto-womanist thinker, 164; public intellectual, 166, 167; *The Purple Flower*, 171; Queen mother, compared to, 174; *Race Rhymes*, 164, 167–69; slavery, critique of, 166, 168, 172; *Sowing for Others to Reap*, 165; teaching and activism, 174; theology of, 165, 174–75; "Votes for Children," 164, 165, 175, 176; "Votes for Women," 176; West African religions in poetry of, 173; *The Widening Light*, 164, 167, 169, 170, 174; women's suffrage, 165

Collier-Thomas, Bettye, 16, 18, 22, 121
Collins, Patricia Hill, 32n41, 298; intellectual activism strategies, 8
Cone, James, *God of the Oppressed*, 164, 171, 177. *See also* Black liberation theology
Cooper, Anna Julia, 10, 11, 154; *A Voice from the South*, 17, 35
Crenshaw, Kimberlé, 14, 32n41, 183, 238
Crisis, The, 25, 129, 165, 169, 175, 243. *See also* NAACP
Cullors, Patrisse: abolition activist, 314, 315, 316, 326, 327, 330n33–35, 333n79; ancestors (African), 319, 322, 326, 327; art as protest, 317; Black female/feminist public intellectual, 315, 324, 327; Black (self-) love, 310, 311, 312–13, 320, 321, 322, 323, 326; criminal justice system activist, 26, 28, 319, 330n32; Jehovah's Witness, 30, 321; prison industrial complex, critique of (criminal justice system), 28, 312, 314, 315, 319, 330n32; reparations, 315, 330nn33–35; West African Yoruba religious practices, 6, 322; *When They Call You a Terrorist*, 312, 324

Douglas, Kelly Brown (Kelly Delaine Douglas), 5, 27, 278, 311, 314; *Resurrection Hope*, 27, 278; *Stand Your Ground*, 278, 283
Du Bois, W. E. B., 22, 125, 126, 129, 139, 152, 165, 170, 246

education. *See* Burroughs, Nannie Helen; Clifford, Carrie Williams; Hackley, Madame Azalia; Reconstruction

Garrison, William Lloyd, 61, 67, 73–74, 78. *See also* Prince, Nancy
Garza, Alicia, 310, 312
Gilkes, Cheryl Townsend, 6, 95, 121, 166, 172, 173
Gramsci, Antonio, 7, 221, 230n38
Grant, Jacquelyn, 30n11, 165, 171, 177
Gumbs, Alexis Pauline: ancestors, respect for, 287, 288, 290, 292–93, 296, 301; as Black feminist public intellectual, 302; Black feminist spirituality (spiritual practice), 32, 287–88, 302; Black love, 286, 288, 290–91, 293, 298; Black women's breathing project (chorus), 28, 292, 300, 302; relationality, expressed in relationships among Black women, 295, 302; slavery, critique of, 287, 291; West African Yoruba practices, informed by, 288

Hackley, Madame Azalia: Adams and, 140; beauty, 141–42, 145–48, 152, 156; classical music, 139; *The Colored Girl Beautiful*, 140–43, 146–49, 152, 154, 156, 157–58, 159, 160; education, importance of, 139, 142–43, 145, 154, 156, 160; Edwin Henry Hackley, husband, 139, 147; God, belief in as central to activism, 138, 139, 149–51, 156–58, 160; gospel and activism, 159, gospel of Black motherhood, 146; Jim Crowism, 159; motherhood, importance of, 143, 145–46, 149, 156, 160; public intellectualism and, 141, 148, 152, 153, 154; racial uplift activist, 139, 155, 156, 160; slavery, critique of, 141, 145; womanist, theological perspective of, 159, 160
Hamer, Fannie Lou, 22, 292
Harlem Renaissance, 23; Hurston's literary production during, 176
Harper, Frances Ellen Watkins: activism, 94, 96–97, 101, 102, 103, 106; African American autobiographical tradition, 94–95, 97–98; antislavery work, 93, 96–98, 101; autobiographical exploration of discipleship, 101; holiness, 96, 98; poetry, biblical themes in, 96, 98–99, 102; poetry, devotional, 103–4; poetry, first-person speakers in, 93–96, 98–101, 103–6; poetry, I-voiced expression of antislavery stance, 97, 111n57; publication strategies, 97–98; racial uplift, 105; reader as convert, 98, 103, 105; temperance, 96, 98, 101, 102, 103–5; Unitarian theology, 96, 101, 102, 103; *The Widening Light*, 164, 166–67, 169–75
Hedgeman, Anna Arnold: autobiography (self-life-writing) and, 216, 217, 218; Black feminist, 226; Black freedom struggle and, 212, 216, 219, 220, 224, 227; civil

Hedgeman, Anna Arnold (*cont.*)
rights movement activism, 212–13, 216, 217, 220, 223–24, 225; education, importance of, 214, 228; Fair Employment Practices Commission and, 214, 219–20, 224, 227, 228; *The Gift of Chaos* (memoir), 214, 216, 218; interracial (cross-racial) cooperation, 219, 220, 222, 223, 224, 227; intersectionality, 213, 216; Jim Crow racism, experience of, 218; March on Washington, leadership in, 218–19, 228; Methodist Church and theology, influence on, 214, 215, 218, 222, 227; NAACP, 212, 226; National Organization for Women (NOW) cofounder, 212, 238; pragmatic (Christian) feminist theology, 221, 223; public intellectual, 25, 216, 220, 221; *The Trumpet Sounds*, 215, 216, 218, 219; Wesleyan theology, 222; YWCA, affiliation with, 212, 213, 218, 223, 228
hooks, bell, 12, 16, 313
Hoover, Theressa: Black church, critique of women's role in, 190; education, 184–86, 188, 193, 195, 202; family of, 184–85; feminism of, 182, 189–91, 193; feminist theology of, 197; field secretary, 188; hope, theology of, 197; Jim Crow, 184, 187; laypeople, importance of, 188, 194, 206n21; Methodism, influence of, 193–94, 197–98; public intellectual, 181; public intellectualism informed by religion, 215; United Methodist Church, 181, 184–86, 188; United Methodist Church women's division, 160; United Methodist Women, 189, 195, 201, 203n1; voter registration, 201; womanist theology, 189; Women's Division (WD) of the General Board of Global Ministries, 181–82, 184, 187–89, 201–2, 203n1, 207n25; women's history, in Methodism, 194–95, 201; YWCA, 185, 196, 201
Hurston, Zora Neale, 176, 296, 303n22

intellectual. *See* public intellectual
intersectionality, 3, 4, 5, 10, 14, 24, 25, 26, 32n41, 106, 190, 213, 216, 220, 221, 230n34; Crenshaw and, 14, 32n41, 183, 238

Jim Crow, 21, 159, 218, 312; Alexander's writing on, 21, 312; *The New Jim Crow*, 314

Khan-Cullors, Patrisse. *See* Cullors, Patrisse

Lee, Jarena: and Allen, 53; and AME church, 51, 54; as mystic, 23, 41; and preaching, 45, 47–55; public intellectual, 43, 44; *Religious Experience and Journal of Mrs. Jarena Lee*, 41; slavery, condemnation of, 53; spiritual autobiography, 20, 42–43, 47; womanist theological framework, 44–47, 48, 49, 55
liberation theology (theology of liberation): Black feminist liberation theology, relationship to, 28; Black women's oppression, elision of, 6; Cone and, 5–6, 185, 191
Liberator, The. *See* Prince, Nancy
Lorde, Audre, 12, 288; Cullors inspired by, 315; Gumbs, ancestor of, 292, 293, 299
lynching (and anti-lynching): Black women's activism, 18, 23, 165, 176; creative works, critiqued in, 166, 168; movement, 12; Reconstruction, failure of, 20; Wells-Barnett's anti-lynching crusade, 20, 21, 22

Martin, Trayvon, 28, 278, 310, 324
Murray, Pauli: Black feminist, 25; civil rights leadership, 237, 241, 243, 253; counter-memory, 25, 242, 246, 250; embodiment theory of, 248; *The Entreaty*, 252, 254–56, 259; Episcopal faith, 240, 251, 255; Episcopal priest, 239, 258; ethic (love, relational), 255, 257, 259; Jim Crow myths critiqued, 246, 247; legal scholar, 24, 25, 238; matter (remattering), conception of, 240–41, 253, 254, 256–57, 259; public intellectual, 237, 239, 253, 258; racism, critique of, 237–38, 243–46; sexuality, 251–53; slavery, critique of, 244–45, 246, 248; time, concept of in poetry, 254, 255

NAACP (National Association for the Advancement of Colored People), 123, 124, 222; Baker's leadership in, 22; *The*

Crisis, publication of, 165; Niagara Movement, as precursor to, 170
National Organization for Women (NOW), Hedgeman's affiliation with, 212, 213, 228

preaching: as political discourse, 49, 54; as religious discourse, 44, 46, 55; as sacred speech, 49. *See also* Lee, Jarena
Prince, Nancy: Afro-Jamaicans, 67, 68, 76; antislavery movement affiliation, 63, 67, 73–75, 80; emigration debates, 68, 78–79; free Blacks, commentary on, 77–78, 81; about Jamaica, 61, 62, 64, 67, 70, 73, 75, 78–81; Jamaica, cause of freed slaves in, 71, 72; *The Liberator*, 71, 74; mobile subjectivity of, 83; racial uplift, 69, 75; resistant truth-telling, 62, 64–65, 68, 72, 79, 80; and Reverend Abbott, 75–76; Russia, travels to, 60, 61, 72, 87n37; Russian peasants compared to American slaves, 70–71; Russian peasants and serfs, treatment of compared to Afro-Jamaicans, 64, 72; slavery, condemnation of, 53, 61, 62, 66, 67, 69–71, 80, 81; as spiritual autobiographer, 67–68, 82; travel narrative, as writer of, 61, 66
public intellectuals: activism, 8, 13, 16, 24; Black feminists as, 8, 10, 15, 16, 29; Black feminist Muslim women as, 32n43; Black womanist as, 15, 16; Black women as, 15, 21, 1; Chomsky, 8; Collins, 8; conception of, 7; Cooper, 171; counterhegemonic, 8; Gramsci, 7, 221, 230n38; history, 10, 13, 84, 220, 221, 231n40, 268, 269, 277; organic intellectual, 7, 8, 221; production, 4, 6, 10, 11, 13, 14, 28, 268, 270, 272; religious, 120; spiritual, 3; Wheatley, 29n3
public sphere: Black, 9; #BlackLivesMatter activists in, 323; Black women's activism in, 16, 97, 196, 327; Christian discourse in, 120; counterhegemonic, 9; global, 60; kitchen table, 9; religious, 44; standpoint, demonstration of, 4

racial uplift: Black women's efforts in, 6, 11, 12, 16, 17, 18, 21, 23. *See also* Burroughs, Nannie Helen; Hackley, Madame Azalia; Harper, Frances Ellen Watkins; Prince, Nancy
Reconstruction: educational opportunities during, 19; failure of, 20; Freedmen's Bureau, 19; post-Reconstruction and Jim Crow, 21; voting rights of African American women and men, debate over, 106

slavery: Black female body and, 69; Black women preachers' protest of, 43; Black women's activism against, 18; Christian principles used to critique, 53; Freedmen's Bureau and, 19; post-Reconstruction and, 19, 34n58; womanist theology's roots in, 6
spiritual autobiography (spiritual narrative), 18, 20, 42, 43, 47, 67, 68, 82, 98, 109; theology and, 45, 82. *See also* Hackley, Madame Azalia; Harper, Frances Ellen Watkins; Hedgeman, Anna Arnold; Hoover, Theressa; Lee, Jarena; Prince, Nancy
standpoint. *See* Black feminists/feminism

Tometi, Opal, 310, 312
Townes, Emilie, 6, 45, 242, 246
travel narrative. *See* Prince, Nancy

voting/vote: 18; Black women and, 164; Chapman, 74; Hamer, 22; Jehovah's Witness stance on, 321; National Woman Suffrage Association (NWSA), 18; registration, 23, 201; suppression of, 20, 243; Three-Fifths Compromise, 245; women's right to, 18, 25, 164, 175. *See also* Clifford, Carrie Williams; Harper, Frances Ellen Watkins

Walker, Alice, womanism of, 5, 183, 191, 192, 296, 313
Wells, Ida B. (Ida Wells-Barnett): anti-lynching campaign, 20, 21; National Association of Colored Women, 172
Wheatley, Phillis, 29n3
white supremacist ideology, 6, 8, 15, 24, 26, 27, 29, 41, 63, 71, 80, 121, 127, 219, 220, 273, 278, 294, 299, 300, 323, 324, 332n69

Widening Light, The. *See* Clifford, Carrie Williams
womanism/womanist, justice-based spirituality of, 6. *See also* Cannon, Katie Geneva; Townes, Emilie; Walker, Alice
womanist theology, 5, 6, 27; Black liberation theology, 5; Christianity, 6, 27; description of, 6, 27, 25; political and cultural critique, 45, 49; survival, concept of, 5; theological framework, 164–65; theology of liberation, 5

Yoruba, 32n43. *See also* Cullors, Patrisse; Gumbs, Alexis Pauline
YWCA. *See* Hedgeman, Anna Arnold; Hoover, Theressa

www.ingramcontent.com/pod-product-compliance
Lightning Source LLC
Chambersburg PA
CBHW021112270326
41929CB00009B/835
* 9 7 8 1 4 9 6 8 4 5 6 8 9 *